THE
A·F·R·I·C·A·N·S
A TRIPLE HERITAGE

THE
A·F·R·I·C·A·N·S
A TRIPLE HERITAGE

ALI A. MAZRUI

Little, Brown and Company
Boston   Toronto

To the memory of Valerie Ward

This book was developed to accompany "The Africans" television series and related college course. The television course consists of nine one-hour public television programs, a study guide and a faculty guide. The series was produced by WETA-TV, Washington, D.C. and the BBC with major funding provided by the Annenberg/CPB Project. Additional funding comes from public television stations and the Corporation for Public Broadcasting.

Second Printing

Library of Congress Cataloging-in-Publication Data

Mazrui, Ali Al'Amin.
  The Africans.

  1. Africa—Civilization.   I. Title.
  DT14.M39 1986   960   86–2753
  ISBN 0–316–55200–3

Published simultaneously in Canada
by Litttle, Brown & Company (Canada) Limited
Printed in the United States of America

Contents

Acknowledgements

Perhaps never in the history of African scholarship has so much been owed to so many – by so few. My debt is to a very wide range of people, scattered in three different continents. Those who challenged, stimulated, irritated, and enlightened me constantly were those directly involved in making the television series, *The Africans*, jointly produced by the British Broadcasting Corporation and WETA (Public Broadcasting Service). In the television series I was to look at Africa – and the BBC and WETA were supposed to translate my ideas into lively television.

In reality, the interaction was much more complex than that. I did indeed present my ideas to the production team of the television series at meetings which were themselves held in three continents – from Mombasa in Kenya to London, England, from Jos in Nigeria to Washington, DC. But it was not of course a simple case of articulating my academic ideas on Africa while the television experts scratched their heads about how to translate my story into pictures. It was a constant give and take. My ideas were analysed, challenged, contradicted, and scrutinised by a group of very intelligent people from another profession (television). In the final analysis I could of course stick to my position on a particular issue and refuse to budge. But much more often we attempted to persuade each other and were responsive to each other's arguments. What is more, my television colleagues soon learnt so much about Africa on their own that purely in terms of information they had as much to tell me on Africa as I had to tell them. My edge of advantage lay in my being an African and in my having spent more than thirty-five years of my life on the continent. Nevertheless, I learnt an awful lot more about my own continent as a result of this project.

It was out of this intense interaction in the course of making the television series that this book in turn evolved and developed. In a curious manner, this book is both the mother and the child of the television series. Many of the ideas of the book helped to give shape and direction to the television series. But other ideas emerged out of the research for filming, and much of the information was obtained as a result of contacts and experience on the ground as we travelled from one African country to another. In this latter sense, the book is the child of the television project. William Wordsworth was right in his ambiguous observation that 'the child is father of the man'. This book bears additional testimony to that eternal truth.

But of course my intellectual and informational debt is not purely 'incestuous' within the BBC/WETA project. Especially for this book, there has also been the special role of Michael Tidy, my co-author in a previous book entitled *Nationalism and New States in Africa* (London: Heinemann Educational Books, 1984). In this new BBC/WETA publication, Michael Tidy has been commissioned not as co-author but as editor and research support. Michael Tidy has indeed discharged those twin responsibilities of editing and research assistance with impressive thoroughness. In some cases I have provided the skeleton (the theoretical framework) and Michael Tidy has provided the flesh (the illustrative information). Without Michael Tidy and the data emanating from the BBC/WETA television series, this book would have been much thinner in terms of information and historical illustrations. Michael's wife, Anastasia Obuya Tidy, graciously lent a hand both as editorial advisor and typist.

In addition, every African country we filmed had its own experts, academic and otherwise. Many of them went out of their way to educate us about their country, making themselves available without compensation. Some of them were personal friends or professional acquaintances of mine, selflessly eager to help. In these brief remarks they will recognise themselves. I do not have to mention them by name. But neither the television series nor this book would have made it without this kind of professional altruism and co-operation. This son of Africa extends his gratitude to many brothers and sisters in Africa itself and in the African Diaspora in all its complexity.

A team of consultants was put together by WETA and the BBC to advise on the scholarly content of the television series. This group consisted of Professors Jacob Adeniyi Ajayi, Ali Hussein Darwish, John Donnelly Fage, I. M. Lewis, Elliott P. Skinner, Joseph Harris and Christopher Davis Roberts. This book is indebted to them all, and to Professor J. Isawa Elaigwu at the University of Jos and Mrs Angeline Kamba at the National Archives of Zimbabwe.

Two universities had to bear the burden of neglected routines as a result of my long absences for this project. The universities were those of Jos in Nigeria, where I am Research Professor of Political Science, and The University of Michigan in the United States where I am Professor of Political Science and of Afroamerican and African Studies. Both universities have shared me with this project over a period which has extended well over three years. Without the patience and understanding of these two universities, I would have been in the wilderness. Particularly relevant are the two Departments of Political Science at Jos and Michigan, and the Center for Afroamerican and African Studies at Michigan.

Since I am indebted to hundreds of other names, I am trying to avoid mentioning too many of them in this acknowledgement. Perhaps I should highlight research assistance and secretarial support as the most *immediate* pillars. Research assistance most directly supportive of this book came from Omari H. Kokole at the University of Michigan, Diana Frank at WETA in Washington, DC, Judith Andrews at the British Broadcasting Corporation, and Sam Max Sebina, Ezekiel Okeniyi, Vianney Bukyana and John Munene at the University of Jos. Kay Kokole was also a major contributor to the smoothness of the work in Michigan.

But the manuscript had to be got ready for publication. Anthony Kingsford of BBC Publications and Roger Donald of Little, Brown warned me quite early against excessive academic jargon, on one side, and, on the other, against 'talking down' to my non-specialised audience. I took the advice to heart. Later on the editorial staff of the two publishers helped more directly with style editing. Valerie Buckingham helped me prune the original hefty manuscript, Frances Abraham tracked down thousands of photographs and helped in selecting them, and Martin Gregory was responsible for the design of the book. Other people involved in preparing the manuscript included Judith Baughn at the University of Michigan as the central co-ordinator, assisted by my former secretary, the late Valerie Ward, and her daughter, Karen Ward. Their dedication at short notice was exceptional.

At the University of Jos the secretarial assistance came mainly from the Department of Political Science, with special reference to Evelyn Iroegbu. At the British Broadcasting Corporation Kate Harris, Caroline Wolfe and Judith Andrews were crucial both as liaison officers and as production aides.

Apart from Judith Baughn and Valerie and Karen Ward at Michigan, it was mainly the secretaries of the Center for Afroamerican and African Studies who were involved in typing drafts of this book. At WETA in Washington, DC the secretaries were busy keeping track of relevant press reports of African news on my behalf and then mailing the photocopies to me wherever I was.

No less immediate in their support were, of course, those involved in the actual production of the BBC/WETA television series. David Harrison, Charles Hobson, Peter Bate, Diana Frank, Timothy Copestake, Alan Bookbinder and Jenny Cathcart were constantly involved in discussing the ideas affecting the television series. Some members of the filming crew also took considerable interest in Africa and discussed the continent with me. So did Judith Andrews and Caroline Wolfe. I am indebted to them all for stimulation, information and support.

But I would have had to give up the whole project if my three sons had appeared cool and resentful of the enterprise. On the contrary, Jamal, Al'Amin and Kim Abubakar were supportive and enthusiastic – though they insisted on fining me a modest sum of money for every week I was away. (I suspect the fine was more to augment their pocket-money than to express their wrath.) My wider extended family and other friends in Kenya responded to their sacred duty in our traditional manner – they helped a compatriot in need all the way from Nairobi to Malindi, from Mombasa to Lamu.

Two women bore the brunt of looking after the children in my absence. Their mother first and foremost. Molly was, as usual, a tower of strength. But when she was not there, Brenda Kiberu took over – as a friend to the children and to me. Without those two women, I would have had to return home and 'babysit' – away from 'the madding crowd' and away from television and field research.

An indirect influence on this book has been a special *Reader*, a collection of essays commissioned by WETA to accompany the television series as supportive material for a college television course. Major Africanist scholars have contributed to that *Reader*. My interaction with those scholars helped to enrich my own book.

In editing the contributions of those scholars for that *Reader*. I have been greatly helped by Toby Levine as co-editor and co-ordinator. Without her energetic involvement, it would have been difficult for me to be educated by this particular team of scholars. This book of mine would therefore have learnt less from the prior reaction of other scholars to my tentative ideas.

Major funding for *The Africans* was provided by the British Broadcasting Corporation and the Annenberg/CPB Project. Additional funding is from the National Endowment for the Humanities, the Public Broadcasting Service, and the Corporation for Public Broadcasting. Subsidies for research by the author also came from the University of Jos, Nigeria and the University of Michigan in the United States.

The faults of this book belong at the author's door. But the author is still indebted to everyone else for a singular intellectual experience.

Ali A. Mazrui

Jos, Nigeria

Ann Arbor, Michigan

BBC, London, England

WETA, Washington, DC

Introduction: A Celebration of Decay?

Westernisation and Decay

The ancestors of Africa are angry. For those who believe in the power of the ancestors, the proof of their anger is all around us. For those who do not believe in ancestors, the proof of their anger is given another name. In the words of Edmund Burke, 'People will not look forward to posterity who never look backward to their ancestors.'[1]

But what is the proof of the curse of the ancestors? Things are not working in Africa. From Dakar to Dar es Salaam, from Marrakesh to Maputo, institutions are decaying, structures are rusting away. It is as if the ancestors had pronounced the curse of cultural sabotage. This generation of Africans is hearing the ancestral voice in no uncertain terms proclaiming,

> Warriors will fight scribes for the control of your institutions; wild bush will conquer your roads and pathways; your land will yield less and less while your offspring multiply; your houses will leak from the floods and your soil will crack from the drought; your sons will refuse to pick up the hoe and prefer to wander in the wilds; you shall learn ways of cheating and you will poison the cola nuts you serve your own friends. Yes, things will fall apart.[2]

If this is the curse of the ancestors, what is the sin? It is the compact between Africa and the twentieth century and its terms are all wrong. They involve turning Africa's back on previous centuries – an attempt to 'modernise' without consulting cultural continuities, an attempt to start the process of 'dis-Africanising' Africa. One consequence takes on the appearance of social turbulence, of rapid social change let loose upon a continent.

Franklin D. Roosevelt once said to Americans, when faced with the economic crisis of the 1930s, 'The only thing we have to fear is fear itself.' For my turn I am tempted to say to fellow Africans, facing a series of severe political, economic, social and cultural crises in the 1980s, 'The main thing we need to change is our own changeability.'

African states since independence have experienced a bewildering and rapid sequence of military coups and economic shifts and turns. In addition, over the last generation or two there has been a remarkable pace of cultural dis-Africanisation and Westernisation. If the Jews in the Diaspora had scrambled to change their culture as fast as Africans in their own homelands seemed to be doing until recently, the miracle of Jewish identity would not have lasted these two or three additional millennia in the wilderness. Many Africans even today seem to be undergoing faster cultural change in a single generation than the Jews underwent in the first 1000 years of dispersal.

Yet there may be hope in the very instability which Africa is experiencing in the wake of this unnatural dis-Africanisation. The fate of African culture may not as yet be irrevocably sealed. With every new military coup, with every collapse of a foreign aid project, with every evidence of large-scale corruption, with every twist and turn in opportunistic foreign policy, it becomes pertinent to ask whether Western culture in Africa is little more than a nine-day wonder.

Africa is at war. It is a war of cultures. It is a war between indigenous Africa and the forces of Western civilisation. It takes the form of inefficiency, mismanagement, corruption and decay of the infrastructure. The crisis of efficiency in the continent is symptomatic of the failure of transplanted organs of the state and the economy. Indigenous African culture is putting up a fight. It is as if the indigenous ancestors have been aroused from the dead, disapproving of what seems like an informal pact between the rulers of independent Africa (the inheritors of the colonial order) and the West – a pact which allows the West to continue to dominate Africa. It is as if the ancestors are angry at the failure of Africans to consult them and to pay attention to Africa's past and usage. It is as if the apparent breakdown and decay in Africa today is a result of the curse of the ancestors. Or is it not a curse but a warning, a sign from the ancestors calling on Africans to rethink their recent past, their present and their future and calling on them to turn again to their traditions and reshape their society anew, to create a modern and a future Africa that incorporates the best of its own culture?

What is likely to be the outcome of this drama? Is the Westernisation of Africa reversible? Was the European colonial impact upon Africa deep or shallow? Was the colonial impact a cost or a benefit to Africa?

The Epic of Colonialism

Let us take the epic school first, the insistence that these last 100 years were not a mere century but a revolution of epic proportions. The arguments for this school include a number of apparently decisive turning points.

First, there is the argument that colonialism and the accompanying capitalism effectively incorporated Africa into the world economy, for good or ill. It started with the slave trade, which dragged African labour itself into the emerging international capitalist system. This was the era of the *labour* imperative in relations between Africa and the West.

But colonialism was the era of the *territorial* imperative, as the West demanded from Africa not just labour but territory and its promise in all its dimensions. Capitalism had come knocking on the doors of the continent and enticed the host into the wider world of the international economy.

Then there was Africa's admission into the state system of the world emanating from the European Peace of Westphalia of 1648. It was that particular set of treaties which has been regarded widely as the beginnings of the modern system of sovereign states. Africa might have been dragged screaming into the world of capitalism, but it was not dragged unwillingly into the world of the sovereign state system. On the contrary, one colonial society after another framed its agitation and anti-imperialism in terms of seeking admission to the international community whose rules had grown out of European diplomatic history and statecraft. Independence for every African country was in fact a voluntary entry into the sovereign state system.

Then there is Africa's incorporation into a world culture which is still primarily Eurocentric. The major international ideologies – liberalism, capitalism, socialism, Marxism, communism and indeed fascism – have all been European-derived. To that extent, the world of ideology is in part the world of European dominance in the field of values and norms.

Another aspect of Africa's incorporation into world culture concerns the role of European languages in Africa. The significance of English, French and Portuguese especially in Africa's political life can hardly be overestimated, at least in the short run. Rulers are chosen on the basis of competence in the relevant imperial language. Nationwide political communication in the majority of African countries is almost impossible without the use of the relevant imperial medium.

Then there is Africa's incorporation into the world of international law, which is again heavily Eurocentric in origin. Many aspects of international law are named after European cities – the Geneva Convention, the Vienna Convention and the like. One looks in vain in the body of international law for conventions named after such Third World cities as Bombay, Maiduguri or Rio de Janeiro. But nevertheless African states seem to be firmly and irrevocably tied to the body of legal precepts governing international diplomacy in the twentieth century.

Also part of the epic theory of the significance of colonialism is the technological variable. It is quite clear that the West has been in the lead in scientific and technological change for at least 300 years. Western colonisation of Africa could therefore be interpreted as an invitation to Africa to be incorporated into the modern technological age. At first glance this ranges from medical science to the automobile, from the tractor in African agriculture to the missile in African military establishments. Again, this would seem to be an incorporation into a global system which is basically of epic proportions and seemingly irreversible.

Information Flows and the Moral Order
Next is the issue of information and data. Africa has been swallowed by the global system of dissemination of information. What Africa knows about itself, what different parts of Africa know about each other, have been profoundly influenced by the West. Even in the field of the mass media, Africa is overwhelmingly dependent on the wire services of the Western world for information about itself. What Nigerians know about Kenya, or Zambians know about Ghana, is heavily derived from the wire services of the Western world transmitting information across the globe. African newspapers and radios subscribe to these wire services and receive data for their

news bulletins from Western sources.

Also apparently epic in significance was the *moral* order which had come with colonialism and Christianity. Important Western and Christian ethical factors entered the domain of African systems of restraint. Can a man have more than one wife? Is female circumcision morally legitimate? Is there such a thing as an illegitimate child if the father admits paternity and the mother acknowledges the child? How sinful was sexuality outside marriage?

All these were major moral dilemmas for Africa, *implying* a permanent change as a result of colonisation and Christianisation. How then could their impact be anything but an epic drama? How then could European influence be anything but a totally transformative force?

Colonialism as an Episode
Yet there is an alternative case for regarding the European impact as no more than an episode in millennia of African history.

There are two main versions of this idea. One insists that Africa could have entered the world economy and the international state system without being colonised by Europe. After all, Japan is now a major power in the world economy and has at times been a major figure in the international state system without having undergone the agonies of European colonisation and imperialism. Japan was able to acquire Western tools without succumbing to Western subjugation. But Africa was denied that option.

Related to this is the argument that modern science and technology were bound to convert the whole world into a global village. Twentieth-century science and technology had become too expansionist to have left Africa untouched. If this body of expertise could reach the Moon without colonising it, why could it not have reached Africa without subjugating it?

What follows from this is the conclusion that European colonisation of Africa was not the only way of Africa's entry into the global system of the twentieth century. Africa could have made such an entry without suffering either the agonies of the slave trade, or the exploitation of colonialism or the humiliation of European racism.

The second version of the episodic school asserts that the European impact on Africa has been shallow rather than deep, transitional rather than long-lasting. It is not often realised how brief the colonial period was. When Jomo Kenyatta was born, Kenya was not yet a crown colony. Kenyatta lived right through the period of British rule and outlasted British rule by fifteen years. If the entire period of colonialism could be compressed into the life-span of a single individual, how deep was the impact?

The kind of capitalism which was transferred to Africa was itself shallow. Western consumption patterns were transferred more effectively than Western production techniques, Western tastes were acquired more quickly than Western skills, the profit motive was adopted without the efficient calculus of entrepreneurship, and capitalist greed was internalised sooner than capitalist discipline.

All this is quite apart from the anomaly of urbanisation without industrialisation. In the history of the Western world the growth of cities occurred partly in response to fundamental changes in production. Urbanisation followed in the wake of either an agrarian transformation or an industrial revolution. But in the history of Africa urbanisation has been under way without accompanying growth of productive capacity. In some African countries there is indeed a kind of revolution – but it is a revolution in urbanisation rather than in industrialisation, a revolution in expanding numbers of people squeezed into limited space, rather than a transformation in method and skill of economic output. It is these considerations which have made capitalism in Africa, such as it is, lopsided and basically shallow.

But alongside this phenomenon is the post-colonial state in Africa, which is also quite often in the process of decaying. The African state since independence has been subject to two competing pressures – the push towards militarisation and the pull towards privatisation. In the capitalist Western world state ownership is regarded as an alternative to or even the opposite of private ownership. The privatisation of the steel industry (its return from state nationalisation to private ownership) in England, for example, is an alternative to state ownership and state control.

In post-colonial Africa, on the other hand, the question arises whether the state in itself can be privatised or become privately owned. Is there a new echo in Africa of Louis XIV's notorious dictum, 'I am the state'?

There is an echo of a sort, but with distinctive African variations. What must be remembered is that the pressures of privatisation in Africa are accompanied by pressures towards militarisation. The pull towards privatisation is partly a legacy of greed in the tradition of Shylock, Shakespeare's creation in *The Merchant of Venice*. The push towards militarism, on the other hand, is a legacy of naked power in the tradition of Shaka, the founder of the Zulu kingdom and empire. Africa is caught between Shylock and Shaka, between greed and naked power – and the decay of the post-colonial state is one consequence of that dialectic.

In Nigeria between 1979 and 1984 the two tendencies of privatisation and militarisation appeared to be alternatives. Under civilian rule from 1979 privatisation gathered momentum. The resources of the nation were, to all intents and purposes, deemed to be the private hunting ground of those in power and of their supporters. Lucrative contracts for trade or construction were handed out on the basis of personal considerations. Foreign exchange was privately allocated and arbitrarily distributed. Millions of dollars and naira disappeared into the private accounts of key figures abroad.

This rampant unofficial and unlegislated privatisation of the state's resources seemed to have set the stage for the state's militarisation. Nigeria's armed forces – restive for a variety of reasons – found additional grounds for impatience with the civilian politicians. On 31 December 1983 the soldiers once again intervened and took over power. The push towards militarisation had triumphed over the pull towards privatisation of the Nigerian state. The soldiers justified their intervention on the basis of ending the private pillage of the country's resources. The action of the soldiers this time seemed calculated to arrest the decay of both the Nigerian economy and state.

The Private State: Three Versions

Although in this phase of Nigeria's history the two pressures (privatisation *versus* militarisation) appeared to be alternatives, in much of the 1970s when the soldiers were in power the two tendencies reinforced each other. The soldiers were themselves inclined to raid the coffers of the state, though not quite on the same scale as the civilians did from 1979 to 1983.

Three forms of the privatised state appear on the political landscape of Africa — dynastic, ethnic and anarchic tendencies of privatisation. Again, these are not necessarily mutually exclusive categories, though their characteristics are often quite distinctive.

The case of Nigeria between 1979 and 1983 was primarily anarchic. The state's resources went into private hands partly because there was no effective control. President Shehu Shagari might himself have been personally 'clean', but he did not check or control the process of privatisation.

A case of combined ethnic and anarchic privatisation was Idi Amin's Uganda (1971–9). On the one hand, the moral order in the society collapsed and both the state and the economy fell into serious decay. On the other hand, there was little doubt that the Kakwa and the Nubi soldiers in the army enjoyed a disproportionate share of the resources of the state and the opportunities of the economy. To that extent, the privatisation was in part a diversion of resources from public ownership and control to narrow ethnic possession. But the Amin case was not merely an illustration of ethno-anarchic privatisation. It was also combined with the militarisation of the state. Contradictory trends were discernible in a complex phenomenon.

Some of the evidence seemed to suggest that in a technologically under-developed society in the twentieth century, ultimate power resided not in those who controlled the means of production but in those who controlled the means of *destruction*. The Asian community in Uganda, the new Black bourgeoisie and some of the more prosperous farmers controlled a substantial part of the means of production. But it was Uganda's lumpen-militariat, the rough and ready military recruits, who captured the state and proceeded to privatise it. The means of production were not modern enough to serve as levers on the power of the state, nor were they complex enough to produce countervailing social groups such as effective trade unions.

Uganda was to reveal another historical contradiction: how societies which were themselves stateless in the pre-colonial era could then inherit the post-colonial state. The Kakwa — Idi Amin's 'tribe' — were stateless in pre-colonial times and were in an area which now constitutes part of eastern Zaire, part of southern Sudan and part of northern Uganda. Their traditional institutions were not centralised enough, or politically distinctive enough, to add up to what we normally mean by 'the state'.

On the other hand, pre-colonial centralised societies such as Buganda and Bunyoro were indigenous and authentic states. The colonial period under the British helped to demilitarise the Baganda and the Banyoro by introducing licensing laws for guns and through new forms of socialisation, acculturation and Western education. Modern schools and cash crops diverted the new élite of Buganda and Bunyoro away from the warrior tradition and towards the new money economy. The people of these pre-colonial states lost the military foundations of what had once made them states.

In contrast, some of those societies which in pre-colonial times had been basically stateless now became recruiting grounds for the new colonial army. In Uganda the Nilotic 'tribes' of the north were regarded by the British as particularly suitable for recruitment into the King's African Rifles. By the time the British left Uganda, the security forces of the newly independent country were disproportionately Nilotic in composition. Although all the Nilotic 'tribes' together in Uganda add up to only a small minority of the population, the stage was already set for a Nilotic supremacy in at least the first few decades of post-colonial Uganda. This Nilotic power prevailed both under Milton Obote, under Idi Amin and under Tito Okello. Whether it will last much longer remains to be seen.

Uganda is by no means the only case in Africa where members of pre-colonial stateless societies have inherited the post-colonial state. In Ghana under Jerry Rawlings we find a comparable case. The most complex pre-colonial state of Ghana – the Confederal Empire of Asante – was also demilitarised during British rule. Under Jerry Rawlings the Ashanti by the 1980s were overshadowed by the Ewe who had been comparatively stateless when the British, the Germans and the French began to carve up their land nearly four generations earlier.

Mobutu Sese Seko in Zaire lies in the same contradictory tradition of pre-colonial statelessness inheriting the post-colonial state. Mobutu does not come from any of the great kingdoms of pre-colonial Zaire. He does not come from among the Bakongo, Baluba or Balunda. Mobutu comes from the far less centralised equatorial area of northern Zaire, along the fringes with the forest. Zaire, like Uganda, has had its lumpen-militariat, inherited from the colonial period – and Mobutu symbolises that heritage. But is this privatisation of the state in Zaire basically anarchic and ethnic, as it was in Amin's Uganda? Or does it reveal different characteristics?

In the earlier years of Mobutu's rule, the 'model' seemed similar to that which later became Idi Amin's style. Zaire betrayed a considerable tendency towards anarchy, combined with ethnic solidarity and nepotism. And the 'raiding' of the state's resources resulted from both tendencies.

But there has since developed in the Zairean state a third tendency – the *dynastic* trend. This is a distinct form of privatisation, crystallising into a kind of royal family with special prerogatives and perquisites. It is a neo-monarchical tendency. In addition to the privatisation of the state's economic resources, and the personalisation of the state's power, there is now also a personification of the state's sacred symbols. A personality cult goes to the extent of sacralising the top man and royalising his family. The ruler's immediate political supporters evolve into a kind of aristocracy, complete with social ostentation, conspicuous consumption, and sometimes the equivalent of aristocratic titles.

Mobutu Sese Seko has not gone to the extent of Emperor Bokassa and his neo-Napoleonic coronation in the Central African Empire (now renamed once again a Republic). But the dynastic tendency is definitely evident in Mobutu's state. The state in Zaire is thus privatised not just economically (by appropriating its resources), not just politically (by personalising its power) but also symbolically (by personifying its sacredness). Yet while this glitter of royalty continues in mineral-rich Zaire, both the state and the economy endure the insidious effects of decay.

On the more positive side of his policies, President Mobutu Sese Seko has made the principle of 'authenticity' the central doctrine of his national commitment. By 'authenticity' Mobutu means the pursuit of life-styles and tenets compatible with Zaire's indigenous and ancestral heritage. But Mobutu's most effective realisation of authenticity lay not in his explicit cultural policies, or in his rhetoric and eloquence on behalf of African culture, but in his mismanagement of Zaire's economy and his form of privatisation of the Zairean state. By helping to damage and even destroy some of the inherited institutions of the colonial order, Mobutu was inadvertently carrying out patriotic cultural sabotage. By reducing modernisation and Westernisation to a farce, Mobutu helped indigenous culture to reassert itself after the massive cultural onslaught of the colonial era. As the roads decayed, and factories came to a standstill, Africans turned increasingly to older and more traditional ways of earning a living.

Also seriously damaged was the Western invention of paper money. The currency, named after the country, zaire, had rather rapidly fallen in value. There were times, for example 1983, when one needed a substantial bag of money in order to pay for a meal in a restaurant in Kinshasa. Mountains of paper money were exchanged for trivia. Faith in the cash economy was being substantially undermined in important sectors of Zairean society. Africans in the countryside are beginning to revert to older forms of exchange, including barter. And many are also beginning to explore alternative forms of saving as the conflict between the indigenous heritage and the Western heritage deepens.

But how does this theme of decay relate to the third leg of our triple heritage in this book – Islam? How do these different levels of social decomposition affect the fortunes of Islam in Africa?

Is the Crescent also Decaying?
The first thing to note is that the most serious forms of decay seem to be occurring in the institutions inherited from the Western world, rather than those bequeathed by Islam.

But this very decomposition of the Western heritage has complex consequences for Islam in Africa. It is arguable that where Islam is already established, the decline of the West is advantageous for Islam. After all, the most important threat to Islam in Africa is not a revival of indigenous culture but the triumph of Western secularism. The materialism of Western civilisation, the superiority of Western science and technology at their home base in the West, the declining moral standards in at least certain areas of Western culture, and the glitter and temptations of Western life-styles, have all combined to pose a significant threat especially to the younger generations of the Muslim world. As these Western institutions grind to a standstill in Africa, causing new areas of poverty and deprivation, the glitter of Western civilisation begins to dim.

But while established Islam is indeed stabilised by this Western decay, Islamic expansion to new areas is probably hindered by the same decay. For example, the economic decline in West Africa has resulted in reduced traffic of Muslim traders and other migrants, many of whom have been unofficial missionaries for the Islamic faith. Also reducing the expansion of Islam are the decaying roads and railways, which reduce social and economic mobility.

To summarise the argument so far: where Islam is already established, the decay of Western civilisation is good for Islam since it helps to neutralise a major threat. On the other hand, where Islam has not yet arrived, the disintegration of African communications and the decline in commercial traffic across African borders has reduced the pace of Islamic expansion.

But the relationship between Islam and Westernism in Africa is more complex than that. While it is true that in Nigeria it is the Muslim north which is less Westernised than the non-Muslim south, in the Sudan the non-Muslim south is less Westernised than the Muslim north by all criteria except the religious one. In other words, the south in the Sudan is more Christianised but less modernised than the north. And since modernity in twentieth-century Africa bears the stamp of Western culture, it is the north which displays more signs of Western technology and institutions, alongside Islam, than does the south. By criteria of depth of decay, northern Sudan reveals more dramatic decline in standards from earlier ones. But southern Sudan has to be assessed in terms of speed of decay since many of the institutions associated with the West are very new in the south and have taken even less root than they might have in the north.

But what does this decay of the economy and infrastructure do to Islamic fundamentalism? Looking at the case of the Sudan, it would appear that increasing poverty and economic frustrations contributed to President Nimeri's policy of Islamisation. The adoption of Islamic Law in Sudan by Nimeri's ex-government was at least partly due to the hardships of economic decline and institutional decay.

On the other hand, Iran had its Islamic revolution not because of poverty but because of wealth; not because Westernisation was being reversed, but because Westernisation was being pushed too fast by the Shah.

It is also arguable that Qaddafy's Libya illustrates a form of Islamic fundamentalism arising out of wealth rather than poverty, a distrust of Western styles of modernisation rather than the decay of those styles.

But in the face of these conflicting examples, what are we to conclude about the relationship between Westernisation and Islamic fundamentalism? A tentative generalisation is that Islamisation from the top (by a ruler) can occur under conditions of either wealth or poverty, depending upon other factors which might influence the ruler in that direction. But Islamisation from below, from the grassroots, is more likely to occur when Westernisation is growing rather than declining, when Western institutions are being built too fast rather than decaying too rapidly. Iran, precisely because it had a social revolution, constituted Islamisation from below, and was substantially a response to increasing Westernisation rather than decline. But Nimeri's Sudan was a case of attempted Islamisation from above, with no major spontaneous movement of the people. Similarly, Islamisation under President Zia ul Haq in Pakistan is from above. As for Qaddafy's Libya, it probably lies somewhere between the Iranian revolution of mass involvement and Nimeri's Islamic reforms by decree. Libya probably includes both mass enthusiasm for Islam and a Muslim Bonaparte (fusing populism, dictatorship and patriotic expansionism) in command at the top, Qaddafy.

Conclusion

European colonial rule in Africa was more effective in destroying indigenous African *structures* than in destroying African *culture*. The tension between new imported structures and old resilient cultures is part of the post-colonial war of cultures in the African continent. The question has therefore arisen as to whether Africa is reclaiming its own.

As we have indicated, the shallowness of the imported *economic* institutions from the West was partly due to the lopsided nature of colonial acculturation. Western consumption patterns prevailed more quickly than Western production techniques, thus promoting Western tastes without developing Western skills.

As for the shallowness of the imported *political* institutions, this was partly due to the moral contradictions of Western political tutelage. After independence these political contradictions took their toll, for the transferred institutions simply did not take root. Africa was torn between the forces of anarchy on one side, in the sense of decentralised violence, and the forces of tyranny, on the other side, in the sense of orchestrated centralised repression. The post-colonial state was in turn torn between the forces of privatisation and the forces of militarism. Privatisation puts a state outside the public sector, as it denationalises it. Militarisation, by definition, abolishes the principle of civilian supremacy.

But in the final analysis, the shallowness of the imported institutions is due to that culture gap between new structures and ancient values, between alien institutions and ancestral traditions.

Africa can never go back completely to its pre-colonial starting point but there may be a case for at least a partial retreat, a case for re-establishing contacts with familiar landmarks of yesteryear and then re-starting the journey of modernisation under indigenous impetus.

In many parts of Africa there is, as we indicated, a war between Islam and Westernism. The decay of Western civilisation is good for Islam in those parts of the continent. But the decay of the infrastructure and the decline of African economies may be bad for Islamic expansion in west Africa.

But when all is said and done, the most important cultural conflict occurring in Africa is between Western civilisation and indigenous forces. If instability in the continent is a symptom of cultures at war, perhaps Africa's identity may survive the ravages of Westernisation after all. It is still true to say that Africans in the twentieth century are becoming acculturated faster than were, for example, the Jews in the first millennium of their dispersal. But the war of cultures is by no means over in Africa. It is almost as if the indigenous ancestors have been aroused from the dead, and are fighting back to avert the demise of Africanity. In their immediate consequences decay and instability are a matter of lament. But in their longer term repercussions, they may be a matter for celebration.

But what is the way out? How can Africa's compact with the twentieth century be amended? How can the ancestors be appeased?

Two broad principles should influence and inform social reform in Africa in the coming decades. One is the imperative of looking inwards towards ancestry; the other is the imperative of looking outward towards the wider humanity. The inward imperative requires a more systematic investigation into the cultural preconditions of the success of each project, of each piece of legislation, of each system of government. Feasibility studies should be much more sensitive to the issue of 'cultural feasibility' than has been the case in the past. Africa's ancestors need to be consulted through the intermediary of consulting African usage, custom and tradition.

But since the world is becoming a village, Africa cannot just look inward to its own past. The compact with the twentieth century has to include a sensitivity to the wider world of the human race as a whole.

In the coming pages we shall explore Africa's decay as a valuable opportunity for fundamental social, economic and political change – an opportunity for a reconciliation with the ancestors and a new relationship with the wider world of the twentieth century. Underlying it all is Africa's triple heritage of indigenous, Islamic and Western forces – fusing and recoiling, at once competitive and complementary.

Islam and Westernism have been part of Africa's response to the imperative of looking outward to the wider world. But Africa's own ancestors are waiting to ensure that Africa also remembers to look inward to its own past.

Before a seed germinates it must first decay. A mango tree grows out of a decaying mango seed. A new Africa may be germinating in the decay of the present one – and the ancestors are presiding over the process.

Where is Africa?

The Universe According to Europe

It could be said that Africa invented Man, that the Semites invented God and that Europe invented the world, or rather the *concept* of the world. Archaeology indicates that Man originated in eastern Africa (as we shall see in the following chapter). The Semitic peoples gave us the great monotheistic world religions – Judaism, Christianity and Islam – a theme which we shall also examine later in these pages (see Chapters 2 and 4). Europe developed the concept of the world in the wake of its voyages of discovery in the fifteenth and sixteenth centuries, but it even imposed its form of that concept on the outlook of peoples in other continents, including Africans.

It is not possible to overestimate the enormous impact of Europe upon our perceptions of ourselves as Africans and upon our view of the universe. Some of these effects are obvious, others are much more subtle. Among the relatively obvious is the choice of Greenwich in Britain as the 'mean time' for the alarm clocks of the human race. The clocks of the world have responded to that choice. Even when we say 'Universal Standard Time' we are really predicating it on Greenwich Mean Time. A spot on the British Isles has changed the clocks and watches of the world. Such is the influence of Britain's former glory on our perceptions of universal time!

Even if we had to choose that particular meridian passing through Greenwich, the same longitude passes through towns and villages in northern and western Africa. Why not name the world's 'mean time' after one of those towns? Why do Africans not unilaterally rename the Greenwich meridian the Gao meridian, to remind themselves not of an English palace built by King Henry VIII but of the great capital city of the emperors of Songhay?

Is Europe *north* of Africa? Is Europe *up* and Africa *down* in geographical location, as well as in income, power and global status? Of course, the maps say Europe is north of Africa (and therefore *up*). But that decision was arbitrary and made primarily by European mapmakers. Whether Europe is *above* Africa or *below* is purely relative because it depends upon the vantage point in the cosmos from which an observer is looking at planet Earth. But no European had been out there in the cosmos before European mapmakers decided that from outer space one 'inevitably' looked at Earth from a vantage point which placed Africa below Europe. Yet there is no reason, from an astronautical or cosmonautical point of view, why the South Pole should not be the North Pole and vice versa.

Even with regard to the size of the African continent, it is quite remarkable how far European ethnocentrism has influenced cartographic projec-

opposite, Sheep market, Ghardaia, Algeria

tions over the centuries. The legacy of Gerhard Mercator, the greatest of the sixteenth-century European cartographers, has continued to distort size on the map in favour of the northern continents of the world. The modern map, based on the Mercator projection, shows North America as one and a half times the size of Africa. On a Mercator projection it is difficult to believe that, on the contrary, Africa is three and a half times the size of United States. On the Mercator projection Greenland appears to be almost in competition with Africa in size, which is of course preposterous, since Greenland (2 million square kilometres) is only a fraction of Africa's size (30 million square kilometres). The visual memories of millions of children across generations have carried distorted ideas about the comparative physical scale of northern continents in relation to southern ones. What is, of course, clear is that Africa is a continent larger than China and India added together, and capable of absorbing several times over the acreage of all the imperial powers that have ravished or conquered Africa throughout the centuries.

This is the dialectic between the map and the master, between the African student of geography and the Western cartographer. Africa might have been denied its full credentials as a part of human civilisation, but must it also be denied its size in square kilometres? Can we not begin to experiment in schools with maps and globes which are less distorting? Should we not include in every school atlas the alternative scenario of 'turning the world the other side up', with South America at the top and North America below, with Africa above and Europe beneath? Should not all geography lessons be more explicit about the danger of ethnocentrism even in mapmaking?

The Mercator map is so distorted because the lines of latitude have been moved further apart the nearer they are to the poles. Exactly 400 years after Mercator produced his world map, another German, Arno Peters, in 1967 produced the Peters Projection Map which represents the size of countries more accurately according to their surface areas. In the field of political philosophy one German, Karl Marx, attempted to put another German, Hegel, the right side up, restoring the primacy of material conditions over ideas. In mapmaking Peters has restored Africa to its true relative size, but he still puts Europe at the top of the world. Future mapmakers may need to put the globe the right side up, restoring a much needed status to the cradle of mankind, Africa, where human history first began.[1]

In this book we shall refer often to the 'Middle East'. That the area concerned is 'Middle' can be objectively argued; that it is 'East' is a subjective *Eurocentric* exercise. The Middle East is objectively 'Middle' in the sense of linking together the three continents of the so-called 'ancient world' – Africa, Asia and Europe. But it would not have been 'East' if the point of departure had been sub-Saharan Africa or India. It was 'East' because the original point of geographic departure was supposed to be western Europe. That is also true of the term 'Far East' – though in this case both the term 'Far' and the term 'East' are Eurocentric and subjective in origin.

Let us consider the actual names of the different continents of the world.

Europeans chose the name of their own continent for themselves – traced to *Europa* and beyond. Europeans also chose the names of the Americas – North, South and Central. Europeans chose the name Antarctica. Europeans decided what would count as the continent of Asia, although the name itself had some ancestral legitimacy in the continent to which it was applied.

As for the name 'Africa', some have traced it to Berber origins; others have traced it to a Greco-Roman ancestry. The ancient Romans referred to their colonial province in present-day Tunisia and eastern Algeria as 'Africa', possibly because the name came from a Latin or Greek word for that region or its people, or perhaps because the word came from one of the local languages, either Berber or Phoenician. Did the Romans call the continent after the Latin word *Aprica* (sunny)? Or were the Romans and the Greeks using the Greek word *Aphrike* (without cold)? Or did the word come from the Semites to refer to a very productive region of what is today Tunisia – a name which meant Ears of Corn? Later, the Arab immigrants 'Arabised' the name *Africa* to *Ifriqiya*. Whatever the origin of the word Africa, two legacies (Semitic and Greco-Roman) have probably helped to define the identity of the third legacy (indigenous Africa).

But although the name Africa may have originally been either Semitic or Greco-Roman, the application of the name in more recent centuries has been due almost entirely to western Europe. In its fifteenth century western Europeans first journeyed to Black Africa, south of the Sahara, and began to apply the old Roman term, originally applied to a part of north Africa, to the lands south of the Sahara. This process of discovery of Black Africa led western Europeans to think of Africa as the land of Black people, as the 'Dark Continent' – no longer as a north African province. The new west European *racial* thinking implied that the 'real Africa' is south of the Sahara, that Africans are Black, that Africa is a *race*, that the northern boundary of Africa is the Sahara. On the other hand, European *geographical* thinking came to assume that Africa is not a race but a *continent*, that the northern boundary is not the Sahara but the Mediterranean, thereby including in Africa the Berber and Arab lands north of the desert. In this case the Europeans decided to leave the matter bewilderingly ambivalent and ambiguous. Incredible as it may seem, Europe, by declaring on the one hand that Africans are a race of Black people and on the other hand that north Africa is also, by reasons of geography, part of Africa, has succeeded in forcing Black Africans themselves to wonder in all confusion whether they are a race or are inhabitants of a continent. Have Black Africans been trapped by Europeans into thinking of their continent as a 'Black continent' in contrast to Europe as a continent of the white race, when in fact Africa is a multi-coloured continent of largely Black Africans south of the Sahara and largely brown Africans north of the desert? Should Africans not begin to regard themselves as multi-coloured peoples? Should Africans think in terms more of their similarity with Asians as multi-coloured peoples than of their difference from white Europeans? Should Africans' self-identity cease to

The face of this black granite statue of Amenophis-son-of-Hahn displays Negroid features

Where is Africa?   25

consist of a racial reaction to a racial identity imposed on them by Europe?

Three Definitions of 'Africa'

The ambivalence has been so deep that in order to demonstrate that ancient Egypt was an *African* civilisation, some have found it necessary to seek evidence that ancient Egypt was a *Black* civilisation. Skeletons and skulls of ancient Egyptians have been checked to see if they were 'Negroid'. Noses in ancient Egyptian paintings have been examined to see if they were flat. The Sphinx has been scrutinised to see if it had Negroid features before wind and sand eroded its nose.

My own feeling is that to insist that nothing is African unless it is Black is to fall into the white man's fallacy. No one insists that the Chinese, on the one hand, and Black Sinhalese or Tamils of Sri Lanka on the other hand, must be the same colour before they can all be regarded as 'Asians'.

The problem originally arose because Europe itself was regarded as a uni-pigmentational continent – the inhabitants of each country being regarded as primarily 'white'. Was Africa going to be as multi-coloured as Asia? Or was it going to be as uni-coloured as Europe? In its hegemonic days of imperialism, European leadership never resolved the issue. Some thought of Africa as having three zones: white-dominated Africa south of the Tropic of

Vasco da Gama, the Portuguese navigator

The Phantom of the Cape of Good Hope appearing to Vasco da Gama

Capricorn, Arab-dominated Africa north of the Tropic of Cancer, and Black Africa between the two tropics. The question of 'Where is the real Africa?' was in this case answered in terms of what lay between the tropics of Capricorn and Cancer.

To summarise, there have until now been three definitions of the 'real Africa'. The racial definition of Africa restricted identity to the Black populated parts of the continent. The continental definition of Africa is the principle on which the Organisation of African Unity is partly based – Africa is a continent as a whole. The power definition of Africa would exclude those parts of Africa which are still under 'non-African' control – especially the Republic of South Africa. But this is, I hope, a very temporary situation.

Is there a fourth definition of Africa, which pushes Africa's boundaries not only across the Sahara but even across the Red Sea? There may be but, in order to consider this possibility, let us first look at the seas. We are sure that the Cape of Good Hope is the southern extremity of the continent. The Cape was, of course, named by Europeans – by the Portuguese. This was at a time when European interest was primarily in Asia. Africa was considered an obstacle on the sea route to Asia. The struggle was to circumvent Africa and find a sea outlet to the Orient. Bartholomew Diaz managed to get to the southern Cape in 1488, and called it the Cape of Storms. The King of

Fort Jesus, Mombasa. The Mombasa city-state was ruled from this fort for 100 years.

Portugal, in anticipation of his sailors reaching Asia, renamed the South African Cape the 'Cape of Good Hope'.

We are also sure that the Atlantic Ocean has been the decisive western boundary of the African continent. There have been differences and territorial disagreements with the Iberian peninsula and with the accompanying islands. But, on the whole, the western boundary of Africa has been relatively consolidated – the Atlantic frontier. The northern extremity of the African continent has been mainly the Mediterranean. As we shall indicate later, those African societies which are on the shores of the Mediterranean have had a triple identity of their own. Are they a southern extension of Europe, a northern extension of sub-Saharan Africa, or a western extension of the Arabian peninsula? The ocean itself was called the Mediterranean by Europeans – precisely because of the ocean's centrality in relation to the three ancient continents. It is the eastern border of Africa which poses important questions about the arbitrariness of continental identities. Should Africa end where the Indian Ocean begins? Should it end where the Red Sea begins?

The juxtaposition of the name of a continent, Africa, and the word *sea* raises a definitional problem. Are we giving the oceans an excessive say in determining where one continent ends and another begins? Can there be continents without the sea to define them? As far as Africa is concerned, we should remember that Africa was connected to Asia at the Isthmus of Suez before Ferdinand de Lesseps created the Canal, which was opened in 1869. Yet the Suez Canal and the Red Sea are considered by many to be part of the boundary between Africa and Asia.

Towards a Fourth Definition of 'Africa'

Where then is Africa? *What* is Africa? How sensible are its boundaries? Islands can be very far from Africa and still be part of Africa – provided they are not too near another major land mass. But a peninsula can be arbitrarily dis-Africanised. Madagascar is separated from the African continent by the 500-mile-wide Mozambique channel. Mauritius lies well over 1000 miles from the African coastline. Greater Yemen, on the other hand, is separated from Djibouti by only a stone's throw at the Strait of Bab el Mandeb. Yet Madagascar and Mauritius are politically part of Africa, while Greater Yemen is not. Much of the post-colonial African scholarship has addressed itself to the artificiality of the boundaries of contemporary African states. But little attention has been paid to the artificiality of the boundaries of the African continent itself. Why should north Africa end on the Red Sea when eastern Africa does not end on the Mozambique channel? Why should Tananarive be an African capital when Aden is not?

There have been discussions in Africa as to whether the Sahara Desert is a chasm or a link. Continental Pan-Africanism asserts that the Sahara is a sea of communication rather than a chasm of separation. Yet there are some who would argue that north Africa is not 'really Africa'. Why? Because it is more

The construction of the Suez
Canal in the 1860s

like Arabia. But in that case, it would be just as logical to push the boundary
of north Africa further east to include Arabia, to refuse to recognise the Red
Sea as a chasm, just as the trans-Saharan Pan-Africanist has refused to
concede such a role to the Sahara Desert. Why not assert that the African
continent ends neither on the southern extremity of the Sahara nor on the
western shore of the Red Sea? Should Africa move not only northwards to
the Mediterranean but also north-eastwards to the Persian Gulf? I am not
suggesting that this is within the realms of practical politics or likely geographical redefinition at the moment; rather that we should question Europe's
decisions about boundaries of Africa and the identity of Africans.

The most pernicious sea in Africa's history may well be the Red Sea. This
thin line of water has been deemed to be more relevant for defining where
Africa ends than all the evidence of geology, geography, history and culture.
The north-eastern boundary of Africa has been defined by a strip of water in
the teeth of massive ecological and cultural evidence to the contrary.

The problem goes back several million years when three cracks emerged
on the eastern side of Africa. As Colin McEvedy put it,

> One crack broke Arabia away, creating the Gulf of Aden and the Red Sea, and reducing the
> areas of contact between Africa and Asia to the Isthmus of Suez.[2]

The 'contact' at the Isthmus was definitional. It depended upon looking at
the Red Sea as a divide. Three cracks had occurred on the African crust – yet
only the one which had resulted in a sea was permitted to 'dis-Africanise'

what lay beyond the sea. The other two cracks resulted in 'rift valleys', straightsided trenches averaging thirty miles across. The eastern and western rifts left the African continent intact but the emergence of a strip of water called the Red Sea had resulted in the physical separation of Africa from Arabia.

The final drama in the separation of the Arabian peninsula from what we now call Africa occurred in the nineteenth century. If the Arabs had been in control of their own destiny they could have been discussing building communications between the two parts of the Arab world. But, in fact, Egypt in the nineteenth century was oriented towards Europe. And so the Suez Canal was built, by a Frenchman, Ferdinand de Lesseps, not in order to facilitate traffic between Africa and Arabia but to make it easier for Europe to trade with the rest of the world. An estimated 120,000 Egyptians lost their lives in the ten years it took to build the Suez Canal (1859–69). A natural cataclysm which had occurred several million years previously and torn off the Arabian peninsula from the rest of Africa was now completed at Suez through its canal. European power and European pre-eminence in map-making decided that Africa ended on the western side of the Red Sea and on the west bank of the Suez Canal, in spite of the similarity of the geology of north-eastern Africa and Arabia on either side of the Red Sea, in spite also of the similarity of language and culture, and the artificiality of a continental boundary based on a man-made canal.

The 'traditional' Mercator map

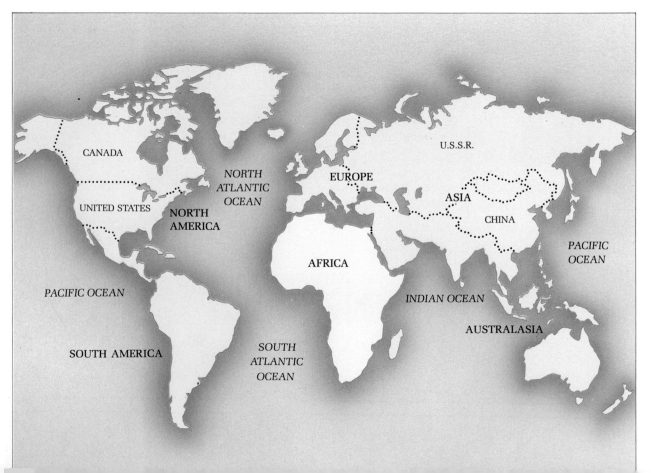

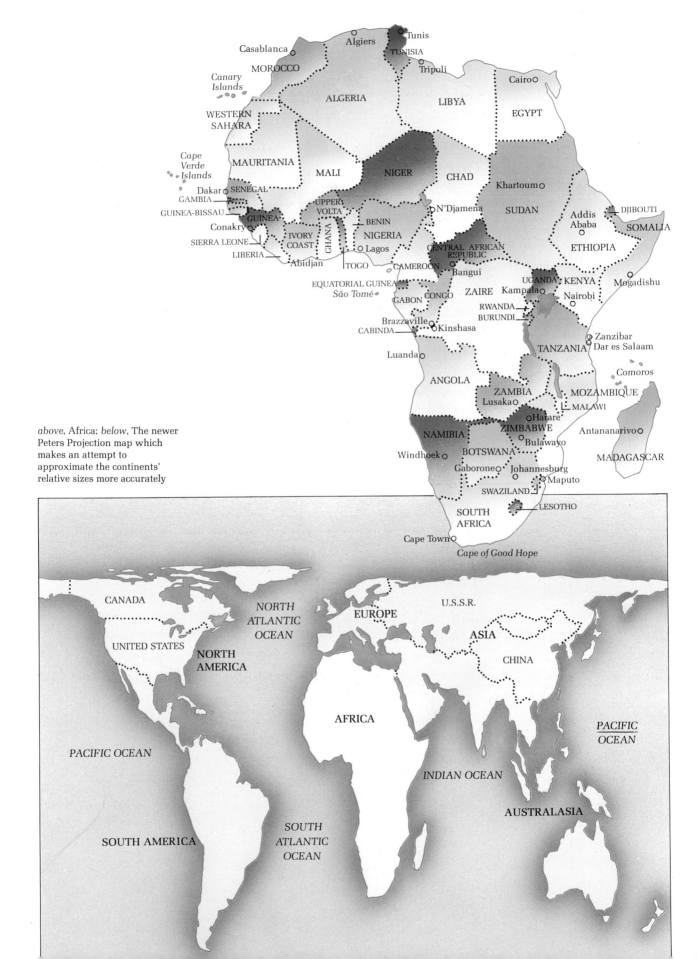

above, Africa; *below*, The newer Peters Projection map which makes an attempt to approximate the continents' relative sizes more accurately

The separation of Arabia from Africa by the Red Sea is not even geological separation. As Paul Bohannan put it,

> Geologically, the whole of the Arabian peninsula must be considered as unitary with the African continent. The Rift Valley that cuts through the whole begins in Anatolia, in northern Turkey, stretches through what is now the Jordan Valley and the Dead Sea; it then follows down the length of the Red Sea (which is best thought of as an inland Lake with a small opening into the Indian Ocean), and down through Lake Rudolf.[3]

In spite of the geological unity of Arabia and Africa and the former land link between the two continents at the Suez Isthmus, European geographers classified Arabia as being part of Asia.

What a geological crack had once put asunder, the forces of geography, history and culture have been trying to bind together again ever since. Who are the Amhara of Ethiopia if not a people probably descended from south Arabians? What is Amharic but a Semitic language? What is a Semitic language if not a branch of the Afro-Asian family of languages? Was the Semitic parental language born in Africa and then exported across the Red Sea? Or was it from the Arabian peninsula originally and then descended upon such people as the Amhara? How much of a bridge between Arabia and Africa are the Somali? All these are lingo-cultural questions which raise the issue of whether the geological secession of Arabia several million years ago has been in the process of being neutralised by the intimate cultural integration between Arabia, the Horn and North Africa.

In the linguistic field it is certainly no longer easy to determine where African indigenous languages end and Semitic trends begin. There was a time when both Hamites and Semites were regarded by European scholars such as C. G. Seligman as basically alien to Africa. In due course Hamites were regarded as a fictitious category – and the people represented by the term (such as the Tutsi of Rwanda and Burundi) were accepted as indisputably African. What about the Semites? They have undoubtedly existed in world history. But are they 'Africans' who crossed the Red Sea – like Moses on the run from the Pharaoh? Or are the Semites originally 'Arabians' who penetrated Africa? These problems of identity would be partially solved overnight if the Arabian peninsula was part of Africa.

Islam: A Bridge Across the Red Sea

The cultural effort to re-integrate Arabia with Africa after the geological divide several million years previously reached a new phase with the birth and expansion of Islam. The Muslim conquest of north Africa was a process of overcoming the divisiveness of the Red Sea.

Twin processes were set in motion in north Africa from the seventh century AD onwards – Islamisation (a religious conversion to the creed of Muhammad) and Arabisation (a linguistic assimilation into the language of the Arabs). In time the great majority of north Africans saw themselves as Arabs – no less than did the inhabitants of the Arabian peninsula. In short, the Islamisation and Arabisation of north Africa were once again cultural countervailing forces trying to outweigh the geological separatism perpetrated by the birth of the Red Sea millions of years earlier.

If the Red Sea could perhaps be ignored in determining the north-eastern limits of Africa, why cannot the Mediterranean also be ignored as an outer northern limit? There was indeed a time when north Africa was regarded as an extension of Europe. This goes back to the days of Carthage, of Hellenistic colonisation, and later of the Roman Empire. The concept of 'Europe' was at best in the making at that time. In the words of historians R. R. Palmer and Joel Colton,

> There was really no Europe in ancient times. In the Roman Empire we may see a Mediterranean world, or even a West and an East in the Latin and Greek portions. But the West included parts of Africa as well as of Europe.[4]

One might add that for the same reason there was no Africa in ancient times either. Even as late as the seventeenth century the idea that the land mass south of the Mediterranean was something distinct from the land mass north of it was a proposition still difficult to comprehend. The great American Africanist, Melville Herskovits, has pointed out how the Geographer Royal of France, writing in 1656, described Africa as a 'peninsula so large that it comprises the third part, and this the most southerly of our continent'.[5]

This old proposition that north Africa was the southern part of Europe had its last frantic fling in the modern world in France's attempt to keep Algeria as part of France. The desperate myth that Algeria was the southern portion of France tore the French nation apart in the 1950s, created the crisis which brought Charles de Gaulle to power in 1958, and maintained tensions between the Right and the Left in France until Algeria's independence in 1962, with an additional aftermath of bitterness in the trail of the career of Charles de Gaulle.

The effort to maintain Algeria as a southern extension of a European power took place at a time when, in other respects, north Africa had become a western extension of Arabia. From the seventh century onwards Arabisation and Islamisation had been transforming north Africa's identity. Because Africa's border was deemed to be the Red Sea, the Arabs became a 'bicontinental' people – impossible to label neatly as either 'African' or 'Asian'. Indeed, the majority of the Arab people by the twentieth century were located west of the Red Sea (that is, in Africa 'proper') although the majority of the Arab states were east of the Red Sea (deemed to be west Asia). The Arabic language has many more speakers in the present African continent than in the Arabian peninsula. Arabic has become the most important single language in the present African continent in terms of number of speakers.

The case for regarding Arabia as part of Africa, though very controversial, is now much stronger than for regarding north Africa as part of Europe. Islamisation and Arabisation have redefined the identity of north Africans

Saoura Beni Abbes, Algeria,
with the French Fort in the
background

more fundamentally than either Gallicisation or Anglicisation have done. In spite of the proximity of the Rock of Gibraltar to Africa, the Mediterranean is a more convincing line of demarcation between Africa and Europe than the Red Sea or the Suez Canal can claim to be as a divide between Africa and Asia. All boundaries are artificial but some boundaries are more artificial than others.

Towards Africanising Judaism and Islam

Mahatma Gandhi said that all the world's great religions originated in Asia. He was referring to Hinduism, Buddhism, Confucianism, Zoroastrianism, Judaism, Christianity and Islam. The last three are what might be called the great Semitic religions. Whether these started in Asia very much depended upon where Africa's north-eastern boundary was drawn.

Of course there are other issues which could affect the continental origins

of the Semitic religions. There is first the issue of whether Moses was an African in our continental sense of the term. Biblically he is supposed to be of the Levi tribe from among a group in Egypt called the Hebrews. But originally the term 'Hebrew' was not racial or ethnic but was class-related. It seems to have been derived from the word *Habiru* or *Hapiru* which referred to a class of people in Egypt who hired out their services in exchange for goods or other forms of payment. For some reason they became a threat to a particular pharaoh, and he enslaved them. The stage was set for the biblical story of Moses and the final Exodus.

One historical debate is whether those Hebrews, or *Habiru*, were in fact a class of Egyptians – in which case they were 'African' in our continental sense of the term. Another debate, fuelled in part by Sigmund Freud, is whether Moses himself was an Egyptian – regardless of whether the Hebrews were or were not Egyptians themselves. His name Moses (*Moshe* in Hebrew) is originally Egyptian. The ancient Egyptian term *mose* ('is born') can be seen in such names as *Tutmose* ('The God Thoth is born'). The question becomes particularly compelling if we accept early Jewish and Christian traditions which attributed to Moses the authorship of the Torah ('Law' or 'Teaching'), otherwise known as Pentateuch ('Five Books'). These are the initial five books of the Bible which are still widely regarded by biblical fundamentalists as being written by Moses. If Moses was Egyptian, the Torah is a work of north African origin.

In the bid to escape from Egypt, Moses took his people to the water's edge. Was it the Red Sea or the Sea of Reeds (papyrus)? If it was the latter, it was probably a lake in north-eastern Egypt, since papyrus grows in fresh water.

Africa's heritage of different influences is shown in the contrasting dress of this mother and daughter in Tunisia

But scholars disagree as to the precise location of the crossing. If it was the Red Sea, then this stretch of water experienced under Moses its most distinctive ecological transformation since the great convulsion of the Rift Valley several million years previously. According to biblical and Qur'anic accounts, the Red Sea parted. A land link between Africa and the Arabian peninsula was re-established for one short moment in biblical times. What an earthquake millions of years previously had put asunder, God briefly put together again by providing a land link for Moses' escape. The waters parted — and Africa was momentarily redefined to include what was later called the Arabian peninsula. The fate of Judaism was temporarily intertwined with a new African frontier.

What about the fate of Islam? It is arguable that Europe dis-Africanised the Prophet Muhammad by declaring the Red Sea rather than the Persian (or Arabian) Gulf as Africa's north-eastern boundary. It is true that Islam had its own early links with Africa west of the Red Sea. Ethiopia was a haven of peace, an asylum, for early Muslims on the run from persecution by pagan Mecca. Ethiopian tourist literature to the present day draws attention to that trend during the lifetime of the Prophet Muhammad himself. Ethiopia helped nascent Islam to survive.

By the twentieth century of the Christian era Islam in Black Africa itself had sufficiently developed to the extent that African followers of Muhammad experienced their own crisis of identity. Precisely because Europeans had dis-Africanised Muhammad by making Africa end at the Red Sea, there were African Muslims who felt a need for an African prophet. Among the more politically dramatic were the Nigerian followers of the Cameroonian, Mohammadu Marwa, otherwise known as Maitatsine. Periodic eruptions of political violence were part of the story of the Nigerian sect, especially from 1980 onwards. Maitatsine himself was killed in one such confrontation between his sect and the authorities in Kano in 1980. The most distinctive yearning within his sect was a burning desire for the Africanisation of Islam, which later became a burning desire for an African prophet. Maitatsine himself was elevated by his followers to the status of such a prophet. It must remain an issue of conjecture and speculation whether the yearning for an African prophet would have been partly assuaged if the Prophet Muhammad had himself been perceived as an African. Would the desire for the Africanisation of Islam have been politically diffused if it was demonstrable that Islam itself was an African religion? By drawing the boundary of Africa at the Red Sea, European mapmakers may have caused more havoc than we even realise. Many a life killed in the Maitatsine riots of 1980, or the riots of Maiduguri and Yola (Gongola State) and Kaduna in 1984, or in Gombe in 1985, could conceivably have been spared if the fourth definition of Africa had prevailed — and Mecca and Medina been African religious capitals for centuries before the birth of Nigeria.

This means that the oldest of the Semitic religions, Judaism, and the youngest, Islam, are eligible for consideration as originally African, as well as Asian. The ancestry of Moses and the origins of the *Habiru*, the role of Ethiopia in helping to rescue nascent Islam, and the ecological secession of the Arabian peninsula and its exploitation by European mapmakers, are all part of the case for reconsidering the continental origins of Judaism and Islam.

What of Christianity? Unlike the other two religions, Christianity has basically been rejected by its founders. Islam is a religion of the Arabs; Judaism is a religion of the Jews – but Christianity is a religion of Europe and has relatively few adherents in Palestine. Ethiopian Christianity is an island, proving once again that Christianity was rejected by its own cradle and flourished elsewhere. But if the Semites were originally African, so surely was Christianity, which was born out of the Semitic womb.

Conclusion

We live in an age when a people's perception of themselves can be deeply influenced by which continent or region they associate themselves with. Until the 1950s the official policy of the government of Emperor Haile Selassie was to emphasise that Ethiopia was part of the Middle East rather than part of Africa. Yet it was the Emperor himself who initiated the policy of re-Africanising Ethiopia as the rest of Africa approached independence,

An artist's impression of the armed conflict between government forces and the militant Maitatsine religious movement in 1980. Hundreds of people were killed, including the religious leader.

Gamal Abdel Nasser of Egypt
and Anthony Nutting of Britain
sign the Anglo–Egyptian
Agreement in Cairo, 1954, by
which British Forces agreed to
leave Egypt

Haile Selassie and
Winston Churchill in
London, 1954

fearing to be outflanked by the radicalism of Nasser of Egypt and Nkrumah of Ghana. In particular, Nasser's strong support for continental Pan-Africanism and active support for anti-colonial liberation struggles both north and south of the Sahara encouraged Haile Selassie to emphasise that Ethiopia, too, was part of Africa. Yet cultural similarities between Ethiopia and the rest of Black Africa are not any greater than cultural similarities between north Africa and the Arabian peninsula. Nevertheless, a European decision to make Africa end at the Red Sea has decisively dis-Africanised the Arabian peninsula, and made the natives there see themselves as west Asians rather than as north Africans.

Several million years ago the crust of Africa cracked and the Red Sea was born. As we indicated, this thin strip of water helped to seal the identity of generations of people living on either side of it. Yet cultural change has been struggling to heal the geological rift between Africa and Arabia. It is time the tyranny of the sea as a definer of identity was at least moderated if not ended.

In any case, the tyranny of the sea is in part a tyranny of European geographical prejudices. Just as European mapmakers could decree that on the global map Europe was above Africa instead of below (an arbitrary decision in relation to the cosmos) those mapmakers could also dictate that Africa ended at the Red Sea instead of the Persian 'Gulf'.

Where is Africa? Our location in the rest of this book will have to be mainly west of the Red Sea and both north and south of the Sahara. We have to accept the continental definition as presently defined internationally. But I personally regard the present boundaries of Africa as not only arbitrary but artificially conceived by European geographers in a former era of European dominance. For the purpose of this book I accept the Red Sea as one of Africa's boundaries – but I do so decidedly under protest.

The most difficult people to convince of a greater territorial Africa may well turn out to be the inhabitants of the Arabian peninsula. They have grown to be proud of being the 'Arabs of Asia' rather than the 'Arabs of Africa'. They are not eager to be members of the Organisation of African Unity, however helpful such a move would be for the OAU's budgetary problems. Yet if Emperor Haile Selassie could initiate the re-Africanisation of Ethiopia, and Gamal Abdel Nasser could inaugurate the re-Africanisation of Egypt, prospects for a reconsideration of the identity of the Arabian peninsula may not be entirely bleak. At the moment the re-Africanisation of the Arabian peninsula is only an idea in the head of a scholar. It may never become a cause in the hearts of men. But its advocacy may help to keep alive the issue of where Africa ends and Asia begins, and encourage other individuals on either side of the Red Sea to re-examine the validity of Africa's north-eastern boundaries and question the arbitrariness of this boundary.

Christian teacher and pupil, Ethiopia

Anatomy of a Continent

Geography is the mother of history. Nowhere in the world is this more powerfully illustrated than in Africa. The most potent indigenous force in Africa's experience is Africa's environment – the combined elements of geophysical features, location and climate. Together they have given rise to three momentous paradoxes of the African ecology. First, Africa has been a continent of abundant life but speedy death. Partly because of this paradox, Africa has been the first habitat of Man but the last to become truly habitable.[1] And linked to these two ironies is the third contradiction of Africa as a cradle of civilisation but a war cemetery of cultures.

Genesis of Man, Nursery of Civilisation

The excesses of a tropical climate have had a great deal to do with the paradox of abundant life and speedy death. The continent sometimes fluctuates between flood and drought: its vegetation ranges from desert to tropical forest. Where vegetation is abundant, there, too, one finds malaria, yellow fever, bilharzia, river blindness and sleeping sickness. Sometimes it is hard to believe that human life began in this continent. Yet when one confronts places such as the Olduvai Gorge in northern Tanzania, one witnesses how long Man has inhabited the African continent. In Africa Man has been around for so long that nature itself has had time to be the grand excavator, digging away across the centuries and revealing layers of life.

In 1931 Louis Leakey of Kenya discovered on Rusinga Island in Lake Victoria a creature in the ape line, called *Proconsul*, with a larger brain than any preceding primate and eyes more clearly focused in stereoscopic vision. *Proconsul* was found in a geological stratum dated to about 25 million years ago. Then in 1959 Leakey and his wife Mary found in the Olduvai Gorge the skull of a more advanced creature they called *Zinjanthropus*, man of Zinj (the early Arab name for east Africa). *Zinjanthropus* was found in association with chipped 'pebble tools'. Potassium argon dating carried out by scientists from the University of California at Berkeley established that *Zinjanthropus* lived between one and a half and one and three-quarter million years ago. Since then, six fossils of the even more advanced *Homo habilis*, 'skilful man', have been found at Olduvai. Further evidence to suggest that Africa is probably Man's first home came in 1984, when two Kenyans, Kamoya Kimeu and Richard Leakey, son of Louis, discovered much of the skeleton of a twelve-year-old boy in a swamp on the western shore of Lake Turkana (formerly Rudolf). The boy seems to have been an example of *Homo*

opposite, Pyramid at Giza, Egypt

Louis and Mary Leakey examining finds at Olduvai Gorge, 1959

A felucca on the Nile

erectus, one step along in the evolutionary scale between *Homo habilis* and *Homo sapiens*, the 'thinking man' or modern man. All these archaeological discoveries increase the possibility that human genesis occurred in Africa; that if there was a Garden of Eden where the first man and woman lived, that garden was in Africa.

But Africa is not merely the probable cradle of Man and his initial culture: the continent is also the genesis of civilisation. Eastern Africa provided the birth of humanity and culture: several regions of Africa made a major contribution to the development of agriculture; and northern Africa initiated grand civilisation. The domestication of certain plants for food actually originated in Africa, being carried out by villagers living in a vast belt of the continent between the Atlantic coast of west Africa and the Indian Ocean coast of east Africa. On the basis of present evidence, Africa is, for example, the primary 'genecentre' (centre of origin of cultivated plants) for such crops as sorghum, African rice, sesame, castor bean, cotton, watermelon, cowpea, coffee, oilpalm, kola-nut and the like. Africa is also a secondary genecentre for many varieties of wheat, barley and oats.

Especially noteworthy was the civilisation of ancient Egypt, the legacy of the pharaohs, the heritage of the pyramids. Again, a combination of geographical and human factors helped to produce one of the great miracles of

human ingenuity. The River Nile provided the geographical stimulus to the emergence of settled cultures along its banks, culminating finally in Africa's first grand or urban civilisation which, given its scale, was probably also the world's first grand civilisation.

Ancient buildings in the Sudanese desert

But, of course, the Nile by itself did not create ancient Egypt. The ingenuity of the people had to exploit the Nile in order to create such a miracle of innovation and construction.

Egypt's proximity to other cultures provided additional stimulation, even though they were often weaker. The interaction between Egypt and her neighbours produced one of the greatest configurations of civilisations in history – the Mediterranean civilisations. The interaction between the Egyptians on one side and, on the other, Mesopotamians, Assyrians, Babylonians, Persians, Nubians, ancient Greeks and ancient Romans resulted in the explosion of one of the most dazzling galaxies of cultures in human history. Had there been no Egyptian civilisation would there have been Greek civilisation in ancient times? Debates of this kind are probably eternal. For this author the balance of evidence would seem to suggest that ancient Egypt was a necessary condition, though not a sufficient one, for the flowering of the Greek intellectual miracle a little later.

In the millennium prior to the birth of Christ the Greeks and the Romans conquered and ruled Egypt, creating our ancient triple heritage of indigenous factors, Greco-Roman forces and the emerging world of the Semites. It should be borne in mind that it was not just the civilisation of ancient Egypt which the Nile helped to create: there were other civilisations which have since become even more dynamic.

Remember the little baby who floated alone on the Nile and who was rescued by the household of the Egyptian pharaoh of the day? Without that little boy, there would have been no Judeo-Christian tradition as we know it, for he grew up to pronounce new laws to humanity. Without him there would have been no Islam as we know it – for he came to be counted by Muslims as one of the three greatest prophets of the faith. According to tradition and faith, the boy that had floated on the Nile and had been rescued was Moses. Whether the tale is symbolic or real, the location is significant.

But the Nile does not begin in Egypt. It has its origins in the lakes of Ethiopia and Uganda. If without Egypt there would have been no grand civilisation in north Africa, without the Nile there would have been no Egypt. In some ways the pyramids began around Lake Tana in Ethiopia and the Jinja outlet from Lake Victoria in Uganda. Sub-Saharan Africa provided the

Baby Moses being discovered among the reeds of the Nile.

City of the Dead, Cairo, Egypt

indispensable sustenance for this north African achievement.

Partly because of Africa's paradox of abundant life and speedy death, the Egyptian civilisation evolved one of the most complex cultures of death in history. That is what the pyramids are all about. Some cultures have built great monuments as a tribute to the dead: the Egyptians built the pyramids as a refuge for the dead. In a sense that is the difference between the culture which produced the Taj Mahal in India and the culture which produced the pyramids in Egypt. The Taj Mahal is a tribute to a departed wife, a love poem in marble. But the pyramids are immortality itself, created in stone. The culture of pyramids recognised no fundamental break between living and dying. The pharaoh who was about to be buried needed the 'standard of *living*' to which he was accustomed. The elaborate wealth which accompanied him to the hereafter was designed for such a purpose. To die was like moving to a new residence. One had to collect one's possessions, pack them in readiness for the move. To die was like changing your address.

Within this summary of Egypt's elaborate subculture of death lies a message which has continued to the present day. Many Egyptians still refuse to recognise any sharp break between living and dying. Egyptian families in Cairo today still invest in dwellings for the dead, almost complete houses where the loved ones are buried and the living pay visits on specific days. The places look not like graveyards but like derelict towns, consisting of houses which provide a setting for graves. In other words, contemporary Egypt maintains an indigenous tradition which goes back to pharaonic times.

Ancient Egypt's way of dealing with death somewhat frightened succeeding rulers of Egypt under new civilisations. Isis was the last great Egyptian goddess to be seriously worshipped well into the Christian era. She guarded the first cataract of the Nile as it entered Egypt, a custodian of the sacred river and a symbol of fertility. But after a while the new Roman rulers of Egypt were uncomfortable with the cult of Isis. By the time of Emperor

Ancient Egyptian gods, *left to right*, Horus, Osiris and Isis

Justinian the cult could no longer be tolerated and was thus outlawed.

But the real destroyers of the religion of ancient Egypt were the Christian rulers of the country, especially between the fourth and sixth centuries AD. The Christian rulers were nervous about the pre-Christian symbolism of the pyramids and the sphinx, often regarding them as potential signposts of subversion and sin. The new Christianity of Egypt destroyed the gods of the pharaohs.

In the seventh century AD Islam was brought to Egypt by the Arab conquerors. They, too, were somewhat intimidated by what they saw as the pagan splendour of the pyramids and the enormity of sin carved in stone. Islam is particularly hostile to what it regards as idolatry, and finds graven images particularly repugnant. Islamised Egypt was forced even further into an induced amnesia about its past. Over time Egyptians became not only Muslims, but also Arabs. Their identity had changed.

It was the last conquerors of Egypt who removed the dread from the pyramids. These final conquerors were, first, the French under Napoleon who ruled Egypt briefly, and then the British who occupied Egypt in 1882 and controlled it well into the twentieth century. These western European conquerors came with a new science and a new technology undaunted by the apparent inscrutability of either the pyramids or the sphinx. On the contrary, the new western Europeans came into Egypt animated by the curiosity of the Industrial Revolution. It was they who attempted afresh to break into the mysteries of ancient Egypt. It was the western Europeans who finally deciphered the writing of the ancient Egyptians, and initiated a new era of archaeology and Egyptology. And it was a British Egyptologist who in 1922 finally discovered the only tomb of a pharaoh that was undisturbed and intact, complete with the golden standard of living to which the pharaoh was accustomed. The romance of Tutankhamun had come into being.

Howard Carter and an assistant clearing an entrance to Tutankhamun's tomb in 1922

Under the new western European impact the pyramids were no longer the sacred objects that they were designed to be for god-kings when they were originally built. Nor were the pyramids now the symbols of Satan and sin as they had been perceived under both the early Christian and Muslim rulers of Egypt. The pyramids and the sphinx, following the work of western European Egyptologists, could now at very long last be regarded neither as sacred nor as profane – but simply as among the great achievements of mankind.

The Cultural Geology of Egypt

It is due to all these considerations that Egypt is a supreme model of cultural geology, revealing layer upon layer of previous civilisations. One of the more dramatic illustrations of this is a mosque in Luxor in Upper Egypt built upon a church, itself built within the walls of an ancient Egyptian temple. Captured in those structures is one dominant theme in Egyptian history: Man in competition with God on a large scale. The huge temple, the grand monastery, the great mosque – many of these structures were built in the service of God. However, sometimes they were built in imitation of God at His most flamboyant, in a search to rival Him against the background of resplendent mountains and awesome rocks.

The mosque at Luxor, Egypt, built within the walls of an ancient temple

But while large-scale construction has persisted, values have been changing. The flooding of the Nile is no longer the most sacred part of the year; it has been replaced by the fast of Ramadhan. The flood used to be a symbol of abundance; Ramadhan is a symbol of abstinence. The ancient Egyptians often worshipped the sun in all its rotund splendour; Islamised Egyptians looked at the new moon in search of Ramadhan. The culture of scale continues in Egypt, the way of life and the way of death do find areas of mutual accommodation, and the Nile still provides a link between survival and salvation, between economics and religion, between sustenance and immortality.

According to the Coptic Church, Christianity was brought to Egypt by St Mark himself. The earliest Egyptians learnt about Jesus not from the Gospel according to Mark written elsewhere, but directly from the mouth of St

Mark. But whether one accepts the precise version of the coming of Christianity espoused by the Coptic Church or not, there is no doubt that Christianity first arrived in the African continent through Egypt very early in the Christian era. What were the conditions which made the society of the pharaonic scale of social visibility produce at the same time a monastic tradition of social withdrawal? Part of the explanation lies in the contradictions of the Trinity as it interacted with ancient Egyptian beliefs. How much of a *man* was Jesus? How purely *divine* was He? Early Egypt debated the issue of whether Jesus had one nature or two (human and divine) with a degree of passion almost unequalled anywhere in the Christian world. The question arises: why was this issue of Jesus' dual identity so important to ancient Christians in Egypt and their Byzantine overlords residing in Egypt?

It is worth remembering first that the idea of a man being also a god was as familiar to ancient Egyptians as their centuries-old pyramids. Jesus was both man and god? This was hardly an innovation. After all, most pharaohs were both men and gods. But ah! There was something new. Jesus was not a pharaoh, at least not of this world. He was not even a priest in the usual Egyptian sense of attachment to a temple and organised religion. Jesus was a common man. It was this notion of godliness without pomp, divinity without earthly royalty, which inspired some of the earliest Egyptian Christians into seeking the desert for solitude and humility. The neighbouring desert was a temptation of a different kind – a temptation away from temptation, beckoning the devout towards the life of self-denial. The splendour of the desert was a splendour of desolation, compatible with a view of a god who was also a common man, divine majesty in humble clothing, the grandeur of creation in the form of miles upon miles of emptiness.

The monastic tradition remains one of Egypt's great influences upon the rest of Christendom. In Egypt the tradition began to flourish in the third century after Christ. The influence of the tradition reached the ancient church of Ireland and even influenced England in those early phases of Christianisation before the coming of St Augustine to Canterbury. Ancient

St Catherine's Monastery, Sinai, Egypt

Egyptian ideas of monasticism reached as far north as Scandinavia, and as far south as Ethiopia.

But within Egypt itself, although monasteries continue to exist to the present day, Christianity is no longer the triumphant religion it was in, say, the fifth or sixth century after Christ. Egypt is an illustration of a historic contest between Christianity and Islam, in which Islam basically emerged as victor. Once again a part of Africa had been a battlefield between cultures; a part of Africa had served as a military cemetery for at least a particular version of Christian doctrine and Christian organisation.

Christianity did also thrive for a while (between the sixth and fourteenth centuries) in the Upper Nile, among the Nubians and further within what is today northern Sudan. In the second half of the twentieth century we think of southern Sudan as Christian-led, and northern Sudan as non-Christian. But historically northern Sudan was Christianised centuries earlier than southern Sudan. But from the fourteenth century northern Sudan, as well as Nubia in Upper Egypt, were Islamised. Battles between cultures and religions have continued along the Nile Valley for centuries. For the foreseeable future those battles appear relentless and unending. The entire Valley of the Nile continues to be not only the fertility symbol of civilisation but also the cumulative silt of new cultures upon old.

Model of an Egyptian cat

> The stream of experience meanders on,
> In the vast expanse of the valley of time,
> The new is come and the old is gone
> Yet the Nile provides eternal rhyme.[2]

Nature and African Pantheism

The phenomena which change in Africa are not always entire cultures or civilisations; they are sometimes elements of a way of life, factors in relationships. Especially fascinating from the point of view of the ecology of the African condition is the relationship between human beings and the animal world. This entire area is itself subject to the principle of a triple heritage operating in conditioning that relationship. If one is looking at Man and animals in terms of historical epochs, one could identify first the more purely indigenous epoch of pantheism when no sharp distinction was made between God and nature and no sharp separation in habitat was mandatory between Man and animals.

Then came monotheism to much of Africa, basically insisting that God be something separate from nature. At least until the twentieth century the most successful form of monotheism in Africa was Islam, though for a while both the Nile Valley and the Horn of Africa accommodated a vigorous form of Christianity. Ethiopia's Christianity has, of course, persisted from the fourth century AD to the present. But on balance it remains true to say that until the twentieth century the most triumphant form of monotheism in the African continent was Islam; and Islam considerably transformed the relationship between its followers and the animal world.

The third historical epoch in Man's relationship with animals is the coming of Western secularism, sometimes modified by Western Christianity. The phase of secularising human attitudes to animals is distinct from either the original indigenous linkage between God and nature (Afro-pantheism) or the intervening monotheistic relationship between God, Man and the rest of creation.

What were the different characteristics of these three cultural and historical epochs of links between humanity and nature? What constituted the differences between indigenous African approaches to animals, monotheistic attitudes to the animal world, and the new secularisation of nature? Let us take the three socio-historical epochs in turn, bearing in mind that in much of Africa they have co-existed in the twentieth century.

In those parts of the Upper Nile inhabited by Black people all the way up to Uganda on one side and Ethiopia on the other, there emerged before the coming of either Christianity or Islam a Nilotic concept of a force which unified the whole of nature. Among Luo-speaking peoples, this force is sometimes referred to as *Jok*. J. H. Driberg defined this concept among the Langi of Uganda in the following terms,

> *Jok*, like the wind or air, omnipresent, and like the wind, though its presence may be heard and appreciated, *Jok* has never been seen by anyone . . . His dwelling is everywhere: in trees it may be, or in rocks and hills, in some springs and pools . . . or vaguely in the air.[3]

A distinguished Kenyan Nilote, Bethwell A. Ogot, helped to confirm this interpretation of a force permeating all things,

> The spiritual part of Man, the only part which survives death, is *Jok*, and it is the same power which is responsible for conception as well as for fortunes and misfortunes. Hence to the Nilote *Jok* is not an impartial universal power; it is the essence of every being, the force which makes everything what it is, and God himself, the greatest *Jok*, is life-force in itself.[4]

The manifestation of a dead man who could continue a ghostly life in the tomb was the *Ba*, represented as a bird with a human head, as in this inlaid gold piece of jewellery from the tomb of Tutankhamun

This idea of a force permeating nature, and indistinguishable from God, is evident in other African cultures away from the Nile. In many African societies social groups have identified themselves with objects or other animals as symbols of solidarity. This is what totemism is all about. Clans have adopted totemic symbols which have established a sense of continuity between nature and Man. Indeed many African belief systems still include animistic tendencies which attribute a soul to natural objects and blur the distinction between Man and nature, the divide between the living and the dead, the difference between the divine and the human.[5] The indigenous belief systems of Africa did not assert a monopoly of the soul for the human species alone. A tree, a mountain, could have a soul. A river, in spite of its flow, could retain a soul. African religion is respectful of living creatures other than Man. Some African communities will not kill a snake because of a bond of brotherhood between the snake and members of a clan. The lion clan of the Baganda has the eagle as a secondary totem. Kintu, the royal ancestor of the clan and indeed of the nation, did himself kill a lion and an eagle, and turned their skins into royal rugs. But by so doing the lion and the

The Royal Garden Palace, Tunis. Islam's distrust of representational art has strengthened the decorative skills of its craftsmen.

eagle were thenceforth made sacred. Members of the leopard clan may not eat meat which has been torn or scratched by an animal. Here is a sense of identification so deep that one shrinks from abusing the totem by satisfying an appetite.

Nature and the New Monotheism

Monotheism is by definition a monopoly of divine power in a single, usually anthropomorphic, deity. Because of this, monotheism tends to have Creator on one side and creatures on the other, God on one side and nature on the other. What is created is deemed distinct from the First Cause.

In the monotheism of the Judeo-Christian and Islamic tradition, God existed before He created anything. Indeed Judaism and Christianity see the process of creation as a single week in the life of God – and on the seventh day He rested.

But one particular product of creation, one particular creature, enjoys a special status in this monotheistic paradigm. That creature is Man. It is true that the Semitic monotheistic religions also refer to angels, both saved and fallen. But among the usual inhabitants of planet Earth, Man alone is endowed with a soul, with moral responsibility and accountability, and with a capacity for immortality.

In light of this monotheistic perspective, there is a sharp divide not only between God and nature, but also between Man and the rest of creation.

Partly because Semitic monotheism limited the possession of a soul to *Homo sapiens*, all other creatures were deemed to be in the service of Man, and sometimes for the pleasure of Man, almost without restraint. This is ecological racism.

Islamic monotheism went a stage further in its profound distrust of anything which smacked of idolatry. Pre-Islamic Arabia had been a society which worshipped graven images and created imitations of the animal world. The Prophet Muhammad had first been persecuted in Mecca, and fled to Medina. When he finally returned in triumph to Mecca, his first targets included the idols in the holy Kaaba. From then on, in order to discourage any return to idolatry, Islam discouraged even representational art involving the figures of animals or human beings.

Against this background of Islamic distrust of idolatry, animals were no longer sacred but could sometimes be protected from excesses of cruelty. The cultural accident that Islam was born among a desert people who valued and almost humanised the camel helped to mitigate those aspects of monotheism which were sometimes harsh to the animal world. The camel is almost the totem of Islam. Had animals been capable of being converted to religions, the first convert to Islam in the animal world would presumably be the camel – just as the first animal convert to Hinduism might well be the cow. The infatuation of the Arabs with the camel, although not directly linked to Islam, helped to ameliorate the tendency of monotheism to deny the sacredness of animals.

Despite the special status of the camel in Arabian culture, Islam – unlike indigenous African civilisations – recognises no sacred animals. But does this mean that Islam has denied the entire animal world any moral status? The answer is no. For while Islam has abolished sacred animals, it still recognises profane ones. The pig especially is a profane animal from which Muslims are required to maintain a distance. This is not simply a matter of diet – avoiding eating pork. It is a matter of cleanliness in the spiritual sense. Contact with a pig creates *najs*, an unclean state. A person with *najs* on his hands or on his clothes is not supposed to enter a mosque or even pray in the street. Such a person is not clean enough to be in communication with the Almighty.

The dog is also widely regarded as a profane animal though less universally so in the Muslim world. Muslims may have dogs as guards, but are usually discouraged from having dogs as pets in the house, in constant contact with them. Most Muslims would say that contact with a dog's nose, or a lick from a dog on your face, creates *najs*.

There is less agreement among Muslims regarding the status of the dog than there is about the status of the pig. However, the essential point to grasp is that these are concepts of profanity in animals which have survived, in spite of Islam's abolition of the concept of sacred creatures.

Nature and Creeping Secularism

There is a third cultural theme which has affected the animal world in Africa – the theme of secularism. While indigenous religions recognise both profane and sacred animals, and Islam limits itself only to profane animals, Western culture recognises neither sacred nor profane creatures. Partly because of this denial of a moral status to animals, the commercial status of animals has acquired extra significance in Western materialist civilisation. Under the influence of Westernisation, the attitude of Africans towards their fellow creatures in the continent has tended to become less moral and more economic with every passing business day. The hunting of the rhinoceros continues in Zambia to provide decorative handles for ceremonial Arab daggers in the Yemen, ivory finds its way to the markets of Khartoum, Kenya fluctuates between animal conservation and racketeering in trophies – and the animal orphanage in Nairobi has become both a conservation symbol and a piece of mere tokenism. In other words, capitalism is now destroying the moral relationship between Man and nature.

But how have the three cultural tendencies (indigenous pantheism, imported monotheism and Western secularism) affected the wider life-styles of Africans in relation to animals?

To begin with, indigenous African culture permitted and sometimes promoted a good deal of living together of human beings and animals. There was often a close proximity in the compound between family quarters and those of their cattle, and people with extensive herds often slept among the cattle.

left, Somali nomads in Kenya use camels for transport; *right*, Cattle at a waterhole, Upper Volta (Burkina Faso), Sahel

Under Islam, co-habitation was also important, arising partly out of the strong tradition of the camel in Bedouin culture. And so Muslim societies with camel cultures, such as the Somali of the Horn of Africa, permitted a considerable degree of co-habitation.

On the other hand, Islam is much more particular about dung and excreta as unclean elements than most indigenous African cultures. While Africans like the Masai would build houses partly with the dung of their animals, Islamic precepts often put excreta on the same level as the pig – a condition of *najs*. This Islamic concern about distancing oneself from the excreta of animals discouraged the degree of intimacy between human beings and animals which one sometimes encounters in non-Islamic Africa.

The most resistant cultural tradition to co-habitation between human beings and animals is Western secular culture. It is out of this third culture that the idea of game reserves and tribal reserves emerged. Western culture introduced into Africa a kind of ecological apartheid, explicitly designating certain areas exclusively for animals, and others for human beings. Game reserves have been established in different areas of Africa. Sometimes human beings have been deliberately marginalised, pushing them further and further away from protected wild animal species.

In indigenous life-styles livestock, wild beasts and human beings sometimes drank water together at the same springs and lakes, wells and boreholes. To the present day it is still possible for one to witness this link between human beings, their livestock, the zebras and wild beasts

Rift Valley, Kenya

as they refresh themselves alongside the same river bank or pond.

But what remains of this co-habitation and co-pasturing in Africa in the post-colonial era is sometimes in spite of government policy, rather than because of it. The strongest tendency until recently has been towards segregating human beings and their livestock on one side, and wild beasts on the other. Those wild beasts that are hoofed and need grass become rivals to domesticated animals that pasture. There are pastoralists in countries such as Tanzania who have reason to complain that wild beasts have been favoured over human beings and their cattle. The era of ecological apartheid has indeed truly arrived.

Part of the background is that old paradox about abundant life in Africa, followed by speedy death. The marginalisation of some of the pastoralist groups has resulted in their speedy death. Wild animals have sometimes multiplied at the expense of human pastoralists on the margins of Tanzanian and Kenyan game reserves.

But the romance of abundant life still persists, sometimes linking African legends with newly imported Semitic traditions. There are stories of the Rift Valley and the Ngorongoro Crater having floods similar to those experienced by Noah. In these, the ark was at the Ngorongoro Crater and elsewhere new lakes and new valleys were created. At the crater the animal world disembarked, blinking at the new tropical sun, far from Palestine. No wonder the full diversity of animal creation is much more evident along the Rift Valley and the craters than in the ancestral holy land of the Semites. The cruel African paradox of abundant life and speedy death finds a biblical link in the floods which caused speedy death yet saved enough animals for abundant life later on.

But what about the eating of animals? What about animals as diet rather than companions, as food rather than room-mates? How do these questions relate to the triple heritage of indigenous pantheism, Semitic monotheism, and Western secularism?

The first apparent anomaly to note is that while indigenous African cultures recognise both sacred and profane animals, those cultures accept as food a wider variety of animals than does either Islam or Western civilisation. I have been to a butcher's shop in equatorial Zaire which had a range of meats from beef to crocodile, from goat to monkey, from chicken to bush rat. Many Africans are as catholic in their acceptance of flesh as the Chinese. Sometimes when the Chinese eat almost everything, it is accepted as just a unique civilisation; but when Black Africans eat almost everything it is equated in Europe or North America with savagery. In reality there is no great difference between the dietary catholicism of the Chinese and the diversity of Zairean cuisine.

Islam, on the other hand, is more restrictive not just concerning the pig but also concerning a variety of other animals, albeit for different reasons. For example, some Muslim denominations discourage the eating of creatures which are amphibious.

Western secularism, in spite of its apparent broadmindedness, also has its own self-imposed cultural dietary restrictions. Dog meat is not likely to be served on English dining tables in the foreseeable future no matter how secular the diners may claim to be. The eating of monkeys also tends to offend Western sensibilities, though the eating of snakes has become widely accepted in desert America and in California. The eating of snails in France has even become prestigious, influencing tastes in former French Africa. However, it should be noted that the eating of snails under indigenous cultural traditions had been widely accepted in western Africa, especially in Nigeria and Ghana, centuries before the arrival of Europeans.

But why is it that the indigenous cultures which treat animals so morally in both the sacred and profane senses should be at the same time more willing to eat those animals? Of course, some clans associated with the monkey would not eat the monkey but instead eat a zebra; whereas the zebra clan might be more prepared to eat the monkey. What this means is that although a greater number of animals is eaten, that variety is not accessible to every part of the particular society. Some discrimination occurs partly on the basis of restrictions within clans rather than within religious orders.

Second, it must be remembered that eating a wider variety of animals does not necessarily mean eating a greater quantity of meat. Africans eat far less meat than do Westerners, but the meat which Africans eat under indigenous traditions comes from a wider variety of animals than that eaten by Westerners. When you add up the gazelles, hippos, elephants, monkeys, chickens, goats and rats that Africans kill to eat, they are still a mere fraction of the cattle that the Western world kills for its food.

Let us consider the role of hunting. Indigenously, hunting in Africa is overwhelmingly for food, though occasionally it is for a *rite de passage*. In Islamic civilisation hunting is for both food and sport, though the choice of animals to hunt is greatly regulated by dietary considerations.

Only in the culture of Western secularism is hunting almost purely for sport, with the food factor being virtually incidental. Because the West had evolved an elaborate subculture of personal achievement and individualism, the animal world was vulnerable to a new danger. It was vulnerable to the danger of the excitement of a chase, of the thrill of stealth, of the sheer exhilaration of closing in on the prey.

Again it is one of the ironies of the situation that while Western secularism has tended to reduce animals to their economic value, that economic value itself has sometimes tended to be divorced from issues of food value. Hunting has become big business in certain parts of Africa and in certain aspects of Western civilisation; but not hunting for food. The economic value of the animals does not lie in their capacity to satisfy an empty stomach, but in their capacity to satisfy a greedy thirst for blood and a greedy yearning for masculine performance.

The Ecology of Islamisation and Westernisation

Until improvements in European technology of travel were made, Africa was for centuries merely a land mass obstructing (or frustrating) Europe's quest for a route to the East Indies. When European curiosity about Africa, and

White hunter with his 'trophy', *c.* 1890s, East Africa

appetite for Africa, were at last aroused, European explorers and adventurers found formidable resistance in west Africa. Word started getting around among British sailors, and songs were sung about west African defences:

> Beware and take care
> Of the Bight of Benin;
> For one that goes out
> There are forty go in.

It is one of the ironies of European penetration of Africa that it was not the wild and gigantic beasts of eastern and southern Africa which frightened Europeans away; it was in fact the tiny insects of the west coast and central Africa which made Europeans nervous. Not by the roar of the lion but by the buzz of the mosquito were the fears of the white man aroused.

On the other hand, many of the areas which had spectacular wild animals were precisely the areas which attracted the white man. Certainly by the nineteenth and early twentieth centuries the lions and elephants, the cheetahs and zebras, flourished in those tropical highland and temperate zones which turned out also to be congenial to settlement and cultivation by the white man, especially on the eastern and southern sectors of the continent. Partly because of that, it was later to Kenya and to the countries of southern Africa that the white man wanted to cling most tenaciously. The large numbers of white settlers there made those countries distinctly different from those which were merely administrative units of a world-wide empire. Algeria, Kenya, Zimbabwe, Angola and now South Africa have suffered the pains of racial conflict in the last third of the twentieth century precisely because they were once geographically too attractive and too unprotected by mosquitoes to keep the white man at bay.

As for the spread of Islam, it was probably checked less by the mosquito than by the tsetse fly. The Arabs were desert people who had succeeded in taming the camel and the horse and had used these animals partly for the expansion of Islam elsewhere. The fact that north Africa had so much desert facilitated the initial Arab penetration. The desert was familiar to the new conquerors. But density of vegetation growth as well as the presence of the tsetse fly in some areas kept the camels and the horses at bay and checked the advance of Islam in at least certain parts of sub-Saharan Africa.

But it is not just location and climate which have so profoundly influenced the political and cultural history of Africa. More recently it has also been Africa's geology. Among the great geological accidents of recent African history is the fact that southern Africa is so well endowed with minerals. The settlement of whites in climatically congenial areas has coincided with geological wealth in those areas.

There are related areas of interaction between geology and our triple heritage. The distribution of Africa's mineral resources has been conditioned by that triple heritage in mysterious ways. Muslims are in control of much of the oil (a liquid mineral) produced primarily by Africa and the

neighbouring Arabian peninsula; whites and Westernised Africans are in control of the solid minerals of this area. A geological accident has concentrated most of the oil of *Afrabia* (Africa and Arabia) discovered so far in either Muslim societies or Muslim-led countries. The Organisation of Petroleum Exporting Countries (OPEC) is two-thirds Muslim in composition and is Arab-led. The population of its African members (Algeria, Nigeria, Libya and Gabon) is also two-thirds Muslim. The Islamic factor in the political economy of the oil of *Afrabia* is considerable. But, as we have indicated, southern Africa (where Islam is weakest) has a particularly heavy concentration of gold, platinum, chrome and other *hard* minerals. And even outside southern Africa, the solid minerals are more the preserve of Christian countries than of Muslim ones. There are, of course, exceptions to both generalisations about Muslim liquid power and Christian solid power, but the implications of this broad distribution have been fairly significant.

In one particular respect, geology and location seem to have been relatively considerate to Africa. Among all the continents of the world, Africa so far has been perhaps the least subject to major earthquakes or major earth tremors, although nothing can be taken for granted for very long. Africa's shores have also been among the least susceptible to typhoons, hurricanes and related forms of elemental devastation. Disease and drought rather than

Breathtaking scenery near the Ivory Coast

earthquakes and hurricanes, seem to have so far been nature's cruelties against Africa.

But nature is not simply a cause of death and devastation, or a source of riches and wealth. Nature can also be a panorama of beauty, and this in turn could profoundly affect history.

This is an issue which is often overlooked in the study of political and economic history. What made ordinary English men and women, ordinary Europeans, leave their native countries and set up new homes in exotic areas of distant lands, sometimes quite inaccessible? The economic and political reasons as well as some of the psychological and climatic choices, are familiar enough. These Europeans were looking for new opportunities, new worlds to conquer. Sometimes they were running away from their own homes in Europe. There were also occasions when people were forced by their governments in Europe to migrate to the colonies. This is best illustrated by the export of convicts to Australia, though in the early years of west Africa's colonisation shipping out white 'undesirables' was still part of the European psychology in the metropole.

All these factors have influenced the white traffic and white settlements in Africa. But what is seldom understood is the imperative of beauty, *the aesthetics of imperialism.* Man is, among other things, *Homo aestheticus* — the only creature that really appreciates beauty. The flame tree against the tropical sunset, the valley and the hills — were these important factors behind European colonisation of Africa? Personally I think they were. One must remember that European colonisation in this phase took place in the wake of the Industrial Revolution in the metropole. The expanding squalor, the ugly facts of technological change, were imposing new aesthetic horrors upon Europe's landscape.

Many Europeans groped for an escape. Some found a Byronic answer — a search for ancient Greece and its glory, a retreat into the romance of the roots of European civilisation. Other Europeans attempted to return to nature. Poets proclaimed that 'Nature is but art unknown to thee'. But then there were some white settlers who came to Africa looking for the grandeur of nature, for places to live in elegance, for the experience of a splendid sunrise and a splendid sunset almost every day of the year. Many found such places in the White Highlands of Kenya or in the green fields of southern Africa.

Because of their leadership in the industrial and technological revolution, and because of the destructiveness of the two World Wars which they initiated, Europeans are the greatest creators of ugliness in human history. Their very command of nature has made them capable of distorting it, their mastery of their universe has made Europe the Goddess of Ugliness. And yet Europeans are probably also the greatest appreciators of beauty in the contemporary world.

That particular battle between beauty and technology is also now joined in Africa. European culture may have helped to enhance African appreciation of its own beauties; but European technology and capitalism have also strengthened Africa's capacity and propensity to destroy them. Africa, the cradle of civilisation, still serves the grim role of graveyard of cultures.

Conclusion

Africa is the world's second largest continent, a continent of 11·7 million square miles. As we reminded ourselves, the continent is associated with such human ancestors as *Zinjanthropus*, *Homo habilis* and *Homo erectus*. We must seek our Adams and Eves from among these ancestors.

But although Africa is the continent where Man originated, it is not the continent where Man has multiplied the most. Abundant life in this continent has been accompanied by speedy death. Climatic and other geographical factors have ensured that the first habitat of Man is virtually the last to become truly habitable.

If eastern Africa was the cradle of Man, northern Africa was the cradle of civilisation. We have drawn special attention to the grand-scale civilisations which emerged along the Nile Valley, covering the areas which are today Egypt, Sudan, Ethiopia and interacting with many neighbouring societies in both Africa and beyond. Climate, location and human ingenuity played a major part in this flowering of creativity. Relations between Man and animals were influenced first by pantheistic indigenous cultures, later by monotheistic religions from the Semitic world, and more recently by the aggressive secularism of Western civilisation.

But underlying it all is the simple fact that Africa's geography is the mother of Africa's history to a large extent. Even more than in most other cultures of the world, Man, God and nature in Africa have been in closest contact, in deepest intimacy – for better or for worse.

Africa's Identity: The Indigenous Personality

The Culture of Hunters

Since Africa is where the human species first started experimenting with different routines in the process of creating culture, it is not surprising that the continent has witnessed a great variety of ways of life across the centuries. In the beginning there were the gatherers of fruit and raw vegetables, soon to become carnivorous and evolving into skilled hunters. In parts of Africa, societies still exist whose economic activities are primarily focused on gathering and hunting. These are the BaMbuti (so-called 'Pygmies') of the Ituri Forest in Zaire and the Khoisan (so-called 'Bushmen') of the Kalahari in southern Africa.

The phenomenon of collective identity in ancient times may well have begun in these economic activities, especially as they matured into competitive activities. An early version of the territorial imperative in human behaviour probably inaugurated the distinction between insiders and outsiders, between 'we' and 'they'. Who had a right to hunt in this particular area? Who had a right to gather fruit or roots in that area? These were questions involving the territorial imperative, and probably initiating the foundations of human differentiation and therefore human identity.

Skills in hunting were also an early version of competition and of the quest for glory – what John Milton, author of *Lycidas*, described as, 'That last infirmity of noble mind.' The skills concerned, of course, varied according to the animals being hunted, the instruments used for hunting, the physical characteristics of the hunters (whether they were tall or short people, lean or inclined to be fat), and the whole area of human ingenuity and calculation.

Hunting was the mother of technology, and technology began to deepen human differentiation and identity. The early weapons for hunting included sticks and stones for bird hunting, special clubs and 'flying sticks' such as the African knobkerrie, and the more distinctive trombash which was developed along the upper Nile. Africa also evolved a variety of spears, ranging from rudimentary sticks (with one end pointed) to more elaborate implements with a separate foreshaft and a head of sharpened bone, stone or, later, metal. The bow and arrow were also widely used for hunting in Africa, and continue to be an aspect of contemporary life in the more remote parts of Africa.

While hunting began primarily as a method of survival, in time it became interlinked with other aspects of culture. Initiation ceremonies and rites of

opposite, A hunting scene in south-west Africa

passage have sometimes included a demonstration of hunting skills and prowess. Ceremonial hunting has also been used to deepen a sense of collective identity in a society.

Further north along the Nile Valley hunting influenced class identity, as well as cultural and ethnic identity. The more elaborate civilisations of the lower Nile towards the Mediterranean, sometimes evolved a whole social class of hunters. This was certainly the case for long stretches of the history of ancient Egypt when a class of 'huntsmen' hunted on its own and sometimes performed as guides and attendants of the nobility, and took charge of the dogs, and co-ordinated the retrieval of the game. There was a considerably larger abundance of animals in ancient Egypt than the present situation in the country would imply. The animals which were hunted by this social class of specialists included ibex, oryx, gazelle, wild ox, Barbary sheep and hare. The ostrich was often hunted for its plumes, and the leopard, jackal, wolf, hyena and fox were hunted for their skins and sometimes because they were a menace to a farm or a household.

If hunting was the mother of technology and helped to initiate the influence of the territorial imperative in human differentiation, technology and the territorial imperative together were in turn the parents of war. The rise of disputes as to who can hunt where, or gather fruit in what area, when combined with the emergence of the instruments of hunting resulted in the earliest examples of military confrontations between human beings. Identity and differentiation were becoming a matter of mutual injury and armed struggle. Again these ancient examples are still contemporary in Africa. Quarrels between groups over hunting ground or over animals are still part and parcel of social relations and conflict of identities.

A Benin bronze depiction of a hunter

Lovers of Land *versus* Lovers of Animals

In some African societies there has been a remarkable transition from the ancient ethos of hunting for wild animals to the continuing ethos of raiding domesticated animals. For example, the Masai believe that they are the custodians of all the cattle of the world, wherever they might be. The Masai are thus God's chosen people in a special sense – not in charge of the soul of Man but in charge of Man's most important companion on earth, the cattle species.

Because of this belief, the Masai regard themselves as fully justified to seek cattle wherever they might be. The cattle complex among them is part of their identity. Their style of life as herdsmen and pastoralists intermingles with the ancient possessiveness of the hunter. But in this case the Masai are not animated by a territorial imperative; they are animated by a cattle imperative, regardless of territorial boundaries. The tendency towards cattle raiding across ethnic boundaries is thus a fusion of the ethics of hunting with a pastoral way of life.

There are other groups in eastern Africa which are similarly inspired by the cattle imperative, often resulting in major disputes and even in military confrontations of the ancient kind. Groups whose behaviour has caused headaches among policymakers in modern African capitals include not only the Masai but also the Turkana of Kenya, the Karimojong of Uganda and the Bareg of Tanzania.

But from the point of view of our concern with the triple heritage, there is an additional factor of remarkable cultural relevance among these groups of pastoralists and herdsmen. On balance they are among the most resistant to Western influences, and sometimes also to Islamic influences, unless the impact is sustained over a long period of time.

The rural world of Africa is divided between lovers of land and lovers of animals. Lovers of land in this context are those Africans who have responded to the challenge of cultivation and agriculture, and have learnt to take advantage of the soil and seeds as a means of production. These are the Africans who plant, tend their farms, and harvest their corn or yams.

Lovers of animals, on the other hand, are those Africans whose entire way of life is bound by a cattle complex or a camel imperative, or a concern for sheep and goats. Land is important to these Africans, but primarily for the sake of pasture for their beasts. Nor do they necessarily cultivate the pasture. They accept it as nature's bounty, very much as the ancient gatherers accepted the wild fruit and wild roots.

The most striking illustration of pastoralists on one side and cultivators on the other is perhaps the remarkable proximity between the Masai of Kenya and their neighbours, the Kikuyu. For centuries the two groups have lived close together, sometimes fought each other and sometimes intermarried. The Masai have remained primarily people of the cattle, fanatically pastoralists. The Kikuyu have for centuries been cultivators. Then came the West in the form of white settlers and administrators at the turn of this century, who settled in the lands of both groups. The agricultural Kikuyu before long responded to the new economy and the new culture which had come with white settlers. Although the Kikuyu interest in cultivating cash crops was sabotaged by white settlers out of fear of economic competition, there was no doubt about a Kikuyu response to the temptations of money-making and the inducements of the profit motive. Culturally the Kikuyu also responded dramatically to the new forms of education which had come with white missionaries and the new universe of Western civilisation. During the colonial period, the Kikuyu even initiated their own independent schools, in the face of inadequate facilities provided by the colonial order. And even after independence the *Harambee* schools of Kenya, based on local self-reliance in erecting the building and raising money for the teachers, have been in part a continuation of Kikuyu initiatives during the colonial period and their response to both the new Western economy and the new Western culture.

In striking contrast, their pastoralist neighbours – the Masai – maintained during the colonial period an obstinate cultural distance from both the new capitalism and the glamour of cultural Westernisation. The Masai have walked tall and often semi-naked, ferociously possessive about their cattle – often treating them as members of their own family – and indifferent to the new culture of Western suits and ties, Western hats and even Western shoes. Not for the Masai the cash crops or the obsession with earning foreign exchange. These herdsmen have sometimes been such deep idealists about their animals that rather than sell them in times when faced with drought and inadequate pasture they have let them grow thinner and then die. The reluctance to sell and the cultural obsession with maximising one's herd have often resulted in over-grazing and caused crises of starvation and death. On a purely pragmatic basis, one of the solutions to the crisis of famine in Africa is the commercialisation of cattle breeding and the life-styles of cattle societies such as the Masai and the Turkana. Attempts have been made to influence these groups in the direction of responding to select-ive capitalism and the profit motive, engendering some economic value for the cattle instead of almost pure cultural value. But most efforts towards replacing a cattle culture with a cattle economy have so far failed. The pastoral people have remained defiantly idealistic in their attachment to both their ancestors and their animals.

Cattle-herding societies value their cattle for cultural reasons and do not see their animals primarily as economic objects

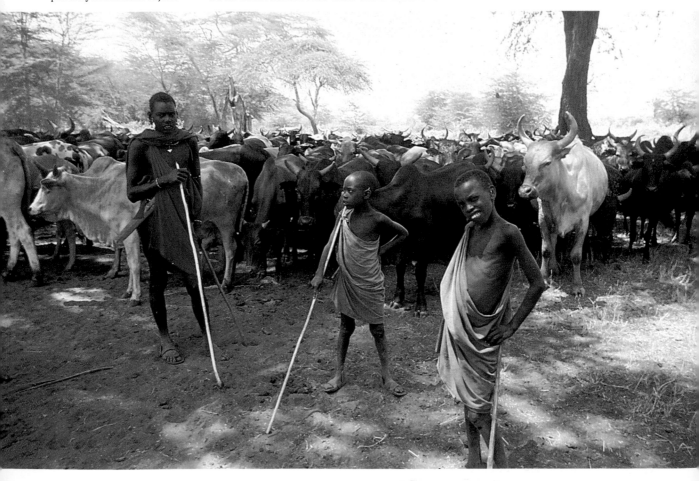

On States and Stateless Societies

These differences in attitudes between lovers of land, the cultivators, and lovers of animals, the pastoralists and herdsmen, have had considerable political and social consequences *historically* as well in the contemporary period. We know that before the white man came, Africa had a wide range of political formations and types of political communities. Some of these were states with elaborate centralised structures of authority and coercion, while others were basically stateless societies. For our purposes in this chapter, a state is a political organisation in which authority is substantially centralised and in which force is a fundamental part of political control. Because of the tendency of the state to be centralised, statehood is more conscious of territorial boundaries and limits of authority than would otherwise be the case.

Stateless societies, on the other hand, are less obsessed with territorial boundaries as limits of authority, and are more inclined to rely on consensus rather than coercion as a fundamental method of political cohesion. Authority in a stateless society is likely to be diffuse and decentralised, relying more on the sanctity of custom and tradition rather than command and legislation.

Barges carrying sugar cane in Egypt. Europe's sweet tooth had a great impact on the history of the world.

There is a school of thought among African scholars which tends to feel that Africa is insulted if it is 'accused' of having had stateless societies. I personally believe this particular school of thought is mistaken. For one thing, to insist that every African society before colonialism was a state is to deny the concept of state any pretence of organisational or institutional specificity. To call both Somali nomadic life, on one side, and the Empire of Ramses II of ancient Egypt, on the other side, 'states' is to abandon all conceptual precision.

Second, this insistence that every African society was a state betrays a kind of intellectual dependency upon European criteria of political respectability. It is true that European colonisers were more likely to respect those African societies which seemed to be relatively centralised and had recognisable monarchs than those societies which appeared to be like 'tribes without rulers'. It was easier for European conquerors to impose treaties and pretend to be involved in diplomatic relations with African kings than with decentralised African elders. But just because Europe did not respect decentralised societies and was more impressed by groups such as the Baganda with their king than by groups such as the Karimojong is no reason to impose the stigma of statehood on all and sundry in pre-colonial Africa.

Third, the state is in any case a less egalitarian construct than a stateless society, and often more brutal and more forceful almost by definition. It is therefore unfair to accuse those African societies which attained a high degree of egalitarianism of the levels of stratification implicit in statehood. It is also unfair to accuse them of having achieved social cohesion through force (again implicit in statehood) rather than through custom and consensus (implicit in stateless societies).

When we relate this distinction between states and stateless societies to the earlier distinction between cultivators and pastoralists, we find that virtually all states were born out of the agricultural and cultivating tradition. Settled agriculture is a necessary but not a sufficient condition of statehood.

Of course, societies with settled agriculture often also reared animals. But the animals were reared as a supplement to cultivated food, rather than as a cultural way of life. As we indicated earlier, Africa's first urban civilisation and most elaborate state was that of ancient Egypt. The Nile Valley provided the silt and fertility for an agricultural way of life before statehood was established. All subsequent states in pre-colonial African history had for their economic foundation a system of agricultural food production, though this was often supplemented by some degree of animal husbandry for food and transportation, and in some cases there was also excavation and mineral wealth, as well as trade.

But what should also be borne in mind is that although settled agriculture is indeed a necessary condition of statehood it is not by itself a sufficient condition for the emergence of statehood. And so Africa has had societies which have been primarily agricultural but not states, though it has never had states which were not at the same time agricultural. Among the stateless societies which are agricultural one has to include the Tiv of Nigeria. This was a group without centralised authority or kings, without traditional codified law and, in the pre-colonial period, without any regular system of taxation or tribute. Social cohesion was obtained through custom and consensus, not only within families but within clans and, as far as possible, between clans. Internally within the group there was minimal use of force and coercion, and greater reliance on traditional precedent.

On the other hand, no pastoralist society has ever become a state on its own historical initiative without either conquering cultivators (as the Tutsi conquered the Hutu) or being conquered by them. Pastoralists normally create stateless societies rather than centralised political structures. Without much exaggeration it can be affirmed that in Africa almost all pastoralist societies have been stateless when left to themselves, whereas all state societies have been based on settled agriculture. Statehood has been built by lovers of land rather than lovers of animals in Africa's history.

When Islam has interacted with an agricultural African society which has not yet become a state, the impact of Islam has been towards state formation. In most parts of Africa the evidence confirms the centralising effect of Islam in terms of political structures and authority. This has been mainly because Islam arrived with codified law, the Shari'a; with a system of taxation based on the Islamic Zakat; with a system of authority based on written scripture consisting of the Qur'an and the Hadith tradition of the Prophet Muhammad; with an idealised notion of centralised theocracy, implying by definition the sovereignty of God; and with an allegiance to a universal community of believers. It is partly because of these elements that the Islamic influence on situations of settled agriculture has tended to be towards centralisation and state formation.

Muhammad Abdilleh Hassan, 1901, modern Somalia's leading hero

These Islamic states have either been city-states, such as the Swahili city-states of eastern Africa, or empire-states, such as ancient Mali and ancient Songhay in west Africa. The empires were usually dynastic and multi-ethnic in composition, with extensive agricultural areas. These city-states and empire-states both engaged in agriculture as a foundation of survival and sustenance, but also engaged in considerable trade, across the Indian Ocean or across the Sahara.

But what about the impact of Islam on a pastoralist society? Even Islam has often failed to push that society towards centralisation and state formation. A pre-eminent example is that of the Somali of the Horn of Africa. The people have been deeply Islamised, so deeply that their Somali identity now is inconceivable without an Islamic foundation. Indeed, Somali nationalism is a fusion of three forces – nomadism as a way of life and culture, the Somali language and Islam. And yet until the coming of European colonisation the Somali were basically a stateless society, and their identity was based on family and clan rather than allegiance to a state or to a single nation. The

Fasilides Castle, Gondar,
Ethiopia

Somali were a decentralised people, held together by language and clan ties,
rather than by state structures of coercion and control.

The role of the Somali language has been particularly striking. No society
in Africa is as deeply wedded to poetry and verse as the Somali, and no
society has evolved as elaborate a culture of verbal composition and
eloquence, a ritual use of the Muse, as these nomads have done. Their
greatest hero of the twentieth century was Muhammad Abdilleh Hassan,
whom the British designated as the 'Mad Mullah'. He fought the British and
Italians with great cunning and dexterity; but he was also a great user of the
Somali language. The so-called 'Mad Mullah' was in fact an inspired Muse.
In a land where almost every third person is a poet, Muhammad Abdilleh
Hassan stands out as one of the greatest Somali poets of all time. In him
patriotism and poetry were married to each other, resounding among the
hills and sand-dunes of the Horn of Africa. The career of Muhammad Abdilleh Hassan was probably the most dramatic illustration of how the Somali
as a stateless society managed to achieve substantial social cohesion partly

through the role of language among the clans. In the place of structures of control the Somali evolved a culture of co-operation.

It was not until the impact of the West that the Somali at last found themselves subjected to true statehood. The colonial powers had split the Somali people five ways. There was during the colonial period a British Somaliland, an Italian Somaliland and a French Somaliland. A section of the Somali people was also absorbed separately into Kenya under British colonial rule. The fifth component became the Ogaden, a section of Ethiopia. The dream of independence for the Somali was in part a dream of reunification. Two of the components were indeed reunited at independence – former Italian Somaliland and former British Somaliland coalesced into the new Republic of Somalia. But neither Kenya nor Ethiopia were prepared to relinquish those areas of their colonial boundaries which were inhabited by ethnic Somali. As for French Somaliland, this became the separate independent Republic of Djibouti.

Most other African countries are colonially created states in search of a sense of nationhood. The Somali, by contrast, are a pre-colonial nation in search of a unified post-colonial state. Most other African countries are diverse peoples in search of a shared national identity. The Somali are already a people with a national identity in search of territorial unification.

What is more, the Somali people today are an emphatic affirmation that it is possible for a sophisticated culture to thrive without structures of state control; that a culture of poetry can mature without kings and queens; that nomadism and pastoralism can constitute an impressive civilisation.

Ruins at Gedi, Kenya – part of the history of the Swahili civilisation

Young Fulani man, Nigeria

On Grandeur and Primitivism

Yet strictly by the measurement of technology there seems to be little doubt that African societies which developed into states were often significantly more advanced in the use of sophisticated tools than African societies which were still primarily based on a pastoral or herding way of life. Some of the African states evolved into cultures of monuments, brick and mortar civilisations. At the pyramids of the Nile or the castles in Ethiopia, or at the awesome ruins of Great Zimbabwe, or at the remains of Gedi in Kenya, one is visually reminded of this monumental side of African history, the history of kingdoms and dynastic empires which also believed in using stone and brick to erect durable testimony to their life-styles. This is the theme of gloriana in African history.

But alongside these African societies of centralised complexity and gloriana have lived people who are either still hunters and gatherers primarily or, at a more advanced stage of technology, have become societies which deal with domesticated animals. The hunters and gatherers include the Khoisan ('Bushmen') of the Kalahari and, with even more complex skills, the BaMbuti ('Pygmies') of Zaire. The pastoral and herding communities have included, as we indicated, the Somali and the Masai, and also a substantial section of the Fulani who are spread over much of west Africa (not to be confused with the Hausa-Fulani), the Tuareg of the southern Sahara and other pastoralists on the march. For centuries all these so-called 'tribes without rulers', illustrating civilisations of subtle simplicity rather than complex structures, have co-existed alongside the more elaborate states and monumental gloriana. Even the term 'simplicity' underestimates the underlying intricacies of these pastoral and hunting societies, but there is little doubt that their technology has been significantly less developed than the technology either achieved indigenously or imported by African states and the makers of Africa's monumental history.

But by the time Europeans started penetrating and colonising Africa, European technology was more advanced than that achieved by either African states or African stateless societies. Europe's partition of Africa occurred in the aftermath of Europe's Industrial Revolution with its modern factories, the Maxim gun and other instruments of the new military technology, the revolution in railway transportation, and the increasingly sophisticated steamship. Inspired by an unprecedented sense of mission and boundless self-confidence, Europeans did not try to conceal their contempt for African cultures, either centralised or decentralised.

The massive cultural arrogance of Europeans was later to influence the indigenous personality of the continent, and create at times schizophrenia among the Westernised Africans. Defending themselves against European contempt, one school of African thought emphasised that Africa before the European had had its own complex civilisations of the kind that Europeans regarded as valid and important – civilisations which produced great kings, impressive empires and elaborate technological skills. This particular school of African thought looked especially to ancient Egypt as an African civilisation, and proceeded to emphasise Egypt's contribution to the cultures and innovations of ancient Greece. A particularly striking illustration of this attitude is the work of the Senegalese historian and scientist, Cheikh Anta Diop. Diop's efforts to demonstrate that the civilisation of ancient Egypt was not only African but *Black*, and that it provided the foundation of the intellectual miracle of ancient Greece, have been influential among Black people not only in Africa but also in the African Diaspora in the Americas.

We may call this school of African assertion a school of *romantic gloriana*. It seeks to emphasise the glorious moments in Africa's history defined in part by European measurements of skill and performance, including the measurements of material monuments.

In contrast to this tradition of romantic gloriana is what might be called *romantic primitivism*. In this the idea is not to emphasise past grandeur, but to validate simplicity and non-technical traditions. Romantic primitivism does not counter European cultural arrogance by asserting civilisations comparable to that of ancient Greece. On the contrary, this school takes pride in precisely those traditions which European arrogance would seem to despise. In the words of Aimé Cesaire, who invented the word *negritude*, 'Hooray' to,

> . . . Those who have invented neither powder nor the compass
> Those who have tamed neither gas nor electricity
> Those who have explored neither the seas nor the skies . . .
> My negritude is not a rock, its deafness hurled against the clamour of the day;
> My negritude is not a thing of dead water on the dead eye of the earth;
> My negritude is neither a tower nor a cathedral;
> It plunges into the red flesh of the earth . . .[1]

Kwame Nkrumah of Ghana meets Anastas Mikoyan, Deputy Leader and Minister of Trade of the USSR at Accra, 1962. Mikoyan's visit foreshadowed closer economic ties between the two countries.

As Jean-Paul Sartre pointed out, this revelling in not having invented either powder or the compass, this proud claim of non-technicalness, was a reversal of the usual cultural situation, 'That which might appear to be a deficiency becomes a positive source of richness.'[2]

Now, let us juxtapose those two African responses to Europe's cultural haughtiness. Romantic gloriana in the African context looks to the pyramids as a validation of Africa's dignity, takes pride in the Great Zimbabwe ruins and adopts the name for a newly independent country, and turns to the ancient empires of Ghana and Mali for official names of modern republics. Idealised primitivism, on the other hand, seeks solace in stateless societies, finds dignity in village life and discerns cultural validation in the traditions and beliefs of rural folk.[3]

Romantic gloriana is inspired by a faith in rationality and science, trust in technology and technical achievements. But for Leopold Senghor, former president of Senegal and the most distinguished proponent of negritude within Africa, the great genius of Africa lay not in European concepts of rationality, but in indigenous capacities for intuition; not in the principles of scientific method and objectivity, but in the wisdom of custom and instinct;

Village democracy: local
government by consensus

not in cold analytical reason but in warm responsive emotion. Hence
Senghor's controversial dictum, 'Emotion is Black ... Reason is Greek'. To
the French philosopher Descartes' assertion, 'I think, therefore I am',
Senghor counterposed the African genius as being, 'I feel, therefore I am'. It is
in this sense that Senghor has sometimes been accused of reducing the
African genius to the poetic concept of the Noble Savage. Romantic primitivism is given the mind of the savage.

Romantic gloriana, on the other hand, tends to have a sense of awe towards the written word, a high respect for written evidence as contrasted
with oral tradition, a glorification of literate civilisation. Under the presi-
dency of Kwame Nkrumah in Ghana, romantic gloriana sometimes sought to
trace almost all the ingredients of literate culture and written science to some
African origin. I have a collection of postcard reproductions of paintings.
These were issued from the archives of Accra during Nkrumah's reign. One
postcard shows Tyro, an African secretary of Cicero, and attributes to Tyro
the invention of shorthand writing in the year 63 BC. Another postcard
shows Egyptian figures, and points to the African origins of paper. Yet
another postcard claims that the science of law originated in Africa and was
practised in the ancient empire of Ghana. Yet another portrays an African
teaching mathematics to the Greeks. Also in the collection is a painting of an

African teaching the alphabet to the Greeks. Chemistry, medicine and written versions of other sciences are also accredited to Africa. This collection is an illustration of Africa's romantic gloriana at its most extravagant.

The school of African idealised primitivism, on the other hand, praises those who invented neither the alphabet nor the pen, those whose fingers never itched for the keys of a typewriter, those whose mode of communication did not require the destruction of trees. As Julius Nyerere of Tanzania once said, the very origins of African democracy lay in ordinary oral discussion – the Elders sat under a tree and talked until they agreed.

On the other hand, idealised primitivism is not interested in the effort to capture the past in bricks and mortar. Cesaire affirmed that his negritude was no tower and no cathedral. Instead, idealised primitivism in the African style is a romance of rhythm, of the drum and the dance, of continuity through living traditions.

Romantic gloriana is also an ethos of urbanism – the growth of cities, the gods of trade and manufacture, the locations with more people and less nature. Idealised primitivism, on the other hand, is an ethos of rural intimacy, a fellowship of face-to-face societies.

Finally, romantic gloriana in its very admiration of kings, emperors and eminent scholars of the past, is predicated on a respect for hierarchy and stratification, with its capacity to produce historical achievements. Idealised primitivism, on the other hand, is predicated on village egalitarianism. Important schools in African thought assert that traditional Africa was classless. Societies without rulers, and certainly without kings, were based on limited class differences and very modest disparities of power between and among the different sub-groups. Julius Nyerere combined this egalitarianism with the fellowship of village life to provide what he regarded as the ancestry of his own brand of socialism. Nyerere used the Swahili word *ujamaa* (familyhood) for the fellowship of modern Africa rooted in the ancient virtues of equality and co-operation. As Julius Nyerere once wrote,

Kenneth Kaunda of Zambia

> We in Africa have no more need of being taught socialism than we have of being taught democracy. Both are rooted in our past, in the traditional society which produced us.[4]

President Kenneth Kaunda of Zambia's ideas on Africa's humanism also include this assumption of equality in African traditional life. Kaunda once described his policy of decentralisation as a form of returning power to the people. He expressed faith in the people's capacity to exercise power properly, in their natural wisdom as ordinary rural people and in the tradition of egalitarianism in Zambia from pre-colonial days. To some extent Kaunda's conception of traditional Africa is somewhere between romantic primitivism and romantic gloriana.

But in its purer form romantic gloriana is a branch of idealised African history. It tends to accept European values while rejecting European 'facts' about Africa. The gloriana tendency betrays a readiness to agree with the proposition that respectable societies are those with relatively centralised political systems, with kings or imperial structures, preferably with monuments in bricks and mortar, and ultimately based on the organisational principle of statehood. What the gloriana school disputes is the European assertion that such societies did not exist in pre-colonial Africa. And so the thinkers in this tradition are quick to draw the attention of Europeans to the great monumental civilisations of ancient Egypt and Ethiopia in the north and ancient Zimbabwe in the south, and the great empires of western Africa like Ghana, Mali and Songhay in the Sahel and Benin, Oyo and Asante nearer the coast. This form of reasoning is a rejection of European 'information' about Africa (that pre-colonial Africa was decentralised and without towers or palaces) but an acceptance of European values which regarded towers and palaces as the necessary symbols of civilisation.

In contrast, romantic primitivism rejects the European values in favour of towers, palaces and centralisation – but accepts European 'information' and 'facts' that pre-colonial African societies were not marked by any talent of innovation, invention or discovery.

All these debates are the historical contradictions between pre-colonial African states and pre-colonial stateless societies, between cultivators and pastoralists, between centralised and decentralised communities. These have been some of the important dualisms of both African history and African identity across the generations.

But how much do we really know about those past generations? Can there be African identity without *an African memory*? How much does Africa remember about its own past, be that past gloriana or primitive, centralised or decentralised, agricultural or pastoralist? It is to this linkage between *memory* and identity that we now turn.

Archival Memory *versus* the Oral Tradition

How important are archives for consciousness of the past? How do they relate to the problem of identity? How has the problem of historical memory affected the African condition?

The archival tradition may be defined, quite simply, as a cultural preoccupation with keeping records, a tradition of capturing the past through preserved documentation. This means more than establishing national archives; it means a particular readiness for recording the dates of births and marriages, collecting maps, preserving love letters, keeping household accounts, as well as documenting treaties, contracts and the like. Because the archival tradition was weak in Africa, the scientific tradition became weak, sometimes our languages atrophied and so did philosophical tradition – with ghastly consequences for our people across the centuries.

Sometimes the process of atrophy or amnesia was induced by a foreign conquest or the triumph of a new civilisation which made the older one seem something to be ashamed of. But elsewhere in the African continent why was the archival tradition weak? First, because most indigenous African cultures have basically refused to regard the past as a bygone or the present as transient. The ancestors are still with us in Africa, and we ourselves are would-be ancestors. If the present is not transient why bother to record it?

A related reason for the weakness of the African archival tradition is the weakness of the calendar tradition (including the tradition of the clock). This was not true of ancient Egypt which was quite sensitive to the movement of the sun and its implications. But in much of the rest of the continent the calendar and clock traditions were underdeveloped. Many of my fellow students at school in Mombasa, Kenya, in the 1940s did not know exactly when they were born. The first president of my country, Jomo Kenyatta, did not know when he was born. There is indeed a Gregorian calendar in the world, an Islamic calendar, an Indian calendar, a Chinese calendar – but no African calendar apart from the revised Orthodox Christian calendar of Ethiopia.

A third reason for the weakness of the archival tradition in Africa is the weakness of the written word except in Ethiopia and north Africa. Many African societies have only come to know the written word during the last century or so. Somalia chose its alphabet only in the 1970s.

This is not to suggest that Africa is homogeneous in this respect. Quite apart from other differences the continent as a whole continues to operate within that triple heritage of cultures – indigenous, Islamic and Western traditions. Modern archives are mainly Western in conception, but they are also Islamic to some extent. The question which arises is whether these can be indigenised outside those two traditions? Or are they inevitably part of the imported sections of Africa's triple heritage? To the extent that archives, until recently, had been viewed almost entirely as collections of *written* records, the indigenous aspects of the triple heritage have not been viewed as archival material. Muslim Africa has been better endowed with written records than non-Muslim indigenous Africa. These records in Islamic societies have been sometimes in the Arabic language, but they have also on other occasions been in indigenous African languages using the Arabic alphabet. There are, in any case, remarkably few surviving written records.

For a long time this literary deficit resulted in the assumption by outsiders that Africa was a continent without history. The absence of castles, cathedrals and written contracts in much of Africa made the civilisational gap appear wide. There is a good case for the argument that Africa's crisis of documentary deficit had a good deal to do with the origins of racism, with the condemnation of Africans to centuries of marginality and servitude, to the slave trade and colonialism. Indeed, why did Europeans pick on Africans to enslave? Why did they not enslave Arabs or south Asians or Indonesians? It was partly because most of Black Africa seemed to have neither concrete remains nor written records.

What then is the new archival order for Africa? In his *Ode on Intimations of Immortality* the English poet, William Wordsworth, talked about the child being father of the man. In the West the national archive was the child of the archival tradition. The national archive was a consequence of a pre-existent cultural preoccupation with record-keeping. In Africa, on the other hand, the national archive may have to father the archival tradition, or at least help that tradition become strong.

Much more than dusty documents are at stake. Africans must stop believing that the present is not temporary, that the past is still strongly with us even if we do nothing to preserve its records. We must keep accounts, record births, marriages and deaths, keep picture albums, and protect contracts.

Perhaps above all, we need not only to respect intellectual heresies, but also to create a climate where they do not perish into unrecorded oblivion. A new archival order in Africa could help change the continent fundamentally. And a world with a fundamentally different Africa cannot but be a fundamentally different world.

While African memory needs to find new foundations, Africa's identity is at stake. The collective self of Africa needs not only better recorded history, but also stable languages, dynamic science, shifts in paradigms of philosophy and technology, and more creative conditions for intellectual and ideological innovations. Identity without self-awareness is a contradiction in terms; and self-awareness requires the foundations of a strong archival tradition.[5]

Conclusion

In this chapter we have addressed ourselves to the complex problem of identity in an indigenous cultural context in Africa. We have traced the history back to the emergence of the territorial imperative and competition in hunting and gathering among the earliest Africans in history. Some of these traditions have just taken new forms across millennia, and co-exist today with more complex economic processes and institutions.

In time Africa and the world initiated the momentous process of domesticating plants, on one side, and animals on the other – thus laying the foundations of the future distinction in Africa between cultivators and pastoralists. In general the most endangered cultures in Africa are precisely those of pastoralists and nomads – threatened both by ecology and modernity. Drought is certainly more devastating when it hits pastoralists than when it disrupts cultivators, although both forms of damage can be very severe. When rainfall returns at last, cultivators can revive their way of life more quickly as the plants begin to grow again, but rainfall by itself cannot replace the dead animals after a severe drought.

This basic distinction in African identity and life-style has resulted in other dualisms. We have discussed the phenomenon of gloriana in African history, including the builders of stone and brick monuments, the architects of empires and creators of centralised kingdoms. In contrast, there are African societies of subtle simplicity, technologically underdeveloped. Out of this dualism emerged two schools of thought among Africans themselves – the tradition of romantic gloriana, priding itself on the achievements of the more complex societies of pyramid builders and architects of Great Zimbabwe, on the one hand, and the tradition of idealised primitivism, revelling in the triumphs of simplicity and the virtues of non-technicalness, on the other.

But both types of African civilisation have been weakened by an under-developed archival tradition, a weak capacity to record and preserve both consensus and heresy across time. The raw African memory has been too strong, permitting the past to retain excessive relevance today; and refusing to recognise the present as transient and temporary. There is a desperate need for a consolidation of Africa's capacity to record its own languages and philosophies, to permit its own heresies to be conserved, and to enable the flow of its history to have more diverse forms of documentation than it once had. Africa's own identity requires self-awareness; and Africa's self-awareness requires a scientific and human archival tradition.

The absence of such a tradition is sometimes in danger of leaving Africa in a coma, inadequately aware of its context with a memory which is numbed. Perhaps no African poet captures this idea of an Africa in a coma more powerfully than A. M. Fayturi. Fayturi had a profound ambivalence about Africa, with a crisis of identity which needed reassurance. And yet Africa seemed oblivious, breathing deep in a blissful coma. The poet seeks to wake Africa. Writing in the Arabic language Fayturi desperately shakes the continent of his birth, seeking to pull it out of its coma,

> Africa Oh Africa
> Wake up from your dark self . . .
> Many times has the Earth rotated,
> And many times have the burning planets rolled.
> The rebel has built what he destroyed,
> And the worshipper debased what he once adored.
> But you are still as you have always been,
> A rejected skull, a (mere) skull.[6]

If the continent is still in a coma, the antidote may well be a reinvigorated archival tradition, a reawakened sense of identity.

Africa's Identity: The Semitic Impact

The most successful Semitic *religion* in the world is Christianity; the most successful Semitic *language* is Arabic; the most successful *people* globally are the Jews. In this chapter we shall look at the issue of identity in Africa from a particular perspective. We shall focus on the impact of the Semitic peoples (especially Arabs and Jews) upon the cultural personality of the African continent.

Contemporary Africa's triple heritage of indigenous, Islamic and Western legacies is just the modern culmination of a much older triple heritage – the heritage of indigenous, Semitic and Greco-Roman influences on Africa. The ancient Semitic strand has now narrowed and focused more firmly on Arab and Islamic influences; the ancient Greco-Roman strand has now *expanded* to encompass wider European and American intrusions.

The expansion of the Greco-Roman (Western) strand is probably irreversible. But is the reduction of the Semitic strand to the Arabo-Islamic trend now under challenge? Is the Semitic factor in Africa's political experience destined to re-incorporate a Jewish element in the years ahead? If we estimate political influence in proportion to the numerical size of a people, then the combined influence of the Jews of the United States and the Jews of Israel has a far greater impact on the foreign policy of the world's main superpower than does the influence of the Arabs. But this global balance of Semitic influence is not necessarily reflected in Africa, where Islam has been at least as influential as Christianity, and where the Arabs have had a much bigger impact than the Jews.

The best embodiments of the ancient triple heritage (indigenous, Semitic and Greco-Roman) are north Africa and Ethiopia. The best embodiments of the modern triple heritage (indigenous, Islamic and Western) are Nigeria and Sudan. The cultural history of Africa is captured in the transition from the triple ancient personality of north Africa and Ethiopia to the triple modern personality of Nigeria and Sudan. In population Ethiopia is probably the second largest African country south of the Sahara. Nigeria is the largest. Sudan is third or fourth largest. Culturally the three countries together tell the whole story in their own way.

The Jewish Impact

The Jewish impact on African identity has taken a variety of forms, of which the most important are: the actual presence of Jews in Africa; the direct religious impact of Judaism; the indirect religious impact of Judaism through

opposite, Interior of El Ghriba synagogue, Jerba, Tunisia

Christianity and Islam; Jewish experiences as a comparative metaphor for Africa; Jewish economic and political penetration of Africa, especially in the twentieth century.

First let us examine the actual presence of Jews in Africa – beginning with the observation that Africa accommodates, on the one hand, some of the richest Jews in the world, and, on the other, some of the poorest.

The two main divisions of world Jewry have also been well represented in Africa. North Africa has accommodated clusters of Sephardic Jews, mainly immigrants from Spain and Portugal who entered Africa in the fifteenth and sixteenth centuries, and Ashkenazic Jews, immigrants from northern and eastern Europe who entered Africa in the nineteenth and twentieth centuries. Outside the Republic of South Africa, the numbers of these European Jews in sub-Saharan Africa are modest. But in countries such as Kenya, Jews are often influential and some are exceptionally wealthy.

The biggest number of Jews in the Arab world today is in Morocco. Before the creation of Israel, Morocco had more than a quarter of a million Jews. By 1956 well over 60,000 Jews had emigrated to Israel. Some also left for France. Every Arab-Israeli war created new fears among Moroccan Jews. The number of Jews now remaining there is probably in the region of, at the most, 50,000. Egypt had approximately 100,000 Jews before the Second World War. There are now very few Jews left in Egypt. As for Algeria, there were more than 135,000 in 1960:

> Mass exodus of the Jewish population began in May 1962 after the signing of the Evian Agreements which secured independence for Algeria. Within a few weeks, from May to July, almost all of Algeria's Jews left the country; they were joined by most of the Europeans. Being French citizens more than 125,000 went to France and about 10,000 to Israel.[1]

The history of the Jews in Algeria goes back 2000 years, but most of them acquired French citizenship through the Cremieux Decree of 1870.

But let us now take a different look at the Jewish presence in Africa from the unusual vantage point of a comparative study – a vantage point which includes issues of race, class and power.

Comparative Jewry

The Jewish presence in Africa, though much more modest than that of the Arabs, has had a fascination of its own. The most Black of all Jews are the Falasha of Ethiopia – self-conceived as the lost tribe of Israel (Beta Israel). Most of them were at last transferred to Israel in 'Operation Moses', a massive airlift via the Sudan that began in 1983 but was at its height from November 1984 to March 1985, in the wake of another Ethiopian famine. Economically, the Falasha in Ethiopia were among the poorest of the poor. Politically, they were often persecuted under a Christian theocracy. Religiously, they continue to be despised even by fellow Jews. It was only in the 1970s that Israel's Law of Return was at last allowed to be selectively applicable to the Falasha Jews. They could 'return' to Israel, but under careful

opposite, In the El Ghriba synagogue, Jerba, Tunisia

conditions. By early 1984 about 3500 Falasha had settled in Israel. It took a large-scale ecological 'holocaust' in Ethiopia in 1984 to tilt the balance of Israeli sympathy. Another 10,000 arrived in Israel in the airlift. Only a few thousand Falasha now remain in Ethiopia.

In Israel the Falasha have met with hostility, cultural arrogance and exploitation. They have experienced hostility from the unemployed who see the newcomers as a threat to their future hopes of employment; they have encountered cultural abuse from conservative rabbis who treat the Falasha as 'impure' Jews and demand they undergo a special 'purification' ceremony; and they are exploited by politicians who regard the Falasha as manpower and have reportedly settled some in the occupied West Bank, which is Arab territory. Many young Falasha even received call-up papers from the Israeli army within a few weeks of arrival. Culture shock, bitterness and homesickness were soon noticeable among the Falasha in Israel.

The Falasha of Ethiopia, even when transferred to Israel, are among the poorest of the Jews. In Ethiopia they are among the poorest of the Africans. But among the richest of all Jews of the world are those of the Republic of

Like all Israeli citizens, the Falasha from Ethiopia must do three years of military service

South Africa. What they contribute to the treasury of Israel is next only to the contribution of the Jews of the United States. Indeed, per head of the population, the donation of South Africa's Jewry has in some years been larger than that of American Jews.

Among white South Africans the Jews have a higher per capita income than the ruling and politically more influential Dutch-speaking Afrikaners. In class terms this means that, while the Falasha Jews have been either serfs or peasants across the centuries, the Jews of South Africa have been in the main either in the liberal professions or members of the commercial bourgeoisie. Until 1985, the Falasha were disadvantaged Jews in a land ruled by privileged Black gentiles, from Black emperors in the past to Black Marxists of latter years. South African Jewry have been privileged white Jews in a land ruled by privileged white gentiles, bound together by the bonds of racial advantage. The Falasha were racially part of a Black majority but religiously a minority. On the other hand South African Jews are racially part of a white minority though religiously also a minority. The Falasha were for a long time Jews under a Christian theocracy, a state based on sectional *religious* supremacy. South African Jews have been part of white supremacy, a state based on sectional *racial* supremacy.

A Falasha potter near Gondar, Ethiopia

The Falasha were politically submissive in Ethiopia. South African Jews have remained ideologically liberal and sometimes progressive and radical. The Falasha Jews briefly gained from a left-wing revolution in Ethiopia in 1974. The Marxist regime in Ethiopia was beginning to treat the Falasha with a greater sense of equal citizenship than almost any of the previous Ethiopian governments across the centuries. On the other hand, the Falasha lost through a right-wing swing in Israel under Menachem Begin in 1977. The Orthodox right-wing in Israel have tended to be more anti-Falasha than the secular Jews. The Jewish purists often regard the Falasha as unacceptable Black pretenders if not heretics.

But while the left-wing radicalisation of Black Ethiopia did briefly aid the fortunes of the Falasha, any future left-wing Black revolution in South Africa is bound to hurt white Jewry as well as white gentiles. A large part of South Africa's Jewry seems to be inevitably destined for settlement in Israel or the United States within the next generation. And yet the two Jewish communities of Africa (Falasha and South African) have posed problems about the definition of an *African*. The Falasha were indigenous by every appearance, but they insisted that they were immigrant. They were the 'Lost Tribe of Israel'. On the other hand, South African Jews are immigrant by every appearance, but they increasingly claim that they are no less indigenous to South African soil than Blacks claim to be. The whites claim that many of the Blacks came from the north of the continent at just about the same time that whites arrived from across the seas. And yet it seems very obvious that the Falasha (even when transferred to modern Israel) are culturally African in almost every respect, while the South African Jews are almost completely European culturally. The Falasha claim to be alien, while

left, A Falasha woman in the highlands of Ethiopia; *right*, A Falasha woman grinding corn

their culture betrays their Afrocentric actuality.

It is clear that the issue of how 'African' white Jews are has to be related to the question of how 'Black' is Africa generally. If we have accepted that Arabs are Africans, how can we reject north African Jews? After all, Jewry in the African continent is older than Islam. We have already referred to the history of the Jews of the Maghreb (north-west Africa) – a history which goes back 2000 years. That is 500 years older than the history of Islam. How can we accept Muslim Arabs as Africans if we reject the Jews, who were in Africa before the Muslim conquest of north Africa?

On the other hand, how can we accept the Jews of South Africa and reject the Dutch-speaking Afrikaners? What would ever make a white man an 'African'? Is the definition subjective – demanding that the person must *feel* African? Or is the definition temporal – depending upon whether whites have become African by sheer durability and time in Africa?

One solution is to insist on both subjective and temporal criteria of Africanity. The remaining Jews of Arab Africa, especially those not of European origin, qualify as 'Africans' under the combined subjective and temporal criteria. But the European Jews of sub-Saharan Africa, mainly Ashkenazic Jews, are in the same situation as the rest of the white presence in Africa. They have to demonstrate both a sense of belonging to an African society and a long period of geographical location in Africa.

The Star, the Cross and the Crescent

Every society tends to have two paramount myths: the myth of ancestry (how the society started and developed) and the myth of mission or purpose (what is special about that society in terms of human values).[2]

Ethiopia's myth of origin is heavily Hebraic. Even under a Marxist regime most Ethiopians probably believe that their overthrown Royal House could trace its origins to King Solomon and the Queen of Sheba, and that the Emperor's title of 'Lion of Judah' was historically accurate.

Historians of Africa have speculated about King Solomon's empire. Did it expand to southern Arabia? Did some Jewish migration take place from southern Arabia to Aksum, the heartland of ancient Ethiopia? Did these early Jewish immigrants into Africa help to shape future Ethiopian history?

Kamal Salibi, Professor of History at the American University of Beirut, has recently propagated a theory that the Israelite kingdom of David and Solomon lay not in present-day Israel but in the southern Arabian provinces of Hejaz and Asir.[3] Salibi says that with a modern gazetteer of Saudi Arabia he has succeeded in pin-pointing up to 80 per cent of the hundreds of biblical place-names that he has examined. The events of the Old Testament occurred, according to him, much further south than originally imagined.[4]

If he is correct then the existence of heavily Hebraic elements in Ethiopian religious and political culture becomes easier to understand, although there are other factors by way of explanation.

Ethiopian Christianity – Black Africa's oldest Christian legacy (dating from the fourth century) – is Judeo-Christian in more than the usual sense. It is reminiscent of the religion of the Christian Jews of Jerusalem in the first century after Jesus, Christians who incorporated many Jewish practices into their Christianity (in contrast to the less Judaic Christians of Antioch).

Ethiopian Christianity (like the Christian Jews of the first century) practised circumcision and also adopted some of the dietary practices and laws

A church painting from Gondar, Ethiopia

of ritual cleanliness of Judaism. However, we should also note there is a persuasive school of thought that says Ethiopian circumcision is pre-Christian.

In spite of the Hebraic elements in Ethiopian Christianity, the Ethiopian Orthodox Church was not particularly tolerant across the centuries towards Ethiopia's Black Jews, the Falasha. The Falasha had defiantly rejected Christianity – and the Christian theocracy, while it lasted, was not amused.

The Jewish influence on Africa is also indirect, through both Christianity and Islam. Virtually all Jewish prophets are honoured by both Christians and Muslims in Africa. The Jewish myth of origin (Genesis and Adam and Eve) has been replacing Africa's own tribal myths of origins from one corner of the continent to the other. Monotheism has been conquering Africa under the banner of either the cross or the crescent but behind both banners is the shadow of Moses and the Commandments he conveyed.

The third Jewish impact on Africa is through the Jewish experience as a metaphor for the African predicament. The Jewish release from Egypt under Moses's leadership has captured the imagination of many an African nationalist. South Africa's Albert Luthuli, Black Nobel prizewinner for peace, entitled his book *Let My People Go* after Moses's demand to the Pharaoh. On the other hand, Luthuli's Dutch oppressors in South Africa saw their own trek north from British control as the equivalent of Moses's exit from pharaonic Egypt. The Afrikaners' more recent isolation among hostile neighbours is often equated with Israel's 'heroic isolation' in the Middle East.

This brings us to the fourth impact of the Jews on Africa: the economic and political penetration, especially in the twentieth century. Joseph Chamberlain, as Colonial Secretary, offered the Zionist movement parts of Uganda and Kenya for the establishment of the state of Israel. Theodor Herzl, the leader of the Zionist movement, preferred to keep east Africa as a potential colony of Jewish surplus population – but the initial Jewish home had to be Palestine. East Africa was thus spared a long-term Israel in its midst.

In 1948 Israel was created in Palestine rather than in eastern Africa. Much of Africa was still under European colonial rule in any case. Israeli penetration of Africa had to wait until Africa's independence. In 1957 Ghana became independent under Kwame Nkrumah, and the Israelis wasted no time in cultivating the new African leadership. The decade from 1957 to the June Arab-Israeli War in 1967 was the honeymoon of African-Israeli relations when Israel committed itself to a variety of African development projects, providing mainly expertise rather than capital, while the setting was one of rivalry with the Arabs. The historic competition between the two Semitic peoples – the Jews and the Arabs – had entered a new phase, with Africa as the theatre of rivalry.

From 1967 to 1973 a deterioration in African-Israeli relations was discernible. But it took the October War of 1973 to shake most of Africa into breaking off diplomatic relations with the Jewish state.

In May 1982, President Mobutu Sese Seko of Zaire resumed relations with

Israel. Did he do it to improve security in Zaire? Was he exasperated with the Arabs? Was he also looking for additional funds from Capitol Hill?

At any rate, Israel seems to have had some success in reducing its isolation in Africa, however modestly. Was this a revival of the Jewish component in Africa's Semitic equation? It is too early to be sure.

The Arabs in African History

More weighty than the Jewish factor in Africa's historical experience has been the Arab factor. What forms has the Arab impact on Africa's history taken?

One form is the linguistic impact which includes, first, the role of Arabic in strengthening fellow Afro-Asiatic languages in Africa. The Afro-Asiatic language group, according to the linguist J. H. Greenberg's classification, has five main branches: Semitic (including Arabic), Ancient Egyptian, Berber, Cushitic (including Somali) and Chadic (including Hausa). The impact of Arabic on Somali is a particularly striking illustration. Somali is not as close to Arabic as is Ethiopia's Amharic, which is a Semitic language. And yet the impact of Arabic on Somali imagery and vocabulary is comprehensive. In northern Nigeria, Arabic linguistic influence has been far less profound than in Somalia, which is geographically close to Arabia, but many Arabic nouns have found their way into the Hausa language, which is spoken not only by the Hausa but by those Fulani who have settled in Hausa towns and villages. Many of the Fulani in Hausaland also speak their own language, Fulfude. It is a curious fact that the Fulani are closer to the Semites biologically (for example, they have similar physical features) but the Hausa are closer to the Semites linguistically. Further north, from the vicinity of Timbuktu to the shores of the Mediterranean, the various Berber languages have also benefited, like Somali and Hausa, from numerous Arabic words and terms.

Mobutu Sese Seko of Zaire, the monarchical tendency in political style

In addition to the Arab impact on related languages within Africa, there is, second, the direct impact of Arabic on the emergence of *new* languages altogether. The most important of these new languages is Kiswahili in east Africa. There is little doubt that Kiswahili is the product of interaction between Arab culture and African linguistic structures. Though 'new' in this sense, Kiswahili can be traced back eight centuries if not longer.

Third, there is the indirect impact of Arabic through other languages already influenced by Arabic. Kiswahili in east Africa has influenced many other African languages, bequeathing to them some words and Swahili imagery. Hausa in west Africa has influenced many neighbouring languages. There is also the danger that Arabic-influenced languages such as Kiswahili and Hausa may, in their own success, cause the death of dozens if not hundreds of other smaller indigenous languages. The death of a language in Africa is often the death of an ethnic identity with mixed consequences for national integration.

Fourth, there is the role of the Arabic language itself as a medium of communication. More and more Africans are learning it as a language in its own right. It is being introduced into universities in Africa as a special area of study. The proportion of African Muslims who have a command of Arabic is increasing. It is clear that Arabic is already, in terms of speakers, the most important single language in Africa. At least one out of every five inhabitants of the African continent speaks Arabic.

Fifth, there is the receding impact of the Arabic alphabet south of the Sahara. Kiswahili is abandoning the Arabic alphabet in favour of the Roman. The Somali, after decades of hesitation, have at last chosen the Roman alphabet instead of the Arabic.

And yet the creation of *new Arabs* is still continuing. Let us now turn to the history of this remarkable process of 'Arab-formation'.

The Making of New Arabs

The Arab conquest of north Africa in the seventh and eighth centuries initiated two processes – Arabisation (through language) and Islamisation (through religion). The spread of Arabic as a native language created new Semites, the Arabs of north Africa. The diffusion of Islam created new monotheists but not necessarily new Semites. The Copts of Egypt were linguistically Arabised and therefore became Semites but they are not, of course, Muslims. On the other hand, the Wolof and Hausa of west Africa were preponderantly Islamised – but they were not Arabised.

The process by which the majority of north Africans became Arabised was partly biological and partly cultural. The biological process involved intermarriage and was considerably facilitated by the upward lineage system of the Arabs. Basically, if the father of a child is an Arab the child is an Arab, regardless of the ethnic or racial origins of the mother. This lineage system could be described as *ascending* miscegenation, since the offspring ascends to the more privileged parent.

It is precisely because the Arabs have this lineage system that north Africa was so rapidly transformed into part of the Arab world (and not merely Muslim world). The Arab lineage system permitted considerable racial co-optation. 'Impurities' were admitted to higher echelons as new full members, provided the father was Arab. And so the range of colours in the Arab world is from the whites of Syria and Iraq to the browns of the Yemen, from blond-haired Lebanese to the Black Arabs of the Sudan.

Within Africa the valley of the White Nile is a particularly fascinating story of evolving Arabisation. The Egyptians were, of course, not Arabs when the Muslim conquest occurred in the seventh century AD. The process of Islamisation, in the sense of actual change of religion, took place fairly rapidly after the Arab conquerors had consolidated their hold on the country. On the other hand, the Arabisation of Egypt turned out to be significantly slower than its Islamisation.

But this is all relative. When one considers the pace of Arabisation in the first millennium of Islam, it was still significantly faster than average in the history of human acculturation. The number of people in the Middle East

opposite, Hausa man celebrating a Muslim festival in Nigeria

who called themselves Arabs expanded dramatically in a relatively short period. This was partly because of the exuberance of the new religion, partly because of the rising prestige of the Arabic language and partly due to the rewards of belonging to a conquering civilisation. Religious, political and psychological factors transformed Arabism into an expansionist culture which absorbed the conquered into the body politic of the conquerors. In the beginning there was an 'island' or a peninsula called 'Arabia'. But in time there were far more Arabs outside Arabia than within. At the end of it all there was an 'Arab world'. Along the valley of the White Nile, northern Sudan was also gradually Islamised – and more recently has been increasingly Arabised. Again a people who were not originally Arabs have come to see themselves more and more as Arabs.

Is there a manifest destiny of the White Nile – pushing it towards total Arabisation? This process began with the Egyptians and their gradual acquisition of an Arab identity. The northern Sudanese have been in the process of similar Arabisation. Are the southern Sudanese the next target of the conquering wave of Arabisation within the next 100 to 200 years? Will the twin forces of *biological mixture* (intermarriage between northerners and southerners) and *cultural assimilation* transform the Dinkas and Nuers of today into the Black Arabs of tomorrow? It is not inconceivable, provided the country as a whole holds together. Southern Sudanese are the only sub-Saharan Africans who are being Arabised faster than they are being Islamised. They are acquiring the Arabic language faster than they are acquiring Islam. This is in sharp contrast to the experience of such sub-Saharan peoples as the Wolof, the Yoruba, the Hausa or even the Somali, among all of whom the religion of Islam has been more triumphant than the language of the Arabs. This rapid Arabisation of the southern Sudanese linguistically has two possible outcomes. The southern Sudanese could become Sudan's equivalent of the Copts of Egypt – a Christian minority whose mother tongue would then be Arabic. Or, the Arabisation of the southern Sudanese could be followed by their religious Islamisation – in time making southern and northern Sudanese truly intermingled and eventually indistinguishable.

Meanwhile, the Swahili language has been creeping northwards towards Juba from east Africa as surely as Arabic has been creeping southwards from the Mediterranean. The Swahilisation of Tanzania, Kenya, Uganda and eastern Zaire has been gathering momentum. With the spread of Arabic up the Nile towards Juba and Kiswahili down the same valley, the southern Sudanese will find themselves caught between these two forces. Historically, these two cultures can so easily reinforce each other. It is because of this pattern of trends that the manifest destiny of the valley of the White Nile appears to be a slow but definite assimilation into the Arab fold.

The Religious Impact of the Arabs
There is a school of thought which regards the religious penetration of the Arabs as the most important Arab influence in Africa. Certainly the popu-

lation of Africa converted to Islam is far greater than the population linguistically or biologically linked to the Arabs. And Islam is a form of identity as well as a religion. The distribution of Islam in northern, western and eastern Africa leaves southern Africa almost untouched, but not quite. In May 1983 President Banana of Zimbabwe addressed an Islamic Conference in Harare. The delegates represented the Muslims of southern Africa. Zimbabwe alone had 800,000 Muslims.

It is in west Africa, however, that Africa's new triple heritage can be studied at its most vigorous. If Ethiopia is the laboratory of the ancient triple heritage (indigenous, Semitic and Greco-Roman) south of the Sahara, Nigeria is the grand laboratory of the new triple heritage (indigenous, Islamic and Western). Sometimes the different identities are in conflict with each other. Estimates of Nigeria's population of Muslims vary considerably, from a third of the population to an absolute majority. The Organisation of the Islamic Conference (OIC) has reportedly reclassified Nigeria from the category of 'country with Muslim minority' to 'Muslim country'. Although not a member itself, Nigeria has been granted observer status by the OIC.[5] Certainly the Islamic presence in Nigeria is considerable, especially in the north and west of the country. Each time Nigeria has had a general election since independence, the Federal Government has passed into the hands of a Muslim-led political party. In 1981 Nigerians topped even Pakistanis as the largest contingent of pilgrims to Mecca from any part of the world. This pattern would probably have continued but for new foreign exchange regulations in Nigeria in 1982 which resulted in a federally-imposed rationing of the number of pilgrims per state.

Ways of controlling the number of Nigerian pilgrims to Mecca have been devised by the Muslim-led Federal Government. The conditions announced for the registration of pilgrims in 1983 included the automatic disqualification of anyone who had been to Mecca on pilgrimage in the preceding three years. There was also a sectarian disqualification of Muslims who were of Ahmadiyya persuasion (an evangelical proselytising Muslim movement which was founded by Mirza Gulam Ahmed in British India and has been doing missionary work in different parts of Africa).

These are illustrations of an Islamic presence in Nigeria which is dynamic and vigorous, at times a little too vigorous. In distribution at least half the Yoruba are probably Muslim and so are an overwhelming majority of the Hausa-Fulani. In other words, if Nigeria consisted only of its three largest 'tribes' (Hausa, Yoruba and Ibo) over two-thirds of the country would be Muslim. It is the presence of smaller 'tribes' in Nigeria (the so-called 'minorities') which has reduced the percentage and proportion of the Islamic presence in the country. Yet even among the minorities in the north and west both Christianity and Islam continue to make inroads. On the whole the European colonial impact failed to arrest the spread of Islam in west Africa, though it may have slowed it down in some parts. It is estimated that Guinea (Conakry) and Niger are each over 90 per cent Muslim, Senegal and Mali

Reverend Canaan Banana, first President of Independent Zimbabwe (1980)

Invalid pilgrims being carried to the Ka'aba, Mecca

each over 80 per cent, Chad over 60 per cent, Sierra Leone over 50 per cent, Cameroon over 40 per cent, the Ivory Coast over 30 per cent, and so on. The heartland of Black Africa's Islam is definitely west Africa.

In east Africa (as distinct from the Horn and the Nile Valley) European colonial rule was more successful in arresting the spread of Islam. In Uganda, Kenya, Rwanda, Burundi and Zaire Islam remains at best a minority religion, though at times politically significant. Indeed, under Idi Amin, the Muslims of Uganda were a politically privileged and powerful minority for eight years. In Tanzania there are probably more Muslims than Christians numerically, but there are still large numbers of Tanzanians who do not belong to either category and continue to uphold their own traditional creeds and beliefs. Christians in Tanzania are a powerful and privileged minority, but a large one at that.

In the Horn of Africa and the Nile Valley Islam is numerically preponderant, though patchy in southern Sudan and uneven in Ethiopia. The population figures of Ethiopia have so far been hazy, but the Muslims are estimated to be in the region of 50 per cent, in spite of the history of Ethiopia as a Christian theocracy. The ruling or central ethnic group, the Amhara, are mainly (Coptic) Orthodox, but Islam is strong among many other ethnic groups, including the separatist regions of Eritrea and the Ogaden.

In the Sudan and Egypt Islam is more clearly triumphant, though both countries have large non-Muslim minorities. Egypt's Christian minority has strong cultural ties with Europe; the Sudan's southern minorities have strong cultural ties with the rest of Black Africa. The expansion of Islam within Egypt has probably reached its limits, it is unlikely to make further inroads into the Coptic population. However, the expansion of Islam in the Sudan will probably continue. The process of Islamising and Arabising the south may no longer be the official policy of the central government in Khartoum, especially now that Nimeri is no longer in power, but the sociological context of the south in a country under ultimate Arab rule is almost automatically receptive to further spontaneous acculturation.

The impact of Islam on Zaire is more modest and is unlikely to expand to any significant extent except in the east. An offshoot of Islamic culture in eastern Africa, the Swahili language is one of the major languages of Zaire but the religious presence of Islam in Zaire is more limited.

The white presence in southern Africa arrested the spread of Islam further south. But there are Muslims in Malawi, Zimbabwe and Mozambique especially in the northern parts. Islam in the Republic of South Africa is a significant phenomenon mainly among the coloureds, the Indians and the Malays. It is weak in the Black African population, but there have been inroads even there. There may be a rise in conversions as a result of disenchantment with white-dominated Christianity.

This then is the approximate spread of Islam as a religion. The religion captured Saharan Africa and parts of the Nile Valley before it captured west Africa. It penetrated parts of eastern Africa and trickled further inland and further south. But Islam is not just a religion. It is a civilisation.

Islam's Impact on African Political Culture

Another impact of Islam on Africa has been in the realm of political culture. This includes Islam's impact on political values, institutions and vocabulary. Again identity, political identity especially, is at stake.

The origins of the state in west Africa were partly Islamic. Before European colonisation, there were west African states or empire-states. The nation-state had yet to develop fully, as we shall indicate in a later chapter. Empire states such as ancient Mali and ancient Songhay were products of interaction between Islam and indigenous culture. Sometimes the rulers were strong Muslims and became patrons of Islamic scholarship in court and beyond. In turn the scholars could sometimes be strong influences in court and in policy formulation. Examples include the court of Muhammad Touré in his rule in Songhay between AD 1492 and 1528, and the court of Idris Alooma (AD 1571–1603) of the Kanem-Bornu empire.

By the time the European colonisers arrived in the nineteenth century, experience in statecraft had accumulated in west Africa, though not uniformly. As history would have it, it was the Islamic Emirates of northern Nigeria which had the most enduring consequences for the colonial order. The British empire-builders were impressed by the political structures of the Hausa-Fulani. The British conqueror of northern Nigeria, Lord Lugard, was inspired enough by these institutions to develop a new doctrine of colonial rule – the doctrine of indirect rule through Native Authorities.

Indirect rule as a doctrine had repercussions elsewhere in Africa. This doctrine of using Native Authorities did not work effectively everywhere but the fact that it was attempted at all was born out of the British response to the Islamic state structures discovered in northern Nigeria.

Aspects of Islamic law, the Shari'a, were respected by the Colonial Order wherever there were Muslims in any significant numbers. The Shari'a is still operative in post-colonial Kenya in aspects of personal and civil law, though the trend in independent Kenya is towards a gradual integration of Islamic, indigenous and Western-derived law. The latest effort has been a quest to establish an integrated law of succession and inheritance. The Government of Kenya has consulted Islamic opinion and the opinions of African customary law specialists. Although consensus has been elusive, the present Kenyan regime remains obstinate in its pursuit of integrated national law as a long-term objective. The triple heritage in law is in search of a synthesis in a number of African countries. Kenya is most active in this search.

The impact of Islamic culture has not only been in the areas of political institutions and law. It has also been in the field of political ideas and political vocabulary. Languages such as Hausa and Kiswahili still look to the Arabic language and Islamic history as sources of new words for political discourse. In Kiswahili, the contrasts of borrowings from indigenous and Arabic sources are themselves fascinating. The Swahili word for king (*mfalme*) is Bantu or indigenous while the word for president (*raisi*) is Arabic-derived. Indeed, while the word for king (*mfalme*) is Bantu, the word for queen (*malkia*) is Arabic-derived. The word for monarchy (*ufalme*) is Bantu while the word for republic (*jamuhuri*) is Arabic-derived. The word for slavery (*utumwa*) is Bantu, while the word for freedom or independence (*uhuru*) is Arabic-derived. Since independence there has developed the language of 'East/West relations' and 'North/South dialogue'. The former refers to the ideological divide between Western countries and Communist countries; the latter refers to the economic divide between the industrialised countries of the northern hemisphere and the developing countries of the south. In Kiswahili the original words for East and West (*mashariki* and *magharibi*) are Arabic-derived; while the words for North and South (*kaskazini* and *kusini*) are probably Bantu-derived. In Tanzanian Kiswahili the word for socialism (*ujamaa*) is Arabic-derived whereas the word for capitalism (*ubepari*) is Bantu. One of the reasons why Nyerere's translation of Shakespeare's *Merchant of Venice* appears ideologically inspired is because Nyerere entitled the translation *Mabepari wa Vanisi* (Capitalists (*sic*) of Venice). Indeed, the term *ujamaa* in Tanzanian Kiswahili is a fusion of the triple heritage. The word itself is Arabic-derived. It refers to the indigenous phenomenon of ethnic solidarity or the solidarity of the extended family. And yet Nyerere's intention was to find an African equivalent of the European concept of 'socialism'. The word *ujamaa* is Islamic, the ancestral phenomenon of solidarity is indigenous, and the conceptual metaphor equates African familyhood with European socialist fellowship.

Conclusion

Africa is a cultural bazaar. A wide variety of ideas and values, drawn from different civilisations, competes for the attention of potential African buyers. This marketing of cultures in Africa has been going on for centuries but a particularly important impact has come from the 'Semites' (especially Arabs and Jews) and the 'Caucasians' (especially western Europeans).

The most recent Jewish impact on Africa has been due to Arab-Israeli rivalries. But while Israel can compete with the Arabs for political influence, and for a role in Africa's development programmes, it has no chance of catching up with Arab *cultural* influence and the impact of the Arabs on African identity. The modern triple heritage of Africa has produced approximately 100 million Muslims south of the Sahara. This is a cultural reservoir for the Arabs for which the Jews have no real equivalent. In any case, Judaism is a more exclusive religion than Islam, and Judaism is therefore offering no competition to either Islam or Christianity in the scramble for Africa's soul. Nor can Hebrew ever rival Arabic as a major force in Africa's cultural experience, and as a source of words for indigenous African languages. With regard to intermarriage, Jews are more exclusive than the Arabs. The 'Semitic' blood which mingles with African blood will remain overwhelmingly Arab not only because Jews are much fewer than Arabs in absolute numbers, but also because Jewish endogamy and lineage are less receptive to intermarriage than are Arab kinship patterns.

On the other hand, those Jews that are part of Western civilisation are major carriers of Western ideas and major innovators in the Western idiom. Ethnic Jews who have shaped the modern intellect include Karl Marx, Sigmund Freud and Albert Einstein. Marxism – from the barracks of Ethiopia and Mozambique to the cafés of Dakar – is probably the most important legacy from a Western Jew to have influenced twentieth-century Africa.

In ancient and medieval Ethiopia, the Jewish contribution was part of the Semitic aspect of the ancient triple heritage (indigenous, Semitic and Greco-Roman). In Ethiopia, since the revolution of 1974, the Jewish component (including Marxism) is part of the Western leg of the new triple heritage (indigenous, Islamic and Western).

The Semites, both Arab and Jew, continue to be a major aspect of Africa's problems of identity and Africa's political and cultural history. Their roles range from the muezzin calling Africans to prayer to the radical trumpet calling Africans to revolution, from Africa's shared nationalism with the Arabs to Africa's shared martyrdom with the Jews.

Africa's Identity: The Western Aftermath

One of the great ironies of modern African history is that it took European colonialism to inform Africans that they were Africans. This chapter is partly about the white man's creation of the African identity within the African continent, and the white man's destruction of the African identity in the African Diaspora abroad. This is clearer in the case of Black Africa than with regard to Arab Africa north of the Sahara, but even north Africa has been affected by this paradoxical role of Europe in fostering an African identity. To that extent, it is arguable that Europe not only created the African Diaspora by its ruthless export of millions of slaves to the Western hemisphere; Europe also helped to invent Africa as we know it through the ruthless distortions of colonial rule.

How these two processes occurred are the two historical and conceptual challenges which this chapter addresses.

An Identity is Born

Bernard Lewis, a Western analyst of Middle Eastern affairs, once grappled with the question 'What is a Turk?' and finally put forward, virtually as part of the definition, the 'sentiment of Turkish identity' – simply thinking of oneself as a Turk.[1]

Lewis later grappled with the question of 'What is an Arab?' and built into his definition the sentiment of Arab identity. Now the course of world history is once again being affected by people who, on occasion, speak of themselves collectively as 'Africans'. How important to the definition of an African in politics is the quality of thinking of oneself as an African? And what did the Western world do to contribute to this feeling?

The pioneer American Africanist, Melville Herskovits, used to argue that Africa was a geographical fiction. 'It is thought of as a separate entity and regarded as a unit to the degree that the map is invested with an authority imposed on it by the mapmakers.'[2]

In part, the argument here is presumably that climatically the range in Africa is from arid deserts to tropical forests; ethnically from the Khoisan to the Semites; linguistically from Yoruba to Kidigo.

Herskovits referred to that old description of Africa made by the Geographer Royal of France in 1656: Africa was a 'peninsula so large that it comprises the third part, and this the most southerly, of our [European] continent'. And, as indicated elsewhere in this book, a case can certainly be made for the thesis that north Africa was in a sense an extension of southern

opposite, Captives forced into slavery in Central Africa, *c.* 1860

Europe for a long time. If the connection with Europe was to an extent weakened with the advent of Islam, it was only to turn north Africa into a western extension of the Arabian peninsula rather than strengthening its identity as a northern continuation of sub-Saharan Africa. The whole debate can be taken as further evidence for Max Beloff's argument in another context that 'it is easier to understand the contiguities of geography than the continuities of history'.[3]

But how then did Europe Africanise Africa? In what way is the sense of identity that Africans have as Africans an outgrowth of their historic interaction with Europeans?

In fact a number of inter-related processes were at work. First, there was the triumph of European cartography and mapmaking in the scientific and

FUN.—DECEMBER 4, 1875.

THE NEW AFRICAN MISSION.

Rev. Mr. Fun:—"THIS, DEARLY BELOVED BROTHER, IS OUR CIVILISATION. A TEMPTING PICTURE, IS IT NOT?"

intellectual history of the world in the last 300 years. We have already referred to the Gospel of the Universe according to Europe – the impact of European perceptions of the world upon international perceptions generally. As we have indicated in Chapter 1, it was primarily Europe which decided the boundaries of Africa as we know them today. Western Europeans did not invent the name 'Africa' but Europeans played a decisive role in applying it to the continental land mass that we recognise today.

The second process through which Europe Africanised Africa was the process of racism in history. This was particularly marked in the treatment of the Black populations of the continent. The humiliation and degradation of Black Africans across the centuries contributed to their mutual recognition of each other as 'fellow Africans'.

The third inter-related process through which Europe Africanised Africa was imperialism and colonisation. This generated a sufficient sense of shared African identity for the movement of Pan-Africanism to be born.

A fourth process of Europe's Africanisation of Africa was truly dialectical. This was the fragmentation of Africa in terms of artificial state boundaries, in terms of reinforced ethnic nationalisms and in terms of new élite formations. By a curious destiny, these criss-crossing boundaries of sectional identity have sometimes increased the value of a regional or continental African identity.

Let us look at these four processes of Europe's Africanisation of Africa.

The Map and the Master

As we have indicated, what we regard as Africa today is primarily what Europeans decided was Africa. It was therefore Europeans who decided that the western side of the Red Sea and the Suez Canal was indeed Africa while the eastern side was not despite the fact that geologically the Arabian peninsula still shares much with that part of Africa that is nearest to it. Culturally, Islam and the Arabic language have attempted to reunite what was torn asunder. What then prevented a reunification? It was the force of European power and European pre-eminence in cartography and mapmaking. It was this combination which decreed that Africa ended at the Red Sea instead of at the Gulf which separated the Arabian peninsula from Iran. And so, it was not Saudi Arabians who decided initially that they were not Africans; it was not Africans either who made that decision. It was European hegemonic mapmaking.

The final act in the drama about Arabia's separation from its ancestral continent occurred in the nineteenth century. If the Arabs on both sides of the Red Sea had been in control of their own destinies, they could presumably have discussed building a tunnel under the sea or a bridge over it or a special road across the Isthmus of Suez to facilitate communication between the two parts of the Arab world. But in the nineteenth century power was such that priorities were oriented towards Europe. And so the Suez Canal was built, not to increase traffic between the eastern and western sides of

Mid-nineteenth-century map of Africa, before the continent was partitioned following the Berlin Conference of 1884–5. The central regions were still largely unexplored by Europeans at this point.

the Red Sea and thus integrate Africa more fully with the Arab world, but to increase traffic from Europe to the rest of the world through the Canal, and back to Europe. A cataclysm which had occurred several million years previously when the Arabian peninsula was torn off its continent was at long last completed at Suez, severing the physical umbilical cord between the Arabian peninsula and its maternal continent. But although the European adventurers and scientists did not realise it at the time, they were laying the foundations of a new African identity, encompassing the Black peoples south of the Sahara, linking them with the Arabs north of the Sahara – but unlinking them from the Arabs in the Arabian peninsula. What is Africa? It is what Europeans finally decided it was.

European Racism and African Identity

Andrew Young, when United States Ambassador to the United Nations, once accused the British of having invented racism. Young was at once stimulating and exaggerating. It is true that Anglo-Saxon racism has had very distinctive features, and has been one of the great forces which have conditioned relations between white people and Black people. But a variety of alternative forms of racism have existed in the world over the centuries, even before the Anglo-Saxons established world hegemony.

Racism certainly influenced slavery and the slave trade to a great extent, and converted Africans into commodities to be acquired and sold on the world market. Because Africa was hard to circumnavigate, explorers such as Christopher Columbus set sail westwards instead, looking for alternative sea routes to the Orient. Yet history did have its cruel revenge upon Africa. Christopher Columbus did not realise what damage he was doing to the *African* continent by 'discovering' the *American* hemisphere. In a relatively short time the demand for slaves in the 'New World' played havoc with population patterns and social institutions in western Africa. A substantial part of Africa's population was dragged off, kicking and screaming, and shipped to the new plantations of the Americas. The maritime and nautical achievements of Europe and the 'discovery' of new worlds to conquer, did irreparable damage to Black Africa since it coincided with a new wave of racism. Today one out of every five people of Black African ancestry lives in the Americas. That is a rather high proportion. From Africa's point of view, Christopher Columbus and his navigational skills have a good deal to answer for. No people in history have been forcibly exported in such large

A slave auction in Virginia, 1861

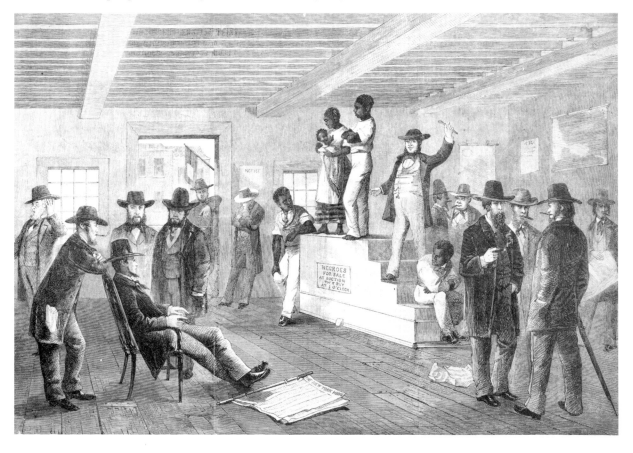

numbers as Africans. And the Americas were the largest recipients of these reluctant exiles. Slavery was at once the consequence of racism and the mother of newer forms of racial degradation.

European racism helped to convince at least sub-Saharan Africans that one of the most relevant criteria of their Africanity was their skin colour. Until the coming of Europeans south of the Sahara, Blackness was taken relatively for granted. It is true that fairer-skinned Arabs sometimes penetrated into the interior of Black Africa, but they were few in number. And they were ready to intermarry with local populations and not emphasise too greatly the colour differentiation.

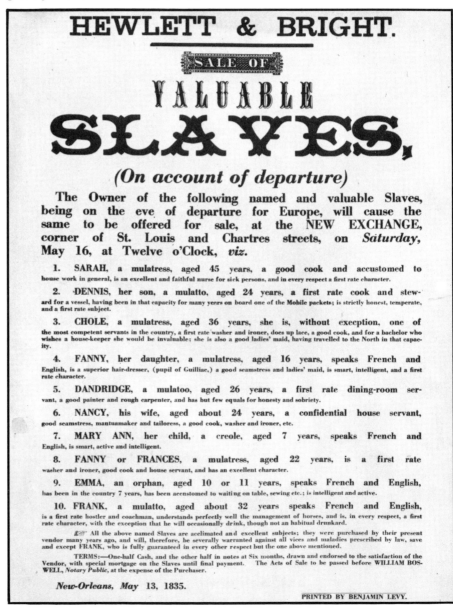

It is true that the Arabs themselves were aware that as they progressed southwards from north Africa they came to a belt which they called the Sudan, a name derived from the Arabic word for blackness. But Arab marriage and lineage systems allowed for the emergence of many Black Arabs. The definition of what is an Arab is more strongly tied to language than pigmentation. As we have indicated in the previous chapter, the colour of Arabs in the Middle East and Africa ranges from blond Arabs of Lebanon and Syria to Black Arabs of Libya, Sudan and parts of Saudi Arabia. The primary criterion of differentiation between Arab and non-Arab is not skin colour. In contrast, Europeans decided that one of the most fundamental

Elmina Castle, Ghana. This was built by the Portuguese in 1482 and occupation passed to the Dutch in 1637.

1875 cartoon showing the plight of the British agricultural labourers. The caption reads, 'Mr Zanzibar: "From what I can see, Mrs Britannia, it would be just as well for you to remedy some matters at home, before interfering so actively abroad."'

lines of differentiation between European and African was the fact that Europeans were white and Africans were black or brown. Nothing reminded sub-Saharan Africans especially that they were Black people more convincingly than European attitudes towards skin colour. To use the words of Julius Nyerere of Tanzania, 'Africans, all over the continent, without a word being spoken either from one individual to another or from one African country to another, looked at the European, looked at one another, and knew that in relation to the European they were one.' This was a central aspect of Black consciousness in Africa, which in turn is an aspect of African identity, at least south of the Sahara.[4]

That form of Pan-Africanism which was based on colour owes a good deal of its original impetus to the Western world's racism. It was partly because of this that Pan-Africanism as a movement was for so long led by Diaspora Blacks. In many ways these exported Africans had had to face the challenge of racism more frontally, from being captured as slaves to being lynched as 'niggers'. Their race consciousness was aroused even more dramatically than that of Blacks who remained in Africa. Names such as Marcus Garvey, W. E. B. DuBois and George Padmore do recur time and again in the annals of Pan-Africanism as a historical movement. And these names are of West Indians and American Blacks. Their indignation had been aroused by the experience of racial humiliation and colour discrimination as people of African ancestry. It is in this sense that Pan-Africanism as a movement of Black consciousness was in part created by the racists who aroused Black anger, just as the burglar alarm is in part created by the reality of thieves in the world.

But racism as a force did not immediately apply the term 'Africans' to any of these Black people, not even to those within the African continent south of the Sahara. It is another irony of history that the Europeans who applied the name 'Africa' to the whole of the land mass were nevertheless reluctant to apply the name 'Africans' to the inhabitants. For a long time the slave dealers preferred to refer to the inhabitants, especially south of the Sahara, either as 'natives' or in even more pejorative terms like 'savages'. The term 'natives' was also applied to north Africans, again in a pejorative rather than purely objective sense of indigenous peoples. The British invented other insulting epithets for Egyptians, while the French chose their own for Algerians, Moroccans and Tunisians.

The white settlers within Africa were even more reluctant to use the term 'Africans' in referring to the indigenous peoples around them. And the structures of power and special policies which were devised had the term 'native' constantly in mind. British colonial rule devised 'Native Authorities' as part of the structure for indirect rule.

In the more deeply racialised societies of southern Africa the reluctance to call Black people 'Africans' lasted even longer. Until the rest of Africa became independent, the whites of South Africa used to call their Blacks 'Bantu' when they were not using more insulting names such as 'kaffirs'. The most astonishing presumption of all in South Africa was the readiness of Dutch-speaking whites to call *themselves* 'Africans' (or 'Afrikaners') while denying the suitability of the word 'Africans' to the Black population for a century or more.

It is in this sense that European imperialism managed to define what land mass constituted 'Africa', while at the same time denying the right of the inhabitants to call themselves 'Africans' until rather late in their history of domination. When we therefore say that Europeans awakened Africans to the fact that they were Africans, we must always remember that this awakening was not intended by the Europeans. A set of historical circumstances created conditions in which African awareness was at last aroused, and the Africans adopted a name for themselves based on what others had called their land mass.

Western Imperialism and African Identity

But the history of racism in the last 200 years is inseparable from the history of colonisation and territorial annexation by the Western world. Imperialism was in turn closely linked to that process of fragmentation which created conflicting identities and, at least some of the time, inadvertently fostered Pan-Africanism as a consequence. In 1944 a British Colonial Office

Slaves in chains, guarded by an Askari soldier

The Berlin Conference, held in 1884–5 to discuss Congo and the partition of Africa

Advisory Committee on Education in the Colonies drew attention to the finding that travel and contact with other nationalities had given rise among Africans to a 'dawning realisation of themselves as Africans, even as "nationals" of a territory like Northern Rhodesia, playing a part in world affairs'.[5]

Indeed, many African nationalists do believe that Western imperialism was an exercise in divide and rule. The argument sometimes sounds like the following, 'We were all Africans until colonialism split us into Ugandans, Kenyans, Ghanaians, and Ivorians'. It is certainly true that there could not have been Ugandans, Kenyans or Ivorians before the advent of colonialism, since colonialism created Uganda, Kenya and the Ivory Coast. The logical jump is the assertion that Africans must 'therefore' have previously been just 'Africans'. It is not a simple case of the very word 'African' being itself non-African in origin, however true that may be. Rather, it is a case of the inhabitants of the continent having known other, often narrower, group identities than 'Ugandans' and 'Ivorians' before colonial rule.

Yet there is a persistent reluctance in the continental school of African nationalism to accept the map which partly grew out of the Berlin Conference of 1884–5 and the ensuing scramble for Africa. Many nationalists have demanded that once foreigners stopped interfering with Africa, Africans could set about putting the continent 'back together again'.

This dilemma as to whether European colonialism divided Africa or united it is a continuing contradiction in the thought and rhetoric of African nationalism. Of course the two impacts on Africa (unifying it and also dividing it) are not impossible to reconcile. Certainly Julius Nyerere seemed to subscribe to both. On many occasions he referred to the divisive tactics of Western imperialists and indeed to the 'policy of divide and rule'. Yet Nyerere was known to argue in a way which suggested that if the imperialists divided (as a policy) in order to rule, they also united (in effect) by the very act of ruling. At a symposium at Wellesley College, Nyerere had emphasised that 'the sentiment of Africa', the sense of fellowship between Africans, was 'something which came from outside'. He elaborated,

> One need not go into the history of colonisation of Africa, but that colonisation had one significant result. A sentiment was created on the African continent – a sentiment of oneness.[6]

It is certainly clear that the mere departure of alien forces from the African scene would not be enough for the task of 'putting Africa back together again'. Indeed, the evidence so far points in the reverse direction. When Africans decide to unite against colonialism and racism, they stand a better chance of sustaining that unity and sometimes achieving really substantive results. Pan-Africanism of liberation, concerned with gaining independence for Africa and ending white minority rule, has basically been a success story. On the other hand, when Africans decide to unite for the sake of economic development or shared regional facilities and utilities, unity is less likely to be sustained. Post-colonial African history is littered with the debris of economic communities and common markets and indeed sometimes political unions which did not last very long. This includes the most promising economic community of them all at the time it was launched, the East African Community involving Kenya, Uganda and Tanzania. At some levels it was even more integrated than the European Economic Community. But one by one the legs of solidarity were removed – and the table of solidarity finally collapsed in 1977. Pan-Africanism of integration, of uniting for Africa's development rather than Africa's liberation, has basically been a failure.

The sense of commitment to the cause of Africa is stronger when Africans are conscious of external threats than when they are left on their own. Even apartheid in South Africa, evil and brutal as it is, serves at least one function which is positive – helping to sustain African solidarity all over the continent in a shared political cause, and increasingly also involving the solidarity of Africa's exported sons and daughters in the Diaspora. The activities of the organisation TransAfrica in the United States, and the impressive demonstrations which the organisation helped to foster against apartheid in South Africa, were part of a new Black awareness in the United States and a new empathy with the African condition.

The Western world has succeeded, at least in Africa, in creating a sense of African identity and African solidarity in spite of the West's intentions. Europe's supreme gift to Africa is neither Christianity nor Western civilisation – it is African identity.

The Dis-Africanisation of the Diaspora

But while the impact of the Western world on Africa has resulted in Africa's increasing awareness that it is Africa, the impact of the Western world on the African Diaspora has been in the reverse direction. A central strategy of

Julius Nyerere and Ronald Reagan

slavery was to make the captives forget as soon as possible where they came from. The slave condition was in this sense a case of engineered or contrived amnesia. In most cases the idea was to reduce the risk of nostalgia and the desire to escape. So much of the history of the slave experience in the Western hemisphere amounted to the following command addressed to the captives, 'Forget you are African, remember you are Black! Forget you are African, remember you are Black!'

Black Americans are almost the only sub-group of Americans whose official name is racially based. All other ethnic groups of the United States carry names which are based on either their geographical origins or their cultural ancestry. Thus there are Irish Americans, Italian Americans, German Americans, Greek Americans – all of them bearing the name of their geographical ancestry. Then there are Jewish Americans who are defined in terms of cultural origins. 'Indians'. are, of course, named after a misunderstanding when the first European 'discoverers' of the Americas thought they had arrived in the Indies. But when these are called native Americans, once again it is a term of location. Even 'Orientals' are named after a place of origin. But American Blacks have always been named after a physical feature, a racial characteristic – their skin colour.

What happened to Black identity under the American impact were twin processes: its dis-Africanisation, on one side, and its racialisation on the other. Hence the historical imperative addressed to the Black captives by their experience, 'Forget you are African, remember you are Black!'

The dis-Africanisation of the imported captives took a variety of forms. There was first the dis-Africanisation of personal identity for each individual. It was decided by the masters that the slaves should not carry the names they had borne in their own cultures – all that wealth of African names drawn from Yoruba, Mandinka, Ewe, Wolof and other African cultures. Again, as a group, Black Americans became the only ethnic group in the United States whose personal names almost never give a clue about their cultural or geographical ancestry. Slavery forced them to adopt Anglo-Saxon, Hebraic or related Western names.

Alex Haley's book, *Roots*, captures this theme of the dis-Africanisation of the personal names which the slaves arrived with. Kunta Kinte was faced with the challenge of having to give up his African name and submit to being called 'Toby'. His friend, the Fiddler, was all too aware that Kunta Kinte was defiantly trying to cling to his cultural identity. Fiddler said,

> 'You got to put away all dat stuff [African charm]. You ain't goin' nowhere, so you might's well face facks an' start fittin' in Toby, you hear?'
>
> Kunta's face flushed with anger [at hearing the name 'Toby']. 'Kunta Kinte!' he blurted, astonished at himself. His brown companion, Fiddler, was equally amazed,
>
> 'Looka here, he can talk! But I'm tellin' you, boy, you got to forgit all dat African talk. Make white folks mad, an *scare niggers*. Yo' name Toby.'[7]

All this illustrates part of a dis-Africanisation of individual identity. But there is also the dis-Africanisation of the collective identity of the imported captives. The ethno-cultural names from Africa (Yoruba, Mandinka, and the like) were forced out of existence relatively rapidly. The slaves ceased to be called 'Africans' or anything related to their geographical ancestry, and rapidly became 'niggers' or 'negroes'.

This was accompanied by the dis-Africanisation of collective pride. The captives' capacity for African nostalgia was undermined or destroyed by a ruthless negative indoctrination. The captives were gradually taught to believe that being a slave was almost a form of deliverance away from the savagery and primitiveness of their ancestral homes. The Blacks in the Americas were systematically taught to be *ashamed* of where they came from. In the words of Fiddler to Kunta Kinte, 'White folks says all Africans knows is livin' in grass huts an' runnin' 'roun' killin' an' eatin' one 'nother!'[8]

There was also religious dis-Africanisation of the imported slaves. Traditional religious African tendencies survived less in the United States than they did in other parts of the Black Diaspora such as Brazil or some of the Caribbean islands. However, some aspects of the style of Black worship in the United States are still very African in origin: for example, the involvement of the congregation in response to either the sermon or the service on the basis of individual spontaneity, and emotive response to the ultimate. There are in Black services and Black churches echoes of the sense of being possessed reminiscent of many religious ceremonies in Africa. The spontaneous cries of Hallelujah are sometimes as persistent as the chanting in an exorcism ceremony in Africa.

The African Diaspora, Atlanta, Georgia

These emotive elements in Black religious experience in the United States have survived in spite of the brutal process of dis-Africanisation. On the contrary, the sadness of it all was perhaps reinforced by the brutalities. The sense of being possessed in a religious service may have something in common with the origins of the Blues as a musical form, the sad humming of a people possessed both in the sense of being owned by others and in the sense of being religiously inhabited by a supernatural force.

Islam, too, first arrived in America in chains. Many of the slaves captured from West Africa, especially in the eighteenth century, had already been converted to Islam. Like the Hebrews under pharaonic subjugation, African Muslims served in bondage under the plantation barons of America.

As for the linguistic dis-Africanisation of Black Americans, perhaps it was the most inevitable fate of them all. The captives arrived with multiple languages. There was presumably a need for a lingua franca; and it was very unlikely that the lingua franca would be one of the African languages imported into the Americas. The masters felt a need for a language of command to get the captive labour organised and disciplined. The language of the master prevailed with a certain inevitability, but not entirely without qualification.

James Baldwin, the Black American novelist, once agonised over a very distinctive hatred – he hated Shakespeare. As the supreme genius of the use of the English language, Shakespeare symbolised to Baldwin the ultimate oppression of the enslaved. Baldwin had been forced to adopt the language of his oppressor to such an extent that not a thought, not an idea, had occurred to his secret mind without using the vocabulary of the 'master race'. Baldwin profoundly resented this ultimate invasion of the inner recesses of his mental experiences. It was as if he was permanently naked before an oppressor with a whip.

And then James Baldwin went to spend some time in France. There, in the midst of a language far less familiar to him at the time, he rediscovered afresh the role of the English language in his own identity. He discovered something else – that Blacks in America's history had not simply borrowed or imitated white usage of the English language. Blacks had put their own stamp on that language, used it as an instrument of survival and as a mechanism of their own collective solidarity and identity. Baldwin gradually came to terms with Shakespeare and ceased to hate the supreme bard of the Anglo-Saxons.[9]

But as these linguistic, religious and other forms of dis-Africanisation were taking place, a parallel process was also under way: the racialisation of the Afro-American identity. The imported Afro-Americans came to see themselves primarily in pigmentational terms. The white man had decided that the most important aspect of their identity was their black skin and the Afro-Americans accepted that fate for generations. In a sense, the white man had also used the same methods with Africans south of the Sahara, but in that case there was the paradoxical role of Africanising the identity of the Africans within the continent. But the Diaspora fate was both dis-Africanisation and racialisation. It is partly because of this that Black Americans tend to be far more race conscious than Africans.

In their controversial study, *Beyond the Melting Pot*, Patrick Moynihan and Nathan Glazer asserted that the 'negro' was only an American and nothing else. He had no values and culture from his ancestry to guard and protect. This was certainly the intention of the slave system – to force the 'negro' to forget the values and culture of his ancestry. But in reality, of course, the Blacks of the United States evolved their own third culture. And in any case, the 'negro' was by definition *Black*. Over time he was forced to protect and to value precisely that racial identity imposed upon him by his oppressor. The Afro-American had indeed responded to the historic imperative, 'Forget you are African, remember you are Black!' Until recently the overwhelming majority of Afro-Americans not only did not know much of Africa, or care to identify with it; but those who knew anything about it were still ashamed of their place of origin. The destruction of the Afro-American capacity for cultural nostalgia was complete in the bulk of the population.

The question for the future is whether a partial re-Africanisation is under way, with its roots in the movement of Pan-Africanism in the Diaspora. The story of the quest for re-Africanisation includes not only the movement generated by Marcus Garvey and commanding the following of millions of Afro-Americans early this century, but also the establishment of Liberia as

Demonstration in Memphis, Tennessee, after the assassination of Martin Luther King in 1968

an example of Black Zionism, a physical Black return to ancestry.

There has been the Pan-Africanism of liberation which responded to such figures as W. E. B. DuBois and his legacy, and the leadership of Diaspora Blacks in Pan-African congresses of the first half of the twentieth century.

Black Islam in the form of the Nation of Islam, which was later renamed the World Community of Islam in the Western Hemisphere, has also been a version of re-Africanisation in a special sense. Elijah Muhammad started the movement; Malcolm X was part of re-Africanisation through Islamic conversion. And, of course, Muhammad Ali, the boxer, is probably the most famous American Muslim of them all.

Re-Africanisation has also taken the form of new group names, like the name 'Afro-Americans' (instead of Blacks) or even 'African Americans'. Cultural revivalism also includes in a few cases the adoption of African personal names by Afro-Americans, and African styles of dress and of hair.

But the most promising development of the 1980s is the new identification by Afro-Americans with African causes, especially the fight against apartheid and the struggle against famine and drought. Compassion has been aroused among Afro-Americans for the starving millions of Africa; and anger has been provoked against racism in South Africa. The achievements of these new moves are relatively modest. The re-Africanisation of Black America is still in its infant stages. But there are signs that the past is not completely irreversible. In spite of the width of the Atlantic, the Blacks that were enslaved and taken away and the Blacks who remained behind may yet stretch out their arms towards each other, seeking to touch across the gulf of the ocean and the chasm of history.

Malcolm X (1925–65) speaking at a rally in Harlem, New York, 1963

Conclusion

We have attempted to show in this chapter that the impact of the West upon Africa has been towards Africanising the identity of the people of the African continent; while the impact of the West upon the African Diaspora has been towards dis-Africanising the identity of the exported sons and daughters of the ancestral continent.

Europe especially awakened Africans to the fact that they were Africans. This Africanisation of Africans was accomplished first through cartography; then through European racism and racial classifications; third, through the impact of colonisation and imperialism; and fourth, through the fragmentation of Africa and the resulting quest for a transcending continental or racial identification.

When we say that Europe Africanised the identity of the inhabitants of the continent, we mean that this was in spite of the wishes of Europe. Europe's greatest service to the people of Africa was not Western civilisation, which is under siege, or even Christianity, which is on the defensive. Europe's supreme gift was the gift of African identity, bequeathed without grace and without design, but a reality all the same.

Marcus Garvey (1887–1940), Black American leader from Jamaica

Africa at Play: A Triple Heritage of Sports

It is, of course, widely recognised that sport is linked to broader cultural and sociological forces. In Africa the links are to indigenous culture, on the one hand, and to imported culture, on the other. Race, class and religion have all had a bearing. So indeed has gender.

But underlying these factors is once again Africa's triple heritage of cultures. Indigenous traditions, Islamic ways and Western tendencies have exerted their influence upon the history of sports in Africa.

The Indigenous Tradition in Sport

The warrior tradition of indigenous Africa has created a link between play and warfare in Africa. In many African cultures initiation into manhood and initiation into warrior status have been indistinguishable. It is against this background of the masculinity of the warrior that we have to understand indigenous African sports.

Wrestling is one of the most widespread games in Africa. Among the Nubians of Upper Egypt and the Sudan the arts of wrestling seem to be thousands of years old, going back to pharaonic times. What has persisted about wrestling throughout history and throughout much of Africa is the game's obstinate masculinity in the warrior tradition. This is demonstrated in *tigil*, the Ethiopian form of wrestling,

> In the countryside, the young males are paired off more or less according to age and strength; sometimes within a village, but more often one village against another . . . Fights are usually held near a village after the harvest and stacking of the grain, but before the threshing and winnowing . . . The contestants are clothed in white breeches and tunics, with bare feet.[1]

Even more colourful are Ethiopian games involving horse riding. Horses may have been imported into Ethiopia by the Oromo (Galla). The Oromo successes eventually convinced Ethiopians of the military value of horses so in time horses in Ethiopia were used mainly for battle and more rarely as beasts of burden. Donkeys and mules served the latter purpose. The third major use of horses (after carriage and combat) was for sport and entertainment. Particularly colourful is the *Feres Gugs* game,

> The game of gugs is based on warfare, but where a cavalryman carried two spears, a light one for throwing, and a heavier job for infighting, the gouks (gugs) player uses only light wood wands. The object is for members of one team to gallop off followed by the others who are supposed to hit them with their wands, either by hurling at them or by catching up and hitting them. Those being pursued are protected with traditional circular shields in

opposite, Julius Korir of Kenya

Masai people in Kenya examine the results of a spear-throwing challenge

hippo or rhinoceros hide, some covered with coloured velvet and decorated with gold and silver. As they tear away across the plain, they may dodge, hang off the horse or ward off with the shield. The riders are often in traditional costume, or at any rate the cloak and gold-fringed lion or baboon headdress![2]

Spear throwing for entertainment has managed to survive in countries such as Uganda and Zaire. The competition in spear throwing is not usually based on aim and marksmanship but on strength, velocity and distance of throw. The game is still highly localised and has yet to become Pan-Africanised. The chances of it becoming an international sport between African countries are slim.

Much more organised is langa, a traditional sport in many of the northern states of Nigeria. Langa is similar to wrestling because opponents run into each other, trying to throw the other off balance. Langa is being revived under the leadership of the prominent businessman, Alhaji Dr G. N. A. Hamza, who hopes to involve women in the game.

It is one of the more curious gaps in African sport that archery has not evolved into a major form of entertainment. One reason may be that bows and arrows are still part of the technology of hunting and defence in parts of Africa, and people are self-conscious about converting them into skills of entertainment. The westernised African élites particularly are often embarrassed by the bow and arrow as an illustration of Africa's 'primitive technology'. These élites are often the ones who make decisions about which sports should be promoted in their countries. Archery, though an activity in which Africans could excel internationally, is therefore carefully relegated to oblivion by the urban sophisticates.

The Crescent of Sport

The Arabs once served as the transmission belt of the civilisation of ancient Greece into medieval Europe. The works of Greek thinkers and scholars were translated into Arabic and studied in the academies of the Muslim world: from Damascus to Timbuktu, from the courts of the Moghul emperors in India to Al-Azhar University in Cairo, from Baghdad in Iraq to Cordova in Spain. The rest of Europe paid some attention, and learnt about Plato and Socrates from the writings of Arab scholars.

But there was one aspect of the civilisation of ancient Greece which the Arabs did little to promote or transmit. This was the field of sports and athletics – the legacy of the Olympic games.

To begin with, Islamic civilisation was a little too earnest to incorporate a sub-culture of leisure. The arts of relaxation and entertainment in the Arab world have survived in spite of Islam rather than because of it. Love songs and romantic music are just on the borderline of Islamic toleration.

The Islamic rules of dress are also so stringent that the development of athletics has been hampered in much of the Muslim world as a result. Exposed knees are a form of nakedness in Islam, and wearing shorts in a public arena is a violation of the moral code of dress. Wearing briefs for swimming in public also stretches Islamic rules. The code governing female attire is even more stringent, making the training of female athletes exceptionally difficult in much of the Muslim world.

Another Islamic factor which has militated against the development of sports is opposition to *maysir* or games of chance. The commercialisation of sports in Islam has encountered the Shari'a's discouragement of profit-making on the basis of chance and speculation. In the first instance the Shari'a outlaws betting on races and other sports. But even less obvious forms of 'speculation', such as rewarding a winner in a bout or a fight, have been frowned upon by Islamic law. This has slowed down the expansion of sport by slowing down its commercialisation, and has reduced the resources available for training, promotion, the attraction of new talent and general enhancement of sports as a social activity.

Fourth, there is the nature of Islamic education, which in most Muslim societies refrains from mixing training with organised leisure.

A fifth Islamic factor which militates against systematic training in sports is the fast of Ramadhan. The fast is supposed to be a discipline in consumption – abstinence from food, liquid, smoking and sexuality from before dawn until sunset during the whole month of Ramadhan. The discipline has relevance for fitness and for restraining indulgence.

From this point of view of weight-management, most Muslims emerge slimmer from Ramadhan than when they entered the fast. Perhaps many are therefore fitter as a result. This is good for sporting effectiveness. What is dysfunctional is the debilitating impact of the fast during its duration. In the daytime during Ramadhan (with neither water nor food) many feel drained and short of energy. '*Leo saumu ni kali kweli kweli*', ('Today the fast is truly

above, Contemporary display of horse-riding skills in Morocco

left, A Turkana woman drying fish from Lake Rudolf, Kenya. These people do not fish for sport but to sell.

ferocious'). This is a common topic of conversation during Ramadhan in the Swahili world. How draining is today's fast as compared with yesterday's! And tempers usually run short and general productivity declines.

In the rest of the Muslim calendar there are substantive sports which Islam has helped to foster in Africa. The most colourful are connected with animals. In northern Nigeria the horse is used not only as a beast of burden but also as a sporting animal. Polo is a highly developed sport among the Islamic Emirates of the north. The Englishman Richard Lander in 1831 saw a horse race at Kaiama held to celebrate the Muslim festival of 'Bebun Salah' or 'Great Prayer Day'. In the Horn of Africa the camel is used not only for milk and transportation but also for some kinds of entertainment – including camel races.

The Gulf Arabs have learnt to train certain birds as couriers and messengers, and use them sometimes for retrieval when hunting. Some of these skills have found their way into Arab Africa.

On Hunting and Fishing

Hunting generally is a feature of all three cultures in Africa – indigenous, Islamic and Western. The most efficient technology of hunting is now Western. With a rifle under his arm my father used to take me hunting near our country home. His targets were usually the large wild pigeons of the east African coast. He would shoot two or three for our own food. I served as retriever for him. That exercise in the 1940s was itself a fusion of indigenous, Islamic and Western customs and traditions.

Until recently the modernisation of hunting in Africa was supposed to be a transition from the bow and arrow to the gun. But under American stimulation a new school of thought now allows for the modernisation of the bow and arrow, rather than its replacement by the gun. Within the United States, hunting with the bow and arrow is becoming fashionable again. The official season for this primordial form of hunting is usually separated from the season of hunting with the gun. But the technology of the bow and arrow in the United States is becoming increasingly sophisticated; hunters are equipped with a scientific telescope for aiming and the arrow has been redesigned to be breeze-proof and can therefore attain a new velocity.

For the time being the indigenous African hunter either uses the more rudimentary and primordial bow and arrow of the past or turns to the greater precision and destructiveness of the gun. It remains to be seen if indigenous African hunters will follow the American lead to modernise ancient instruments of hunting rather than replacing them with the technology of the bullet.

One major question arises. Has indigenous African hunting ever been a sport at all? Or has it always been either an economic activity for acquisition of food or a cultural activity for masculine initiation and related rituals? The evidence would seem to suggest that hunting purely for pleasure is more characteristic of Western culture than of indigenous African traditions. On that issue the culture of hunting in Islam lies somewhere between the wide-ranging sporting functions of Western hunting and the more purely economic and ritualistic hunting of indigenous Africa.

A similar contrast applies to the functions of fishing. Traditionally Africans have fished almost exclusively for food and trade and very rarely just for pleasure. The idea of a rich person going fishing, or a major leader owning a fishing line or net, was quite alien to most African cultures. Fishing was left to the specialists: fishermen with their boats. It was exclusively a 'proletarian' activity rather than a sport of the élite. Fishing was specific to a class.

On this issue Islamic traditions are much closer to African ways than they are to Western customs. Muslim dhows did traverse the seas in trade, often dealing in dried fish from the Persian (Arabian) Gulf and neighbouring waters. Fishing as a pastime of the élite is virtually as alien to Islamic culture as it is to indigenous African civilisation. But Westernisation is beginning to change this configuration. The Westernised élites of Africa and the Muslim world are beginning to take to fishing waters and hunting grounds.

Sport: The Western Legacy

The Western impact has not been homogeneous or monolithic even in the narrow field of sports and play. In Africa there are some games which are specific to particular colonial powers. Cricket, for example, is almost exclusively associated with countries previously ruled by Britain. What is more, Africa's cricket is also race-specific. It has failed to capture the imagination of Black Africans, but immigrant Asians, as well as immigrant whites, have embraced it as one of their sports. (On the other hand, Black West Indians are as great cricket-lovers as brown and white West Indians.) Also race-specific is the game of hockey in Africa. Where it is played at all, it tends to be dominated by citizens of South Asian ancestry, from the Indian sub-continent. (Yet Zimbabwe's team which won the women's hockey gold medal at the 1980 Olympics in Moscow was an all-white team and Kenya's men's hockey team at the 1984 Olympics in Los Angeles contained a number of Black African players.)

As for games which are class-specific, these include tennis and golf which are monopolised by the new middle classes of Africa, regardless of race. But class in Africa is sometimes culturally rather than economically defined. Immersion into the new conquering culture of the West can change a person's status and class affiliation. Some imported sports from the West are culture-intensive – one has to be substantially Westernised before one can be attracted to the sport. African lawn-tennis players are all substantially Westernised. Nigeria's Nduka Odizor who lives in the United States of America and Cameroon's Yannick Noah who lives in and plays for France, are examples of highly Westernised African tennis stars.

On the other hand, soccer is almost culture-neutral in Africa. In Britain, its homeland, soccer is *not* class-neutral as it is mainly a working-class game;

and in the USA soccer is an acquired taste and therefore semi-élitist. In Africa, however, soccer is culture-neutral because it is classless, a game for the whole population, as it is in Latin Europe (Italy, Spain, Portugal and France) or in Latin America. Rugby in Africa seems to demand much greater Westernisation than soccer. There are small groups of Black African rugby players in Kenya, Zimbabwe and South Africa, nearly all of whom are middle class and highly Westernised. Rugby is, therefore, like lawn tennis, a culture-intensive game in Africa. (Rugby in Britain is not culture-neutral, as it is a middle-class game. However, in New Zealand rugby is played by all classes. Rugby's equivalent in the USA, American football, is classless.)

Some colonial powers emphasised acculturation more than others. France especially is widely credited (or debited) with policies of intensive assimilation of colonial subjects. In the French-speaking part of Cameroon the élite is more attracted to culture-intensive games (for example, tennis) than in English-speaking Cameroon. On the other hand, in the field of international sports Cameroon's most notable success so far has been in a culture-neutral sport, soccer. Aided by their star goalkeeper Thomas Nkono and their star forward Roger Milla, Cameroon's soccer team did exceptionally well in the 1982 World Cup Finals in Spain, being unbeaten, drawing with Peru, Poland and the eventual champions, Italy, failing to go through to the next round only on goal difference, and displaying the world-class quality of African

left, Nduka Odizor, originally from Nigeria, now living in America; *right*, Yannick Noah from Cameroon, now living in and playing for France

left, Soccer players Stephen Keshi from Nigeria and Roger Milla from Cameroon; *right*, Nigeria's 'Baby Eagles' – the team that won the 1985 Kodak World Cup for under-16s

football. Then in 1985 Nigeria's 'Baby Eagles' stunned the world and delighted much of it by winning the Kodak World Cup for under-16s, a feat achieved mainly through African coaching and management. A higher age-group, the 'Flying Eagles', came third in the World Youth Cup soccer tournament in the USSR, also in 1985.

Sports in general have a more institutionalised place in British-style educational establishments than they have in French-style schools. In the British educational system sport is a crucial part of upbringing and education whereas in French schools there is very little emphasis on sporting activities. The competitiveness of sports in the British school system has been transported to schools in Anglophone Africa. One possible result is the greater Anglophone African success in the Olympic Games than successes by Francophone Africans from south of the Sahara. The great African Olympic and Commonwealth Games heroes have come disproportionately from countries such as Kenya, Tanzania, Uganda, Ghana, Nigeria and (partially Anglophone) Ethiopia. Anglophone Africa has produced Olympic champions such as Kipchoge Keino, Naftali Temu and Julius Korir of Kenya and John Akii-Bua of Uganda, and Ethiopia's Olympic gold medallists include the double marathon champion Abebe Bikila and Mirus Yifter. Filbert Bayi of Tanzania held the 1500 metres world record from 1974 to 1979, Henry Rono held three athletics world records in 1978, while the Black South African Sydney Maree held the 1500 metres world record for a time in the early 1980s.

However, there are other reasons, apart from British influence on educational systems, for the achievements of African athletes from Anglophone countries. One is the environmental factor: Africa's Olympic champions and world record holders have come disproportionately from the east African

Nawal el Moutawakel from Morocco at the 1984 Olympics. Under Islam women rarely compete at public events so el Moutawakel's achievement is especially remarkable.

and Ethiopian highlands, a factor which gives a major advantage in middle-distance and long-distance running. Second, many of east Africa's and Ethiopia's great athletes are products not so much of the educational system as of the physical training of the armed forces and the police. Third, many of these athletes originate from communities where the indigenous culture places high value on athletics and sports. Fourth, athletics is a culture-neutral sport and there are no cultural barriers to African participation in it.

There is still evidence that the imported British educational system has helped Anglophone Africans succeed more than Francophone Africans south of the Sahara in international sports: this evidence comes from west Africa and from Uganda, where the highland environmental factor is lacking, and whose sportsmen and sportswomen generally have performed comparatively far better than those of their Francophone neighbours in a range of games. In athletics, for example, there have been achievements such as those of Ghana's Alice Annum, Karikari and Ernest Obeng and the 1974 Commonwealth Games triple jumpers Owusu and Amoah, and Nigeria's 4 × 100 metres relay team which won the gold medal in the 1982 Commonwealth Games at Brisbane.

Linked to this issue of comparative colonial legacies in sport is the fact that the Francophone world has no real equivalent of the Commonwealth Games: large-scale competitive sports events in which countries previously ruled by Britain test out each other's skills. The Commonwealth Games are often a rehearsal for the Olympic Games.

French-speaking Africans north of the Sahara have a different history, uniquely affected by both Islam and the Mediterranean world across the centuries. Muhammad Gamoudi of Tunisia won a gold medal at the Mexico City Olympics in 1968. Both Morocco and Algeria have played well in recent soccer World Cup finals. Morocco won two track gold medals at Los Angeles in 1984, when Said Aouita won the men's 5000 metres (and a year later set new world records for both 5000 and 1500 metres) and Nawal el Moutawakel won the women's 400 metres hurdles. El Moutawakel's achievement was all the more remarkable considering the normally inhibiting effect of Islam on public performance by women. The explanation for the success of sportsmen and sportswomen from the Maghreb may be that north-west Africa is one of the most secularised and Westernised parts of the Muslim world and therefore among the least affected by traditional Islamic restrictions on sport.

In Africa as a whole women are under-represented in both culture-intensive imported sports such as lawn tennis and golf and in culture-neutral sports such as sprinting, long-distance running and high jumping. The reasons for female under-representation in the two types of games overlap but are not identical. The culture-intensive imported sports are élite-specific. Of course there are Westernised women in Africa but in general the level of Westernisation in the continent is still more pronounced among males than among females.

In Search of Rural Sportswomen

In general, both in sports as a form of play and in warfare itself, females have been given a subsidiary role. This goes back further than Aristotle but Aristotle summed it up when he asserted in the fourth century BC that the 'author of nature gave man strength of body and intrepidity of mind to enable him to face great hardships, and to woman was given a weak and delicate constitution, accompanied by a natural softness and modest timid ity, which fit her for sedentary life' (*Physiognomics*). Much later a professor at Yale observed, 'One way of dealing with these disparities between the athletic promise and achievement of men and women is to view women as truncated males. As such they should be permitted to engage in such sports as men do ... but in foreshortened versions.'[3]

What Islam shares with most sports is segregation of women. Women internationally are segregated from male rivals in tennis, running, jumping and swimming. International sports and the rules of orthodox Islam have found a shared principle. But, of course, Islam at its most conservative would prefer to segregate spectators as well as players.

Throughout the world women continue to be grossly under-represented in major sports but there is evidence to suggest that Africa is almost on a par with the Muslim world in degree of keeping women out of sporting activities. Those two overlapping regions are probably the least androgynised in sporting activities in the world.

In the case of the world of Islam the reasons are perhaps a little clearer than they are in Africa. Orthodox Islam tends to protect women from both public glare and general intermingling with male strangers. Major sporting activities involve dealing with a variety of male strangers, from players to managers, from reporters to spectators, from rivals to fans. Thus the majority of Muslim women in the world feel culturally embarrassed in such situations.

These considerations apply far less to indigenous African culture. Why then have African women in non-Muslim areas been almost as under-represented in public sporting activities as have their Muslim counterparts elsewhere in the world?

There may sometimes be an assumption that the chivalry which protects women from heavy physical labour also prevents them from developing sporting physical skills. The assumption may make some kind of sense in the Muslim world where, comparatively speaking, women are both spared physical labour and denied physical skills. But in much of Black Africa this is simply not true. Black African women often do more physical work than their men. In at least some African societies women often walk longer distances, carry heavier loads and have to learn a greater variety of balancing skills than their men.

If the culture of work does indeed help to condition the culture of sports, if African women can be so 'physical' in their economic activities on the land, why have they been so slow in excelling in the physical world of sports? One

Carrying a heavy burden along the beach at Assouinde, Ivory Coast

reason may be that decision-makers in Africa have been encouraging the wrong kind of sports. Perhaps more attention should be paid to the possibility of promoting marathon walks as a major sporting activity in Africa. Children begin to walk long distances to school quite early. Women have been walking longer and longer distances to diminishing supplies of firewood and water. The tradition of long-distance walking could be used to detect talent and structure new patterns of competitive sports. The very chores of collecting firewood could be given a new enthusiasm and liveliness as they are purposefully linked to training young girls for competitive walking.

Weight-lifting could also be more systematically promoted among African women, as well as men. In rural Africa one continues to be astonished by the enormous bundles of firewood on the backs of women walking long distances. Huge baskets of farm produce may be balanced on their heads at the same time. Rural culture would find new levels of animation if these simple chores were given greater value and prizes were awarded to young men and women who excel in purposeful weight-lifting and graceful carriage.

But the purpose of this integration between work culture and rural sports could not simply be to give women greater access to new competitive games. The purpose should also be to encourage men to share the chores which were previously exclusively for women. Turning these skills into proud competitive qualities of triumph and honour would help to give them greater respectability as forms of work, as well as forms of play.

As for the linkage between work culture and sporting culture, it could itself be an honourable form of professionalisation. The Olympic movement has long resisted, perhaps understandably, the idea of turning sports into a profession. The proposed new rural games for Africa are, in a sense, intended to turn rural professions into sports — an inversion of the Olympic movement's position. The rural professions of farming, herding, collecting firewood, long-distance walking for pasture or water, are all potential material for imaginative minds to help relieve the tedium of labour and androgynise the heritage of sports.

Sports and the Aesthetics of Sex

We have discussed the issue of sports-gender in relation to the work ethic. We now turn to the relationship between sports-gender and the aesthetics of sexuality itself.

What makes a woman physically attractive? What makes a woman physically fit? If the measure for sexual attractiveness in Africa is *fatness* and the measure for fitness is *slimness*, we have a wide *sexercise gap* between the criteria of sexual beauty and the criteria of fitness through exercise.

Traditionally in most African societies the sexercise gap for women was wide. Putting on weight was part of the process of acquiring elegance and poise. For example, among the Fantes of south-eastern Ghana and among the people of the Rivers State of Nigeria, an institution called the Fattening Ceremony has been specifically designed to enlarge the hips and 'behind'. Paul Crispin reminds us of the issue in the past tense but, in fact, these aesthetics are still very much alive. Crispin says,

> Body adornment in Africa has gained varying emphasis depending on the ethnic symbols or aesthetic dimensions of the people ... It is particularly fascinating that the muscular development of the whole body is a sign of health and wealth ... Many years ago, before it became the fashion to trim down to scientific streamlining like 36–26–36 ... it used to be the pride of a man in the village to exhibit his 'fat', stately, elegant wife who responded to the admiration of visitors by gorgeous royal slow steps delicately shifting the behind rhythmically from left to right with supple, well-nourished hands flexibly swaying from side to side to complete the picture of 'the wife of a well to do man'.[4]

In spite of his own claim that 'those times have virtually passed', Paul Crispin goes on to tell us how the 'fattening ceremony' is still practised by the people of Calabar in eastern Nigeria. There the fattening process these days occurs in December or January but can last for a whole year or a year and a half. The ceremony is for adolescent girls between fifteen and eighteen. Apart from receiving a special diet, the girls are also taught traditional etiquette, manners and the sex roles of the society.

The principle of big buttocks as a sexual asset for a woman is more widespread than just in Calabar. It is a standard preference in most parts of Black Africa. In Nigerian humour, the term 'bottom power' refers to the sexual tricks that a woman can play to get her own way. Sometimes the idea of 'bottom power' is virtually the equivalent of a woman's sex appeal. On the other hand, the demands of athletic prowess require a trimming down of 'bottom power' and a more commensurate balance between weight and height. The athletics of weight are in conflict with the aesthetics of sex – and the resulting sexercise ratio is wide.

Islam has had a similar though less direct effect on the sexercise ratio. By separating women from hard physical labour and confining most of them to the home, conservative versions of Islam have encouraged *de facto* fattening of women from a fairly early age. 'Bottom power' may not be an aspect of Islam aesthetics *per se*, but the limited exposure of conservative Muslim women to either physical exercise or physical labour has resulted in declining standards of fitness among them.

It is in the third legacy of our triple heritage – the Western legacy – that the sexercise gap is narrowed. Slimness is a measure of both sexual appeal and physical fitness. The struggle to be athletically fit does not contradict the struggle to be sexually attractive. Athletics and aesthetics are fused at some level. The vital statistics of Olympiad are compatible with the vital statistics of Venus.

Westernised African women are less likely to be involved in hard physical labour than women in traditional indigenous roles. Traditional women are more likely to walk long distances for water and firewood, and more likely to be involved in digging and tilling, than Westernised women are.

And yet Westernised African women watch their weight a little more closely and are more likely to mix with Westernised men, whose aesthetics of sex have been modified by European values of slimness. Traditional rural women are probably more fit in terms of daily exercise than are their urbanised sisters but rural folk are less informed about hygiene and have less access to modern medicine than do the Westernised sophisticates. The contradictions of the triple heritage continue to play havoc with both aesthetic standards and athletic measurements. In Africa these contradictions have exacerbated the marginalisation of women in sports.

In Search of Female Warriors
The marginalisation of women in African games has not merely been due to the current contradictions of divorcing sexual aesthetics from rural work and competitive sports. Even more fundamental is the divorce between

women and both the warrior tradition of indigenous Africa and the Jihad tradition of Islam. In all human societies the ethos of armed men and protected women was the most persistent and most primordial of all forms of stratification. Women became marginalised not because they had lost control of the means of production but because they permitted themselves to be eased out of the use of the means of destruction. Nothing in human history has been more responsible for the political subordination of women than their own demilitarisation.

In Africa and the Muslim world that demilitarisation took the form of exclusion from the warrior tradition and the Jihad tradition. In one society after another, the fighters were the sons – and almost never the daughters. Given the link between sports and warfare, and given the exclusion of women from warfare, it stood to reason that women should also be excluded from the more demanding sporting endeavours. The taxing physical exertions of war were supposed to be partially reproduced in the physical exertions of sporting combat. If women were not eligible for the former, why should they be eligible for the latter? In Britain, such calculations led to the exclusion of women from rugby and soccer and even cricket. In the United States, it kept women out of American football and baseball.

In Africa, similar trends have been discernible across history. Apart from such occasional exceptions as pre-colonial Dahomey with its Brigade of

Lagos Polo Club, Nigeria

Moroccan horseman

Amazons, the warrior tradition in Africa has been heavily masculine. Young boys have been initiated into warrior virtues of valour and endurance. The cultures which practise male circumcision have linked at times the symbolism of sexual prowess with the symbolism of the burning spear. The sexual virility of the male has been part of his armoury of martial valour.

It is against this background of the masculinity of the warrior and Jihad traditions that we have to understand the masculinity of the game of polo among the Hausa-Fulani in northern Nigeria, the masculinity of the bullfight on Pemba Island off the coast of Tanzania, and the masculinity of various African forms of wrestling. Horse riding games and skilled horsemanship in northern Nigeria and Ethiopia are forms of sport which carry heavy martial associations. Because of that, they are also games of high masculine profile.

Race, Class and the Boxers' Gender

Boxing came to Africa with colonisation but it did have links with indigenous culture through the tradition of wrestling. Since boxing was a fight, it was implicitly a bridge between the culture of war and the culture of play. Perhaps nobody symbolised this more than Idi Amin, long before he became Uganda's President. Amin was once the heavyweight boxing champion of Uganda, a title which he held for nine years. In his rise to importance within the King's African Rifles during the British period in Uganda, Idi Amin certainly combined the skills of play with martial qualities. In the words of David Martin,

> He was the type of material the British officers liked in the ranks – physically large at six feet four inches and uneducated. The theory was that material of this type responded better to orders and were braver in battle. He endeared himself to his commanders by becoming the Ugandan heavyweight boxing champion . . . and by taking up rugby where, even if his skills were limited, his weight as a second row forward was a valuable contribution.[5]

There were variations among European colonial policies. The British went the furthest in encouraging sports in the colonies, sometimes among girls as well as boys. Schools in the British colonies put more emphasis on sports than schools did in either the French or the Portuguese colonies. But in the field of boxing there were additional reasons why English-speaking Africans became more involved in boxing than did their counterparts elsewhere in the continent. Indeed, many Anglophone Africans actually studied in the United States – and many Black Americans established contacts with English-speaking Africa. Exposure to American boxing was more sustained among English-speaking Africans as a result.

There were consequences for Africa's participation in international boxing in future years. Performance in boxing by Anglophone Africa has usually been more pronounced than that by boxers from either French-speaking or Portuguese-speaking countries. Anglophone Africa has produced professional title fighters such as Hogan Kid Bassey and Dick Tiger of Nigeria, Roy Ankarah, Floyd Robertson and Azumah Nelson of Ghana and Cornelius Boza-Edwards, Ayub Kalule and John Mugabi of Uganda.

John Mugabi (*left*) of Uganda

What has remained constant is the masculinity of the game of boxing. Indeed, the most fundamental similarities between American boxer Muhammad Ali, on one side, and Ugandan soldier Idi Amin, on the other, were two simple attributes – they were not only *Black* but also both *male*. Those attributes encompassed in themselves important relationships between race, class and sex in sports as well as war. Why has heavyweight boxing at the global level been so overwhelmingly dominated by Black men in much of this century? Why have those Black men been disproportionately from the Black Diaspora in the Western hemisphere rather than from the heartland of Africa itself? We may be back to the issue of technological pre-eminence and international stratification. The commercial sophistication of the United States, the techniques of promotion and intensive training, have played their part in ensuring that such a high proportion of Black athletic giants have come not from Africa itself but from among the 'exported' Africans.

Yet even that is not the complete story. On the one hand, Black Americans by being citizens of the United States, subject to the commercial and economic culture of the United States, and modern beneficiaries of American technological affluence, have become the most affluent single group of Blacks anywhere in the world. Their standard of living, ranging from possession of cars and television sets to the number of calories available in the diet, places them on a pinnacle of relative advantage compared to the great majority of Black people anywhere else in the world. On the other hand, because Black Americans experienced some of the harshest forms of slavery in recent times, they have also borne worse scars of humiliation and degradation than those sustained by the majority of Blacks left behind in the African continent.

Both the relative advantage of affluence for Black Americans and their background of degradation and subjugation have contributed in ways, not always easy to grasp and comprehend, to their domination of boxing. 'In the days of slavery, white planters would sometimes put two or more of the strongest neighbourhood slaves into a ring and make them fight it out, for the amusement of white men, until all but one were pulverised into unconsciousness.'[6] When slavery was abolished, and Blacks sometimes sought boxing as a sport or a career, the white champions of the day usually refused to fight them. It was not until 1908 that the white heavyweight champion, Tommy Burns, agreed to fight Jack Johnson, a Black stevedore. Johnson won and kept the crown for several years.

Yet discrimination in the sporting world in the United States continued. Until the Second World War boxing was the only integrated sport in the United States. And even in amateur sports Black athletes permitted to emerge into national prominence were few and far between.

> Jackie Robinson's debut with the Brooklyn Dodgers in 1947 was an event in American social history almost comparable in importance with President Harry Truman's integration directive to the armed forces the following year. By 1970 the proportion of Blacks in major league baseball and football was three times their percentage of the population; more than half the players in the National Basketball Association were Blacks. The exploits of Black athletes have made them heroes in the ghetto and focal points for race pride and identity.[7]

It is this painful predicament of Black Americans, caught between affluence and discrimination, which has sharpened their performance in selective areas of sporting life. The trend has begun to affect Blacks in other affluent societies such as Britain and Canada, as Blacks there too have risen to sporting pre-eminence in more recent times.

By helping Blacks to achieve wealth and admiration, boxing has been a weapon against racism. But boxing has remained at once an arena of triumph for Black people and an area of exclusion for all women. By being at once the most masculine of all sports, boxing has been a brutal symbol of sexism. Calling a rival a 'woman' in boxing is regarded as the most demeaning insult of all. Muhammad Ali went to the extent of describing Sonny Liston as a big ugly woman who had successfully fought her way to the grand opportunity of confronting Ali in a battle of the sexes:

> It was only a nightmare, only a dream.
> But it tortured me all through the night;
> Six women fought to make love to me.
> And the ugly one carried the fight.[8]

The cause of racial equality has gained through Black triumphs in the boxing ring — but the cause of sexual equality has lost through the masculine orientation of this combative sport.

Conclusion

The warrior tradition in Africa affected the pattern of indigenous sport. Martial sports such as wrestling, spear throwing and horse riding were very popular and have survived up to the present day in parts of the continent. Some martial activities such as archery have not been taken up as sport partly because of their association with economic necessity (hunting) and partly because of self-consciousness on the part of the westernised élite about apparently 'primitive' technology.

Islamic civilisation has largely inhibited the development of sport in many of the Muslim parts of Africa. But in north-west Africa — one of the most secularised and westernised parts of the Muslim world — Western sports such as athletics and soccer have been developed with considerable success.

The Western sports which have been embraced the most enthusiastically in Africa have been *culture-neutral* games, such as athletics and soccer, rather than *culture-intensive* games, such as tennis and golf. The British influence on educational systems, the experience gained in the Commonwealth Games tournaments, the influence of indigenous culture and the high altitude factor in east Africa together account for the disproportionate achievement of athletes from Anglophone countries as compared with the performance of Francophone athletes.

African women have, on the whole, performed extremely poorly in sports compared with their male counterparts. The demilitarisation of women is the biggest single cause for the marginalisation of women in sport and politics. In war, women have continued to be, even in Israel, subsidiary to the main war effort. The warrior tradition in societies which are otherwise culturally vastly different has tended to be dominated by males. Both sport and combat have been areas of masculine monopoly. Muslim Black boxers Muhammad Ali and Idi Amin have been just sheer rugged symbols of a tradition at once primeval and current.[9] There might have been a time when the technology of warfare justified such a division of labour, when wars were fought by muscular power. But now it no longer needs a masculine hand to press the button of the B-52 bomber, or to release intercontinental ballistic missiles. Yet the masculine presence is still overwhelming. Class and gender have profoundly interacted in this particular division of labour.

Underlying it all within Africa is the triple heritage of cultures. The Jihad legacy reinforces the warrior tradition of indigenous Africa. Islam and African culture sometimes fuse and sometimes recoil from each other — only to turn around and confront the powerful sporting forces of the Western world. The whistle has sounded. The match between cultures has begun.

Africa at Prayer: New Gods

Long before the religion of the crescent or the religion of the cross arrived on the African continent, Africa was at worship, its sons and daughters were at prayer. Indigenous religions had a concept of divinity which was decentralised. God is not in heaven, or on a throne, or necessarily in the shape of Man. The concept which some indigenous eastern Africans call *Jok* is primarily the process of being the essence of universal power, which inheres in life as a force in its own right. In indigenous religion, Man was not created in the image of God; nor must God be conceived in the image of Man. The universe and the force of life are all manifestations of God.

Totemism in Africa led to groups identifying themselves with objects or other animals. Clans among communities such as the Baganda adopted totemic symbols which established a sense of continuity between nature and Man. Indeed, many African belief systems still include the so-called animistic tendencies, which blur the distinction between Man and nature, between the living and the dead, between the divine and the human, between the natural and the supernatural. All the different elements in nature can be expressions of God – the sunrise can be God's smile, the drought the wrath of the ancestors, and thunder and lightning is sometimes interpreted as divine orgasm.

Then came Islam and Christianity with a greater focus on Man as being in the image of God, and with a God often defined and described in the image of Man. In the case of Christianity, God even had a begotten son.

How have the new religions in Africa fared against each other and against the old religion?

As the European colonial period was coming to an end in the 1950s, calculations were made about the balance of religious forces in the African continent. In the year of Ghana's independence (1957) the Paris Academy of Political and Moral Sciences received some pertinent estimates. Between the years 1940 and 1946 the annual increase of professing Muslims in the French African colonies was nearly a quarter of a million every year. Between 1931 and 1951 the number of Muslims in the whole of Africa had risen from 40 million to 80 million in comparison with a Roman Catholic rise from 5 million to 15 million.

Of the total Black population estimated at the time as being 130 million in Africa south of the Sahara, 28 million were Muslim, 13 million were Catholics, 4 million were Protestants and 85 million still followed their own indigenous religions, even though some of these traditionalists were nominally

opposite, Masks from the Ivory Coast

Muslim or Christian. Islam in Africa as a whole, including Arab Africa, commanded the allegiance of approximately 40 per cent of the continent's population.

Islam: Regional Differences

Islam had entered the continent quite early in the Hijra (Islamic) era. Soon after the Prophet Muhammad's death in the year AD 632 Islam took on the challenge of non-Arab parts of the world. The Arab conquerors snatched away Egypt from the Byzantine Empire in the year AD 642 and soon afterwards overran the Maghreb up to the Atlantic.

Christianity in north Africa was now on the defensive and suffered severe setbacks as a result of Islamic conquest. The bulk of north Africa was dis-Christianised permanently, although a sizeable minority of Egyptians managed to hold fast to their Coptic Christian faith.

We can certainly say that the Islamisation of north Africa took place primarily through political means (conquest, control and suzerainty) but on the other hand, Islamisation in Black Africa has tended to occur primarily through *economic* means (trade and economic migration). Islam came to Black west Africa on horseback across the Sahara, mainly as part of economic traffic between the northern societies of the continent and the western. Islam came to east Africa on dhows, usually with the monsoons. Again, the dhow traffic from the Arabian peninsula and the Gulf areas was essentially economic, involving trade in both directions. Muslim traders were often also part-time missionaries and informal proselytisers.

In the continent as a whole the distribution of Islam has taken the shape of an inverted crescent. Islam is strongest in north Africa, west Africa along the bulge of the continent, and in eastern Africa including the Horn of the continent. Islam in the middle of the continent is relatively weak, and in southern Africa it is very thin indeed. The nature of the European impact on Africa had something to do with the distribution of Islam. The spread of Islam in eastern and southern Africa was effectively arrested by the consequences of European colonisation. Just as Islam spread north of the Sahara through conquest, so did Christianity spread south of the Sahara by the same means. If north of the Sahara Islam spread by the sword, south of the Sahara Christianity spread by the gun. As Hilaire Belloc once put it,

> Whatever happens we have got
> The Maxim gun and they have not.

But in spite of the importance of the gun in the consolidation of Christianity south of the Sahara, the European influence was not even. Islam in west Africa continued to conquer in spite of European colonisation, while in eastern Africa it was held in check by European colonisation. The question arises, why the difference?

One explanation for the vigour of Islam in west Africa could be its greater degree of indigenisation and Africanisation. Islam had ceased to be led by the Arabs and had acquired an independent dynamism in western Africa. The great leaders and religious preachers, the great warriors of Jihad, such as the Fulani Uthman dan Fodio in northern Nigeria in the early nineteenth century, were indigenous Africans. This contrasted quite sharply with religious leadership in many parts of eastern Africa, where immigrant Arabs or visiting Arabs played a disproportionate role. Throughout much of the colonial period east Africa under British rule allocated positions of Kadhis and Chief Kadhis disproportionately to Islamic jurists of Arab rather than African ancestry. This was particularly so in Zanzibar, Tanganyika (now mainland Tanzania) and Kenya. The fact that Muslim leadership in these countries was disproportionately in the hands of immigrant Arabs helped to reduce the dynamism of Islam in eastern Africa, and contributed to the slowing down of the spread of Islam during the colonial period.

Another factor behind the arrest of Islam's expansion in eastern and southern Africa was the high visibility of the European presence in those sub-regions. The prestige of European civilisation within Africa was reinforced by the physical presence of European settlers in those areas. Quite often the aggressive exclusivity of European civilisation helped to close the gates against any further Islamic expansion southwards. This was very different from the situation in west Africa where the absence of white settlers and the Africanisation of Muslim leadership ensured for Islam a substantial measure of local authenticity and sheer vibrancy.

But even in west Africa the impact of Islam varied considerably from one African country to another. Islam among the Hausa in Nigeria, for example, is very different from Islam among the Yoruba in the same country. For one thing, Yoruba Islam is significantly less politicised than Hausa Islam. In their political behaviour the Yoruba can often be as volatile and even violent as any other Nigerians. But the Yoruba are more likely to explode in defence of ethnic interests than in pursuit of religious concerns.

On the other hand, both religion and ethnicity can get very political among the Hausa in Nigeria. Periodic religious explosions have occurred involving Muslims of different denominations in the north of the country, sometimes costing a lot of lives. The Jihad tradition among Nigerian Muslim northerners is latent and potentially revivable. The links between religion and politics among the Muslims of northern Nigeria are deeper and more durable than such links among the Muslims of southern Nigeria. The major reason is that historically the pre-colonial Hausa city-states often attempted to enforce the Shari'a (Islamic law) and fused church and state. Yoruba states and kingdoms before European colonialism tended, on the other hand, to be based on indigenous Yoruba customs and traditions, rather than primarily on the Shari'a. Yoruba Islam in these post-colonial times remains less Arabised and less subject to politicisation than Hausa Islam has tended to be. It is because of these considerations that Yoruba Muslims have sometimes been regarded as Yoruba first and Muslim second – while Hausa Muslims have been perceived as the reverse.

The Crescent and the Clock

But whatever the precise combination and weight between indigenous loyalty and Islamic allegiance, the Muslim presence in Nigeria has deep roots. And the number of Muslims in the country is greater than the number of Muslims in any Arab country, including Egypt. In other words, Islam in Nigeria has more followers than Islam in any single Arab country, mainly because Nigeria itself is, of course, much larger than any country in the Arab world. There have been occasions when Nigerians going on pilgrimage to Mecca constituted either the largest or the second largest contingent of pilgrims from any part of the Muslim world. In 1981, the number of Nigerian pilgrims reached 100,000, the largest contingent from any Muslim country. The decline of the number of pilgrims in subsequent years was due mainly to foreign exchange problems in Nigeria. This resulted in greater control of numbers of pilgrims permitted to go by the federal government. The inhibitions of the modern state system and the constraints of the world economy intruded more decisively into Islamic calculations in post-colonial Africa.

In a sense these new international horizons within Africa are an extension of a process which was initiated by Islamisation in some parts of Africa.

Courtyard in the Medersa Ben Yusuf, Marrakech, Morocco

Islam introduced a new understanding of distance and space, as well as a new understanding of time and duration. The obligation on every Muslim to go on pilgrimage to Mecca at least once in his or her lifetime was an extended perception of distance. Africans newly converted to Islam were forced to think of a far-away place called Mecca not simply as the birthplace of the Prophet Muhammad but as a target to reach in their own lifetime.

In the centuries of Islam many Africans marched overland over many months, not running away from pestilence or drought, not seeking new worlds to conquer, but simply in quest of Mecca. The grand trek to the twin cities of Islam, Mecca and Medina, became a kind of annual migration, a revolution in mobility for many sectors of African society.

Islam also introduced its own disciplines of time in societies which previously felt less pushed by considerations of punctuality. Again, Islam's discipline of time was related to the five prayers of the day. These prayers were precisely spaced out during each twenty-four-hour period. It was a sin to postpone the prayer unless there were exceptional and compelling reasons. Sensitivity to the time of the day was a pre-condition for avoiding the sin of ritual procrastination.

Mosaic wall in Meknès, Morocco

Mosque on the shores of the
River Niger, Mali

What this means is that the ethos of punctuality in much of Africa did not come initially with Western culture and its obsession with precision in time. The ethos initially came with Islam. But did both imported civilisations fail to take Africa into the discipline of punctuality? The answer is that Islam succeeded in promoting punctuality in the religious sphere but failed to extend it to the secular domain. Muslims do observe their five prayers each day, usually within the prescribed times allocated to those prayers. Muslims search the skies for the sight of the new moon in order to ensure that the rituals of the different lunar months are satisfactorily observed. The fast of Ramadhan, from the hours before dawn to sunset, is prescribed with precision. It is a sin to eat at or after dawn, so one has to be sure precisely what time it is. It is also a sin to eat before the sun has gone completely down, and this requires a sensitivity to minutes and seconds, and not just to hours. As for the pilgrimage to Mecca, this takes place during a certain week or two of the year, and each stage is carefully timed within the rituals of the Hajj.

Islam appeared set to inaugurate a revolution in time among its converts in Africa, as well as in the Arab world. The revolution in the discipline of time succeeded strictly within the religious domain. Both the Arab world and Africa have had to await the greater impatience of Western civilisation before the ethos of punctuality could be secularised. Even then the West failed to make Africa observe the clock with the same attentiveness with which it observed the clock under Islamic stimulation. Appointments with visiting businessmen and professors in transit in African cities are sometimes broken with impunity or at any rate subjected to delay. But appointments with God are a different case. That is why the muezzin calling believers to prayer is a more compelling alarm clock in Muslim Africa than all the chimes of Big Ben and the Greenwich time signal.

The Language of God

Prayers in the mosque are preceded not only by the muezzin calling believers to prayer but also by a sermon. In many parts of Africa the sermon is still entirely in Arabic, although the bulk of the congregation south of the Sahara might not understand the Arabic language. In Zanzibar since the 1964 revolution some degree of Africanisation of the ritual has taken place, including the introduction of a Swahili section to the sermon. The rest of the sermon is still in Arabic, notwithstanding the language of the congregation. The prayer itself, involving bowing to God, kneeling and prostrating before God, is usually accompanied by oral recitations from the Qur'an. Again, the words recited throughout the formal prayer are entirely Arabic.

This brings us to a striking feature concerning Islam in relation to Christianity in Africa. Strictly from the issue of the language of worship, Islam has been less compromising than Christianity. It is as if the God of Islam understood only one language, Arabic. Formal prayer and ritual in Muslim Africa, as well as in the bulk of the rest of the Muslim world, is conducted almost entirely in the Arabic language. Most Muslim children have to learn the art of reading and reciting the Qur'an even if they do not understand what the words really mean. That is why many Muslim schools in Africa are referred to as Qur'anic schools, emphasising the verbal mastery of the Holy Book. Most of the hymns in the mosques in Africa are in the Arabic language, and are memorised and recited, not necessarily with a command of their meaning. It is in this sense that Islam in Africa is linguistically uncompromising, demanding due conformity with the language in which God communicated with humankind.

In contrast, Christianity has quite often communicated with Africans in the language of their own societies. The Bible was often translated into indigenous African languages decades before the Qur'an. Services in African churches are often conducted in indigenous African languages. Many hymns, though originating in Europe, have been translated and are often sung in indigenous African tongues. At least at the level of language, Christianity has made more concessions to Africa than has Islam.

Yet in other respects Islam has appeared to be more accommodating to the wider culture of Africa, more ready to compromise with African ancestral customs and usages. For example, the use of the drum in certain Muslim ceremonies in Africa contrasts with the stricter disapproval of the drum in comparable Christian ceremonies until quite recently. Islam has also been less militant against certain practices which are both un-Islamic and un-

Christian. One illustration is female circumcision. European Christianity has often taken a strong position against this custom which is practised by a minority of African societies.

It is possible that by the canons of orthodox Islam female circumcision is equally alien and un-Islamic. And yet such deeply Muslim societies as Somalia and northern Sudan practise female circumcision on a relatively wide scale. Islam has interfered less with this pre-existent African custom than Christianity has done.

There is also the issue of areas of accidental similarity between Islam and traditional Africa. A widely discussed area of congruence concerns attitudes to polygamy. Islam has a limit of four wives, whereas traditional Africa has an open-ended policy. Normally African Muslims have not been tempted to go beyond four wives in any case. It has been widely suggested that part of Islam's success in Africa is precisely its toleration of polygamy as compared with the monogamy taught by Christianity.

But this kind of argument overlooks other disciplines which Islam imposes and which Christianity does not. Among these is Islam's prohibition of alcohol. Many traditional African societies used alcohol for a variety of cultural and ritual ceremonies. African Islam has not made concessions on this issue.

On the whole, while it is indeed true that Islam in Africa has gained from not preaching monogamy, Christianity in its turn has gained by not banning alcohol. Africans being courted by the two religions have had to choose between the discipline of being satisfied with only one wife and the discipline of being satisfied with only soft drinks. In many instances the choice has not by any means been easy.

But on the wider spectrum of comparison, it remains true that Islam has

Islam allows polygamy on the condition that each wife is treated absolutely equally (taken to extremes here in dress!)

been more accommodating to indigenous African custom and traditions than European Christianity has been. I use the term 'European Christianity' to distinguish between the religion which came with the European missionaries in the nineteenth and twentieth centuries, and the centuries-old Christianity of Ethiopia and north Africa and the new Independent African Churches of the twentieth century. Ethiopian Christianity has, for example, tolerated female circumcision. Some of the Independent Churches have accepted polygamy.

What are the reasons for Islam combining linguistic intolerance in the mosque with a wider cultural accommodation? Why has it insisted on the primacy of Arabic as a medium of prayer yet shows a spirit of compromise towards the wider aspects of African traditions and life-styles?

To take the first part of the question first. Why has Islam displayed linguistic intolerance? To understand the answer, we need to know a little about the Islamic world-view. Islamic theology has divided the world conceptually into *Dar el Islam* and *Dar el Harb* (the Abode of Islam and the Abode of War). The Abode of Islam is, of course, the Muslim world as a whole, the lands where Islam is supreme as a way of life if not as a system of law. The Abode of War is the rest of the world, but only in the sense which Thomas Hobbes, the English philosopher, meant by 'a state of war'. Both Islam and Thomas Hobbes are really referring to a situation where there is no recognised central authority, and where everyone is for himself with the possibility of war constantly on the horizon. But within the Abode of Islam there is an official language – just as every African country in the second half of the twentieth century has had an official language. The official language of Islam is Arabic: the language in which the Qur'an was revealed to the Prophet Muhammad. The fact that the Holy Book of Islam is actually available and read in its original language has much to do with the possessiveness with which Muslims treat Arabic.

There is no Christian equivalent of the Arabic language as the language of revelation. Only a few scholars ever read the Bible in the languages (Hebrew and New Testament Greek) in which it was originally written. No Christians recite anything from the New Testament in the language in which Jesus Himself spoke, because He spoke Aramaic and Hebrew, not the Greek in which the New Testament was written. This is in sharp contrast to Islam, where the words of the Qur'an are precisely the words that the Prophet Muhammad used to communicate to his followers what he felt was the message of God.

Gods in Exile

The Bible from very early times has been primarily a work of translation. After all, Christianity did not triumph among the people to whom it was first revealed – the ancient Hebrews. Christianity had its greater successes away from its own cradle. It became pre-eminently the religion of the foreigner, the religion of the gentiles. By becoming the religion of the stranger, Christianity entered into the realm of translation almost from the beginning.

The message of Jesus started as a sect of Judaism. Early Christians accepted Jewish rituals, and the Jerusalem church insisted on circumcision and saw itself as operating under Mosaic Laws. But the Christian Jews of the Diaspora started the trend towards universalism. The Christians of Antioch in Syria began something which was to transform the world – they began to convert gentiles and to insist that gentiles did not have to circumcise. The Antioch Church of young Christianity then started to send missionaries to neighbouring provinces. Paul was probably the first to preach a thoroughgoing and complete Christian universalism. As he declared in his letter to the Romans, 'There is no distinction between the Jew and the Greek; the same Lord is Lord of all and bestows his riches upon all who call upon him.'[1] Even Rome itself was to witness before very long a small Christian community. Multi-lingualism was beginning to be a feature of the new Gospel. The Christian religion was spreading, becoming internationalised in the sense of making converts among new cultural groups and across provincial frontiers, but at the same time it made little progress in its cradleland in Palestine where Judaism remained very strong.

The next major divide in the history of Christianity came in the fourth century. Christianity had grown to such an extent that recognition by the Roman emperor seemed politically desirable. The edict of Milan was proclaimed in AD 313 by Emperor Constantine I, giving toleration to Christianity on an equal footing with other religions. Emperor Constantine delayed his own formal conversion to Christianity until rather late in his life. At least on the eastern part of his empire he never abandoned the concept of God-Emperor but he laid the foundations of Christianising the Roman Empire. That foundation served as the genesis of European Christianity, with its acceptance of imperial authority, and increased the estrangement of the message of Jesus from the people among whom it was initially revealed.

Islam had no such experience in estrangement. The people among whom it was first revealed were converted overwhelmingly to that religion. It is true that only a fraction of the Muslims of the world today are Arab. The population of Muslim Indonesia alone is almost the equivalent of the population of the Arab world as a whole. The Muslim population of the Indian subcontinent or South Asia alone (Muslims of Pakistan, Bangladesh and India) outnumber the population of the Arabs in the world. The Muslim population of the African continent is greater than the Arab population *outside Africa* by a ratio of two to one. Seventy per cent of the Arab people and 65 per cent of Arab lands are now in Africa. But while it is true that Islam has expanded beyond the Arabian Peninsula, and far beyond the Arab world, the Arabs themselves are overwhelmingly Muslim in allegiance.

Two factors have maintained Arab centrality in the fortunes of Islam, the Arabic language and Mecca. There is little doubt historically that the Qur'an as it exists today was the Qur'an of the days of the Prophet Muhammad and contains the words in which the Prophet communicated the message of God to his followers. That degree of authenticity is assured in Islam to a degree which is far greater than that which can be guaranteed with regard to the authenticity of the Christian New Testament. But in addition the major capitals of Christianity for Africa in the twentieth century are places such as the Vatican in Rome and Lambeth Palace in London. It is very doubtful that Jesus Christ visited either Rome or London. The estrangement of Christianity is captured in that very contradiction. Indeed, the Papacy has been dominated by Italians almost from the beginning and the few non-Italian Popes there have been have, none the less, all been Europeans. Christian leadership on a world scale was an exercise in estrangement and Eurocentrism.

It is against this broader background that we can understand why it is that in Christian churches in Africa today there is acceptance of foreign languages as media of communication with the Almighty. Where would European Christians be if they could not communicate with God in languages other than those used by either Jesus or His Apostles or the writers of the Gospels?

On the other hand, the Abode of Islam could rightly take pride in the official language, bequeathed in entirety across the centuries from the pulpit of Muhammad. Indeed, the Qur'an has been the greatest stabilising factor behind the Arabic language itself, preventing literary Arabic from too drastic a departure from the style of the Qur'an.

A Roman Catholic church in Khartoum, Sudan

But why is it that the religion which is linguistically monopolistic should at the same time be more tolerant on a wider scale? Why should Africans, on the one hand, be expected to pray to God in the Arabic language, and on the other hand be permitted to uphold female circumcision and the use of the drum in at least certain areas of worship?

This in turn is related to the origins of Islam before the African phase. To begin with, Islam envisaged itself as being a fusion of three religions and ways of life: Judaism, Christianity and the religion fostered by the Prophet Muhammad. In Islam, Moses and Jesus were the greatest prophets before Muhammad. And so doctrinally, almost from the beginning, Islam had the seeds of multi-culturalism. The origins of cultural accommodation in Islam go back not only to the conquests we referred to earlier but also to the shift quite early in Islam from the Umayyads in Damascus to the Abbasids in Baghdad. The Umayyad empire after the death of the Prophet was still primarily Arab. The ruler Muawiya assumed authority in the year AD 650. Islam was still an Arab democracy in essence, with its power based on a federation of Arab tribes.

But then came the Abbasid revolution in Baghdad, and the consolidation of authority from the year AD 744 to the year 754. This was the period when the Arab factor in Islam had to confront the non-Arab factor.

The question of the equality of Arab and non-Arab Muslim was put to its most direct test during the Abbasid Caliphate. The great division between Sunni Islam and Shiite Islam remained unresolved. Most Arabs are Sunni Muslims; most Shi'a Muslims are non-Arab. The stage was set for a sectarian divide which was to last the bulk of the remaining period of Islamic history. But behind that very mixture of culture and orientation was a predisposition towards syncretism. Islam was ready to accommodate divergent customs and cultural orientations. Sometimes these new elements enriched Islam, quite fundamentally. Certainly the Persian contribution to the artistic and cultural wealth of Islam has been inestimable. Many of the stories of the Arabian Nights are really Persian or Iranian stories, rather than Arab legends. The Moghul empire of India has also been a major enriching experience in Islamic history, architecture and art. After all, the Taj Mahal is one of the great architectural monuments to Islamic civilisation.

It is against this background that we can say that Islam in Africa has been culturally accommodating, in spite of being linguistically monopolistic.

Comparative Organisation and Structure

But there are other reasons why Islam in Africa was more culturally accommodating and less subject than Christianity to dis-Africanisation. The fact that the Islamic religion is not under a formal priesthood, and not subject to formal structures of decision making, has been a major element in the cultural flexibility of Islam. There is no priestly hierarchy, no Vatican, in Islam's infrastructure. Much of the business of the religion has been completely decentralised. To that extent Islam, unlike Catholicism, does not

have to look to a fountainhead of authority to legitimise particular departures from mainstream ritual. The decentralisation of Islam in terms of church organisation has been a major element in its accommodating nature.

Islam in Egypt: *left*, a young boy learns the Koran; *right*, a young girl is instructed in Islamic teachings

This is really another irony in the history of the two religions. After all, Muhammad was to all intents and purposes a head of state when he died. Islam had become substantially centralised politically before its founder left the scene. Mecca and Medina constituted a tale of two cities, two capitals of a new and expanding civilisation. A new political community had come into being, complete with its own juridical system under the Shari'a, a tax system based on the Islamic Zakat, a constitutional order based on Islamic theocracy. Muhammad died virtually as a head of state, presiding over a centralised social and political order.

And yet the same religion which produced a founder of Islamic centralism also produced an order of missionary decentralisation. The priesthood was not formal or specialised. The missionary activity was neither organised nor institutionalised. The religion which had produced a centralised political order did not produce a centralised missionary order. Muslim missionaries had been disproportionately individual, informal and almost casual.

On the other hand, the religion which had produced the underdog on the cross, the man who could pronounce neither temporal legislation nor

above, White Fathers
missionaries in northern
Rhodesia, now Zimbabwe

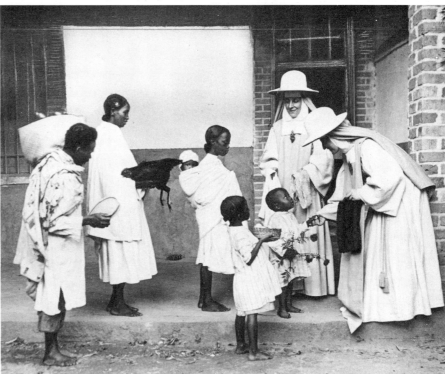

right, Roman Catholic
missionaries were active in
Madagascar after French rule
was imposed in 1896

temporal taxation, the man who was tried by the laws of others, could at the same time inspire a relatively centralised church and a hierarchical system of authority. Christian denominations, especially Roman Catholic, Greek Orthodox and, to some extent, Anglican, have been denominations of more centralised authority than anything within the missionary activity of Islam. Whatever may have happened in the seventh century in terms of Islamic centralisation, Islam has become a religion of informal conversations with God. On the other hand, whatever may have happened in the crucifixion of Jesus and the denial of Christian power to the founder of the religion, Christianity has since become a language of cultural hegemony and a structure of church authority and hierarchy.

Western Christianity and Secularism

It is one additional irony of African history that Christianity, so often identified with European imperialism, should at the same time have produced so many African nationalists. The struggle against imperialism, as well as the struggle for imperialism, owes a good deal to the Christian impact upon Africa. But European Christian missionary activity in Africa has always been prepared to dig its own secular grave. Christian mission schools in the African continent have been among the major carriers of secularism in the total African experience across generations. All Christian schools were simultaneously carriers of Western secular skills and values. The missionary schools taught mathematics as well as religious studies; sometimes philosophy as well as the catechism; social studies in the here and now as well as theology about the hereafter. Young Christians such as Kwame Nkrumah, products of missionary schools, once considered becoming priests – only to change their minds and become politicians with a rendezvous with history.

This means that Christian missionary schools were ambivalent, while Muslim schools were single-minded. Christian schools split allegiance between Western Christianity and Western secularism, whereas Muslim schools concentrated allegiance to Islam. The schooling wing of Islam never undermined the beliefs of Muslims. But the schooling wing of Christianity often undermined religiosity through secularism.

In a sense this is the masochistic side of Christianity which goes along with its theme of estrangement. At least in Africa Christianity has come with a death wish, an orientation towards self-nullification. I suppose this is because by the time Western interests emerged in Africa, Western secularism was beginning to gain ascendancy over Western Christianity. The result from an African point of view was an African Christian masochism, promoting the Gospel by destroying it, inculcating faith by promoting secularism, creating a new religious order by building a new secular order. The Christian church is soon identified with those who seek more than souls. It has been one of the more bizarre orientations of religious history ever. 'When the missionaries came,' said Jomo Kenyatta in a famous aphorism, 'the Africans had the land and the Christians had the Bible. They taught us to pray with our eyes closed. When we opened them they had the land and we had the Bible.'

One result has been the remarkable irony that Christianity has been both an ally of colonisation and a partner in liberation. African nationalists who are products of missionary education include not only Jomo Kenyatta of Kenya and Kwame Nkrumah of Ghana, but also Julius Nyerere of Tanzania, Kenneth Kaunda of Zambia and Robert Mugabe of Zimbabwe. Perhaps it is no surprise that one of the first acts of the Afrikaner Nationalist government on coming to power in 1948, was to close some of the mission schools for giving Africans, as Verwoerd later put it, 'the wrong expectations'. South Africa continues, though, to produce Christian nationalists, from Alan Boesak's leadership of the World Council of Reformed Churches to Bishop Desmond Tutu's leadership of Christian opposition to apartheid.

Towards Africanising New Gods

There are at least two main ways by which both Islam and Christianity have been Africanised. One is through relatively blind social forces at work across time, causing cultural mixture and sometimes synthesis. The other mode of Africanisation is through a prophet or social reformer, intent on giving greater native meaning to the imported religions or seeking to close a cultural and psychological gap which Islam and Christianity have sometimes created in Africa.

So far in this chapter we have discussed indigenisation through blind social forces leading to cultural mixture. Let us now take a closer look at the phenomenon of indigenisation through prophetic intervention and purposeful religious reform. Let us start by examining Islamic efforts. Heretical prophets in African Islam have been relatively few, partly because Islam has responded more readily to informal Africanisation except on the issue of the language of worship.

It should be borne in mind that dis-Arabisation of Islam is not necessarily the Africanisation of Islam. One of the best-organised movements in Muslim Africa is the Ahmadiyya sect, operating both in east and west Africa. The founder of the sect was Mirza Ghulam Ahmed of Old India under the British Raj. Doctrinally the movement upholds the Prophet Muhammad of Arabia as the most important of God's prophets but not the last. This is a major departure from mainstream Islam which insists that Muhammad was both the greatest and the last of all the prophets.

The Ahmadiyya movement has quite extensive missionary activity in Africa. It is often bitterly opposed by Sunni Africans, who are the great majority in the continent. My own father wrote a number of passionate essays against the Ahmadiyya movement, and was constantly at loggerheads with the Indian-derived sect.

In east Africa the Ahmadiyya movement was also the first to translate in full the Qur'an into the Swahili language, the most widespread indigenous language in the continent. Sunni Muslims strongly reacted against the

Missionary building at Kilema, Tanzania

Ahmadiyya translation. My father as Chief Kadhi of Kenya once again took the leadership in this reaction. He started translating the Qur'an himself, and made some progress, but he did not live to complete the job. His fragment of the translation was published posthumously. Later on, another Chief Kadhi of Kenya, Sheikh Abdullah Saleh Farsy, provided a more complete Qur'an in Kiswahili. The central charge against the Ahmadiyya movement, which still commands many followers in eastern and western Africa, remains that of claiming the status of a new prophet after Muhammad. But the fact that the new prophet, Mirza Ghulam Ahmed, was an Indian attempted to shift the focus of Islam away from the Arabian peninsula. To that extent the Ahmadiyya movement has in part been an effort to dis-Arabise Islam although stopping short of Africanising it.

But not all Messianic African movements under Islam are necessarily heretical. Islam has a concept of the Mahdi, a renewer and reviver of religion, but not necessarily a full-scale prophet in the technical Islamic sense. Perhaps the most famous and most enduring Mahdist movement has been in the Sudan. A substantial section of northern Sudan was aroused in the late nineteenth century against British penetration and to some extent against Egyptian overlordship. Again the movement took the form of the Jihad, and initiated military action against the foreign intruders. In 1885 General

left, The Mahdi's mosque, Sudan; *above*, The Mahdi, 1881

Gordon from Britain was killed in the Battle of Khartoum. The Mahdist movement has continued in more peaceful forms to the present day but it has retained a considerable political orientation.

Less militant in the military sense have been the Mourides of Senegal, an Islamic brotherhood that grew out of the Qadiriyya movement of the Sufi branch of Islam. The Mourides came into being in the second half of the nineteenth century under the leadership of Amadou Bamba. Like the Mahdist movement in the Sudan, the Mourides were responding to an external threat. In the latter case it was the reaction to French imperialism and the social environment which resulted from French penetration. Bamba was neither as militaristic as the Mahdi in the Sudan nor as revolutionary as the Ayatollahs of Iran, but he alarmed the French enough to induce them to exile him twice for a total of twelve years.

There has been a final triumph in some senses. Although Amadou Bamba was not an organiser, the movement grew around him. Some claim that up to three-quarters of the population of the country are now Mouride, though that estimate may be exaggerated. What is clear is that the Mouride movement has had a major impact on both the economy and the politics of Senegal. The capital of the brotherhood is Touba, a three-hour drive from Dakar, and founded by the brotherhood. The town is dominated by a giant mosque.

> The giant mosque is a towering symbol of Mouride unity and strength, a proof of the devotion of the Talibes [disciples] and of their capacity for hard work. The central minaret is 86 metres high (almost 300 feet), apparently the highest in Africa, and it is even provided with a ... lift. There are four other minarets, fourteen domes and two ablution baths ... The size of the building is most impressive, and in the flatland around Touba surrounded by single-storey dwellings, it seems all the more immense.[2]

Touba as a town is growing. A palace for the Khalifa-General or successor to Amadou Bamba is about to be completed. An Islamic university and a major Islamic library are also under construction. Touba has become virtually another Mecca to the Mouride Muslims of Senegal. Indeed, there are some who believe that a pilgrimage to Touba could, under certain circumstances, substitute for a pilgrimage to Mecca, but this is a heretical point of view. Certainly during the major festival of the Great Magal, usually held annually in December, many thousands of people converge on this town, reminiscent of the early days of Mecca when the Muslim community was limited to the boundaries of the Arabian peninsula. The celebrations in Touba today are as spectacular as those of ancient Mecca. (Those in contemporary Mecca are even more overwhelming, due to the scale of the number of pilgrims, which sometimes reaches 3 million in a year.) When the Khalifa-General appears at the Great Magal all are silent. The African Khalifa has arrived. The spirit of Islam lives on in the Black world. But the struggle for further Africanisation of the religion of the crescent continues.

What about efforts to Africanise Christianity through prophetic intervention? In the middle of the countryside in Central Africa, quite far from any major city, there stands a startling structure. It is a temple of the Kimbangu-ist religious movement, mainly based in Zaire. The founder of the movement was Simon Kimbangu. The Congo, as the country was then called, was still under Belgian rule when Simon Kimbangu began to challenge the white monopoly of religious leadership in the country. There were Congolese who were already framing the question in racial terms. If God wanted to communicate with the Black races, would He have chosen the white man to serve as His messenger? Such worries have sometimes affected Christian Africans from generation to generation. But in the case of Simon Kimbangu's followers, the answer was at last clear. This prophet was at least African; this messenger was Black.

But was this a case of merely Africanising the messenger without necessarily Africanising the message? Has the message of Jesus changed as a result of channelling it through Simon Kimbangu?

Although the symbol of the cross has not completely disappeared in the Kimbanguist church, it plays a significantly more modest role than it does in the rest of Christianity. Indeed, the huge Kimbanguist Temple at Nkamba has no cross inside the building. To that extent the building is startlingly un-Christian within.

However, there is a theological reason for the low profile of the symbol of the cross in the Kimbanguist church. The Almighty had always warned His people to beware of graven images and idolatry. A cross with a statue of Jesus came pretty close to a graven image, according to Kimbanguist theology. But even a cross without a figure of Jesus should not be elevated too highly lest it becomes yet another version of the graven image, yet another form of idolatry.

The people from among whom the Kimbanguist church emerged were matrilineal. The matrilineal tendencies of the wider traditional society helped to enhance the role of women in the Kimbanguist church. Women in this church can become pastors and deacons. Debates in Europe and America about whether women can become priests had not yet gathered momentum when the Kimbanguist church gave women a firmer role. Female pastors in the church are just an extension of the mother symbol in indigenous matrilineal culture. Indeed, female religious figures and reformers are more likely to emerge from indigenous traditions than from either orthodox Islam or European versions of Christianity. The range of major female religious reformers in Africa is from women in pre-colonial Ashanti to Alice Lenshina in colonial and post-colonial Zambia, leading her Lumpa Church.

Sometimes African women have shown enormous courage and readiness for martyrdom in defence of religious ideas. Back in the year 1706 a woman in Central Africa was burnt at the stake holding her baby son. This was Donna Beatrice, otherwise known as Kimbaveta. She, too, was in the tradition of trying to Africanise Christianity. Some of the changes she espoused were quite fundamental, perhaps more fundamental than those of the Kimbanguist church. For example, she argued that many of the Apostles of Jesus

Pilgrim in Touba, Senegal, for
the Grand Magal

were not Hebrew at all – they were Africans. She insisted that the Patron
Saint of Portugal was an African. She argued that Jesus Christ never prohibited polygamy. But her most controversial assertion was that a virgin
birth was not a monopoly of the mother of Jesus – that an African woman
was as capable, with God's help, of having a virgin birth as any woman in
Bethlehem or Nazareth.

These were of course very radical assertions. And when Donna Beatrice
tried to demonstrate the virgin birth theory by having a baby son of her own,
it was almost too much for those converted to Europeanised versions of
Christianity. The Portuguese missionaries and Portuguese officials advising
the old Congo kingdom set to work, persuading the converted rulers of the
kingdom to take action against this female messiah. And so she was burnt at
the stake holding her son. Out of those ashes arose new movements struggling once again to narrow the gap between African cultural realities and
Christian doctrine. One such movement, as we have indicated, is the one
which Simon Kimbangu initiated.

Kimbangu himself was also a martyr. The Belgians arrested him after a
while, the arrest partly instigated by Western missionaries in the new Congo
of the colonial period. Kimbangu spent almost as long in jail (1921–51) as
Jesus Christ spent on Earth. Kimbangu entered a series of Belgian cages
when he was just a young man, and died in jail three decades later at a
relatively advanced age. His own martyrdom was not on the cross; his
martyrdom was in a cage.

Today the Kimbanguist Church in central Africa claims some 4 million
followers. It may not sound like many but that is more followers than Jesus

Mouride pilgrims crowd on to a train to Touba, Senegal

Christ had in the first three centuries of the Christian era. It is far more than attend Christian worship throughout Britain each Sunday, out of a population of over 50 million.

The Kimbanguist Church is only one of many independent African churches flourishing in Africa today. There is evidence that the faster growing Christian churches in Africa in the years since the Second World War have been the African or syncretic churches. Many, like Kimbangu's in the Belgian Congo (Zaire) and Lenshina's in northern Rhodesia (Zambia), arose in the colonial period as a reaction against white domination of the missionary churches from Europe. The syncretist churches synchronise or blend Christianity with African custom and practices, putting far more stress than do missionary churches on music and dance in worship, communal self-help and prayer related to faith-healing. These syncretist churches range from the Aladura ('prayer people') of west Africa to the Zulu Zionist churches of south Africa. The Aladura churches originated in the prophecies of Babalola in Yorubaland in the colonial period but have spread to many parts of Nigeria as well as to Ghana and even London. In Ghana the most notable independent church is the Eden Revival Church founded by its prophet Charles Yebea-Korie in 1963. Kenya and Uganda also contain a variety of syncretist churches, founded by prophets, rejecting foreign guidance and emphasising African cultural practices.

Any analysis of Africanised Christianity must, of course, take account of Ethiopian Christianity, which not only pre-dated Christianity in most of Europe but was adapted to local conditions. In the fourth century of the Christian era King Ezana of Aksum was converted to Christianity which then became the religion of the whole Aksumite kingdom. Ethiopian Christianity has strong indigenous and Hebraic (Jewish) elements. Unlike in European Christianity, circumcision is generally practised, as a religious duty, as is levirate marriage and ritual cleanliness. The heritage of Ethiopian Christianity is alive today not only in Ethiopia itself (in spite of a measure of persecution by the Marxist regime of Mengistu Haile Mariam) but also throughout Black Africa, among the millions of members of African independent churches, sometimes called the 'Ethiopian' churches.

New Gods and the Gender Question

We have seen that Simon Kimbangu's church has women pastors and that from Donna Beatrice to Alice Lenshina, central Africa has provided women prophets. Have the independent churches of Africa won as much support as they have, especially from women, because of new approaches to the gender problem in religion?

Of the three approaches to God in the modern triple heritage, the most masculine in orientation is perhaps Islam's concept of God. This is also the God of the Old Testament of the Jews and Christians: tough, decisive, more concerned with justice than with love, prepared to be ruthless in pursuit of principle. It is the God of hard masculine virtues (toughness, endurance, courage, ruthlessness) rather than soft feminine virtues (meekness, gentleness, love, patience). Islamic rulers on earth are decidedly male. Where Islam is triumphant in politics, society is male-dominated. Northern Nigeria is the best African illustration.

There are exceptions to this general pattern of male domination in Muslim Africa. For example, Egyptian Islam is moderated by Westernism and conservative extremists like the Muslim Brotherhood have been restricted by

A Doep healing ceremony in Senegal

Presidents Nasser, Sadat and Mubarak. In Libya and the Maghreb states Muslim women have achieved much social emancipation in recent years. In Algeria, for example, Muslim women played a crucial role in the War of Independence against France (1954–62) as weapon couriers, messengers, organisers of supplies and even as fighters. In Libya, the social emancipation of women has accelerated under the Qaddafy regime. North Africa in the last three decades has seen some progress in the position of women. Perhaps the most stunning physical symbol of this progress was Nawal el Moutawakel of Morocco's gold medal victory in the women's 400 metres hurdles in the 1984 Olympic Games. But in religion and politics, Muslim women in north Africa as elsewhere have been even more subordinate than their sisters of other faiths.

Indigenous cultures in Black Africa are sometimes matrilineal and even matriarchal. Female religious figures and reformers are more likely to emerge from indigenous traditions than from either Islamic or foreign Christian traditions in Africa. The range has been from powerful religious women in pre-colonial Ashanti and the Queen Mother Yaa Asantewaa, who used indigenous religion to help inspire the anti-British revolt of 1900, to Alice Lenshina leading the Lumpa Church in Zambia in the 1950s and 1960s, though with tragic results which led to civil strife and several hundred deaths after Alice rejected the authority of the government and refused to allow her followers' children to attend school. Alice was jailed and the Lumpa Church banned.

Indigenous religion may have female prophets and female pastors. It is, therefore, considerably less sexist than African versions of European Christianity (for example, Roman Catholicism and the Church of England in Africa) which, in turn, are more sexist than Western versions of the same denominations.

Conclusion

Africa has both the oldest forms of Christianity, such as those of Egypt and Ethiopia, and some of the newest forms of Christianity such as those of the Kimbanguists. But the balance of power has shifted. In Egypt Islam has dominated the Coptic Church. In Ethiopia the Coptic Church has dominated Islam. In Egypt Islam has been more hostile to the pharaonic legacy of Ancient Egypt than Coptic Christianity has been. In Ethiopia both Christianity and Islam have accommodated indigenous Semitic religious practices. In the twentieth century, traditional religion has declined in the sense that many of its adherents have become Muslims or Christians but it has maintained its force in the sense that a number of Muslim sects and many Christian churches are indigenously inspired. The old religion interpenetrates with the new religions even as the new religions compete with each other for converts.

All over Africa the processes of both synthesis and dissonance continue. Three visions of God seek to capture the soul of a continent.

Tools of Exploitation: A Triple Heritage of Technology

The argument of this chapter rests on three interconnected theses concerning technology and the triple heritage. Our first thesis is that in the last 300 years Africa has helped substantially in building the West's industrial civilisation. The phases of Afro-Western interaction are from the days of the trans-Atlantic slave trade to the coming of the nuclear age. At each stage Africa helped construct the wealth of Europe and North America.

Our second thesis is that the Western reverse impact on Africa may have had the effect of hampering Africa's own construction of an industrial civilisation. Again the period covered is from the days of the slave market to the era of the nuclear reactor.

Our third thesis is that the resulting technological gap between the West and Africa explains the triumph of Western power so far over the forces of both Islam and indigenous culture in Africa.

Let us take each of these theses and explore their ramifications.

The Era of the Slave Trade

It is widely believed that Africa is indebted to the West for rapid industrialisation and development. This chapter seeks to demonstrate that in fact the balance of indebtedness is in the reverse direction. In other words Africa's impact on Western industrialisation during the last 300 years has been greater and more profound than the impact of the West on industrialisation in Africa.

Which African resources helped to transform the West? There was at first *slave labour*. Just as European voyages to Asia (during the fifteenth and sixteenth centuries) were once greatly influenced by Europe's interest in spices, so were European slaving expeditions to Africa (during the sixteenth to nineteenth centuries) once influenced by the growing European taste for sugar. In the history of the slave trade, Europe's sweet tooth has much to answer for. Expanding demand for sugar in Europe resulted in expanding demand for slave labour in South America and the West Indies from the seventeenth century onwards.

In the eighteenth century technological change in the West resulted in even greater 'need' for African labour. The new factories of Europe needed more labour-intensive crops such as cotton and indigo. And the new prosperity created new tastes in the West – which resulted in the growth of such additional labour-intensive crops as rice, coffee and tobacco in South America, the Caribbean and the southern states of the United States. All

opposite, Imported copper piping being unloaded at Dar es Salaam, Tanzania

This depiction in bronze of a Portuguese soldier holding a matchlock shows the advanced skills of Benin craftsmen

these developments seemed to require more imported labour in the Americas and Africa was raided more intensively to provide that labour. The industrial revolution in the West was, in part, riding on the backs of Black slaves on distant plantations.

On the other hand, while African slaves were part of the technology of production in the West, Western slavers were part of the technology of destruction within Africa. The slave trade coincided with the gun trade. African slaves arriving in the Americas helped the West to be more *productive*; Western guns arriving in Africa helped Africans to be more *destructive*.

Then further technological change in the West began to make slave labour less and less efficient. An ailing worker hired for wages could be fired and replaced at next to no cost, but the worst time to sell a slave is when he is ailing. Buying a slave was a long-term risk, but hiring a worker for wages was a short-term investment. With urbanisation in the West, one did not have to brave the seas to risk the diseases of west Africa to get cheap labour. It was now increasingly available not far from Manchester or Philadelphia. Slave labour was outpaced by the new technology. It was at last possible to regard slavery as wrong. The high technology of wage labour had made the high morality of abolitionism possible at long last. Britain, which had been the biggest shipping nation in the slave trade in the eighteenth century, became the leading abolitionist power in the nineteenth.

Did the abolition of the slave trade end Africa's contribution to Western industrialisation? The answer is in the negative. The new technology may have made the West more hostile to slavery, but it also made the West more favourable towards imperialism. Britain was at once the leading abolitionist power and the leading empire-builder. The era of the slave trade in the history of Africa's contribution to Western industrialisation was now to be followed by the era of colonial exploitation.

The Colonial Era

In 1884–5 fourteen Western states met in Berlin and agreed both to end slavery and facilitate imperialism. The voices which were raised against the Arab slave trade were also raised in favour of King Leopold's 'Congo Free State'. In King Leopold's domain the most brutal forms of forced labour were practised. The Berlin Conference was a classic case of the contradictions of imperial exploitation.

The economic impact of the African colonies on Western industrialisation took several different forms. First, colonisation was part of the search for new sources of raw materials. King Leopold wanted to turn the 'Congo Free State' into a huge rubber plantation, sustained by forced labour. The British helped to promote cotton produced along the Nile Valley in Egypt, the Sudan and Uganda. Other fibres were produced in other colonies.

In addition to producing raw materials, the dependencies were geared towards catering for the new consumption patterns of an increasingly prosperous West. Economies began to emerge in the colonies, disproportionately focused on producing some beverage or dessert for affluent Europe's new dining tables. Crops for dessert and beverage included cocoa (from Ghana), coffee (from Uganda) and tea (from Kenya).

Third, the colonies provided new opportunities for some of the more enterprising individual citizens of the imperial powers, opportunities which included settlement in the colonies. The problem of white settlers was thus born in countries which ranged from Algeria to South Africa, from Zimbabwe to Kenya.

Fourth, the colonies were potential markets for goods produced in the metropole. The Imperial Preference in Britain's trade with the colonies (later renamed the Commonwealth Preference) was a device for securing colonial markets for British goods. The French created long-term trading and investment ties with the colonies which survived into the post-colonial period.

Meanwhile a strange thing had happened. Whereas the West's expanding technology of production had once resulted in the enslavement of Africans and the colonisation of their continent, the West's expanding technology of destruction in two World Wars helped to liberate Africa. The Second World War was especially critical. The war weakened the great imperial rulers irreversibly, as France, Belgium and Italy were humiliated; Britain was impoverished; and Portugal and Spain were morally bankrupt as a result of their association with fascism and Nazism. These imperialist countries still maintained their hold over their African colonies but the grip was weakening in the aftermath of a masochistic European War which had become world-wide.

Nationalism and anti-colonial fervour erupted all over Africa almost as soon as the Second World War ended. Barely fifteen years after the end of this war the bulk of the African continent had attained formal political sovereignty. Never was a whole continent so swiftly subjugated, and then so rapidly emancipated. Europe's pursuit of production in the industrial revolution had once resulted in the colonisation of Africa. Europe's pursuit of destruction in the Second World War had reversed the process and helped to initiate Africa's decolonisation.

Has this political decolonisation ended Africa's contribution to the industrial development of the West? Has the industrial lifeline from Africa to Europe been cut now that European rule in most of Africa has ended? The answer is once again in the negative. The West is no longer interested in African territory but it continues to be interested in Africa's resources, especially minerals.

Minerals in the Post-Colonial Era

Western industry still relies greatly on a wide range of strategic minerals from Africa. The great proportion of minerals extracted from Africa is for Western industry – very little is for Africa's industrialisation. The Third World generally produces a third of the key minerals of the world economy, but the developing countries use only one-twentieth of those minerals.

Miners at the Elsburg gold mine, South Africa. Do they dig for wealth or for the collective burial of a people?

Africa's share of consumption is small, even by Third World standards, but Africa's shares of reserves and of production are impressive.

In terms of reserves, Africa has 90 per cent of the world's cobalt, the bulk of which comes from Zaire. Africa has over 80 per cent of the world's reserves of chrome, more than 50 per cent of the reserves of gold, nearly half of the planet's reserves of platinum, and nearly all of the non-communist world's reserves of industrial diamonds. These are just some of the strategic industrial minerals.

Then there are the exchange minerals of which the most important is gold, to which we have already referred. Although most of the African reserves are in southern Africa, there has been considerable gold production in other parts of the continent as well. Gold has provided part of the support of the international monetary system. A disrupted gold market could endanger the world's system of exchange.

Third, there are Africa's fuel minerals. The continent has a third of the world's reserves of uranium. Africa's share of natural gas is expanding, especially in the Muslim areas. And, of course, Africa is well represented in the Organisation of Petroleum Exporting Countries (OPEC) by Nigeria, Algeria, Libya and Gabon. It should also be noted that Zaire is the chief source of the world's radium, located in the uranium ores of the Shinkolobwe-Kasolo area.

Kolwezi copper mine, Zaire

Then there are gems and precious metals. The bulk of the world's gem diamonds come from Africa. Africa has 80 per cent of the world's tantalum. Africa's share of the world's silver is small, but Africa's precious stones are diverse, ranging from sapphires to topaz, from malachite to opal, from rubies to tanzanite. Africa's metallic deposits also include substantial amounts of manganese, iron ore, copper, vanadium (a rare element to toughen steel), bauxite (the chief aluminium ore), lead and zinc.

Then there are Africa's non-metallic deposits. Muslim Africa has large deposits of phosphates, from Morocco to Senegal. Other phosphate deposits occur in the area of the great lakes in eastern Africa. In Madagascar Africa possesses the largest known accumulation of flake graphite deposits in the world. And the People's Republic of the Congo has potash deposits which are regarded as among the largest in the world.

The biggest beneficiary of all this mineral wealth is the West and its industries. Since the 1970s the United States has been importing nearly half of its manganese from Africa. A major reason why the West has been supporting Mobutu Sese Seko is the importance of Zaire's cobalt for Western industry. It has been said that the West would be prepared to go to war to keep Zaire within the Western orbit. Niger's uranium mining was designed and developed in the 1970s specifically for the French nuclear programme. Iron ore from Swaziland goes directly into Nippon steel.

The transfer of technological skills: a French foreman advises a Nigerian worker

In addition to being the main consumer of Africa's mineral wealth, the West is the main manager of that wealth. A few Western firms control the processing, manufacturing and marketing of most of Africa's mineral resources. Anglo-American, DeBeers, Roan Selection Trust, the old Union Miniere are only a few of the names that have shaped this phase of Africa's contribution to Western industrialisation. This is quite apart from the oil giants – Shell, British Petroleum (BP), Gulf, Exxon, Mobil, Chevron, Texaco and smaller independent firms. Even the smaller ones often have capital value which is greater than the Gross National Product of most African states.

Of the two major areas of African production, agriculture and mining, mining is both the more capital-intensive and the more skill-intensive. It needs a lot of money to initiate and needs a lot of skill to operate and maintain. In the absence of an adequate transfer of technical and managerial skills to Africans, and against the background of the multinational corporations dominating the field, mining in Africa has remained a preserve of Westerners even when African governments have ostensibly put it under state ownership. Reliance on Western expertise and Western marketing has perpetuated the Eurocentric orientation of African mining.

When Africa's contribution to industrialism in the West was mainly through the export of labour (the slave trade), the Americas rather than Europe were the main importers of the slave labour. But in this latest phase of mineral contribution to Western industrialism, it is Europe that is the main importer, even after allowing for the fact that Nigeria is the USA's second external supplier of oil after Saudi Arabia. However, in both phases the economic interconnection between European economies and those of the New World has made the African resources fundamental to both parts of the West's industrial civilisation. Today, without Africa's mineral resources, large sectors of Western industrial civilisation would grind to a standstill, throwing millions of Europeans out of work and drastically reducing European living standards.

The West *versus* Africa's Industrial Revolution

As we have indicated, it is not technological change within Africa which has affected recent African history most, it is technological development in the West. And Africa itself has contributed, however unwittingly, precisely to that process in the West. But has the West contributed to industrialisation in Africa? Self-congratulatory Western interpretations abound, giving the West credit for the 'modernisation' of Africa. This chapter seeks to demonstrate that much of that 'modernisation' is shallow: that the West has contributed far less to the industrialisation of Africa than Africa has contributed to the industrial civilisation of the West.

The West harmed indigenous technological development in a number of ways. First, the trans-Atlantic slave trade disrupted west Africa the most; and west Africa was the region which held the greatest promise of independent industrial take-off. It had made the most progress in local textiles and in taming and using metals before the European penetration.

Alongside the slave trade, the importation of European cloth *before* colonial rule dealt a severe blow to local textile industries. Traditional iron smelting declined in most parts of Africa as a result of the European impact. The slave trade took away millions of potentially productive and creative youth. Some slavers specialised in capturing skilled Africans for use as artisans in the New World. European traders generally were less interested in what Africans made with their hands than in what Africans could dig up (for example, gold), capture (for example, slaves) or kill (elephant tusks, etc.). Because of this, African economies were diverted away from resource-enhancing activities such as agriculture and manufacture and towards resource-depleting activities such as mining, slave trading and hunting for trophies and tusks. Trade with Europeans even before colonisation was beginning to consolidate the export bias at the expense of producing for the local African market.

Some African rulers sought to be taught Western technology rather than import Western goods. In Ethiopia, Lebna Dengel in the seventeenth century and Tewodros in the nineteenth century wrote to European rulers for assistance in industrialisation. In the eighteenth century King Agaja Trudo of Dahomey thought the best way of stopping the slave trade was to industrialise west Africa with European help. Opoku Ware of Asante in the nineteenth century also tried to innovate industrially. In each case, Europe refused to help.

Colonial rule helped to build an infrastructure of roads, electricity, railways, postal services and rudimentary telephone systems. Colonial rule also encouraged importation of Western industrial products such as motor cars, lorries and locomotives, and luxury goods such as perambulators, radios and gramophones. But colonial rule did little to transfer technological skills to Africans. At the time of independence many African countries could not even make their own bulbs and plugs.

Cultural Westernisation was promoted more vigorously than genuine technological modernisation. The French policy of cultural assimilation helped to keep the so-called 'modern' sector under French control even after independence. Colonial schools generally were transmitters of Western culture rather than transmitters of Western technical skills. Brilliant graduates were at best potential Shakespeares but almost never potential Einsteins or potential Edisons or Graham Bells.

Colonial conditions encouraged the importation of Western equipment without transfer of Western technology. In post-colonial Africa governments continue to import inappropriate Western equipment at great expense and do little to promote effective technology transfer and effective technical training for their people. Many industrial projects are for prestige rather than production. Below-capacity production is the norm rather than the exception in Africa.

Imported Western tools of destruction have been more potent than imported Western tools of production. Political power in Africa often resides among those who control the means of destruction rather than among those who own the means of production. Hence the many coups. The West has encouraged Africa to abandon its traditional wisdom without necessarily helping Africa to acquire a new scientific expertise.

The balance of technological power entered a new phase with the maturation and further development of nuclear know-how. How has the nuclear age affected Africa's destiny? How has it shaped the history of Islam in the second half of the twentieth century? It is to these atomic concerns that we should now turn.

Africa *versus* the Nuclear Age

It is symbolic of the basic African condition that the first form of African participation in the nuclear age concerned a raw material. Uranium is of course as indigenous to Africa as the 'flame trees of Thika' or the baobab tree of Senegal. Africa in the 1930s and 1940s helped to provide the uranium which launched the Western world into the nuclear orbit. It was in part Africa's uranium from Zaire which helped to set in motion the first nuclear reactor in North America. And, for better or for worse, Africa's uranium may have gone into those atomic bombs which were dropped on Hiroshima and Nagasaki in August 1945. But, of course, Africa had no say in the matter. An African resource had simply been pirated by others, and once again played a major role in a significant shift in Western industrialism.

Not that uranium was all that scarce even in the 1940s. What was significant was that outside the Soviet Bloc and North America, uranium seemed to be substantially available only in Black Africa. As Caryl P. Haskins put it in an article published in 1946,

> [Uranium] stands next to copper in abundance, is more abundant than zinc, and is about four times as plentiful as lead ... however, the outstanding deposits are narrowly distributed, being confined to the United States, Canada, the Belgian Congo, Czechoslovakia and possibly Russia ... The fact that the richest deposits of uranium ore occur in a fairly limited number of places makes international control feasible; but it also foreshadows violent competitive struggles for ownership of the richest deposits (the struggle for oil greatly intensified).[1]

Of course since 1946 other reserves of uranium ore have been discovered in the world, including different parts of Africa, notably Namibia, Gabon and Niger. African uranium has continued to fill many a reactor in the Western world, and to help create many a nuclear bomb.

The second service (after uranium supply) which Africa rendered to the nuclear age was also symbolic. Africa provided the desert for French nuclear tests in the early 1960s. In this case Africa's nuclear involvement had slightly shifted from a purely indigenous resource (uranium) to a partially Islamic context (the Sahara).

The third African point of entry into the nuclear age has been through the

Part of a uranium factory at
Mounana, Gabon

Republic of South Africa. South Africa is either already a nuclear power or is close to it, indirectly as a result of those earlier nuclear tests in Algeria. A circle of influence developed. The progress of the French nuclear programme and its tests in the Sahara probably helped the Israeli nuclear programme. This was a period when France was quite close to Israel in terms of economic and technological collaboration. The French helped the Israelis build a nuclear reactor at Demona and seemed at times to be closer to the Israelis in sharing nuclear secrets than even the Americans were. The evidence is clear

Demonstrators in Accra protest against French nuclear testing in the Sahara, 1960

Dummies wearing Army, Navy and Air Force uniforms were positioned in the Sahara during the French nuclear tests in 1960. Instruments attached to the dummies recorded the effects of the blast.

— the French nuclear programme in the late 1950s and 1960s served as a midwife to the Israeli nuclear programme. And French tests in the Sahara were part of France's nuclear infrastructure in that period.

By a curious twist of destiny, the Israeli nuclear programme in turn came to serve as a midwife to the nuclear efforts of the Republic of South Africa in the 1970s and 1980s. Relations between the two countries cooled a little after the Sharpeville massacre of 1960 and when Israel briefly considered the possibility of extending aid to African liberation movements in southern Africa. But by 1970 there were clear improvements in economic relationships. After Black Africa's almost complete diplomatic break with Israel in 1973, co-operation between Israel and South Africa entered new areas, including the nuclear field. When a nuclear explosion occurred in the South Atlantic in September 1979, the question which arose was whether it was primarily a South African nuclear experiment undertaken with Israeli technical aid, or primarily an Israeli explosive experiment carried out with South Africa's logistical support. A cover-up policy was pursued by both countries, helped in part by their Western allies, especially the Carter Administration in the United States. The cyclical nuclear equation was about to be completed. The Sahara had aided France's nuclear programme, France had aided Israel's nuclear design, and Israel had in turn aided South Africa's nuclear ambitions. Kwame Nkrumah's earlier fear of a linkage between nuclear tests in the Sahara and racism in South Africa had found astonishing vindication nearly two decades later. It was in April 1960 that Nkrumah had addressed an international meeting in Accra in the following terms,

> Fellow Africans and friends: there are two threatening swords of Damocles hanging over the continent, and we must remove them. These are nuclear tests in the Sahara by the French Government and the apartheid policy of the Government of the Union of South Africa ... It would be a great mistake to imagine that the achievement of political independence by certain areas in Africa will automatically mean the end of the struggle. It is merely the beginning of the struggle.[2]

It has turned out that Nkrumah's thesis of 'two swords of Damocles', one nuclear and one racist, was prophetic. The Republic of South Africa is using nuclear power as a potentially stabilising factor in defence of apartheid. The old nuclear fall-out in the Sahara in the 1960s involved a linkage between racism and nuclear weapons which is only just beginning to reveal itself.

Nuclear technology has been a disservice so far not only to Black Africa but also to the Arabs and to the world of Islam as a whole. It is to these anti-Islamic implications of the nuclear age that we must now turn.

Islam *versus* the Nuclear Age

The nuclear age has, at least until the 1980s, been disadvantageous for Islam in general. The new science arrived at a time when Islam had been pushed to the periphery of technological civilisation and the margins of scientific know-how. Who now remembers the days when Muslims were so advanced in mathematics that the very numbers of calculation took the name 'Arabic numerals'? Gone were the days when the Arabs led in pushing back the frontiers of the metric principle. Who even remembered that words such as average, algebra, amalgam, atlas, cyphers, chemistry and zenith were originally Arabic? Then the superpower which emerged as the nuclear leader in world politics happened to contain a Jewish enclave which came to exert a powerful influence on American foreign policy towards the Middle East. The new state of Israel was born within three years of the dropping of atomic bombs on Hiroshima and Nagasaki. Within a single generation the Jewish state itself became a nuclear power. That was ominous for the Arabs and for their supporters in the rest of the Muslim world, including Muslim Africa.

Even in the realm of the peaceful uses of atomic energy, the nuclear age is potentially a disservice to Islam. It is oil rather than uranium ore which has recently given Islam new economic leverage in the world system. The Organisation of Petroleum Exporting Countries (OPEC) is primarily a Muslim organisation in composition. The largest Muslim country in the world, Indonesia, is a member. The heartland of Sunni Islam, Saudi Arabia, often presides over OPEC's fortunes. The heartland of Shi'a Islam – Iran – is a force within the organisation. So are the bulk of the other Gulf states. So indeed, is Nigeria, often Muslim-led. Two of the remaining African members (Libya and Algeria) are, of course, also Muslim.

If OPEC is in composition basically a Muslim organisation, we should remember that it is also the most powerful economic organisation that the Third World has so far created. Anything which threatens the survival and influence of OPEC also threatens both Islam and the Third World as a whole, including Africa. Nuclear energy is one such threat to the pre-eminence of oil.

There are, of course, Muslim sources of uranium in the world. Among the latest discoveries are those of the Republic of Niger, a preponderantly Muslim west African country. But the Muslim world is better placed in the politics of oil than in the politics of uranium. To that extent, an ascendancy of nuclear energy in the world system would decidedly be dysfunctional to the interests of the Muslim world, including the interests of Muslim Africa.

Many people feel that the human race should never have permitted itself to enter the nuclear age. Nuclear physics is, in sum, evil. The genie ought never to have been let out of the bottle. I tend to share that sentiment. Unfortunately, the genie is already out of the bottle. The question is: should Africa participate in taming it? And can Africa do that without the necessary science for nuclear participation?

So far the West has used Africa's uranium mines, and usurped Africa's deserts for nuclear experiments, without transmitting to Africa genuine nuclear know-how. An advanced form of science has exploited Africa without permitting Africa to exploit it in return.

Towards a Global Technological Solution
The broad technological redemption of Africa requires new alliances and coalitions with other parts of the Third World – especially an alliance between Africa and Arab countries. If the Western part of the triple heritage has technologically marginalised the indigenous and Islamic parts, it is up to these two other branches to join forces and correct their own handicap. An Afro-Arab coalition could be the nucleus not only of an Afro-Islamic alliance but of Third World solidarity more generally.

At this point it would be advisable to redefine the concepts of the 'Third World' and the 'West'. The 'Third World' is more easily translated into the 'South' in both the geographical sense and in economic terms; this is because the developing countries lie to the south of most industrialised states. The capitalist West, in terms of the world economy, together with the East (the Soviet Union and its European allies), constitutes the 'North' – the term now widely used to describe the industrialised world. In this global system an industrially developed North exploits a South which is still seen as a provider of raw materials and foodstuffs for the North.

Two forms of solidarity are critical for the Third World (South) if the global system is to change in favour of the disadvantaged. *Organic solidarity* concerns South-South linkages designed to increase mutual dependence between and among Third World countries. *Strategic solidarity* concerns co-operation among Third World countries in their struggle to extract concessions from the industrialised Northern world. Organic solidarity concerns the aspiration to promote greater integration between Third World economies. Strategic solidarity aspires to decrease the South's dependent integration into Northern economies. The focus of organic solidarity is primarily a South-South economic marriage. The focus of strategic solidarity is either a North-South divorce, a new marriage settlement or a new social contract between North and South. The terms of the North-South bond have to be renegotiated.

Organic solidarity may be made more real by the use of strategies such as *indigenisation* (the greater use of African personnel, materials, techniques and resources) and *domestication* (making something which is not indigenous more relevant to the African scene, for example, university syllabi). Strategic solidarity, on the other hand, can be achieved by strategies such as *diversification* (of trade partners, products and aid donors, for example) and *counter-penetration* of the North (by using the leverage of Africa's mineral power and even debtor power against the North).

What then is the way out? How can these two forms of solidarity help to

Western luxury goods have now infiltrated many parts of Africa

ameliorate the Afro-Arab predicament of dependency and its persistent economic vulnerability?

One of the more neglected areas of co-operation is manpower and manpower training. A start has been made in manpower exchange between some Third World countries and in the field of manpower training across Third World boundaries. But the importance of this area has been grossly underestimated.

Nowhere is the power of knowledge demonstrated more clearly than in southern Africa and the Middle East. Less than 5 million whites in South Africa have been able to hold to ransom a Black population in the region of ten times their own. They have held neighbouring Blacks to ransom both economically and militarily. The main explanation is not simply because South Africa is rich, but because that wealth has been extracted through African labour and *European* expertise. South Africa's neighbours have African labour too. Some of them are also rich in minerals. What the Blacks have lacked indigenously is the superior technology of production and the accompanying culture of efficient organisation.

The Middle East is a clearer and more staggering illustration of the power of skill over income. At least since the 1970s much of the Arab world has become significantly richer than Israel in sheer income. Indeed, the Israeli economy would have suffered complete collapse but for the infusion of billions of dollars from the United States and from world Jewry. And yet in spite of being outpaced in numbers and wealth, the Israelis have retained the upper hand militarily against the Arabs. The supremacy of skill over income and numbers has been dramatically illustrated in one Middle East war after another.

In both South Africa and Israel the cultural variable is critical. Had Israel consisted entirely of Middle Eastern Jews, the Arabs would have won every war. Indeed, it would not have been necessary to have more than the 1948 war. After all, Middle Eastern Jews are not very different from their Arab neighbours in culture and skill. In a war against fellow Middle Easterners, the numerical preponderance of the Arabs would have triumphed against Jews long before the numerical advantage was reinforced by Arab petro-wealth.

What has made the Israelis militarily pre-eminent is not the Jewishness of 80 per cent of the total population but the Europeanness of less than half of that Jewish sector. It is the European and Western Jews who have provided the technological foundations of Israel's regional hegemony.

If then the ultimate basis of international stratification is skill rather than income, what is the Afro-Arab world to do in order to ameliorate the consequences of its technological underdevelopment?

The most obvious answer is for the Afro-Arab world to obtain the know-how from the Northern hemisphere as rapidly as possible. But there are difficulties. Countries of the Northern hemisphere are often all too eager to transfer certain forms of technology, especially through transnational corporations, but the need of Arabs and Africans for certain technological transfers only helps to deepen relationships of dependency between the two hemispheres. On the other hand, there are other areas of technology which the North is not at all keen to transfer. Pre-eminent among the taboos is the transfer of certain branches of nuclear physics and technology. The computer is part of the phenomenon of dependency through technology transfer; the nuclear plant or reactor is a symbol of dependency through technological monopoly by the North. The transnational corporations are often instruments of Northern penetration of the South through technological transfer; nuclear power, on the other hand, is a symbol of Northern hegemony through technological monopoly.

The dual strategy for the Third World (including China) is both to learn from the North and to share expertise among each other. Those aspects of technology which are being freely transferred by the North should be 'decolonised' and stripped of their dependency implications as fast as possible. Those aspects of technology which are deliberately monopolised by the North should be subjected to Southern industrial espionage in a bid to break the monopoly. Pakistani scientists have been on the right track in their reported efforts to subject Northern nuclear monopoly to Southern industrial spying. If Pakistan becomes Islam's first nuclear power, and decides to share the nuclear secrets with a few select fellow Muslims, that trend would be in the direction of enhanced technological co-operation among Third World countries.

That is one reason why the brain-drain from the South is *not* an unmitigated disaster. What would be a catastrophe is a complete stoppage of the brain-drain. It is vital that the South should counter-penetrate the citadels of technological and economic power. The counter-penetration can take the form of Southern engineers, teachers and professors, medical doctors and consultants, businessmen and scientists, working in the North. The North needs to be made more sensitised to Southern needs, not only by the speeches of Southern statesmen and ambassadors but also by the influence and leverage of Southerners resident in the North.

In any case, there is no law of gravity which says expertise can only flow from the North to the South. There is no gravitational logic which says that European teachers teaching African children is natural – but African teachers teaching European children is not. The structure of scientific stratification in the world should rapidly cease to be a rigid caste system and allow for social mobility in both directions. Of course, too big a brain-drain from the South northwards could deeply hurt the South – but the trouble with the present level of the South's knowledge is not that it is too great, but that it is grossly under-utilised by the South itself. Professor Edward S. Ayensu, a Ghanaian Research Director at the Smithsonian Institution in Washington, DC, has argued that there is a large potential pool of Third World experts, resident in the Northern hemisphere, who would be only too glad to serve for a year or two in developing societies if only their services were solicited. What is more, the Northern institutions where they work would, according to Professor Ayensu, be sympathetically inclined towards facilitating such exchanges if so requested by Third World authorities.[3]

If that were to happen, it would be a case of tapping the brain-drain on the basis of a triangular formula. The flow of expertise would be first from South to North, then North to South, and then South to South – often involving the same Southern experts or their equivalents, sharing their know-how across hemispheres.

There is already some movement of expertise between Third World countries. Dr Boutros Boutros-Ghali, Egypt's Minister of State for Foreign Affairs, assured me in 1983 that Egypt had '2 million experts' working in other countries, mainly in Africa and the Middle East. South Asia also exports a considerable body of expertise to other parts of the Third World.

Some of the traffic in expertise across Third World frontiers is caused by political instability and economic problems at home. Qualified Ugandans are scattered in almost all the four corners of the Third World, as well as in the North. So are qualified Lebanese, Palestinians, southern Africans, Ethiopians and others.

Then there is the inter-Third World traffic of experts caused by the magnetism of petro-wealth. The Gulf states have a particularly impressive variety of manpower from different lands. Two Ghanaian scholars visited the University of Petroleum and Minerals in Dhahran in the Kingdom of

Against the background of oil-works in Nigeria rural life continues in the traditional style

Saudi Arabia in the summer of 1984. They were impressed by the Ghanaian presence in the research complex of the university. They were also surprised to learn about 'twenty-four highly qualified Ghanaian medical officers working in and around this university town of Dhahran'.[4]

To summarise, there is a *push factor* in some of the less fortunate Third World countries which forces out many native experts in search of alternative opportunities in other countries. But there is also a *pull factor* in the wealthier Third World societies which magnetically attracts workers and specialists from other lands. Together the two forces are helping to lay down some of the foundations of organic solidarity within the Third World.

But although the power of skill is at the moment overwhelmingly in the hands of the North, there are other areas of power which the South possesses but which the South has under-utilised.

OPEC is an illustration of producer power. From 1973 to 1983 OPEC grossly under-utilised its leverage. Instead of using that golden decade to put pressure on the North for fundamental adjustments in the patterns and rules of the world economy, OPEC concentrated almost exclusively on the prices game, a game of short-term maximisation of returns.

There is a crying need for other 'producer cartels', no matter how weak in the short run. Cobalt has more promise as a mineral of leverage than copper, and would involve fewer countries. Experimentation in a cobalt cartel could pay off if Zaire asserted herself a little more decisively as an independent

Cabinda oil-rig in Angola – one of the few oil-producing countries in Africa which is not part of OPEC power. After all, Zaire has the credentials of being the Saudi Arabia of cobalt when the market improves in the years ahead.

The Third World has also under-utilised its consumer power, regionally specific and patchy as it is. The Middle East is especially important as a consumer of Western civil and military hardware, technology and household products. The consumer power of the Middle East could be used as leverage for more fundamental changes in the exchange patterns between North and South.

The fourth form of power currently under-utilised by the South is debtor power. We shall return to this in the last chapter. President Julius Nyerere of Tanzania, upon being elected Chairman of the Organisation of African Unity in November 1984, identified development, debt and drought as the three leading concerns of the current African condition. Of course, African debts are modest compared with those of Latin America, but Nyerere identified debt as a source of power and not merely as a source of weakness. At the first press conference after his election, Nyerere lamented that the Third World was not utilising the threat of defaulting more efficiently to induce Western banks to make more fundamental concessions to the indebted.[5]

Fundamental as all these areas of strategic solidarity are, they are no substitute for organic solidarity in terms of greater trade, investment and other interactions among Afro-Arab and other Third World countries themselves. Here the Less Developed Countries (LDCs) are caught up in one of several contradictions. In their relations with the North, the LDCs need to diversify their economies. But in their relations with each other, the LDCs need to specialise in order to increase mutual complementarity. Uganda could revive its cotton industry and sell the fibre to Kenya to process into a textile industry. This specialisation would help the two countries develop in the direction of complementary specialisation. But the imperatives of Uganda's relations with the world economy as a whole dictate diversification of Uganda's industry rather than specialisation. This is an acute dilemma which Afro-Arab and other Third World countries need to resolve as a matter of urgency. They need to find a suitable balance between diversification for North-South relations and specialisation in South-South trade.

Related to this is the imperative of finding alternative methods of payment in South-South trade. The principle of using Northern currencies for South-South trade has been very stressful. The bogey of 'foreign exchange' has bedevilled Southern economies. Tanzania, Zambia and Zimbabwe have been exploring possibilities of reviving *barter* as a basis of at least some aspect of their economic relations. The new detente between Kenya and Tanzania also envisages areas of barter trade between the two countries in the years ahead. And if Uganda's cotton did feed Kenya's textile industry more systematically in the future, it would not be unrealistic for Kenya to pay back Uganda in shirts and processed military uniforms.

Another area of organic solidarity among Third World countries concerns the issue of sharing *energy*. There have been years when Kenya has needed to obtain a third of its electricity from the hydroelectric dam at Jinja in Uganda. Uganda is still a major supplier of power to Kenya.

The Akosombo Dam on the Volta River in Ghana was also designed to be a major *regional* supplier of electricity in west Africa. Unfortunately, the level of water has been so low that, far from supplying power to neighbours, Ghana has periodically had to ration power domestically. We shall return to Akosombo later in the book.

Southern African dams such as Kariba have had more successful regional roles. They all symbolise a kind of Pan-Africanism of energy; organic solidarity through interlocking structures of hydro-electric power. Yet, the struggle for a more integrated Africa has encountered many setbacks – from the collapse of the East African Community of Kenya, Uganda and Tanzania to the substantial drying up of the Akosombo Dam.

Strategies of solidarity are but means to an end. The goal is distant and difficult – but the South's reach should exceed its grasp or what else is a heaven for?

Conclusion

This chapter has focused especially on the political economy of technological change. We have sought to demonstrate that in the last three centuries Africa has helped substantially in building the West's industrial civilisation, while the West may have hampered the evolution of Africa's own industrial culture. Africa's contribution to the West's industrialisation has ranged from the era of the slave trade for Western plantations to the new era of cobalt and chrome for Western factories. The foundations of Western industrial prosperity include African labour, territory and minerals. Africa's contribution to Western industrial development inadvertently helped to create the white technological Brahmins of the world. The West's disruptive impact on Africa helped to create the Black technological untouchables of the twentieth century.

How is the balance to be restored? At the beginning of this book we prescribed for Africa the twin strategies of looking inward to Africa's own ancestry and culture, and looking outward to the wider world at large. Africa's relations with the Arabs are in an intermediate position. Relations with those who are today regarded as 'Arabs' are at once part of Africa's own ancestry and part of Africa's interaction with the world beyond.

In the face of the West's technological pre-eminence, Africans and Arabs need to explore two forms of solidarity – *strategic solidarity* in their negotiations and confrontations with the West and *organic solidarity* in their relations with each other. As part of the Third World, Africans and Arabs need to develop both a more effective alliance when they deal with industrialised states and a more productive relationship when they co-operate with each other. The Third World as a whole needs to exploit its own areas of leverage and influence – such areas as producer power, consumer power, debtor power and the newly emerging skill power.

In Search of Stability

One of the most serious consequences of European colonisation in Africa has been the destruction of Africa's own legitimate institutions and structures of authority. The initial military triumph of European power over the local rulers was itself enough of a strain on the historic prestige of indigenous monarchies and institutions of governance. But that initial European military triumph was followed by decades of European overlordship, with policies deliberately calculated to change the nature of Africa's political processes for ever. Indigenous institutions began to atrophy, though not always completely. Indeed, one of the wonders of the twentieth century is how some of those institutions – from Ashanti to Buganda, from Morocco to Swaziland – managed to find the resilience to survive the cultural and political corrosive power of European colonisation.

A Triple Heritage of Allegiance

However, in spite of the miracle of this resilience, the new artificial boundaries of African colonies sowed the seeds of further political decay in the decades which were to follow. The original indigenous institutions were designed for societies which had vastly different borders from those imposed by European colonialism. Indeed, the colonial boundaries often encompassed a variety of societies with greatly different political traditions. Serious contradictions were created when previously stateless societies were enclosed with ancient monarchies, forming new colonial entities. In the new Uganda the previously centralised Baganda had to accept the post-colonial governmental authority of the previously stateless Langi. The previously imperial Ashanti had to accept, in the new Ghana, the post-colonial military pre-eminence of the previously decentralised Ewe. In the post-colonial state, power has indeed sometimes been inherited by those who were once stateless in pre-colonial times. This has been true not only of Obote's Uganda and Jerry Rawlings's Ghana, but also true of Mobutu Sese Seko's Zaire and Jomo Kenyatta's Kenya. The consequences of these contradictions included stresses and strains which often left Africa caught between the danger of tyranny and the risk of anarchy.

We have defined *tyranny* as centralised political violence in pursuit of governmental ends. We have defined *anarchy* as decentralised violence committed in a governmental void. A majority of post-colonial African countries hover in a balancing act between the chasm of anarchy and the brink of tyranny. The contradictions of colonial rule and the destruction of Africa's

opposite, Flight Lieutenant Jerry Rawlings

Robert Mugabe speaking at a rally at Mutare during the 1985 Zimbabwe elections

own indigenous structures have left the continent a prey to the forces of concentration of power, on one side, and the forces of disintegration of authority, on the other.

In a struggle to cope with this predicament between the devil of tyranny and the deep sea of anarchy, Africa has invented two magic pendula – the pendulum between military and civilian rule and the pendulum between the one-party and the multi-party state. Military rule has often been invoked to arrest a civilian trend towards anarchy. Civilian restoration has often been necessary to arrest a military trend towards tyranny. The second pendulum, between the one-party and the multi-party state, has its own logic. On the whole, the multi-party state in Africa has had a marked inclination towards anarchy while the one-party state shows a marked tendency towards tyranny. When the African nation has longed for discipline, it has been mesmerised by the principle of the one-party state – only to be disappointed by its tendency towards dictatorship. When the African nation has longed for liberty, it has been enchanted by the doctrine of a plural political system with many parties – only to be dismayed by the pluralistic tendency towards chaos.

How have these inclinations and trends been affected by Africa's triple heritage? African champions of the one-party state, like Robert Mugabe of Zimbabwe, have often argued that multi-party competition is alien to African culture and traditions. The idea of a 'loyal opposition' to the king or chief was traditionally regarded as a contradiction in terms. Dissent had to be expressed under the broad umbrella of loyalty and cohesion. The one-party state was therefore the more appropriate.

Julius Nyerere of Tanzania regarded traditional African democracy as a constant quest for consensus through discussion. 'The elders sat under a tree and talked until they agreed.' This was government by discussion; it was also government by consensus. Those two principles could best be modernised through the establishment of the one-party state.

But while each traditional African society might indeed have been best served by a single party, what would best serve a collection of traditional societies now enclosed into a single post-colonial state? The Ibo, the Yoruba and the Hausa separately might have been best served by the one-party principle in their own individual societies. But now that all three were enclosed in a single post-colonial Nigeria, would they not be best served by a multi-party plurality? These dilemmas have yet to be resolved in the vortex of post-colonial contradictions.

As for the role of Islam in Africa, it has shown a remarkable capacity for systematic mixture and ideological syncretism. Outside Africa, Islam expresses itself politically either through monarchies (from Saudi Arabia to Malaysia) or through the military (from Pakistan to Indonesia) or directly through priests (as in Iran). Under any of those three Islamic systems (monarchy, militocracy or direct theocracy) the multi-party system is either under stress or is outright impossible. In Africa monarchical Islam still thrives in places such as Morocco and the Emirates of Nigeria. Militarised Islam has been practised in places such as Libya and Mali. Theocratic Islam has been tried out in Sudan, though not really under the Mullahs as in Iran.

However, Islam in Africa has gone beyond those three legs of king, warrior and priest. Muslim Senegal has proved to be one of the most resilient multi-party systems in Africa. It also showed a capacity for accepting a Christian head of state for the first two decades of independence – a degree of ecumenicalism greater than that achieved by the United States in the first two centuries of its independence. After all, Muslim Senegal accepted Leopold Senghor, a Catholic, for the first twenty years of Senegal's independence – while the United States is still unlikely to accept a practising Jew for President for at least another quarter of a century from now.

Whenever Nigeria has been under civilian rule, it has been under the leadership of a Muslim. Competitive multi-party elections in Nigeria have so far always resulted in a Muslim-led government. In the First Republic (1960–6) the effective political leadership came from a northern party led by Prime Minister Abubakar Tafawa Balewa and the Sardauna of Sokoto, Ahmadu Bello. In the Second Republic (1979–83), the leadership came not so much from a northern party as from a northern-dominated party under Al-Haji Shehu Shagari.

But in Nigeria, as elsewhere in Africa, the party-system is caught between the competing forces of anarchy and tyranny, and the competing pulls of militarism and civilian supremacy. The political aspirations of discipline as against freedom are caught in between.

Africa's Civil-Military Pendulum

Africans are passing through a period when the economic vices of their governments seem to be regarded as more important than their political virtues. Nowhere is this better illustrated than in the fate of the Shagari Administration in Nigeria. The years 1979 to 1983 were perhaps the freest four years in Nigeria this century, certainly from the point of view of the open society and candid dissent. The names and reputations of the rulers were emphatically not spared. Perhaps nowhere else in the Third World were those in power more blatantly denounced in their own country as 'pirates and robbers' than as they were in Shagari's Nigeria. It is arguable that Shagari's four years were the golden years of press freedom in Nigeria. Sometimes the press came close to inciting violence. Sometimes opposition leaders actually did incite violence – and got away with it. If political dissent means anything, it reached its highest peak in Shagari's Nigeria, sometimes higher than in Western countries with their laws against incitement, against 'clear and present danger', and against disclosure of 'official secrets'.

Yet the same Shagari Administration was one of the most economically corrupt and incompetent in Nigeria's history. The nation's oil resources were rampantly abused, its finances substantially depleted, its laws of contract desecrated, its laws against corruption ignored, its teachers unpaid, its people

right, Alhaji Shagari of Nigeria; *far right*, Dr Hilla Limann of Ghana

impoverished. Never was a country's economic promise so quickly reduced to economic rampage. Shagari's balance sheet was stark: impressive political freedom against incredible economic anarchy. The stage was set. The military intervened 'to save the nation'. The nation's applause was loud. Shagari's economic sins of anarchy were deemed to be more relevant than his political virtues of freedom.

Now the Nigerian soldiers are in relative control. They have taken action against economic anarchy with methods which have ranged from stiffer currency controls to an economic war against indiscipline. But they have also taken action against certain political liberties, with secret tribunals to try members of the former government, with restrictions on press freedom, and with public executions.

The Limann Administration in Ghana from 1979 to 1981 was also a case of political openness on one side and economic corruption, drift and decay on the other. Again, the people of Ghana seemed to be more angered by the economic sins of the Administration than pleased by the political virtues of an open society. Flight Lieutenant Jerry Rawlings took over as a redeemer. Political liberties declined partly in the name of greater economic discipline.

Why are so many African countries so coup-prone? A major reason is that the technology of destruction in Africa is ahead of the technology of production. And so ultimate power resides not in those who control the means of production, as Marxists would argue, but in those who control the means of destruction.

A related reason why Africa is coup-prone is that most other institutions in Africa (such as labour unions, professional associations, religious leadership, universities, the judiciary, peasant associations, and even the civil service) are relatively weak. In most cases they are unable to stand up to the military.

A third reason for coups in Africa is the low level of professionalism in the armed forces. Criteria of recruitment and promotion are sometimes ethnic rather than based on merit; methods of professional socialisation are often haphazard; pay is often so low that it encourages corruption. Conditions do vary in different countries, but African soldiers in the streets of African capitals are more likely to display petty arrogance towards civilians than professional pride.

Another reason for military intervention in Africa is boredom in the barracks. Ultimately, what are African armies *for* anyhow? In the majority of cases there are no likely wars with foreign powers on the horizon. In most countries there are no major defence needs. Heroism for African soldiers is therefore to be sought not on the battlefield but in the political arena, not in military command against the enemy but in political command over one's own compatriots. African armies are therefore tempted to proclaim themselves the political and moral custodians of the national interest – rather than the military defenders of the nation's security and sovereignty. It is of such material that coups are made.

But the story of military coups in Africa will not be complete until we also try to understand under what conditions coups do *not* occur and why. Political analysts are often better at diagnosing diseases than at interpreting good health. The analysts are more skilful at identifying what is wrong than at fathoming the underlying causes of what is right. Diagnosis of military coups is easier, much easier, than prescribing preventive medicine.

Why have the longest surviving civilian regimes been so disproportionately one-party states? These include Tanzania, Zambia, Malawi, the Ivory Coast and Kenya. Has the one-party system in Africa been a better safeguard

Nigerian officers at the staff college at Jaji being addressed by the British Deputy Chief Instructor, Colonel Mike Tennant. Officers from the staff college have been directly involved in several of Nigeria's six military coups since Independence.

against a military coup than a multi-party system has proved to be?

We can assume that no government in Africa is 'coup-proof'. But perhaps we should take some comfort in the fact that some governments have proved to be less 'coup-prone' than others. Africans should begin to study the causes of civilian survival with as much earnestness as many have studied the causes of civilian collapse. Among the factors of comparative survival must be included, once again, the competing claims of the one-party state and multi-party system. It is to this critical dimension of the state in relation to the party-system that we now turn.

The State and the Party System

For our purposes in this chapter, we still accept the definition of the state as a structure of power and authority which claims sovereign jurisdiction over a given territory, and which seeks to monopolise the legitimate use of physical force within those boundaries.

Pre-colonial Africa encompassed both states and stateless societies. The states included elaborate empires such as ancient Ghana, Mali and Songhay, as well as city-states such as pre-imperial Sokoto or pre-imperial Zanzibar. Stateless societies ranged from the Nuer in the Sudan to the Tiv in west Africa. We shall return to the triple heritage of the state later in this book. However, our concern in this chapter is with the post-colonial state, perhaps Europe's most important political bequest to the new rulers of Africa.

In those parts of Africa where the state had not existed before European colonisation, it can be argued that state formation began as soon as the colonial order established structures of control. The entire colonial period was therefore an experience in state-building, a phase in the growth of the modern African state. But before independence the colonial state was part of a wider system of power, a wider empire. Independence was an initiation into autonomous statehood. There were also high hopes for democracy.

How is the state faring under the stress of independence in Africa? Also, how does it relate to the party system in the context of class-formation and civil-military relations?

It soon became clear that the post-colonial African state was inherently fragile domestically as well as in relation to the outside world. If the state is fragile in Africa, the political party is even more so. The fact that parties are an even more recent phenomenon than the state aggravates this crisis of general institutional fluidity. Yet African leaders have sometimes looked to their political parties as instruments for state-building. They have sought party strength in order to compensate for state weakness. It is partly in this context that we should place the lure of the one-party principle to such towering architects of African statehood as Kwame Nkrumah and Julius Nyerere. In Ghana under Nkrumah, the case for the one-party state rested on the argument that the country was dangerously divided without it. Ethnic and separatist sentiment cast a shadow on the legitimacy of the state as a whole. The pull towards anarchy was strong. Opposition parties, it was argued, because they were ethnically based, became instruments for the erosion of the legitimacy of the state and a danger to national cohesion. Attempted assassinations of President Kwame Nkrumah, whether real or stage-managed, provided additional grounds in favour of the single-party principle, as well as in favour of preventive detention. In short, the case for the one-party state in Ghana under Kwame Nkrumah rested on the state's need to *create* a national consensus in the face of deep division.

In contrast, the case for the one-party state in Tanganyika under Julius Nyerere rested in part on a pre-existent national consensus. In the last election before independence, the population voted overwhelmingly in favour of the Tanganyika African National Union (TANU). The opposition seemed to consist of a single lone figure in Parliament. In the face of such a massive national consensus, Nyerere understandably argued that it was a mockery to insist on a multi-party formula. There was no real competition for the ruling party. Should the electoral system therefore be internalised? Should the party find ways of giving the electorate a choice under a single-party umbrella, rather than denying the electorate real choice by insisting on a multi-party principle in a situation where electoral consensus behind one party was overwhelming?

Unlike Nkrumah's Convention Peoples' Party (CPP) in Ghana, Nyerere did not move directly towards monopolising power without a careful study. A commission was appointed to investigate how best to achieve the democratic principle of choice under the umbrella of a single party. The commission affirmed that principle of a single party but linked it every five years to an electoral competition among members of the same party, with the people choosing from different candidates at election time. The constitution of Tanganyika underwent a change to meet this innovation.

In 1964, Tanganyika united with Zanzibar to form the United Republic of Tanzania. The Afro-Shirazi party continued to rule Zanzibar virtually as a separate entity, while TANU ruled Tanganyika. It was not until 1977 that the two parties merged to create Chama Cha Mapinduzi (Swahili for 'Party of the Revolution'). Between 1964 and 1977 Tanzania was technically not a one-party state but a country with two single-party systems, parallel to each other. Zanzibar was under the Afro-Shirazi party; mainland Tanzania was under the Tanganyika African National Union. Both were single-party systems – but they were two single-party systems within a single state.

But while the inauguration of the single-party system in Tanzania in 1965 rested on the argument that the country already had a national consensus and the party system should reflect it, the merger of the Afro-Shirazi party with TANU in 1977 partially rested on the argument that the two parts of Tanzania needed to create a national consensus – and a unified party structure was one route towards it.

Milton Obote's Uganda did flirt with the principle of the one-party state in the course of the critical year, 1970. Again the reasons were closer to those which inspired Nkrumah (the country needed to avert anarchy and create a

Field Marshal Idi Amin Dada: a symbol of heroic foreign policy and repressive domestic regime

national consensus) than to those which inspired Julius Nyerere in the early 1960s (the country had so much national consensus that an opposition party could not flourish). In fact, Uganda was even more deeply divided than Nkrumah's Ghana had been. The ethnic cleavages were deeper in Uganda than in Ghana, and the tendency toward anarchy and interethnic violence was stronger in Uganda than in Ghana. Milton Obote understandably felt that the country needed delicate political and electoral engineering to help it create a viable political order. The idea of the one-party state was one strategy of political engineering. Much more interesting, however, was Obote's idea of making each Member of Parliament stand in four different constituencies – one in the north of the country, one in the south, one in the east and the fourth in the west. The design envisaged a situation in which every Member of Parliament would need to owe allegiance to four different ethnic areas of the country. This multi-ethnic accountability in parliamentary life would force the candidates to evolve positions and platforms which attempted to accommodate different groups rather than divide them. Between the elections every five years, each Member of Parliament would need to nurse four vastly different constituencies, and would therefore need to provide leadership in finding national perspectives on public issues rather than advocating narrower sectional and sectarian interests.

But before these innovative ideas could be implemented, General Idi Amin Dada intervened – and the first government of Milton Obote's was overthrown on 25 January 1971. The attempt to transcend ethnic cleavage through political reform was interrupted. The Amin years were to result in a deepening of ethnic animosities and aggravated anarchy in the country, in spite of the shared hatred of his regime. Indeed, under Amin, Uganda experienced both tyranny and anarchy simultaneously.

Leaders such as Nkrumah and Obote had seen ethnic cleavage as one of the main justifications for experimenting with the one-party state. But if the presence of ethnic cleavage is a reason for inaugurating a one-party state, what about the absence of class cleavage in Africa? Does class struggle exist in Africa? And how does that issue relate to the desirability or viability of the one-party state? It is to these issues that we now turn.

Class Struggle and the Single Party

In communist countries, the ruling Marxist party is seen as the ultimate weapon in class struggle. The party is designed to help realise and consolidate the dictatorship of the proletariat, which in turn is ultimately designed to prepare the way for a classless society. The communist parties of socialist countries, far from assuming that their societies have no classes, are normally alert to issues of class privilege, and see themselves ideologically as parties of the working class.

In contrast, Julius Nyerere argued in the 1960s that Africa needed a one-party system because Africa lacked genuine class cleavages:

The European and American political parties came into being as the result of the existing social and economic divisions – the second party being formed to challenge the monopoly of political power by some aristocratic or capitalistic group.[1]

The assertion here was that Conservative and Labour parties in Britain, Republicans and Democrats in the United States, and the multiplicity of political factions in such countries as France and the Federal Republic of Germany, were all a reflection of class antagonisms within the Western world. But in the absence of such class polarisation in Africa, African political organisations had to take different forms.

But what evidence did Nyerere advance for the proposition that traditional Africa had no class conflict? Nyerere used in part linguistic evidence. The word 'class' did not exist in any indigenous language in Africa that he knew about.[2] Nyerere also believed that traditional African collectivism was a form of socialism, and therefore helped to moderate if not actually prevent possibilities of class conflict. As he put it,

> We, in Africa, have no more need of being 'converted' to socialism than we have of being 'taught' democracy. Both are rooted in our past – in the traditional life which produced us.[3]

But if the absence of the word 'class' in African indigenous languages was evidence that classes had not existed traditionally, did not the absence of the word 'socialism' in most African indigenous languages also carry the implication that the phenomenon itself had not existed? At that stage, Nyerere might not have worked out fully the contradictory implications of linguistic evidence in relation to his twin propositions – the proposition that socialism is native to Africa and the proposition that class struggle is not. But other African leaders, such as the late Tom Mboya of Kenya, insisted quite early that 'socialism' had existed in traditional Africa in spite of the lack of a name for it. In an article answering a critic's letter in an east African journal at the

Julius Nyerere with Fidel Castro

time, Mboya accused his critic of 'confusing the word socialism with its reality, its practice'. Mboya asserted,

> I have not suggested that we have to go delving into the past seeking socialism. It is a continuing tradition among our people. Does the writer of the letter think that socialism had to be given a name before it became a reality? It is an attitude of mind towards people practiced in our societies and did not need to be codified into a scientific theory in order to find existence.[4]

In assessing the validity of linguistic evidence on its own, Mboya was more plausible than Nyerere. The absence of a name for a phenomenon does not necessarily prove the absence of the phenomenon itself.

But regardless of whether traditional Africa was socialist or classless, what can we say about contemporary post-colonial Africa in relation to classes and ideology?

Socialism: Good Climate, Bad Soil

As a generalisation, we might say that the intellectual climate for socialism in Africa is quite good, but the sociological and material soil is not fertile enough for socialism. Let us explore this twin proposition more fully, and then relate it to party systems.

The reasons why the intellectual climate for socialism in Africa is good include basic historical continuities and discontinuities. For one thing, many Africans both north and south of the Sahara have conceptually come to associate capitalism with imperialism. In reality, you can have socialism accompanied by imperialism – and the Chinese can soon equip you with the necessary vocabulary concerning 'social imperialism' and 'Soviet hegemony'. It is also possible to be a capitalist country without being an imperialist country – Switzerland and Sweden might be considered by some as good illustrations of non-imperialist capitalism. But in Africa's historical experience it is indeed true that modern capitalism came with imperialism. The enemy of imperialism is nationalism; the enemy of capitalism is socialism. If there is an alliance between capitalism and imperialism, why should there not be an alliance between African nationalism and socialism? Such a paradigm of intellectual and ideological convergence has been found attractive in many parts of Africa.

A second consideration which has contributed to the favourable intellectual climate for socialism in Africa concerns the accumulation of frustration over efforts to develop Africa through Western patterns of economic growth. Many Africans are seeking alternative strategies of social and economic improvement out of a sheer sense of desperation at the inadequacies of the first decades of independence. In reality, socialist experiments in post-colonial Africa so far have not yielded any greater improvement for the masses than other experiments. On the contrary, sometimes the social costs of socialism in Africa have indeed been rather high. It is arguable that while there are relatively successful petty capitalist experiments in places such as Kenya, Malawi, Tunisia and the Ivory Coast, Africa has yet to produce a relatively successful socialist experiment in terms of achieving a significant improvement in the material conditions in which the masses live. The nearest socialist success story is perhaps Algeria – and that needed to sell oil to the capitalist world to buttress it.

In spite of these contradictions, however, many Africans are so disenchanted with the first two decades of independence that they are prepared to experiment with socialist approaches to social transformation.

The third factor which predisposes many Africans in favour of socialism is the rampant corruption among the immediate post-colonial rulers of the continent, all the way from Egypt to Zimbabwe, before the implementation of socialism. Again, corruption is by no means a peculiarity of capitalism, as many of those who have travelled or lived in socialist countries will testify. But there is no doubt that social discipline can at times be more difficult to uphold in conditions of laissez faire economic behaviour than in conditions of relatively centralised planning and supervision. On balance, it is arguable that the socialist ethic is, almost by definition, more opposed to 'kick-backs, goodwill bribery', and even profit itself, than the ethic of acquisitive individualism.

The fourth factor which has contributed to the favourable intellectual climate for socialism in Africa is the widespread belief that traditional African culture was basically collectivist, and 'therefore' socialist. We have already referred earlier in this chapter to claims by such leaders as Nyerere and Mboya that the morality of sharing in traditional Africa, the ethic of responsibility for the young, the old and the disabled, the imperative of collective ethnic welfare, were essentially a distributive ethic akin to socialism.

Because of this broadly favourable intellectual climate, most African governments soon after independence paid some kind of lip-service to socialism. Even regimes like that of Jomo Kenyatta and Leopold Senghor managed to adopt in the initial years of independence a partially socialist rhetoric.

Regimes which planned to go the one-party-state route were particularly tantalised by socialist symbolism. After all, the presumed centralising tendencies of socialism could help justify a one-party monopoly of power. Prospects for socialism in the first decade-of African independence did seem to be congenial. Nasser, Nkrumah, Sékou Touré, Julius Nyerere and Boumedienne were seen as architects of a new socialist Africa.

What then went wrong? This is what brings us to the barrenness of the sociological soil, in spite of the favourableness of the intellectual climate. One obstinate sociological factor was simply the primacy of ethnicity in Africa as against class consciousness. Most Africans are members of their ethnic group first and members of a particular social class second. When under pressure, Ibo peasants are more likely to identify with the Ibo bourgeoisie than they are with fellow peasants in Yorubaland. Jaramogi Oginga Odinga in Kenya attempted to form a radical socialist party. He soon discovered that his supporters were almost exclusively fellow Luo. Chief

Posters of Marx, Engels and Lenin in post-colonial Angola

Obafemi Awolowo invoked socialist rhetoric in both the First and the Second Republics of Nigeria. He soon discovered that he was a hero not of the working class of Nigeria as a whole but of all classes of fellow Yoruba.

A related factor is the strength of élites rather than social classes. The new élites especially have emerged out of the womb of Western imperial acculturation. It has not been the possession of wealth necessarily which opened the doors to influence and power, but initially the possession of Western education and verbal skills. The initial political establishment of post-colonial Africa was disproportionately comprised of a Westernised and semi-Westernised core. This galaxy of Westernised stars has included names such as Nkrumah, Nyerere, Senghor, Kaunda, Ferhat Abbas, Obote, Houphouet-Boigny, Banda, Bourgouiba, Mugabe, Nkomo, Sadiq el-Mahdi, Machel, Neto and others.

This created a basic sociological ambivalence on the African scene. On the one hand, it seemed that the most opposed to imperialism rhetorically, and the ones most likely to link it to capitalism, were precisely the élites produced by the West's cultural imperialism in Africa. Even when these elements became truly revolutionary, there was a basic contradiction. After all, Karl Marx had expected the most revolutionary class to be the least advantaged class in the most advanced societies. This was deemed to be the proletariat in industrial Western society. But when you look at revolutionary leaders in Angola, Tanzania and Guinea, and examine the Western credentials of the leaders, you may be inclined to conclude that the most revolutionary of all classes in those societies were the best advantaged. In other words, Westernised Third World radicals were the most likely to pursue the dream of socialist transformation.[5]

It is a socio-linguistic impossibility for an African to be a sophisticated Marxist without being at the same time substantially Westernised. This is partly because the process of becoming a sophisticated Marxist requires considerable exposure to Marxist literature, both primary and secondary. Access to that literature for the time being is rarely possible through indigenous African languages such as Kiswahili, Yoruba or Amharic.

A third factor of this barrenness of the soil concerns Africa's organisational capabilities in the present historical phase. Many hastily assume that a tradition of collectivism in a traditional setting is a relevant preparation for organised collective efforts in a modern setting. Unfortunately, much of the evidence points the other way. Collective effort based on custom and tradition and kinship ties leaves Africa unprepared for the kind of organised collectivism which needs to be based on command rather than custom, on efficiency rather than empathy, on rationality rather than ritual.

The fourth aspect of the infertility of Africa's sociological soil would take us back to issues of historical continuity. Most African economies have already been deeply integrated into a world economy dominated by the West. African countries which become socialist domestically find that they are still integrated in the world capitalist system. The rules of that system are overwhelmingly derived from principles evolved in the history of capitalism. In international trade countries seek to maximise their return and acquire profit. The rules of business and exchange at the international level, the banking system which underpins those exchanges, the actual currencies used in money markets and in meeting balances of payments, are all products of the capitalist experience. Countries such as Vietnam, Angola and even Cuba discover soon enough that their best economic salvation is to gain international legitimacy by Western standards. Vietnam and Cuba may fail in gaining that legitimacy, but it is part of their ambition to begin receiving Western benefaction and to have easy access to Western markets for their goods, and to Western currency markets as well. So Third World countries can make their internal domestic arrangements socialist while remaining deeply integrated in the international capitalist system. It has also been argued that a country such as Tanzania is today more dependent on the world capitalist system than it was before it inaugurated its neo-socialist experiment under the Arusha Agreement in 1969.[6]

This then is the configuration of factors which reveals that although Africa is ready for socialism intellectually the material conditions for genuine socialist experimentation in Africa are not yet at hand. The intellectual climate is promising; the sociological soil is forbidding.

But how does this configuration of factors relate to the issue of political parties in Africa and to the fortunes of the one-party state?

Mass Mobilisation *versus* Élite Competition

It is a major premise of this analysis that a political party can only thrive under one of two alternative social conditions – a condition where mass mobilisation is feasible or a condition where élite competition is manageable. The question then arises whether conditions in most African countries are congenial to either situation.

One-party states in Africa are at their most pitiful in those societies which have attempted to stifle élite competition without substituting mass mobilisation. Curiously enough, two of these countries are regarded as the most successful cases of capitalist development in Africa. The two are Kenya and the Ivory Coast. Both countries, at least in the late 1970s, revealed quite impressive levels of economic growth. What was not mentioned was that both countries also had a substantial degree of political decay. The party institutions especially had severely atrophied. The governments of those countries are very sensitive about any suggestion that their political parties are mummified parties. In Kenya people have been detained for remarking that the Kenya African National Union (KANU), ostensibly the ruling party, was in fact a mummified ruler. In reality, KANU has been at its most vigorous only when it has had competition from another party. It did have such competition briefly at the very beginning of independence when the Kenya African Democratic Union (KADU) provided the countervailing force of an alliance of minority ethnic communities, seeking to protect themselves from what was presumed to be an alliance between the giant 'tribes' of Kikuyuland and Luoland. Then, when Jaramogi Oginga Odinga inaugurated his Kenya Peoples' Union (KPU), KANU for a while responded with vigorous enthusiasm and aggression. But when after 1969 KANU successfully eliminated all party competitors, KANU itself began to experience the not-so-slow process of atrophy. The dilution of élite competition through intimidation and the elimination of other parties resulted in the dilution of the vigour of the ruling party. This was particularly so since KANU did not even try to experiment with mass mobilisation as an alternative party dynamo to multi-party élite competition.

Across the border in Tanzania, on the other hand, the dilution of élite competition through both the one-party system and the rigorous leadership code of the Arusha Agreement was partially compensated for by an ethic of general social, economic and political organisation of the masses. The Tanganyika African National Union (TANU) remained a relatively active and meaningful party, in spite of the fact that many of its goals and ambitions were never realised. The country became materially poorer almost in proportion to the richness of its idealism. Some regarded it as socialism turned sour; some regarded it as *ujamaa* without *uji* (socialism without porridge). Tanzanians accused Kenya of being a capitalist society where 'man eats man'. Kenyans retorted by accusing Tanzania of being a socialist society where 'man eats nothing'. But strictly from the point of view of party vigour, the Tanzanians had the last laugh. Their ruling party not only ruled but was a party. The Kenyan ruling party may or may not have ruled – but it was certainly less and less of a real party.

The most important difference was that Tanzania, while diluting élite competition, nevertheless attempted to compensate with a real mass mobilis- ation. Kenya attempted to dilute élite competition at the political level, with- out substituting any pretence at mass mobilisation. But, of course, Kenya encouraged élite competition at the economic level even if it attempted to discourage it in the political process. Élite competition at the economic level in Kenya produced relative economic growth; while élite monopoly of power produced relative political decay. In contrast, Tanzania's effort to stifle élite competition in the economy might have contributed to relative economic decay, while Tanzania's bid for mass mobilisation in politics under Julius Nyerere did at least generate institutionalised political vigour.

We should bear in mind that sociologically élite competition need not be generated. Where it is not deliberately impeded it would occur anyhow. Élite competition in Africa and elsewhere is a natural social propensity which can only be stopped if someone takes deliberate steps towards throttling it. In contrast, mass mobilisation is not a natural phenomenon. Someone has to attempt to bring it about, arousing the masses through appropriate symbols of solidarity, inspiring them with the right symbols of motivation, channel- ling them towards appropriate avenues of endeavour. Mass mobilisation needs strong leadership; élite competition flourishes best in conditions of weak leadership. As a result, Africa finds it easier to suffer the contradic- tions of élite competition than to launch mass mobilisation.

A word is also necessary about Marxist one-party states in Africa. The longest surviving neo-Marxist state was Guinea (Conakry) under the late Sékou Touré's rule. His party, the PDG, was supposed to be Marxist-Leninist but Islam was deemed compatible with democratic centralism. The party had its moments of genuine mass mobilisation – going back to the days when it succeeded in inspiring the electorate of Guinea to vote for freedom from France in the De Gaulle Referendum of 1958. But Sékou Touré's one- party state was not always a magnet of mobilisation; it was often a mechan- ism of dispersal as hundreds of thousands of Guineans fled the country and created a massive Guinean diaspora in west Africa and in France. Before Touré's death in 1984, it was estimated that one out of every five Guineans had fled the country. The record of mobilisation within Guinea under Touré had to be balanced with the record of a massive exodus. Élite competition was so brutally suppressed that mass mobilisation as an alternative strategy became at times a sham. There were signs of an improvement in Guinea in the last few years of Sékou Touré's rule. Some degree of liberalisation was on the way. The ruling party became a party again instead of an instrument of repression. And the new mineral wealth of the country began to help Guinea realise economic development and, at the same time, arrest the long-standing political decay. But so weak were the party's roots that the whole system was overthrown in a military coup soon after Touré's funeral.

FRELIMO in Mozambique is, of course, another Marxist-Leninist ruling party. But unlike the PDG, FRELIMO was born out of the armed liberation movement against Portuguese rule. The ethos of mobilisation within FRELIMO has for a while been military as well as political. Organisationally the movement should have acquired considerable advantages over the usual political parties in Africa. The apparently sustained attempt to mobilise the peasantry as part of the war against the Portuguese, and then institutionalise the ethos of purposeful transformation in the liberated rural area, helped to deepen the experience of genuine collective organisation and commitment. FRELIMO's achievements are not to be underestimated. But the country's proximity to South Africa, and the subversion and sabotage perpetrated by South Africa's surrogates (the Mozambique National Resistance – MNR) have left Mozambique's socialist experiment in tatters. Indeed, the organisation of the party at the time of the Portuguese withdrawal had not acquired sufficient administrative sophistication or broad economic competence. The departure of the Portuguese settlers and administrators left a substantial vacuum in the broad national infrastructure. It remains to be seen if FRELIMO will succeed in the effort to arrest both political and economic decay in the society. The party's experience in mass mobilisation against the Portuguese should be an asset in this new struggle for reconstruction and rejuvenation once the MNR subversion is effectively contained.

A less convincing Marxist one-party state is Angola. This is partly because the Popular Movement for the Liberation of Angola (MPLA), far from demonstrating a capability to mobilise the masses of the society, is still barely struggling to assert control over large parts of the country. Far from achieving mass participation, the ruling party is trying to cope with widespread rebellion. A massive internal security problem exists within Angola. This is greatly aggravated by South Africa's aggressive policies towards Angola. Periodically, South Africans have made major military incursions into Angola, playing havoc not only with the South West African Peoples' Organisation (SWAPO) but also undermining Luanda's attempt to pacify the rest of the country and establish control. The National Union for the Total Independence of Angola (UNITA) under Jonas Savimbi has managed to sustain a continuing rebellion against the central government in the country, complete with substantial UNITA control over large geographical areas of Angola. The Angola government's dependence on foreign troops (Soviet-backed Cuban troops) for basic security considerably dilutes the country's sovereignty.

Is not the rivalry between UNITA and MPLA itself a form of 'élite competition' in Angola? If political parties in Africa become vigorous under conditions of either mass mobilisation or élite competition, and if mass mo-

Sekou Touré of Guinea

A revolutionary mural in the
Maputo Museum, Mozambique

bilisation is not viable in Angola at the moment, is not the competition between
Jonas Savimbi and MPLA leaders a form of basic élite rivalry? The answer is
indeed yes. Unfortunately, however, this is militarised élite rivalry rather
than a rivalry between political parties. When a country such as Angola is
experiencing armed conflict between two movements, the rivalry has gone
beyond party competition. War has taken over from party politics.

This brings us back to the broader issue of civil-military relations. This
time we need to look at how these relations affect political parties in Africa.
What does the evidence tell us about this meeting point between political
and military processes in Africa?

Ballots, Bullets and the Party System

Simply in terms of correlations, rather than causation, a remarkable phenomenon emerges out of Africa's record in the first two decades of independence. The most durable civilian governments in Black Africa have been
disproportionately governments of one-party states. The elder statesmen of
African politics towards the end of the 1970s included such names as Julius
Nyerere of Tanzania, Houphouet-Boigny of the Ivory Coast, Kenneth
Kaunda of Zambia, Hastings Banda of Malawi, Gamal Abdel Nasser of Egypt
and Jomo Kenyatta of Kenya. Habib Bourgouiba has also presided over a de
facto one-party or dominant party state in Tunisia. This galaxy of the most
distinguished African statesmen of the first two decades of independence
consisted of presidents of basically one-party states.

On the other hand, many of the casualties of military coups during those first two decades were rulers of countries which still had a multi-party system or had at any rate not yet consolidated a one-party monolithic alternative. Nigeria, the first English-speaking African country to experience a military coup, was a multi-party state in 1966. Nkrumah was also overthrown in Ghana in the same year, against the background of an inadequately consolidated single-party system. Allegiance to former opposition parties in the country was still very strong. Milton Obote believed that he narrowly escaped a military coup in 1966 when his country still had a flourishing multi-party system. When he was overthrown in 1971 by Idi Amin he had not yet had time to consolidate a single-party alternative in Uganda. The Abboud military coup in the Sudan in 1958 was also against the background of a vigorous and articulate multi-party system. Civilian rule was later restored in the Sudan, and multi-party politics once again flourished – only to be succeeded by further military coups. The original Mobutu coup in the Congo (now Zaire) was also against the background of tremendous élite and ethnic rivalries in the country. Civilian rule returned to the Congo, including a phase under the notorious leadership of Moise Tshombe. Again, a military fate awaited a pluralistic and competitive African polity. There are other examples in Africa of multi-party systems capitulating to military intervention.

Of course not all one-party states in Africa have survived; nor is it true to say that all multi-party states have capitulated to military coups. What we are suggesting is that the most durable civilian governments in Africa so far have been disproportionately governments of one-party states; while the casualties of military intervention in Africa have been disproportionately multi-party states. The compelling question which arises is whether this is simply an accidental correlation in the first twenty years of African independence or whether there is a basic causal connection at work in these processes.

It is too early to be sure at this stage. For example, it is conceivable that the durability of civilian rule in countries such as Tanzania, Zambia, Kenya, Malawi and the Ivory Coast has been due more to such factors as towering personalities, Western backing and configuration of sociological factors in those particular countries, rather than to the fact that those countries have a one-party state. The charisma of such figures as Jomo Kenyatta and Julius Nyerere might have been much more relevant as part of the explanation for the durability of civilian rule than the existence of either the Kenya African National Union or Chama Cha Mapinduzi in Tanzania. Similarly, French backing for Houphouet-Boigny in the Ivory Coast and British backing for Jomo Kenyatta and Daniel arap Moi might have been given more as appreciation of their security as leaders than to support the structure of their political parties.

We must also note the apparent inevitability of multi-party solutions in the process of restoring civilian rule where it has previously been replaced by military rule. If, on the one hand, Africa's record in the first two decades of independence suggests that a one-party system could help prevent military rule, it should on the other hand also be noted that a multi-party system in Africa has often seemed to be the necessary cure for military rule.

When the soldiers are about to go back to the barracks, how can they hand over power to a single party? To which single party could they conceivably transfer the instruments of sovereignty? After all, even if they previously took over power from a single ruling party, as they did in Ghana under Nkrumah, they could hardly return the power to the party they had previously condemned. The pattern therefore of recivilianisation in Africa has quite often taken the form of holding competitive multi-party pluralistic elections to determine who should receive the mantle of political authority. In 1979 such elections were held in Ghana and Nigeria as the soldiers returned to the barracks. In 1980 such elections were held in Uganda. Indeed, both Ghana and the Sudan have experienced more than one moment of recivilianisation – and in each case it had been necessary to have multi-party competitive elections before the soldiers could restore power to the civilians.

In politics, as in medicine, it may be true that prevention is better than cure. But cure is still better than ill health. On balance, it would seem that the one-party state is a more effective preventive medicine against military rule than the multi-party system. That at least is what the African evidence in these initial decades after independence seems to suggest. But at the same time the African evidence also suggests that a multi-party arrangement is a necessary cure if the malady of military rule is to be ended, and the soldiers encouraged back to the barracks. The way out of a military era in Africa has tended to be through competitive multi-party elections – for better or worse.

The Dual and the Plural Society

The strongest case for the one-party state in Africa is to be found in those African societies which are ethnically *dual*: consisting primarily of two ethnic groups, one of which is well over half of the total population and the other is a permanent minority. Dual societies in Africa include Rwanda, Burundi and Zimbabwe. Rwanda and Burundi each has a permanent Hutu majority and a permanent Tutsi minority. Zimbabwe has a permanent Shona majority and a permanent Ndebele minority. In each of the three cases the numerical margin between the two ethnic communities is substantial.

Algeria is also a dual society, consisting of Arabs and Berbers. But there has been such a considerable cultural Arabisation of the Berbers through Islam over a very long period of time that the problems of ethnic cleavage are moderated as a result.

On the evidence so far electoral behaviour among Africans south of the Sahara correlates overwhelmingly with ethnic allegiance. In the two most critical elections in Zimbabwe's history (the last under colonial rule in 1980 and the first after independence five years later), the Shona people voted overwhelmingly for fellow Shona, Robert Mugabe, and awarded him

Polling stations in the 1983
Nigerian elections: *left*, Lagos;
right, Muslim women wait in a
separate line to cast their votes

political power. The Ndebele voted overwhelmingly for fellow Ndebele, Joshua Nkomo, and gave his party a minority of seats in parliament. For as long as Zimbabwe remained a multi-party state, it looked as if the Ndebele were sentenced to being permanently out of power while the Shona seemed guaranteed to be permanently in power. A dual society with a multi-party system in Africa seemed to be a prescription for a political caste system, with 'Shona Brahmins' and 'Ndebele Harijans' or their equivalent, for the foreseeable future.

But would a one-party system help to defuse this kind of situation? The evidence elsewhere would seem to support such a hypothesis. Some of the worst moments of ethnic tension in Kenya have come during the days when there was an opposition party – the Kenya African Democratic Union (KADU) soon after independence and the Kenya People's Union (KPU) two years after KADU's dissolution. Interparty rivalry deepened interethnic tensions, and vice versa. But in the periods when members of all ethnic groups competed under the same single-party umbrella of KANU, the tensions were between personalities and their supporters rather than between ethnic groups. In Kenya the single-party system has meant genuine power-sharing among ethnic groups which would otherwise have been mutually exclusive in government. If KADU had survived as a separate party, instead of merging with the more preponderant KANU, Daniel arap Moi, originally a KADU man, would never have become President of Kenya. There were other former KADU leaders who lived to wield considerable power within the enlarged KANU in the years which followed the merger. The single-party system had helped to facilitate greater power-sharing, even if it reduced political participation in the liberal sense of electoral choice.

But while the single-party system does indeed moderate and soften the pull towards anarchy in African political behaviour, there is no denying the fact that the single party risks aggravating the reverse tendency towards tyranny. Although the single party allows for considerable choice in parliamentary elections, as several candidates from the same party compete against each other, the top position of president is almost always left un-challenged. Indeed, there has been evidence in Kenya that any challenge to the reigning president (Kenyatta until 1978 and Moi after that) has usually resulted in repressive treatment of political dissenters.

In much of Africa the choice is often stark – adopting the one-party state in order to reduce the risk of anarchy or rejecting the single-party state in order to reduce the risk of tyranny. There is no easy answer. Each national case has to be considered in its own right.

On the whole, plural societies such as Kenya or Uganda (with multiple ethnic groups) may have more room for experimenting between single-party and multi-party systems. The diversity of groups makes it possible to evolve changing political allegiances over time. But dual societies such as Zim-babwe, Rwanda, Burundi and Algeria face a more pressing problem of ethnic monopoly of power and political exclusivity. The one-party system seems to be one promising umbrella for power-sharing. The case for 'going single' is more urgent in places such as Zimbabwe than it ever was in, say, Kenya on attainment of independence.

Part of Zimbabwe's Independence celebrations, April 1980

Conclusion

We have attempted in this chapter to identify the complicated pattern of party systems in Africa in relation to wider social and political forces. A basic tension has been between the forces and values which have tended to lean in favour of multi-party competition and political pluralism. Behind them are the even more fundamental forces which have tended to pull Africa towards anarchy, on one side, and tyranny, on the other.

Underlying it all is the artificiality and shallowness which Western colonialism created in Africa. Political decay is partly a consequence of colonial institutions without cultural roots in Africa. This includes the general fragility of both the state and democracy in Africa. They have not yet consolidated themselves. The state in Africa sometimes appears all-powerful, overriding or even abolishing other institutions with ease. But even when the African state appears 'almighty' this is less because the state itself is strong than because other institutions (such as industries, churches or labour unions) are even weaker. The post-colonial African state is overtly 'mighty' but inherently vulnerable. It is sometimes excessively *authoritarian*, but in order to disguise the fact that it is inadequately *authoritative*. The state still faces a crisis of legitimacy before the tribunal of African pluralism. After all, the colonial state was born out of wedlock. And the sin is visited upon succeeding generations.[7]

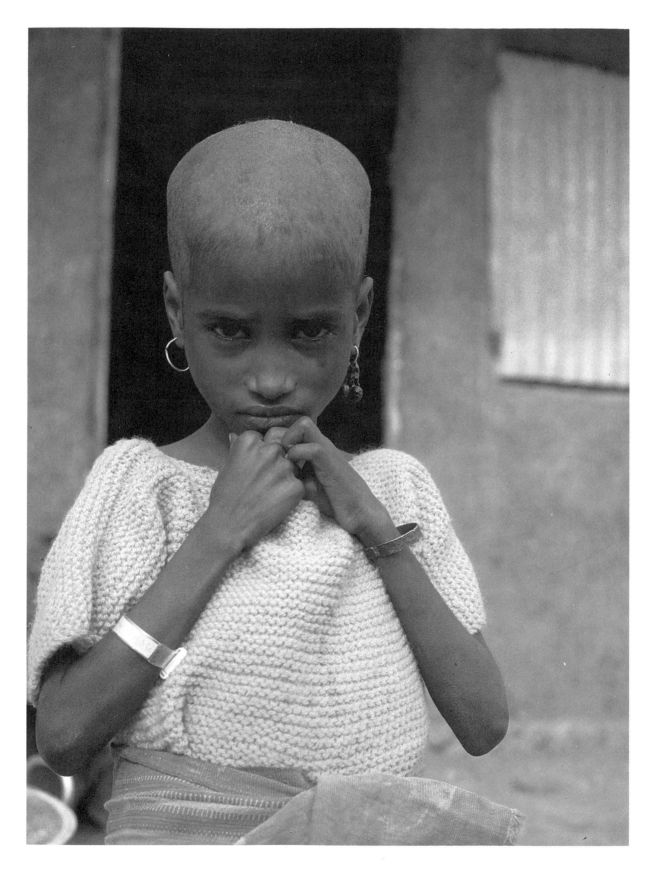

Is Modernisation Reversible?

As we have indicated, Africa is in crisis. Governments are unstable, economies are under strain, infrastructures are decaying. The curse of the ancestors is upon the continent. The present generation of Africans has worked out a compact with the twentieth century – but a compact which is essentially dishonourable and disloyal to the principle of indigenous authenticity. The result has been Westernisation without modernisation. Africa has Western-style armies which are staging military coups, Western-style police forces which are failing in law enforcement, Western-style bureaucracies which are increasingly corrupt, and Western-style agricultural plans which are deficient and unproductive. The ancestors seem to be engaged in resolute cultural sabotage. Are we witnessing dismodernisation? Is the Emperor of Westernisation at last recognised as naked?

It certainly looks as if the post-colonial euphoria about 'modernisation' has been an illusion of modernity, a mirage of progress, a façade of advancement. The reality behind the façade continues to be grim and devastating. Under the curse of the ancestors, Africa is bleeding; the continent is starving. The reasons lie, as we have indicated, in 100 years of colonial history and 1000 years of indigenous and Islamic cultures.

Some modernisation had taken place in Africa under European rule and tutelage. Schools had been established, roads built, railway systems constructed, police forces inaugurated and modern armies recruited. We define modernisation as innovative change based on more advanced knowledge and leading to wider social horizons. We define development as modernisation minus dependency, the promotion of innovative change and the broadening of social horizons without excessive reliance on others.

But even the degree of dependent modernisation which Africa had achieved under colonial rule is in the process of being reversed. As we have indicated in another chapter, Africa is in the process of decay or social decomposition. Instead of African economies growing, they show signs of shrinking. Instead of Africa's per capita production expanding, it betrays a tendency to diminish. Instead of greater experience leading to greater efficiency, Africa's experience paradoxically seems to result in *decreasing* competence. Latest estimates show that thirty of the hungriest nations of the world are in Africa. The World Food Council estimates that population in the African continent may be growing at three or four times the rate of growth in food production. The threat of famine in Africa will persist well into the twenty-first century.

opposite, Famine survivor, Ethiopia

Infrastructure: The Rust and the Dust

One of the more obvious areas of decay is the infrastructure, the system of roads, railways and other broadly supportive facilities and utilities.

The roads of Africa have been taking a terrific beating – there are miles and miles of potholes in some parts of the continent. There is a Ugandan joke about a bad Ugandan road: 'When you see a man driving in a straight line along Kampala road, he must be drunk!' Well, this joke is equally applicable to many other roads throughout the continent. In Ghana the main artery between north and south is the road from Accra to Tamale. The road is fundamental to the nation and yet it is in large parts in utter disrepair. It tells us much about the state of communications in Africa. It tells us much about the African condition. It was Julius Nyerere, founder President of Tanzania, who once said that while the great powers are trying to get to the moon, we are trying to get to the village. Well, the great powers have been to the moon and back, and are now even communicating with the stars. But in Africa we are still trying to reach the village. What's more, the village is getting even more remote, receding with worsening communications even further into the distance.

The poor state of repair of this road in Ghana makes it virtually impassable

Railway systems are also in difficulty in different parts of the continent, with reduced access to foreign exchange for the purchase of spare parts, wagons and fuel and for maintenance. This also applies to lorries and buses which can be seen, often without tyres, languishing by the roadside.

As for telephone systems in Africa, they show in part the usual contradictions of dependency. It is easier to place a call to the Western world from an African country than to place a call to a neighbouring African country. Sometimes it is easier to telephone Michigan from Mombasa, Kenya, than to telephone Thika, another part of Kenya.

Apart from the decaying infrastructure, the system of production in Africa is pitted against severe constraints. Certainly the shortage of foreign exchange and spare parts has made many an African machine grind to a standstill. Dependency upon the West has not made matters easier.

In Pwalugu, Ghana, I followed the story of a tomato factory which tried to be self-reliant, but soon discovered it was up against the hazards of the international market in technology. At first a deal was made with Yugoslavia. The Yugoslavs installed the equipment for manufacturing cans or tins for the tomatoes. For reasons which are unclear, the Yugoslavs were not able to complete the job. The Ghanaians then turned to the Italians who had, in fact, manufactured the machinery in the first place but who had left the installation to Yugoslavs. However, the Italians, for reasons of their own, wanted to sell the Ghanaians new equipment and new spare parts, but the Ghanaians could not afford an additional commitment of foreign exchange. The Ghanaians are still eager to make the right size of tin for their tomatoes, an optimum size for Ghana, but they are unable to do so. Equipment for making the tins is available but unused because the installation was never

Remains of a decaying railway system in Sudan, with a more reliable form of transport in the foreground

Is Modernisation Reversible? 203

completed. The Ghanaians still have to import the tins for their tomatoes.

But the most serious problem of production in Africa concerns agriculture. Part of the problem has arisen because of inadequate returns for farmers and disproportionate use of resources by bureaucracies of marketing boards. In a country such as Nigeria agriculture was, in a sense, murdered by oil wealth. The brief honeymoon of petro-power diverted skills away from cultivation to wheeling and dealing in the temporarily oil-rich Nigeria. In spite of slogans such as the 'green revolution', under President Shehu Shagari Nigerian agriculture was mortally wounded by the petro-bonanza.

Related to this issue is the crisis of the cash economy in Africa. Money in some African societies is a relatively recent phenomenon. Traditionally some of these societies dealt in barter and other forms of exchange, though west Africa had devised ways of using money or its equivalent in shells centuries before the British pound or the French franc penetrated the African continent.

But in much of the rest of Africa exchange of goods in kind was more common than the use of currency. Now this new entity called money is under stress, and is earning for itself considerable distrust among the ordinary people of the continent. The value of the money seems unpredictable, and sometimes changes quite fast at the behest of such incomprehensible foreign institutions as the International Monetary Fund (IMF). Quite often, several devaluations rapidly follow each other.

Also in the process of decay is Africa's schooling system. Teachers are becoming less committed. They are often underpaid and in some countries they are not paid at all for months on end. The teachers have to look for moonlighting opportunities to give them an additional livelihood. The sense of vocation in education is under severe strain in Africa.

There has also been declining support for African universities. In those countries where money has declined in value enormously, professors have to look for additional jobs ranging from taxi-driving to farming, as a method of augmenting their resources.

At Navrongo in rural Ghana, I have witnessed the slow death of a village school. The desks which broke were not replaced. Those which remained were carefully stored away during vacations. Some of the walls began to crumble, the hinges came off doors and windows; the desks were fewer each year. And yet that was not the worst of it. Africa is quite familiar with schools without walls, classrooms in the open. Teaching can go on without desks, learning can take place without walls, but teaching without teaching materials is a different matter. An entire term had taken place at this school without the basics of writing, without paper, without pens. Someone complained, 'Why not write to the head of state?' Someone else retorted, 'Write? With what?'

There was more at stake in that school than a dying classroom. I was perhaps witnessing the slow death of an alien civilisation. Before me was perhaps the gradual death of Western culture as we have known it in Africa.

A classroom without walls:
Liqueleva Primary School,
Maputo, Mozambique

Crime, Punishment and Compensation

Yet another area of decay and dis-modernisation is that of law enforcement in Africa. As in most of the rest of the world, crime in Africa has been increasing. But unlike the rest of the world the law enforcement machinery in Africa seems to be crumbling. In many African countries the police is becoming more corrupt rather than less, the judiciary is becoming more politicised and sometimes less professional, the prisons are not only overcrowded but often falling apart, the legislative system is becoming less predictable and sometimes militarised, the citizens are becoming more confused about the law and so are less and less secure in person and property. Law and order are falling apart not only in the wider society but also within the law enforcement machinery itself.

Much of this law enforcement machinery came with the Western impact upon Africa. Before European colonisation there were alternative forms of law enforcement in operation. These were partly Islamic in those areas which had become Islamised. In the rest of Africa there were other indigenous methods of protecting the innocent in society.

In indigenous terms, the protection of the innocent was precisely the main focus of law enforcement, rather than the punishment of the guilty *per se*. Arising out of this came the victim-focus in law enforcement rather than the villain-focus. When a crime was committed it was more fundamental to have the victim's family compensated, than to have the villain or culprit punished.

I remember when I was a child the case of a young man who was working for my family as a domestic help. One of my aunts sent him to a nearby shop to buy salt and coconuts. It had been raining. On his way back from the shop the young man passed an electric lamp post. It turned out that there was a live wire, and the young man touched it. In the wetness of the occasion the

The British legal system operating in Sudan in 1954

young man was electrocuted immediately. His family came to our family to negotiate compensation. We provided a suitable recompense and prayed for the departed soul of the unfortunate youth.

The coming of Western systems of law enforcement played havoc with African systems of compensation, especially in the field of Western criminal law. There was a sudden and decisive shift from focus on the victim of a crime to focus on the suspect or culprit. The new infrastructure of law enforcement demanded prison houses for violators of the law without adequate machinery for compensating victims of crime. And even when fines were imposed in a criminal case, the money went to the state and not to the victim. Compensation as a principle became almost irrelevant in criminal justice under Western law.

Under Western stimulation, Africa's law enforcement also shifted from emphasis on shame to emphasis on guilt. Shame is a subjective state of mind which implies a state of unease and internal anxiety about something which has gone wrong. Guilt, especially in Western terms, is an objective condition which can be ascertained by laws of evidence and which can be measured in terms of degrees. In other words, shame is primarily subjective, whereas guilt in Western judicial systems is supposed to be objective.

The Western system of law enforcement substituted prison sentences for negotiations about compensation. It also substituted guilt ascertainment for shame arousal. Third, it substituted strict personal accountability by the culprit for collective family and social responsibility for violations committed by a member of the group.

It would not have mattered if the new system had worked. It could then have been asserted that the new and 'modern' method of law enforcement — consisting of judges wearing wigs, policemen wearing uniforms, and the prisoners behind barbed wire – had rescued Africa from a life of violence, destruction and basic criminality. But, of course, what has happened is the reverse. The new system, like many other 'modern' institutions, has simply not been working. The substitution of a cage for the villain in place of compensation for the victim, the insistence on objective guilt instead of subjective shame, the focus on personal individual accountability not collective responsibility, have all resulted not only in escalating violence and criminality, especially in African cities, but also in the relentless decay of the police, judiciary, legal system and prison structures.

In the face of this social and legal disintegration one African government after another has been looking for alternative forms of law enforcement. Unfortunately, almost no African country is returning to the basic principles of indigenous and traditional modes of norm fulfilment. The two most popular approaches towards dealing with rising crime have been either to make the Western method of punishment even more severe or, in the case of Muslim Africa, to return to Islamic law. It is arguable that Islamic law is more conscious of the imperative of shame rather than guilt than Western law has managed to be in the modern period.

The desperate African governments seeking to control crime waves in

This decaying house in Nigeria is still occupied

their societies often forget the distinction between severity of punishment and certainty of punishment. If there is a death penalty for a particular crime, but only a 10 per cent chance that the criminal would be apprehended, this could be less of a deterrent than a life imprisonment with a 60 per cent chance of the criminal being apprehended. In many African countries the chances of arrest and imprisonment are quite low, because police forces are small, and often corrupt, and because systems of detection and investigation are often rudimentary and relatively backward. So African governments do in fact have a choice between making their systems of investigation and detection more efficient and the police force less corrupt, on one side, and making the punishment for crimes increasingly severe on the other. Of course, the latter appears cheaper, easier and seemingly quicker. And so the easy option is adopted, very often with capital punishment for more and more crimes. A number of African countries, including Nigeria and Kenya, have experimented with the death penalty for robbery with violence. There have been occasions when Nigeria has carried out executions of thieves and robbers to a routine, every second Saturday, in public.

The system of executions in public is, in fact, a perversion of the African principle of shame. It is true that many African societies use the device of shaming the culprit, but quite often in front of the victim's relatives as well as the culprit's own extended family. The idea of public executions in front of television cameras was not for the greater enjoyment of an anonymous public. Yet the latter strategy of public executions has been precisely what some military regimes in Africa, including Muhammad Buhari's ex-government in Nigeria, have experimented with to control rising lawlessness.

Islam and Retribution

In Muslim Africa there has always been the alternative temptation of resurrecting the Shari'a or Islamic law. Among the latest to experiment with that option was the Republic of Sudan under President Jaafar Nimeri. Nimeri's government introduced Islamic law in 1983. Robbers and thieves under Islamic law could be liable, under some very strict conditions, to have their offending hand amputated. It is true that a robber in Nimeri's Sudan was better off than a robber in post-Shagari Nigeria. In Nigeria the robber, especially if evidence of violence is clear, is liable to death. In Nimeri's Sudan the robber, even when the evidence of violence was clear, was at the worst liable 'only' to lose his hand.

Islamic law is probably more aware of the principle of shame than are Western concepts of justice. But Islamic law fuses shame and guilt and attempts both to establish guilt and arouse collective shame. It must be remembered that pre-Islamic Arabia had feuds. A member of a tribe who was killed became a basis of collective tribal accountability on the side of both victim and villain. The Prophet Muhammad attempted to control these feuds by promoting new principles of personal accountability and new methods of verification of evidence. The result is a mixture of shame and

Jaafar Muhammad El Nimeri of Sudan, architect of an Islamic state

guilt considerations, and a blending of the personal and collective natures of culpability. Perhaps the least defensible of the Islamic penalties is the stoning or whipping of an adulterer to death. It is true that the evidence required before such a punishment can be imposed is very elaborate, and the loopholes for avoiding such punishment are deliberately contrived by the law. It is almost as if Islamic law itself is ashamed of its own severity on this issue, which is an extreme fusion of the principles of guilt and shame.

Clearly this is in sharp contrast with traditional Black African response to adultery. This views it as a moment of aberration in a marriage, and seeks to solve it by principles of compensation between the adulterer and the aggrieved spouse. Bilateral compensation rather than legal vengeance is indigenous Africa's response to adultery.

What is clear in this picture of law enforcement in Africa is that the continent is being forced to choose between the excesses of the Western system and the excesses of Islamic law, between taking Western concepts of guilt and villain-focus to new extremities of punishment, on one side, and taking Islamic concepts of God's vengeance in relation to both human guilt and human shame, on the other. What almost no African government is doing is returning to indigenous principles of norm fulfilment and methods of compensation and collective responsibility.

But it is worth noting that Islam has one additional insistence in the sphere of morality and the law – the insistence on literal sobriety. Islamic prohibition of alcohol has been a fundamental aspect of Islamic notions of personal and collective responsibility. Can a person be trusted to talk to God if the person is under the influence of alcohol? This was almost the first Islamic dilemma on the issue of sobriety and responsibility. The Qur'an did not at first completely prohibit drinking alcohol. It simply prohibited believers from approaching prayer while under the influence of drink. The idea behind this was that prayer was a communication with God, and complete sobriety was necessary in one's dialogue with one's Maker. There is a school of thought which believes that if the Arabs during the Prophet Muhammad's time had succeeded in postponing their drinking hours to the period after the last prayers of the day (about 8 pm), alcohol in Islam would never have been completely prohibited. But because the believers could not wait until after eight the dispensation was withdrawn. It was evident that those who drank could not be trusted to engage in dialogue with the Lord without first intoxicating their minds.

The next decisive verse of the Qur'an on alcohol was far less ambiguous. It declared less equivocally that drink and gambling were among Satan's activities and believers were to avoid them. Behind this new prohibition was a divine conclusion that alcoholism knew no half-measures, and was insensitive to the distinction between time for play and time for prayer, time for human frivolity and time for divine awe. Personal responsibility in Islam was now more directly linked with personal sobriety.

And so bottles of Scotch whisky, Russian vodka, French wine, German

A large tea plantation in Kericho, Kenya

and British beer, and Ugandan waragi were all poured into the River Nile when President Nimeri declared the Islamic Republic of the Sudan. Drinkers lamented such waste but devout Muslims applauded such promise. President Nimeri was trying to reconcile the principle of personal accountability with the principle of personal sobriety in the field of morality and law.

But there is a fourth path apart from indigenous, Islamic, and Western systems of law enforcement. This is the path of innovation, of trying to find out whether there is an entirely new and unprecedented method of coping with lawlessness, crime and corruption.

One such experiment has been in Ghana under the governance of Jerry Rawlings. The public tribunals which were brought into being after the second coup of Jerry Rawlings in the 1980s attempted new methods of ascertaining guilt and culpability. For example, Western law insists that a person is innocent until proved guilty. There are countries in the world which would insist that a suspect is guilty unless the suspect can prove his or her innocence. In Ghana under the public tribunals inaugurated by Jerry Rawlings's government a suspect is neither guilty nor innocent in advance of the presentation of the evidence before the tribunal.

But such innovations in Africa at the present time are relatively brief, inconsistent and inconclusive. The pervasive atmosphere in much of the land is one of rust and dust, stagnation and decay, especially within those institutions which were originally bequeathed by the West.

Conclusion

In the autumn of 1984 the heart of a baboon was transplanted into a human baby in the United States. It was on 14 October 1984, that Baby Fae was born with a genetic defect called hypoplastic left heart syndrome. Baby Fae had half a heart, and the heart of a baboon came briefly to the rescue. The

baby survived for twenty days, breathing with the aid of an alien heart.

It turned out that the transplant of a baboon's heart to a human being was ahead of its time. Baby Fae finally rejected the alien heart. There is a sense in which Africa, too, has received the heart of a baboon since colonisation. Here, too, Africa's body politic is rejecting the transplanted organ – be the organ an alien university in Kenya or an American constitution in Nigeria, a premature technology or a foreign ideology without adequate roots. Africa is rebelling against Westernisation masquerading as modernity.

In the case of Baby Fae, she was born with half a heart and the resort to the baboon was one method of rescue. In the case of Africa, its culture already had a heart. The West tried to bid that heart be still, and be replaced by a foreign organ. The African body is rejecting the foreign organ. The question which arises is whether Africa's own heart is still strong enough to be reinstated into the body where it belongs. At a more spiritual level, we may be confronting not just a case of hearts but of souls, even a trans-migration of souls. Africa may be in the process of reincarnation. Out of apparent death a new life can emerge. One cultural generation of Africa may be dying – but out of the devastation a new generation may be in formation.

In spite of all the drought and famine, in spite of all the trials and tribul-ations, in spite of the decay and the reversal of modernisation, there is one residual sign of health remaining in Africa, one obstinate symbol of continu-ity – the population of Africa continues to expand at a remarkable rate. We are multiplying ourselves at a rate unequalled in any other region of the world. My own country, Kenya, is supposed to be leading the world now in rate of growth of population, already at a level of 4 per cent a year.

Surely all cannot be lost if, in the midst of all this death and devastation, enough babies survive to outnumber the dead. Africa may be sick, but she seems to be still capable of giving birth.

Canadian-sponsored combine harvesters on the Hanang plains, north Tanzania. Enormous quantities of grain are produced but local Barabaig pastoralists have lost their land and Canadian prairie-style cultivation has resulted in serious soil erosion. The cost of mechanised farming on this scale places a considerable strain on Tanzania's limited foreign exchange.

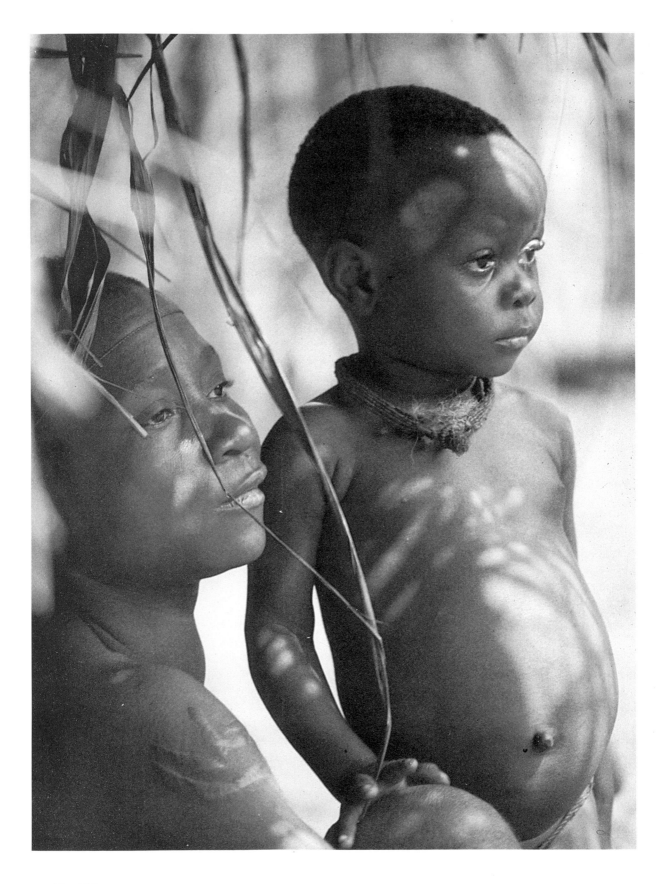

In Search of Self-Reliance: Capitalism without Winter

What has *self-reliance* got to do with *snow*? In this chapter we shall examine the fate of capitalism in Africa from a radically different perspective. We shall explore the convergence of economic and ecological factors as the central explanation of the failure of capitalism in Africa so far.

Let us begin with the picture which confronts us. All the evidence seems to suggest that post-colonial Africa has to try to walk a tightrope between the abyss of decay and the sea of dependency. When an African country tries to break out of dependency, it finds itself and its institutions in the process of decay. Nkrumah's Ghana and Nyerere's Tanzania put up a fight against dependency – and found their economies condemned to decomposition.

On the other hand, Francophone African countries such as the Ivory Coast have so far averted too rapid a pace of economic decay but only at the expense of considerable dependence upon the former colonial power.

Post-colonial Africa is finding it hard to walk that tightrope. Virtually all African countries have fallen into either the abyss of decay or the ocean of dependency. Some countries are desperately swinging between the two.

Although we have used ecological metaphors such as 'abyss' and 'ocean' as figures of speech, part of Africa's predicament is indeed environmentally determined. It is *not* geographically incongruous to talk about the '*winter* of Africa's discontent'. Part of the African condition has been the absence of winter – and the cumulative effect of that absence has been momentous for African cultures. Let us first define the 'winter of Africa's discontent'.

Between Environment and Embourgeoisement
We start from the premise that winter has had a role to play in creating a predisposition to plan among those Western countries which later evolved a capitalist ethos. Before the West developed a culture of industrial capitalism, it had to evolve a culture of calculation and anticipation. We shall demonstrate how a climate of demarcated seasons contributed to this cultural evolution in the West.

We also hope to show that the origins of engineering lie in construction for basic shelter. At least until the coming of Islam and Western culture, tropical Africa's deprivation of winter had resulted in simpler forms of shelter – with long-term consequences for the level of engineering developed in the region.

Third, it should be borne in mind that the origins of sophisticated manufacture for mass consumption lie in textiles and dress culture. Yet, in most

opposite, BaMbuti mother and child, Central African Republic

Masai women outside their home in the Great Rift Valley, Kenya

parts of tropical Africa, dress culture was underdeveloped before the coming of Islam and Western culture. Again, the *winter-gap* was partly accountable for this underdevelopment.

An even earlier differentiation between Europe and tropical Africa could be traced to diverse uses of fire. Europe had to find more varied roles for fire in European culture partly because of the exigencies of climate. It is possible that winter made a contribution to the earlier smelting of metals in European culture as compared with tropical Africa's experience in a winter void.

But we should continue to bear in mind that the causes of Africa's economic underdevelopment do not lie only in ecology and climate; they also lie in political economy. In the modern period the most important force in the field of political economy has been Western imperialism.

Unfortunately, the link between imperialism and capitalism in Africa has not been as simple as most commentators have assumed. The greatest mockery about Western imperialism does not lie in its promotion of capitalism in Africa; it lies in its failure to do so. As discussed in the previous chapter, the West destroyed traditional African economies without really creating capitalist foundations to replace them. In this sense, the problem of dependency in Africa is about who controls capitalism within Africa, rather than about the merits of capitalism as such.

In what sense did Western imperialism fail to create African capitalism? The answer lies in the phenomenon of distorted capitalist transmission. Western imperialism transmitted capitalist greed to Africa – but without capitalist discipline. It transmitted the profit motive – but not entrepreneurial persistence and risk-taking. Western materialism was transferred to Africa, but not Western rationalism.

How did this distortion happen? The fundamental reason is that aforesaid combination of ecological and economic factors. The ecological factors are sometimes manifested through indigenous cultures as products of Africa's climate and geography. The economic factors in recent times are mainly a product of Western colonisation and imperialism. In this chapter we shall address ourselves to this persistent convergence between ecology and economics in Africa's experience across the generations.

The Nile at Luxor, Egypt

There is an ecological war going on in Africa. At one level it is a war between the sun and Africa's water resources. The continent is potentially well-endowed in both solar energy and hydro-power. But the two forces are not pulling in the same direction. Like God, the sun both gives water and takes it away. But in recent times the sun has been taking away water more than giving it in Africa.

Nevertheless there are places in Africa where water has been playing a pre-eminent role – sometimes moving considerable amounts of earth and soil. Along Africa's rivers one witnesses deep unfathomed caves of nature, part of the hidden majesty of the continent, distant from tourists and property speculators. It is one of the games which African rivers have been playing in re-arranging things. Part of ancient Uganda has now been transferred and become part of modern Egypt. And every year part of modern Ethiopia is transformed by the Blue Nile into part of modern Sudan.

At one level, this is a game of Pan-Africanism. Mixing soil between African countries is like mixing blood among adopted brothers – a cut in your arm mixing blood with a cut in my arm. African rivers have been playing a game of Pan-Africanism of soil transfer. My loss as an African is your gain, brother.

Interestingly enough, the Nile was also one of the meeting points between Africa's primordial ecology and Africa's imperial economics. In pharaonic Egypt it was believed that whoever controlled the Nile controlled Egypt. The gods at that time were believed to control the Nile.

By the nineteenth century the British decided to step into the shoes of the gods. The British successfully sought to control the White Nile from the Mediterranean to its source at Jinja in Uganda. They also successfully prevented the Blue Nile in Ethiopia from falling into hostile hands.

It has been argued that British preoccupation with the unity of the Nile Valley was a central factor in the historical episode of the scramble for Africa. The ecological factor of the River Nile was an integral component of the imperial factor of European expansionism.

But on closer scrutiny the most fundamental factor in North-South relations is not the ecological war between the sun and the South's water resources. Within Africa the most fundamental convergence between ecology and economics is not the history of the Nile Valley either.

Even more fundamental than the divide between solar energy and hydro-power is that older ecological tension – the supreme tension of the *winter-gap* in Africa's historical experience.

The Frozen Ecology of Capitalism

Africa is the most tropical of all continents. It is cut almost in half by the equator and it is traversed by both the Tropics of Cancer and Capricorn.

One result of being the most tropical of all continents is being the continent which is furthest removed from the experience of winter. Of course, both the extreme north of Africa and the extreme south do have some kind of

The dam at Jinja, Uganda – the source of the White Nile

cold season but in comparison with other continents even northern and southern Africa's cold seasons are relatively mild. What is indisputable is tropical Africa's exceptional climatic distance from the realities of winter.

As we asked before, what has this to do with the problem of dependency *versus* self-reliance in contemporary Africa? What has Africa's *winter-gap* got to do with the continent's economic problems today?

One question which has arisen is whether contemporary Africa's apparent incapacity to plan ahead is partly due to the absence of winter in our economic experience over the centuries. The inhabitants of the northern hemisphere of the globe learnt quite early that it was necessary to 'make hay while the sun shines'. They knew that there would always be a predictable frozen season every year when the land yielded very little – and that the lives of both animals and human beings would be at risk if advance plans were not made to ensure the availability of food over the several months of barren winter.

Parts of Africa near the desert just outside the tropics do also have the equivalent of barren winter – the dry season. But, of course, drought is not as precisely cyclic as the winter. And neither recurrent drought nor recurrent winter on their own are enough to create a culture of anticipation. In the history of Europe, winter interacted with other variables to create over time such a culture of anticipation. But in the history of tropical Africa there was no real equivalent of winter to foster a culture of planning, the will to anticipate. The long-term consequences for both Europe and Africa were considerable.

Why has tropical Africa been such a poor soil for the transplantation of capitalism in more recent times? Africa's climate is part of the explanation – including the cultural consequences of Africa's winter-gap. Capitalism is a process which involves both accumulation and investment. When purposefully undertaken, investment entails calculation and anticipation. Doctrinally the capitalist ideology abhors centralised national planning. But every rational capitalist corporation has to undertake its own planning. Indeed, capitalism without planning is void. We must therefore view the growth of capitalism as an expansion of the culture of anticipation in the economic history of Europe.

It is not entirely accidental that mature capitalism developed in the colder parts of Europe, rather than along the Mediterranean. Of course, the level of capitalist maturity did not necessarily correlate with the precise centigrade degree of the climatic temperature of a given country. But it may not be altogether fortuitous that although places such as Greece, Italy, Spain and Portugal had dazzled the world in pre-industrial eras, it was the colder climates further north in Europe which inaugurated the twin revolutions of modern industrialisation and capitalism.

Capitalism was later to become the illegitimate mother of economic determinism and helped to provoke the doctrine (espoused by both socialists and non-socialists) that economic forces were the primary movers of history.

Temet's dunes with acacia trees in the foreground, Niger

And yet capitalism itself was a child of *climatic* determinism – mediated through *cultural* response. For more than 200 years the most successful forces of capitalism have manifested themselves in countries which experience cold winters. Not all countries in the winter zone are successful capitalist societies, but almost all highly successful capitalist societies so far (including Japan) are within the winter zone. The culture of economic anticipation has triumphed amidst the chilly winds of colder climates.

But climate does not usually act directly in conditioning patterns of human behaviour. Climate influences behaviour partly by helping to shape culture. And culture in turn includes religion.

There is a school of thought which links the origins of capitalism with the Protestant Reformation. Max Weber develops this theory particularly well in his epoch-making sociological study, *The Protestant Ethic and the Spirit of Capitalism*. According to this theory, it is not a coincidence that the most advanced capitalist countries of the West have tended to be Protestant. Leading Catholic countries of Europe were outpaced by their Protestant neighbours. Spain and Portugal were peripheralised, Italy was relatively backward, Ireland withdrew into its Catholic shell.

The only exception was France. But although France subscribed to Cath-

Cultivators of the land in Nigeria

olicism it had developed a Protestant culture, especially from its liberal revolution of 1789 onwards. The French Revolution was the country's functional equivalent of a Protestant Reformation – complete with a rebellion against the monasteries. But a residual loyalty to Rome was saved, thus making France the exception which proves the rule that Protestantism has been a more fertile ground for modern capitalism than Roman Catholicism.

Curiously enough, while Protestantism was an outburst of religious rejuvenation, capitalism was a major secularising force. And yet on closer look, both movements sought to reduce the role of churches and priests and, in so doing, were helping to shrink the domain of both Caesar and God in favour of the individual. Protestantism – by reducing the role of priests in Man's relationship with God – helped to foster the idea of religion as a matter for the private individual. This was a form of religious individualism. Capitalism, on the other hand, favoured economic individualism, at least at that stage of its development.

The Protestant ethos tended to emphasise that God controlled much less of our lives than was once assumed. The capitalist ethos went further because it tended to emphasise that we were in greater control of nature than we previously imagined. Protestantism was a doctrine of shrinking divine control over Man. Capitalism was a doctrine of expanding human control over nature.

It was as if winter were beckoning western and northern Europeans back to the challenges of nature – back to the problems of survival rather than the problems of salvation. The Middle East was the grand geographical laboratory of religious strategies of salvation. Western and northern Europe became major laboratories of secular strategies of survival. The Middle East and the Mediterranean have been great laboratories of religion. Western and northern Europe became great laboratories of science. The Middle East and the Mediterranean led pre-eminently in quest of God. Western and northern Europe led in quest of nature. The cultures of the winter zone were tilting the balance between the paradigm of the supernatural and the universe of nature. Western and northern Europe (the winter zone) were leading in the natural paradigm.

But sharper than the distinction between colder Europe and warmer Europe is the distinction between Europe as a whole and tropical Africa. What climatic factors left Europe triumphant and tropical Africa vulnerable?

We do know that the winter-gap in Africa – the absence of winter as a problem of survival – affected the construction culture of the African continent. All human societies need food, drink and sex. But human societies differ markedly in their need for shelter. Societies with severe winters need artificial shelter more markedly than most other societies.

In much of tropical Africa shelter could consist either of natural coverage or of modest use of mud and grass or thatch or even animal dung. Human beings in tropical Africa do not have to engage in elaborate constructions against the elements in order to survive. Africans have needed less shelter than Europeans. The imperative of shelter in the course of technological history turned out to be more salient than the imperative of food production.

Out of the culture of construction emerged different forms of engineering as a basis of technological transformation. Building for shelter against the winter was only the beginning. Erecting special homes was the origin of skills of building bridges and hydro-electric dams. Medieval European efforts to shelter from snow or from the cold winds of northern winter were part of the Western expertise which went into the construction of the Akosombo dam in Ghana or the steel mill in Zaire in the twentieth century.

On the other hand, the simpler forms of shelter so characteristic of sub-Saharan Africa, the modest demands of protection against the elements symbolised by our mud-houses with grass thatching, constitute part of the historical background to our own dependency on others for skills of construction.

Those parts of Africa which do have a cold season – the extreme north and the extreme south – did develop skills of construction quite early. The most impressive were, of course, the skills of pharaonic Egypt and the builders of the pyramids, on one side, and the skills of the architects of Great Zim-

St George's Church, the sunken splendour of Lalibela, Ethiopia

babwe, on the other. These were areas of Africa which were subject to significantly colder seasons. In the case of Egypt, there was also the millennia of interacting with other cultures, providing a stimulus for even greater innovation along the Nile.

But in tropical Africa proper – the area between the Tropics of Cancer and Capricorn – almost the only exception to the cultures of mud-houses is Ethiopia. Even in Ethiopia it may be significant that the greatest achievements of skills of construction emerged in the highlands rather than the lowlands. And high on the plateaus of Ethiopia the winds can be as cold as they are during winter in western Europe. Out of that coldness emerged the impressive skills which carved out of solid rock the miraculous sunken churches of Lalibela. And when those skills were reinforced by other cultures, the magnificent palaces of Gondar were erected.

Elsewhere in Africa it has been said that the genius of Black people does not lie in building high but in digging deep. As a Black poet has put it,

> . . . My negritude is neither a tower nor a cathedral;
> It plunges into the red flesh of the earth . . .[1]

But in upper Ethiopia nature has built high; Man has sometimes dug deep. The local people in Lalibela cannot even believe their own ingenuity. Instead, many believe that angels descended from heaven to help carve out the sunken churches. And many native people are convinced that God Himself was the grand architect.

At least as old as the skills of elaborate construction are the skills connected with smelting metals. The origins of those skills probably lie in the diversification of the uses of fire.

Fire was probably first discovered in Africa, but its uses in tropical Africa were limited for a long time to such domestic purposes as cooking, therapeutic burning of a particular part of one's skin, burning off waste and the like. A particularly glaring gap in most parts of tropical Africa was the use of fire for winter-related purposes. Because there was no winter, the use of fire did not become as diversified as it did in temperate zones. One result was tropical Africa's delayed utilisation of metal smelting – though some parts of the continent did stumble upon the skill quite early, and other parts of Africa learnt the art from other cultures.

A clearer impact of the winter-gap is, as we indicated, its effect on dress culture. Climate in tropical Africa did not demand elaborate covering for the body. We know that house shelter was not too elaborate before the impact of Islam and Western culture; neither was dress culture.

Once again there were exceptions. Ethiopia was still very distinctive, and was endowed with sophisticated dress traditions of its own. Parts of west Africa also developed important styles of dress, but partly stimulated by other civilisations. But, compared with the civilisations of the winter zone, most of tropical Africa had a relatively simple culture of attire. There were African societies which did not even bother to dress at all – ranging from pre-colonial Karimojong in Uganda to pre-colonial Tiv in Nigeria.

Weaving and textiles generally are among the earliest forms of indus-

The texture of different civilisations: *main picture*, Tunisian cloth; *inset*, Kano dyers, Nigeria

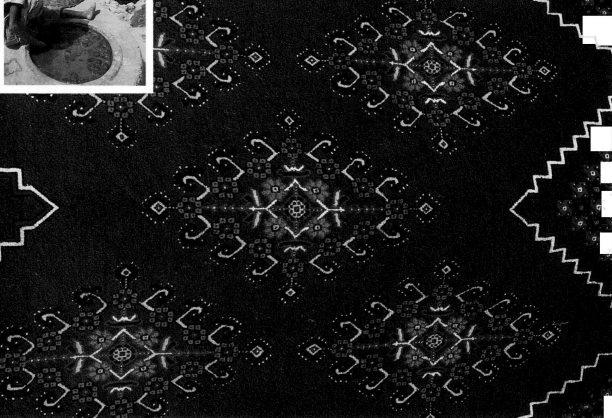

trialisation in the world. The dress-gap in pre-Islamic and pre-colonial tropical Africa deprived much of the continent of the opportunities to deepen and diversify textile industries. Africa's dress-gap was one of the consequences of tropical Africa's winter-gap.

Indeed, England's own Industrial Revolution from the eighteenth century onwards was, as we indicated, substantially stimulated by the textile industry in Lancashire and, later, Yorkshire. The elaborate dress culture which winter had generated in Western civilisation was influential in an economic revolution in world history.

The wheel was about to come full circle. Winter had played a part in the origins of capitalism and the Protestant work ethic. Winter had then played a part in the origins of the Industrial Revolution in Europe. With that revolution came the need for new worlds to conquer. Winter played a part, therefore, in the origins of Western imperialism as well. What Karl Marx called the 'millocracy' of Lancashire and Yorkshire (people owning textile mills) were among the main architects of British expansionism.

The Political Economy of Dependency

Within Africa the Nile Valley was among the first to fall victim to the specifications of the 'millocracy'. Even before direct colonisation Egypt was already devoting its energies to the production of cotton for export. Sudan and later Uganda were to follow 'suit' in more senses than one. The role of Africa as a source of raw materials for the industries of the winter zone began with the raw materials for textile mills. The stage was set for the phenomenon of economic dependency in Africa's relations with the domains of winter in the Western world.

At first this appeared to be like a process of Africa's incorporation into the universe of capitalism. In one sense this was so. Africa was becoming almost inexorably absorbed into the new global system of supply and demand.

But while the resources of Africa were indeed being incorporated into world capitalism, the people of Africa were not being transformed into effective capitalists. Africans were, on the whole, objects in a game of capitalism rather than subjects. They were basically pawns in a bourgeois chess-game; almost never real players in that game.

It is in this sense that Africa's central economic problem in the post-colonial era is not too much capitalism but too little. As we have indicated in another chapter, the genius of capitalism is production. The capitalist countries of the winter zone today constitute the biggest economic producers in human history. But Africa's capacity to produce seems to be declining rather than rising. Effective capitalism has yet to arrive.

If the genius of capitalism is production, the genius of socialism is distribution. And yet one cannot distribute poverty or socialise the means of non-production. Africa will need to develop a productive capacity before it can meaningfully implement a programme of distribution. At least to some extent Africa has to become capitalist before it can genuinely become socialist.

To that extent Karl Marx was right when he identified capitalism as the illegitimate mother of socialism.

Why did capitalist imperialism in Africa fail to re-create the 'Dark Continent' in its own image? Culturally Africa may, in some respects, look more and more like the Western world. But economically and technologically it looks less and less like the West. Why did the goddess of capitalism fail to create a Black image of herself?

We are back to the constraints of ecology, on one side, and the constraints of political economy, on the other. A country becomes successfully capitalist either through acclimatisation (effective response to the exigencies of climate and the imperative of winter) or through acculturation (effective shift in values in response to external stimulus). As we have indicated, tropical Africa's climate had not been ideal for either the capitalist ethos of anticipation and maximisation of returns or for the pre-capitalist stimulus of civil engineering and textile consumerism. The African ecology did not foster capitalist formation. The winter-gap 'condemned' tropical Africa to a pre-capitalist condition.

But could Western imperialism serve as a functional substitute for winter? Could Western economic penetration of Africa compensate for ecological inhibitions to the growth of Black capitalism? Could acculturation be a genuine alternative to acclimatisation as a process of inducting Africa into mature capitalism?

As it happened, Western imperialism failed to compensate for Africa's winter-gap. On the contrary, a number of colonial distortions of African economies aggravated the African condition – and some of these difficulties were later compounded by ill-conceived post-colonial correctives. In other words, some of the problems created by colonialism were made worse by some post-colonial solutions. It is to these distortions of the African condition that we must now turn.

A major factor created by the West's colonisation of African economies has been the stubborn export-import distortion. Here it is worth noting the difference between Islam's impact on African trade and that of the West. For centuries Islam fostered both trade within Africa and trade between Africa and the outside world. The trans-Saharan trade is perhaps the best illustration.

If the Almighty had wanted to convert a beast to a religion, the camel would have been a prime candidate for conversion to Islam. With the Arab conquest of north Africa, trade across the Sahara received a new stimulus. Goods started moving in both directions. Into west Africa came salt, beads and animals (horses and camels). The trade transformed patterns of transportation, economy, diet and warfare. Out of west Africa northwards and eastwards went ivory, gold, wood and sometimes slaves.

In a sense the most important commodity in this trade turned out to be Islam itself. It came to west Africa on camelback and horseback, and proved to be more resilient, less perishable, more capable of expansion than any of

A camel caravan, Algeria

the rest of the merchandise. It is in that sense that Islam in Africa spread more by the camel than by the sword.

On the precise issue of the import-export orientation, it should also be noted that much of the trade fostered by Islam was internal to the African continent, as well as external. Culture and trade were often fellow travellers, across the desert, along the Nile, across the savannah. The beginning of economic Pan-Africanism lay in the movements of Muslim traders – Arab, Berber, Hausa, Swahili and others. To this extent, Islamic trade was a force for regional integration. Muslim Black Africa became culturally dependent upon the Arab world. What Muslim Africa at that time did *not* become was to be *economically* dependent on Islam in any deep sense.

On the other hand, the Western world's economic impact on Africa was considerably more devastating. In a sense it began with Europe's sweet tooth in the wake of the Industrial Revolution. It is a story of economic imperialism which traversed all the way from west Africa to the West Indies – and from the sugar plantations of Jamaica to the tea plantations of Kenya.

It is only in recent times that the enormity of the import-export distortion has been more clearly understood. Have Africans been concentrating so much on incidental food products that they have not given adequate attention to fundamental food products such as grain, meat and root crops? Have we been subordinating the main course of our own diet to the 'desserts and beverages' of European dining tables? Have we been so busy responding to Europe's sweet tooth that we have forgotten our own hungry mouths?

But Africa does not merely export coffee, tea and cocoa. It also exports minerals which are strategic and fundamental to Western economies, as we have indicated in an earlier chapter. And so the exploiters dig up Africa faster than they have ever done before.

The Capital-Labour Distortion

The colonial legacies did not only limit themselves to creating an import-export distortion which inhibited the proper maturation of indigenous capitalism. Colonialism also distorted the very relationship between capital and labour in an African context. Both in the colonial period and in the post-colonial era, Africa has been encouraged to go for capital-intensive, expensive projects, which need considerable foreign exchange – rather than for labour-intensive strategies needing local workers.

This fascination with capital-intensive projects has sometimes been even worse after independence than before. Post-colonial governments, eager to compensate for colonial neglect, have tried to seek high technology and grand scale. Kwame Nkrumah, for example, was a little too impatient to embark on the industrialisation of Ghana with borrowed capital from the lands of the winter zone. Nkrumah, in fact, had two major ambitions in his political life – the unification of Africa and the industrialisation of Ghana. With the hydro-electric dam at Akosombo on the Volta River, Nkrumah sought to realise both aspirations, to give them a 'concrete' expression, as it were. He envisioned electricity for neighbours as well as for Ghana.

Because of Nkrumah's own experiences as a student in the United States,

Valco Aluminium Works,
Ghana

both of his mature political aspirations were rooted in the American dream. He recognised the United States as a model both of continental unification and technological advancement. And so, when he became Ghana's founder-president, he turned with naive simplicity to the Americans to help him realise his dreams. People such as Richard Nixon, Dwight Eisenhower and John F. Kennedy were all involved at different stages of negotiations and discussions about the Akosombo project.

On the whole, the Akosombo Dam is not a monument to genuine co-operation. It is a monument to exploitation. Behind the façade of technological advancement is the reality of economic failure. Ghana's industrialisation might have been delayed by at least two generations as a result of this Volta River project. The American dream had soured into a Ghanaian nightmare.

The original multi-purpose ambition of the project was not only to generate the nation's electricity, but also to provide widescale irrigation, the promotion of a fishing industry, the establishment of additional tourist facilities on the waters of the Volta River, and the promotion of an aluminium smelting industry with inter-related canning factories.

Valco Aluminium Works were given the industrial rights of smelting aluminium. The parent company in the United States, Kaiser, negotiated

Akosombo Dam, Ghana

from Nkrumah's Ghana the cheapest electricity in the world for Valco. These give-away rates of electricity continued to be extended to Valco until the era of Jerry Rawlings nearly twenty years later, when Ghanaian pressures for changes in the arrangements became more insistent. The changes were still a bargain for this company.

But did not the aluminium industry help Ghana utilise its own indigenous bauxite? On the contrary, Valco imported semi-processed bauxite all the way from the shores of Jamaica to be used in the Ghanaian factory. Barely 100 miles away Ghana had its own supplies of bauxite. Why was this resource not used? Why was there no attempt to establish an inter-related industrial complex?

The company claimed that it would be uneconomical to use Ghanaian bauxite. But was this the real reason? Or was the explanation to be sought more in the fact that Kaiser, the parent firm, had Jamaican bauxite already in its possession, and had the facilities in Jamaica to start processing it? What is more, Kaiser had the ships to transport that semi-processed Caribbean bauxite all the way from the shores of the West Indies to Ghana.

With regard to the Akosombo Dam itself, water was, of course, supposed to be the raw material for that power-producing industry. But water in the Volta River has quite often proved to be in short supply. The maximum level of water for the operation of the Dam was 276 feet. The minimum was 248 feet. When I visited the Dam in 1984 the level of water was ten feet *below* the minimum. The result was that at that time four out of the six turbines were not working. What was the cause of this shortfall?

Africans, once mesmerised by the expertise of the winter zone, are only just beginning to discover that Western calculations are not infallible. When the Akosombo Dam was built the Western experts apparently overcalculated by about 20 per cent the likely volume of water available for the dam. Because of that overestimate, there is now a shortfall in electricity generated. This shortfall has been compounded by drought. A combination of Western human error and nature's cruelty has resulted in a relatively empty technological monument.

Directly related to the original grand design of the Akosombo Dam was a canning factory for corned beef. Part of the original idea was the promotion of a cattle industry through irrigation, and the use of Ghana's aluminium to develop the canning complex. A canning plant was built in northern Ghana with EEC, mainly West German, aid, with the intention of buying up and processing the surplus beef of the area. However the new Volta Meat Canning plant managers soon found out that the local people did not want to sell their so-called 'surplus' cattle because it was a form of currency in bride-wealth and other transactions. The attempt to buy beef from across the border in nearby Upper Volta came up against similar problems as the people desired as many cattle as possible for reasons of financial insurance and social status. In the 1970s the factory was able for a time to import cattle from the Sahel as the drought forced owners to sell. Eventually the factory

The Western work ethic and the Black man's burden

was forced to resort to importing beef from as far away as Argentina, a situation which lasted for at least two whole years up to the end of 1983. This in turn led to appalling transport problems as large refrigerated lorries suffered heavy wear and tear and frequent breakdown on the inadequate road from the port of Tema up to Bolgatanga, a journey of over 400 miles. To make matters worse, it was found that cans could not easily be made from local aluminium because a special alloy which was necessary was not available, so cans had to be imported from West Germany. In any case, lack of foreign exchange made it impossible to obtain spare parts for the lorries or the factory itself, or to import beef or cans.

The grand design of the Akosombo Dam and its industrial extensions is one powerful illustration of a capital-intensive approach to industrialisation which went awry. But Africa is replete with ambitious projects of a comparable kind which yielded limited results. The distorted equation of capital intensiveness continues to mesmerise many a decision-maker in the continent.

Imperialism and the Work Ethic

But while it is true that Africa should explore labour-intensive strategies for development more often than capital-intensive ones, the question still arises whether or not colonialism has left the labour option intact. Even if African decision-makers do decide to turn their backs on grand dams and elaborate steel mills, do they really have the alternative of creatively utilising African labour? Or has the winter zone's interaction with Africa helped to destroy the labour imperative, while at the same time enhancing the lure of capital?

A cave in Zanzibar where slaves taken by Arab traders were believed to have been held in transit

The impact of the people from the winter zone upon Africa included considerable damage to Africa's traditional work ethic. It began with slavery and the slave trade. The misery which surrounded slavery was part of the destruction of Africa's own traditions of voluntary work in a collective context.

It was in places such as the dungeons beneath Cape Coast Castle and the Elmina cells in Ghana that the captives waited for the slave ships that would take them aboard. They were often packed in close together, sweating on each other, sometimes lying in their own urine and in their own filth. If cholera broke out a whole cell could be wiped out almost overnight. And yet they were supervised by the same Westerners who very often proved supremely skilful in protecting their cattle or their sheep and yet here they were so appallingly inefficient in protecting the lives of their captives. Yes I know, we've had slavery, too, domestic slavery was not alien to African traditions. But this scale of callousness, this scale of indifference, was totally foreign to African societies. I am just beginning to understand what a Jew must feel like who visits Auschwitz or some other Nazi concentration camp and experiences those powerful emotions of bewilderment, of anger, of infinite sadness. Yet what was at stake in those dungeons was more than the lives of the captives, vital as those were. Also compromised in a longer-term perspective was the concept of voluntary labour in African cultures.

The slave trade rapidly transformed Africans into the most humiliated race in human history. Cages, iron balls, whips, all became part of the totality of the Black experience. Within two centuries alone over 12 million Africans were exported to the New World, to the Americas. The racial map of the world was changed permanently and irreversibly.

Female captives were subject to additional hazards. Very often they were stored separately and they were exposed to the danger of sexual abuse even before they crossed the Atlantic. In those castles along west Africa's coast, for example, European governors used to regard their female captives as reservoirs to satisfy their own sexual appetites. A parade would take place, the governor would survey the contours from up there, choose what he wanted and the female would be presented to him. If the woman became pregnant the woman could gain in two ways: she could either fetch a higher price now that she was the potential mother of a lighter-skinned slave, or she could become the concubine of successive Europeans right there on the west African coast. Such were the obscenities of this commerce in human merchandise. These women were ruthlessly transformed from economic producers on their own farms into sex objects in bondage.

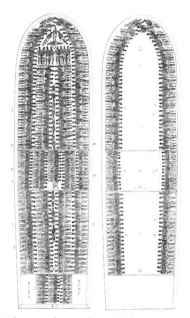

A diagram showing how tightly slaves were packed into slave ships; it is not surprising that up to one-third of slaves died during their journey

In the little boats between the fort and the big slave ships the captives cast their last glance at their ancestral continent. Some of them were quite familiar with the coastline, others captured further inland were seeing this coast probably for the first time, but also for the last time, the land of their ancestors. It was a very complete farewell. The slaves never returned. What was at least as bad – their descendants never remembered. Every Irish-American knows precisely which village his or her parents or grandparents departed from to go to America. Every Italian-American is the same, every Swedish-American. But for African-Americans it is different. They do not know which community they sprang from. They have been denied the privilege of nostalgia because their ancestors, enslaved, were uprooted rudely and blindly. But where did the wiping of memory begin? Right there in Africa between the slave fort and the big slave ship. One last look at Mother Africa before painful forgetfulness began. And one last memory of toil without the whip, of volition in production.

The Africa that the slaves left behind was a significantly more dangerous Africa than the Africa the Europeans first found when they arrived. I don't mean by that simply that the new Africa had cannons. I mean that the gun generally was a much more important feature of life in Africa than it had ever been before. Indeed gun trade and slave trade had been interlocking entities. Guns were used as currency for slaves, one exchanged guns for slaves. Now you realise how bad an exchange, how uneven a bargain this was. Africa had exported to the West men and women, potential implements of production. Africa had imported from the West guns – by definition instruments of destruction. Africa had helped to enhance the industrial revolution of the West through those very slaves sent by force. And yet the guns out in Africa initiated a new culture of violence. The traditional bow and arrow was a very democratic weapon, everybody could make their own bow and arrow. But gunpowder, the gun, that was a revolution in destruction. The era of explosions had arrived.

All this was part of the total cost for the work ethic in Africa. The legacy of the slave trade helped to undermine within Africa traditions of production and enhance the legacy of destruction.

Then under colonial rule came *forced labour* without commercialised sale of 'niggers'. Nowhere was this post-slavery forced labour more brutally realised than in the so-called Congo Free State under King Leopold II of the Belgians. The natives of the Congo were compelled to produce rubber for the rubber monarch under ruthless conditions. King Leopold of the Belgians had elaborate forms of punishment for those who did not deliver: unrelenting forced labour, mutilated limbs, villages razed to the ground because of the 'offence' of a single individual. Populations were decimated. When Leopold's ambition arrived in the Congo, it was not the natives who needed to be civilised; it was the newly arrived white man.

Portuguese colonialism in Africa also opted for forced labour. Under the Portuguese the practice continued for much longer than under the Belgians. Much of economic production in Mozambique and Angola for generations was undertaken under some kind of whip, either literal or on pain of some other kind of punishment. Again a major cultural casualty of this practice was the concept of work as a process of self-fulfilment.

In some of the neighbouring African colonies there were more disguised forms of involuntary labour. British colonial administrators experimented with some of these devious devices. How do you make the natives work for Europeans when they would prefer to remain on their own small farms? Slave labour by the days of Cecil Rhodes as an empire-builder could no longer be countenanced. Direct forced labour in a British colony would lead to awkward questions in parliament in London and general controversy in the newspapers. There was a third alternative – taxing the native. But tax for what? The colonialists decided it did not really matter. The native could be taxed for having a head – a poll tax. Or he could be taxed for having a home – a hut tax. But the tax had to be paid in a currency which the white man himself printed or minted. 'Come and get it!' – the white man summoned. Earn the currency from the white man by working for him.

It took us Africans a while before we realised what was happening. One would have thought that if the white man came and took away my land, and then started talking about payment, it would be payment to me as rent or compensation for the land he unilaterally occupied. But the white man was instead charging me tax and rent! It began to dawn upon us that we had not only lost our land; we were also losing control over our labour. Again the longer-term cultural consequences for Africa's work ethic were severe and profoundly damaging. One's will was being divorced from one's work; one's liberty separated from one's labour.

The fourth factor behind the erosion of the work ethic in Africa was the caste system which colonial rule helped to create. The colonial master did not normally dig his own land physically, or clean his own cattle, or sweep his own barn, or wash his own clothes, or change his own tyres. There was always a Black man around to do the physical chores. The white man's crop was harvested by Black hands, the tea leaves or coffee beans were plucked by Black fingers, the bricks were laid by Black masons, the heavy boxes carried by Black porters, the dirtiest and most dangerous jobs in mining were relegated to Black labour. The impression created was that physical work was a badge of underprivilege, the lot of the lower castes.

At its more elegant level in places such as the White Highlands of colonial Kenya, the white man's life-style was a culture of leisure, of gentility, often of conceit. Its aristocratic equivalent in Britain was already dying before its proponents moved to the colonies. Some people believe in the transmigration of souls – a soul moving from one creature to another. In places such as the White Highlands of Kenya one can still witness a transmigration of cultures – something already dead at its point of ancestry in Britain found a moment of reincarnation in far-away Africa.

This aristocratic legacy of masters and servants had its adverse consequences for the work ethic in post-colonial Africa, just as it had on industrial relations in Britain. White masters in Africa drinking their gin and tonic leisurely while their servants pulled off their boots – this was the colonial caste system which transformed physical labour into a burden of servitude.

A fifth factor which affected the work ethic in Africa was the nature of colonial education with its heavy literary and non-technical emphasis. Even when the missionaries or the colonial policymakers tried to introduce practical or vocational courses, the reception by Africans was often hostile. Most Africans had come to regard Western education as a method of becoming more like the white man – a way of graduating *out* of physical labour. Introducing carpentry or farming in an otherwise Western system of education went against the nature of the colonial caste system. In my own school in Mombasa when I was a child, carpentry was by far the most unpopular subject among the pupils. It was also the only practical subject taught at that time. Learning carpentry in the process of being 'civilised' at a Western school was seen as a contradiction and as a retrograde step.

A sixth factor concerning the fate of the work ethic in Africa takes us back to the ideology of capitalism. The British, especially, arrived in Africa with

New styles of leisure

John Locke's ideas about land being a common heritage of mankind as a whole until an individual puts labour into a piece of the land and makes it his own. A river is owned by everybody – until I dip my bucket into it and take out a bucketful of my own. This was Locke's labour theory of value. European settlers liked to believe that much of the land they occupied was unused when they arrived. European 'labour' made the land European property.

Locke's theory linked the right of property to the exertion of labour. In the White Highlands of Kenya and in much of southern Africa the real labour going into agriculture was primarily African, yet the right to property was European. A divorce had occurred between property and labour.

In the post-colonial era the African élite has borrowed a leaf from its previous white masters and puts more emphasis on accumulating property than on exerting labour. It is one more distortion in the process of capitalist-formation in Africa.

The seventh factor behind the demise of the African work ethic is the erosion of indigenous African safeguards against social parasitism, against the temptation to live off relatives or patrons. Before colonisation indigenous cultures had their own checks and balances between ethnic solidarity and hospitality on one side and the tendency towards parasitism, on the other. Then came colonialism. By its very nature colonial rule was a supreme form of economic parasitism – Europeans living off others. No longer were Africans able to obey the traditional wisdom which is captured in the Swahili adage, '*Mgeni siku mbili; siku ya tatu mpe jembe!*' ('Treat your guest as a guest for two days; but on the third day give him a hoe.') The colonial white man was at best an uninvited guest in Africa; but alas his African hosts were in no position to force a hoe upon him.

A longer-term consequence of European colonial parasitism continues to be its damaging effect on indigenous checks and balances in economic behaviour. African parasitic tendencies have been aggravated by the example of economic blood-sucking which colonialism set.

The final and, in some ways, most wide-ranging distortion of the work ethic in Africa concerns the sexual division of labour in African societies. Colonialism helped to create new dichotomies. These dichotomies included men working for wages while women worked for kind; men in the money economy while women pursued subsistence agriculture. In parts of Africa the sexual divergence in class terms amounted to the emergence of a male proletariat on one side and a female peasantry on the other; an urbanised male population and a more firmly rural female sector. This is particularly true of situations of migrant male labour – either to towns and cities or to mines. In mines in southern Africa a rigid gender apartheid is often enforced – wives are kept firmly in their ancestral rural areas while their men sweat in coal or gold mines hundreds of miles away.

Other colonial consequences for the gender question include the implications of Western deeds and titles for ownership of property on an individual basis. Western economic individualism and private ownership have reinforced male prerogatives in African societies yet women still do the bulk of the work.

The Western credit system usually requires those deeds and titles of private ownership as mortgage. The system in any case tends to regard males as more creditworthy than females. And so African men get the loans while African women continue to toil.

Whenever mechanisation has come to the African countryside, women have become more deeply marginalised. Where the agricultural technology is still based on the hoe, women continue to be pre-eminent as cultivators. When the technology advances to the use of a plough (involving the control of an ox), men begin to take over. When the technology attains the level of a tractor, male supremacy is consolidated. The scene is set where the man drives the tractor, while the woman is on bended knee with her hoe.

The work ethic in Africa continues to be bedevilled by factors which have ranged from the legacy of forced labour to the contradictions of Western literary education, from the impact of colonial parasitism to the interplay between gender and class-formation.

What is clear is that Western colonisation of Africa has failed to compensate for the economic consequences of Africa's winter-gap. The Western colonisers arrived from the cold, complete with the torch of the new capitalism. But the torch of capitalism was never really passed to the expectant Africans. Both the winter-gap and the imperial distortions continue to 'condemn' Africa to the fringes of production and the periphery of capitalism.

Conclusion

We have sought to show in this chapter that post-colonial Africa's central problem is not too much capitalism, but too little. The reasons for Africa's capitalist underdevelopment can be traced, on one side, to ecological factors and, on the other, to the political economy of imperialism.

Particularly important among ecological factors is tropical Africa's *winter-gap*. We have tried to show that the absence of a genuine winter in Africa has had consequences which have ranged from underdeveloped civil engineering for shelter to an underdeveloped indigenous textile tradition, from inadequately diversified utilisation of fire in tropical Africa to a fragile African capacity to plan for major seasonal fluctuations.

The Northern hemisphere in North-South relations is, in fact, the hemisphere of winter, or the winter zone. The Southern hemisphere is crudely the 'sun region'. Although the precise relationship between climate and the origins of capitalism is not as yet clear, we have suggested that there may well be an organic connection between ecology and capital accumulation, between climate and the Protestant Reformation.[2]

Of course extreme winter is far less productive. There are parts of the extreme north in which winter lasts almost the whole year. Such winters allow much narrower ranges of seasonal fluctuations and strategies of anticipation. Such winters also allow for limited cultivation and production. Modern capitalism could not have been born among the Eskimos, though their igloos are often more sophisticated than the traditional dwellings of the Masai or Karimojong in tropical Africa.

The relevant winters for the growth of a culture of anticipation are those which basically do not extend beyond a third of the year, and permit cultivation for the bulk of the year. Russia was in an intermediate position between the winter of prolonged barrenness and the winter of selective production. The Western part of Europe was better placed for the creative interplay between climate and capitalism, between ecology and production.

The inhabitants of this particular winter zone burst forth from their own countries in search of new worlds to conquer. Western capitalism resulted in Western expansionism.

The question which arose was whether this new force of Western imperialism would compensate for Africa's lack of the winter season – and generate African capitalism at last. Yet Africa failed to develop coherent and vigorous capitalism by either of those processes. Western imperialism had failed to compensate for Africa's deprivation of the creative experience of winter.

How did this imperialist failure happen? A number of colonial distortions were responsible – later compounded by ill-conceived post-colonial correctives. Colonial abuses have been compounded by post-colonial solutions.

As for the link between capitalism and dependency, this has turned out to be more complex than some radical analysts have indicated. Making capitalism more efficient in the Third World is a process of *reducing* dependency rather than increasing it. Capitalism in Nigeria is considerably less efficient than capitalism in South Korea. Nigeria has to buy more of what it needs from the West than does South Korea. Nigeria produces less of what it needs, and sells fewer things to the West, than does the Republic of South Korea. Nigeria is economically more vulnerable as a result.

It is in this sense that 'catching up' with Western capitalism becomes a method of reducing vulnerability to the West rather than increasing it. Of course, the most successful example has been Japan. Japanese success in capitalism has made the country less of an economic joke and more of an economic equal of the West than was the case when the Japanese capitalist experiment was much less efficient.

But would making Nigeria's capitalism more effective reduce Nigeria's chances of becoming a socialist country? Not according to the classical theories of Karl Marx and Friedrich Engels, both of whom regarded mature capitalism as the true foundation of the socialist revolution. They both believed that it was impossible to circumvent the capitalist phase if true socialism was to be constructed. How else could a society evolve the crucial antagonistic classes of the bourgeoisie and the proletariat? South Korea has evolved such classes more clearly than has Nigeria. South Korea therefore has stronger foundations for a future 'dictatorship of the proletariat' than Nigeria has as yet evolved.

It is possible that there is a stage of maturation of capitalism beyond which a socialist revolution is almost impossible. Instead of polarisation between the bourgeoisie and the proletariat, one could witness the increasing embourgeoisement of the proletariat. Workers could at the same time be investers and shareholders. Indeed, the middle class rather than the classical industrial working class could become the largest of the classes in society. The United States may have arrived at such a stage. It may be too late to expect a socialist revolution in the United States. Recent studies of Britain have shown an expansion of the property-owning class to embrace a majority of the population.[3]

But African countries can still evolve into genuine socialist societies – provided they first strengthen their capitalist foundations and create the relevant antagonistic classes.

Yet Africa is still in search of a functional equivalent of winter, in search of a fertile ground for capitalist innovation and production. Africa's quest for self-reliance is the pursuit of a dream – perhaps the pursuit of a Mid-winter Night's Dream. If Africa's climate refuses to freeze, can Africa's political economy be permitted to thaw? That is the ultimate question concerning self-reliance as Africa gropes for it amidst the maze of climatic and colonial impediments.

Towards Cultural Synthesis

The interplay of Africa's indigenous cultures with Islam on one side and Western civilisation on the other has had, as we have indicated, political and economic ramifications. But in the final analysis the central process of the triple heritage has been cultural and civilisational. We define culture as a system of inter-related values, active enough to influence and condition perception, judgement, communication and behaviour in a given society. We define civilisation as a culture which has endured, expanded, innovated and been elevated to new moral sensibilities. An interviewer once asked India's Mahatma Gandhi, 'What do you think of Western civilisation?' The Mahatma is reported to have replied, 'I didn't know they had any!' It was presumably the West's 'moral sensibilities' which Mahatma Gandhi was questioning.

But by the other criteria of the concept of 'civilisation', especially that of innovation, the Western world surely scores rather high in the last three or four centuries of human history. For our purposes in this book the word civilisation can be applied to the Western and Islamic as well as indigenous legacies, provided we bear in mind that the term is always relative and somewhat hyperbolic.

Stages of Cultural Integration

A number of stages can be discerned in the evolution of the triple heritage at this cultural level. Initially, there is the simple phenomenon of culture contact, two systems of values being introduced to each other and beginning to be aware of each other's peculiarities.

In African history this was followed by culture conflict, as the two or three legacies began to clash with each other when they discovered areas of incompatibility and mutual incoherence.

Third comes the stage of culture conquest as one legacy establishes a clear ascendancy and sometimes effectively compels the more vulnerable culture to surrender.

Then follows a period of cultural confusion. Among the members of the subordinate or vulnerable culture the choice is between cultural surrender, cultural alienation or cultural revival and the resurrection of original authenticity.

But is there really no other choice apart from surrender, alienation or revival? In reality there is a fourth possible outcome – cultural coalescence or integration, a fusion of two or more cultures into a new mixed legacy.

opposite, A villager and his new acquisition, Mali

What is Correct Behaviour?

It is not very easy to distinguish the stage of culture conflict from the stage of cultural confusion. Analytically, the culture conflict occurs when the indigenous system is still relatively intact and is resisting the encroachments and blandishments of the newly arrived civilisation seeking to impose its own will. The stage of culture confusion follows a partial conquest, a conversion of some of the leaders of the indigenous culture to the new gods of the conquerors, and a conflict of values within the same individuals creating psychological and moral bewilderment.

Nowhere is this better illustrated than on the issue of what constitutes corruption and abuse of privilege. The phenomenon of corrupt practices, conspicuous consumption and perversion of governmental procedures in Africa has its roots in the ideological flux which characterises the transition from indigenous moral restraints, on one side, to the complexities of modern discipline, on the other.

What is at stake, is the phenomenon of cultural transition. Politics in Africa, for example, are sometimes hard to keep clean merely because people are moving from one set of values to another. In no other area of life is this better illustrated than in the issue of ethnic solidarity and kinship obligations. Pressures are exerted on an African official or politician to remind him of those who share his social womb. People from his area or from his clan enquire on how best the well-placed African politician, or even academic, might help his kinsmen to gain admission to a job or to a scholarship. African vice-chancellors have been known to undergo agonising pressure to persuade them to help appoint members of their own 'tribe' to positions of authority and earning power within the universities over which they preside. When I was Dean of the Faculty of Social Sciences at Makerere University in Uganda I was under comparable pressure from relatives in Mombasa seeking to gain admission as students.

The ordinary people who exert these pressures on their more successful ethnic compatriots are often oblivious of the moral inconsistencies of the situation. It was after all traditionally acceptable that God helped those who helped their relatives. It was therefore right that a prospective Ibo porter should look to an established Ibo official for appointment, or that a young Yoruba graduate should look to a more highly placed Yoruba man for promotion. Before a clash of values entered the lives of these Nigerians, there might have been no moral dilemmas involved in such issues. But the Western world had now created a political entity called Nigeria, whose boundaries were not chosen by either the Ibo or the Yoruba, but whose reality cast Ibo and Yoruba in competition with each other for the resources of a colonially created political system. Moreover, with Western ideas came the issue of individual merit *versus* collective solidarity. Individual candidates for a scholarship have to be assessed independently of ideas of ethnic unity. A clash was inevitable between these new values of political communities and the old commitments of a more natural 'tribal' community.

But nepotism is not the only form of corruption which has links with older indigenous traditions. Even bribery can be a cultural residuum. Chinua Achebe, the Nigerian novelist, brings this out effectively in his novel, *No Longer at Ease*. In traditional Ibo values there was a principle of reciprocity involved in the very act of serving somebody else. Dignity often demanded that the beneficiary of a favour should have given something in return.

> They said a man expects you to accept 'kola' from him for services rendered, and until you do, his mind is never at rest . . . A man to whom you do a favor will not understand if you say nothing, make no noise, just walk away. You may cause more trouble by refusing a bribe than by accepting it.[1]

Achebe's character, Obi Okonkwo, a young Nigerian newly returned from his studies in England, had been full of defiance and resistance to all temptations of this kind in the early stages of his career in the civil service in Nigeria. When the temptations of bribery first came his way, he was suitably self-righteous and indignant as he resisted those temptations. We cannot therefore say that in his case the intended recipient of the bribe was unaware of the ethical dubiousness of accepting it under the new rules of the game. On the other hand, the giver of that bribe could be a real case of cultural transition anticipating a favour to himself by extending a favour to his future beneficiary. What is at stake is the principle of *prior appreciation*, an extension of thanks in advance of the favour. What is also at stake is the principle of reciprocity, extending a favour in anticipation of receiving a favour. In the words of the British political economist, Colin Leys:

> While traditional gift-giving [in Africa] can be distinguished from a bribe of money, it is quite obvious that from the point of view of the giver the one has shaded into the other, so that although the practice has taken on a new significance, as the open gift of a chicken is replaced by a more furtive gift of a pound note, it is nevertheless an established fact of life, in which the precise nature of the rule-infringement is partially concealed by a continuity with an older custom.[2]

The central question still persists: is there such a thing as corruption, or is it all a matter of culture? It does seem as if one culture's bribery is another's mutual goodwill.

All over Africa people are no longer sure where traditional prior appreciation ends and the new sin of bribery and corruption begins. Two factors have contributed to this confusion. One is the coming of entirely new institutions such as Western-style banks, with their new rules and new values; institutions which range from the modern civil service to the banking organs and investment agencies of modern capitalism. The other factor behind the confusion is the money economy itself, which is relatively new in many parts of Africa. The modern money economy includes problems of balance of payments, foreign exchange and international transfers. This area has enlarged the scale of economic activity and economic intercourse among Africans. Powerful Africans no longer deal in chickens and cockerels and kola nuts. Quite often they deal in millions of dollars, banked sometimes in

A modern bank built in a mixture of African and Western styles, Botswana

Swiss banks. The massive enlargement of scale puts a different quality on the issue of economic morality and the principles of economic behaviour. These new institutions have given Africans more than one standard of conduct, more than one code of behaviour. And these standards and codes are often in conflict. The result is the simple fact that the continent is no longer at ease morally, no longer sure what is the correct behaviour.

But corruption is not just a case of receiving favours from outside. It is also a question of misappropriating funds from inside. To some extent, the problem goes back to the colonial administration, with all its rootlessness and lack of legitimacy. The colonial regime was alienated from the population not only because, by definition, it was a case of foreign control but also because it was artificial, newly invented. Because the government lacked legitimacy, government property lacked respect. When I was growing up in colonial east Africa, the term *mali ya serikali* (government property) had a kind of contemptuous ring about it, as if that kind of property lacked sanctity.

It became almost a patriotic duty to misappropriate the resources of the colonial government when this was possible without risk of punishment or exposure. After all, to steal from a foreign thief could be an act of heroic restoration. Post-colonial Africa still suffers from the cynical attitudes to government property generated by the colonial experience.

Finally, there is the conflict between patriotism and paternity, between allegiance to the nation and loyalty to one's family. But what is the nation in Africa? Very often it is an artificial entity invented by the colonial order, with boundaries which bear no relation to ethnic limits or traditional kingdoms. The European powers carved up Africa to suit European convenience. Loyalty to Nigeria or to Kenya or Uganda was therefore loyalty to an entity carved out by white intruders without reference to indigenous cultural boundaries. Why should I regard those colonial frontiers as being more

A literacy class in Ethiopia. Ethiopia has been literate for at least 2000 years.

important than the needs of my children? Why should I regard integrity in the service of an artificial national entity as more important than staple food for my children? While I abuse the resources of my artificial nation in favour of my authentic family, let the innocent cast the first stone.

Language and Culture Change

But while on the issue of bribery and corruption Africa is in a state of either cultural confusion or culture conflict, on the issue of such legacies as language and dress culture the continent has been experiencing culture conquest, especially by the Western world. We have referred in a previous chapter to the impact of the Arabic language on Africa, both as a medium of worship and as a source of loan words for indigenous African languages. Taken as a whole, the African continent has more speakers of the Arabic language than any other tongue, either indigenous or alien. But the native speakers of Arabic are overwhelmingly in the north of the continent. The impact of Arabic south of the Sahara as a medium of communication has been indirectly through providing loan words for such languages as Hausa, Kiswahili, Wolof and Somali. Some of these deeply Arabised indigenous languages have in turn influenced neighbouring languages. For example, many other languages in east Africa have borrowed words from Kiswahili which had originally borrowed them from Arabic.

There are occasions when Arabic finds itself in competition with a Western language for influence. Perhaps this is particularly well illustrated in the case of a choice of alphabet. Kiswahili had for centuries used a modified version of the Arabic alphabet for its own writings. But after European colonisation of east Africa, the Roman or Latin alphabet began to gain ascendancy and to be used widely for written Kiswahili. More and more African languages have turned to the Latin or Roman alphabet for their own literary expression. In the case of Kiswahili the ascendancy of the Roman alphabet is rational and justified since it seems to be more efficient in handling Kiswahili than the Arabic alphabet. The cumbersomeness of the Arabic alphabet for Kiswahili applied especially to the issue of vowels, which do need to be inserted for Kiswahili, but are often dispensable when the alphabet is used for its original language, Arabic.

Somalia agonised for a long time over a triple heritage of alphabet. Should the Somali language use the Arabic, the Roman or a new indigenous alphabet of its own? In the end the Somali government opted, to the surprise of many people, for the Roman alphabet – a decision politically controversial in the Muslim world but probably intellectually rational.

But the West has not been winning all the battles of language and literature in Africa. While the Roman alphabet seems irresistible and is conquering all the continent's languages except Arabic itself, the picture concerning Western languages (as distinct from the alphabet) is more complicated. In the struggle between the English language and Kiswahili as the primary language of political discourse in Tanzania, there is no doubt that Kiswahili has been winning. English since Tanganyika's independence in 1961 and Zanzibar's independence in 1963 has been declining as a domestic political medium. Government notices and government discussions are conducted primarily in Kiswahili. Parliamentary debates are conducted entirely in Kiswahili, and so is the business of the ruling political party, Chama Cha Mapinduzi (CCM).

In primary and secondary education, there has also been competition between English and Kiswahili, with the odds in favour of the latter. The increasing Swahilisation of Tanzania's educational system is already having an effect on the standard of English in the country. There is evidence that Tanzanians entering as undergraduates at the University of Dar es Salaam now begin with a lower command of the English language than that of undergraduates twenty years ago.

In neighbouring Kenya the Swahilisation of government and politics has not gone quite as far as it has done in Tanzania, but there is no doubt that Kiswahili has made spectacular progress since independence. The overwhelming majority of public political meetings in the country are now addressed in Kiswahili. President Jomo Kenyatta actually made Kiswahili the language of parliament, compelling almost all business in the national assembly to be conducted in Kiswahili. This decision was made overnight; and overnight yesterday's great orators (in English) became today's weak speakers (in Kiswahili) – and, of course, vice versa. The balance of eloquence was transferred with the stroke of a presidential decree.

There are occasions when the mixture of cultures can be particularly striking. For example, a daily newspaper is not an indigenous tradition in east Africa but was borrowed from the West. On the other hand, when one is sitting at the breakfast table in the Western world, one does not normally expect to be reading poetry in the morning newspaper. But in the world of

Swahili culture, one does. There is a section in Tanzania's newspapers not only for letters to the editor but also for poems to the editor. These poems are on a wide range of subjects: on inflation, or traditional medicine, or some recent government policy.

There is a school of thought in English poetry, represented by such people as Wordsworth and Coleridge, to the effect that poetry should approximate to the ordinary language of conversation. But in Swahili culture there is a school of thought which would argue that ordinary conversation should try to approximate the elegant language of poetry. Those poems to the editor in Tanzanian newspapers, poems of dialogue, are part of this tradition.

But sometimes those verses in the newspapers are provoked by another function of poetry in Swahili culture – poetry as release from stress, as liberation from tense emotion. In the newspapers the emotions may be political, but poetry is used in more personalised anguish as well.

A few years ago two of my three sons suddenly went blind. It was a traumatic experience for all of us. In the course of this period of pain I received poems from friends and relatives, poems of sympathy, shared sadness in rhyme. I responded with my own poem, 'Ode to the Optic Nerve'. When the pain subsided, I could not but reflect afresh upon the nature of Swahili culture – a civilisation which had evolved distinctive ways of communicating compassion between its members.

But the cultural competition for the mind and body of Africa is not only between civilisations, like the competition between Western and Swahili legacies. The rivalry is sometimes within each of those civilisations as they have sought to influence the African condition. Particularly noteworthy in Africa is the rivalry between ancestral European culture and American cultural revisionism. Western Europe and the United States are in the grips of cultural competition for the soul of Africa and much of the rest of the Third World. It is to this comparative area of Westernism that we now turn.

Conquest: Europeanisation *versus* Americanisation

The Western world as a whole has been much more successful in transmitting capitalism than in transferring democracy, though both of them are relatively weak in Africa. Capitalism is the doctrine of competitive economics, resulting in market forces. Liberal democracy, on the other hand, is the doctrine of competitive politics, resulting in political pluralism.

The Carter Administration decided to put an emphasis on the export of liberal democracy. Hence the special premium President Jimmy Carter put on human rights as an aspect of American foreign policy. The Reagan Administration has put an emphasis on the export of capitalism, hence the special premium Reagan's Administration put on private enterprise and fair prices for farmers in American foreign policy towards the Third World.

During the colonial era and at the beginning of independence the versions of Western liberalism which were most influential in Africa were usually in the image of the colonial powers. Indeed, it was widely believed at the time of independence that Britain's greatest legacy to its colonies and former colonies was parliamentary government. The brightest jewel in the British crown was no longer British India; it was British democracy. And so the parliamentary package was shipped out to Africa. 'Mr Speaker, Sir', the mace, the speech from the throne, the Leader of the Opposition, the front and back benches, the white paper – the entire package of Westminster was put together for export.

Unfortunately for the idealists, it did not work. Single-party systems and military rule affected the fortunes of parliamentary government in different parts of Africa. Many buildings which once housed a national assembly have gone silent. No more the loud exchanges of policy disagreements; no more the boisterous laughter of African jokes; no more votes of censure and votes of no confidence. The legislative house in Lagos, for example, is now dead. It bears solemn testimony to the proposition that although one can teach other people how to speak the English language, or how to practise Christianity, one cannot teach them how to govern themselves. That they must learn for themselves.

In the case of Nigeria, the collapse of the Westminster model in 1966 was followed thirteen years later after a military interlude by an American-style

A triple heritage of dress, Tunisia

system of government. The second Republic of Nigeria under Al'Hajji Shehu Shagari collapsed even faster than did the first Republic under Al'Hajii Tafawa Balewa.

A more resilient American contribution to the Nigerian political system is, of course, the federal principle which has been the basis of Nigeria's government since its independence. The number of states within the federation has increased from the original three to nineteen plus Abuja (the new capital-to-be), but the essential principle of federal power sharing has survived many coups and convulsions.

A more widespread indirect American contribution to post-colonial African political systems is the phenomenon of presidentialism. One African country after another has moved away from a focus on parliament to a focus on its president.

But the competition between the United States and Europe for cultural influence in Africa is not merely in the field of capitalism and liberal democracy in their usual forms, but is also in the arena of life-styles and in the sciences and the arts. In the field of education, for example, the American impact is greater on the tertiary level than on secondary and primary levels. In English-speaking Africa the American idea of semester-long courses is

Western influence in South Africa (*left*) and Tunisia (*above*)

beginning to catch on, especially in west Africa. Term papers are beginning to count towards the final grade (instead of basing the grade almost entirely on the final examination, as the British ethos tended to do). The American title of 'Associate Professor' has replaced the old British rank, often unintelligible to foreigners, of 'Reader' which had originally been transferred to the British colonies.

In technology the United States is particularly victorious. Both American varieties of domesticated technology and American successes in high technology have exerted considerable influence on the rest of the world. In Africa much of the technology is only affecting the lives of the élite. American home gadgets, from dishwashers to air conditioners, have become part of the life-style of the more Westernised members of Africa's social echelons.

There is also the issue of dress culture. In a sense, every man in the world has two dress cultures – his own and Western (the Western man has the two traditions fused into one). No one regards a Japanese in a Western suit, or an Arab with a Western tie, as a cultural incongruity. It is only when we see a Japanese in Arab regalia, or an Arab in Japanese dress that we are amazed. The European suit especially has become truly universal. We can therefore confirm that at the level of formal Western dress Europe prevails over the United States in influencing the choices of Africa's Westernised élites.

But in terms of *casual* dress, the picture is very different. The American genius for casual attire is conquering. Casual bush shirts, T-shirts and jeans are capturing the imagination of the young in African cities.

On the issue of food, the American genius is in fast food – while Western Europe continues to prevail in more formal cuisine. The hamburger revolution has begun to penetrate even Africa. Some African cities already have at least one Kentucky Fried Chicken and one American-style pizzeria. American impatience and preoccupation with speed are part of this triumph with fast foods. When you do not have time to spare, eat American. But when you have a whole evening for indulgence, by all means eat French!

There is rivalry over drinks between Western Europe and the United States. In much of Africa, Europe still reigns supreme in alcoholic drinks. French wine, Scotch whisky and Czech and German beer are truly triumphant. Their American equivalents are decidedly poor seconds or thirds in popularity. But where America has communicated effectively is in the field of *soft* drinks. I sold Coca-Cola at the Mombasa Institute of Muslim Education in Kenya back in the 1950s. There is no real European equivalent to either Coke or Pepsi. In the field of soft drinks we have indeed been witnessing the Coca-Colonisation of the world – symbolic of a much wider process of Americanisation of humanity.

In the world of fiction and art, Europe is still triumphant among African connoisseurs of Western heritage. But in the field of science and society, the United States has been establishing a lead. American great novels and great plays are almost unknown in Africa. But in the natural sciences, the applied sciences and the social sciences, the American impact is clear.

At the more popular level there is the triumph of American news magazines, especially *Time* and *Newsweek*. This triumph extends to imitation. Many magazines about Africa printed in London are modelled on *Time* and *Newsweek* magazines in format.

In the field of music the American impact is restricted to the popular variety of Western sounds, from jazz to varieties of rock music – while Europeans continue to lead in Western classical strands. Michael Jackson in the mid-1980s had already become a world figure and not just an American legend. But African lovers of Western classical music, limited in number as they are, are unlikely to know much about either American composers or American performers in this field. In popular music the United States has become a leader but in classical Western music, the United States is still Europe's follower.

In film and television the United States continues to maintain high international visibility in spite of the decline of Hollywood. American soap operas such as *Dynasty* and *Dallas* have wide audiences from Mombasa in coastal Kenya to Maiduguri in northern Nigeria.

American high art and painting is much less known than European high culture of the brush. In much of Westernised Africa names such as Rembrandt, Michelangelo and Picasso have no real American equivalents.

On the other hand, is there a European equivalent of Walt Disney? American genius is revealed more starkly in cartoons than in the art gallery. The United States is Europe's follower in the high art of painting but is the absolute leader in the popular art of film cartoon.

In most areas of life, American genius lies in the popular art form rather than the élite speciality, in mass involvement rather than aristocratic cultivation. After all, America was the West's first *mass* democracy. Why then should its popular culture not be its main claim to global leadership and immortality?

But perhaps the Western world's most important impact on the private lives of Africans lies not in the music they play or the dress they wear but in the sexual mores which govern their lives. It is to this aspect of acculturation that we now turn, bearing in mind once again the influence both of Westernism and Islam.

On Morals and Culture Change

Few things have caused greater confusion than the two sides of Western culture – the Christian legacy and liberal secularism. The initial Western impact on African sexual mores was Christian in the old style of prudishness and distrust of sex for any purpose but procreation. The initial Western missionaries regarded the Africans south of the Sahara as too relaxed on matters of sex, as they tended to look at it as something to be enjoyed as well as a device for perpetuating the human species.

It should be remembered that Africa was being colonised in what the British called the Victorian Age, wherein sexual prudishness was particularly in vogue in the West and Christian uprightness a little too self-

Cotton workers in Gondar, Ethiopia. Cotton is sold for foreign currency.

conscious. Nor must it be forgotten that Christianity itself has traditionally and doctrinally manifested a profound distrust of sexuality. Jesus was regarded as both God and Man, but this particular man was not conceived as a result of a sexual act. The conception had to be so 'immaculate' that the normal biological process of impregnation was divorced from the origins of this particular Son of Man.

The life of Jesus is also protected from any suggestion that He might have had sexual appetites. Once again, God transformed into Man had to have one human drive excluded from His personality – the sexual drive. Scholars have speculated about the relationship between Jesus and Mary Magdalene, but virtually all Christian Churches would shrink in horror if a sexual love affair were suggested between the two. This is in contrast to the founders of other religions such as Judaism, Islam, Buddhism, Hinduism and many African traditional religions, virtually all of which allow that the founding fathers were not only religious agents but also sexual beings.

Making Jesus asexual in His birth as well as in His behaviour set the stage for other forms of prudishness in Christian doctrine. Indeed, perhaps the majority of the Christians of the world belong to the Catholic Church whose priests have to be celibate. Allegiance to God is often regarded as incompatible with an appetite for sex or an allegiance to a nuclear family. The Roman

Western middle-class tastes are catered for in this modern shopping complex in Nairobi, Kenya

Catholic leadership in Zaire has at times proposed to the Vatican that African priests be allowed to marry. Their argument has been that the concept of family is so important to African culture that compelling priests or nuns to lead celibate lives amounts to too big a demand for personal sacrifice and cultural self-denial. But, for the time being, the Vatican has maintained the principle of insulating the priesthood from sexuality and marriage.

If Mary was a virgin, Jesus asexual, the priesthood celibate, what about the rest of humanity? Christianity manifested its distrust of sexuality by a rigorous code of monogamy. This, too, profoundly influenced initial Western responses to Africa's own sexual mores, which were and remain basically polygamous for the men. Many Christian missionaries in the nineteenth century were more horrified by polygamy in Africa than by either domestic slavery or the Atlantic slave trade. In the words of the Reverend Henry Venn, Honorary Secretary of the Christian Mission Society in the middle of the nineteenth century,

The [Foreign Mission] Committee would not interfere with the discretion of a missionary in admitting a slave-holder to baptism. The Word of God has not forbidden the holding of slaves . . . Christianity will ameliorate the relationship between master and slave; polygamy is an offence against the Law of God, and therefore is incapable of amelioration.[3]

A polygamous man was therefore denied baptism, but a slave-owning man could be given baptism at the discretion of the missionary.

But the same Western penetration of Africa which had been so prudish in the middle of the nineteenth century had become sexually permissive by the middle of the twentieth century. The Christian face of the West had been a stern taskmaster on issues of sex at the beginning of colonisation; the secular and liberal face of the West had cultivated a mischievous sexual wink by the end of colonisation. In the 1860s white teachers and Evangelists warned African villagers about their lax sexual ways and their polygamous and sinful tendencies. By the 1960s white women tourists were looking for Black 'beach-boys' along the Kenya coast or in Senegal and Gambia – sex partners on an African holiday. White male tourists with a lust for sexual adventures in Africa had preceded the women by several decades. The new sexual permissiveness of the Western world appeared to be in stark contrast to the original Western sermons against African sexual mores. The moral confusion has left many an African, especially in the cities, in a state of cultural alienation.

As for polygamy, it has proved to be more resilient than many early Christians expected. Women in African societies continue to be valued for two major reasons – as economic producers and as biological reproducers. On the farm women continue to bear a disproportionate burden as cultivators. In some African societies women produce about two-thirds of the total food grown. Men do become involved in cash crops on the export side of agriculture but women shoulder the burden of feeding the society agriculturally.

Women are, of course, also valued for the children they bear. Very often African men are polygamous less because they love women than because they love children. More important than the status of having several wives is the status of having many children.

In any case one of the strange ironies of the Western impact on the issue of polygamy in Africa is that instead of ending it altogether it has begun the process of making it more symmetrical. Far from the Western impact terminating situations where men have more than one wife, the Western impact in parts of Africa has sometimes resulted in women having more than one husband. This is particularly acute in those societies which export a lot of migrant labour to work in mines or cities either in those same countries or in neighbouring more prosperous societies. Southern Africa has been particularly affected by the consequences of large-scale separation of families as men trek to jobs distant from the places where their wives live, and wives in turn take *de facto* additional husbands while they wait. What has already emerged is the strange paradox of a Western world which once aspired to stop African men having more than one wife, and yet created conditions where African women are forced to have more than one husband.

It is not only the intimacy between men and women which has been transformed by the Western impact; it is also the names which men and women call each other by and bequeath to their children.

Identity and Culture Change

Personal names are inseparable from the issue of identity in human affairs. Through identity personal names also become enmeshed in matters such as ideology, ethnicity, religion, sexual differences and social mythology.

Until Christianity and Islam came to Africa, personal names generally were part of the collective uniqueness of each ethnic group. Whatever Polonius may have deduced from his society, in Africa it was not the apparel which proclaimed the identity of the man. It was his name. That told you his ethnic and cultural background. There were Chagga names, Nyoro names, Yoruba names, Ndebele names, pre-Islamic Somali names, Zulu names and the like. The collective uniqueness of the particular society was partly reflected in the personal names of its individual members. At least this was the ideal model, though in practice some names were shared across tribes either accidentally or through cultural influence.

More than any other forces in history, it has been Christianity and Islam which have eroded the link between personal names and the collective uniqueness of each people. By insisting that there are such things as 'Christian' and 'Muslim' names, Christianity and Islam have proceeded to make universal what were originally Semitic names (sometimes in their Europeanised versions). Semitic names such as John, James, Ali, Musa, Peter and Muhammad have been part of the identity of millions of Africans. Some non-Semitic European names have also been elevated to full Christian status.

Among Africa's political leaders it was Mobutu Sese Seko of Zaire who rebelled explicitly against equating Christian names with Hebraic or European names. If Christianity was a universal religion, why were its legitimate christening names limited to the Euro-Hebraic pool? Mobutu precipitated a crisis with the Roman Catholic Church partly on this issue, and compelled his countrymen to use their indigenous African names in their passports.

No other African leader has taken such drastic measures to establish parity of status between indigenous and Euro-Hebraic names. On the contrary, official forms in many African countries include a column for 'Christian name' and a column for 'surname' – both of which are non-indigenous concepts. Western Christianity has transferred to Africa its own concept of 'Christian names' with a pool of names to choose from. Western secular culture has contributed the concept of 'surname' – but has allowed Africans to create their own pools of possible surnames. Thus many Africans have a Semitic or European first name and an African surname. African leaders with such combinations include Julius Nyerere, Kenneth Kaunda, Milton Obote, Joshua Nkomo, Robert Mugabe, Nelson Mandela, Omar Bongo, Abubakar Mayanja and the like.

There are African leaders who have indigenised both their names, such as Nnamdi Azikiwe, Obafemi Awolowo, as well as Mobutu Sese Seko.

On the other hand, there are others both of whose names are either Semitic or European. This is particularly common in Liberia and parts of Sierra Leone because of the impact of the freed slaves who settled there, many of

A scene across centuries: rural cultivation continues against a background of skyscrapers on the outskirts of Lusaka, Zambia

whom already carried European first names and surnames. All Liberia's heads of state since the country's founding in the nineteenth century have had European surnames, including Doe. Recent African leaders with double Muslim names have included Murtala Muhammad of Nigeria, widely admired, and Idi Amin of Uganda, widely denounced.

Nor must we forget that different European imperial powers in Africa promoted different naming cultures. Portugal, especially, pursued policies which encouraged the adoption of Portuguese *surnames* as well as Portuguese Christian names. The founding presidents of Angola and Mozambique – Agostinho Neto and Samora Machel respectively – are two illustrations. All Portuguese-speaking African countries have many Africans (and 'mulattoes') with such Portuguese *surnames* as De Souza, Pereira, DaCosta and so on.

But it is not merely the myth of the collective uniqueness of each African society which has been imperilled by Christianity and Islam. It is also each tribe's myth of origin. At least to the unbeliever, the Adam and Eve story could be seen as the myth of origin of the Jews, which was then adopted by Christians and Muslims. Genesis could be seen as a Hebraic tribal myth which has become universal. Now Africa's own tribal myths of origin are being discarded in favour of the Jewish one – and the name Eve (Adam's companion) in Buganda society in the twentieth century is a strong rival to the name Nnambi (Kintu's companion). Indeed, the word for 'human being' in such languages as Kiswahili has now become *mwanaadamu* (literally, 'child of Adam').

But Western culture has had other consequences for the culture of names in Africa. A wife's adoption of her husband's name upon marriage is an alien custom in most African societies. Traditionally the women of Africa retain their own names upon marriage, a residual link with their own clan and ancestral family. But Western culture is forcing African women to merge their identities with those of their husbands, not on a basis of equality but by adopting the husband's clan name or surname. A new form of sexism has entered African marriage customs, the sexism of shedding a woman's ancestry as represented in her name in favour of her husband's name.

Additional Western intrusions include the tendency to truncate or shorten names, though this has also been encouraged by the multi-ethnic nature of the new African states. A Yoruba name such as 'Olukunle' becomes 'Kunle' not only because the Yoruba have learnt to shorten 'Thomas' into 'Tom' from the British but also because Mr Olukunle now lives in a society which includes compatriots who have some difficulty with Yoruba names. Shortening names in a culturally plural society is one method of helping friends and compatriots from other cultures to cope with your identity.

In spite of the partial erosion of Africa's culture of names as a result of the impact of both the West and Islam, there is little doubt that aspects of that indigenous heritage have remained resilient and stubborn. What is more, there are signs that any further cultural imperialism in the field of names will be resisted by future African parents. Indigenous names are finding a new popularity for new babies. This is a trend which ought to be encouraged. And even when an African child is christened with a Euro-Hebraic name, he might subsequently decide to use one of his indigenous names in his public life. Famous names who have done that include the Kenyan novelist Ngugi wa Thion'go and Ghana's founder President, Kwame Nkrumah.

In addition to this indigenisation trend there are three major innovations which the Africans of tomorrow might wish to initiate. These are the Pan-Africanisation of African names, the ecumenicalisation and the androgynisation of African names.

Why should Ibo names be used only by the Ibo, and Zulu names only by the Zulu? Most Ibo and Zulu have religion-specific first names (usually Christian) and ethnic-specific surnames (derived from their own 'tribal' pool of names). The strategy of Pan-Africanising African names would involve encouraging African parents from one ethnic group to consider using names from other ethnic groups for their children.

A special commission of the Organisation of African Unity could collect a selection of names from different sub-regions of Africa. These names could be made available widely in Africa – in maternity homes, village clinics, social centres, village courts, hospitals and so on. Where the names have a definite meaning, a translation could be included in the relevant leaflet. Propaganda should then be initiated to encourage African parents to adopt trans-ethnic names either from other groups in their own countries or from other parts of Africa. A Somali child bearing a Yoruba name would gradually cease to be incongruous.

If this process went too far it would, however, be culturally disastrous. African names would cease to signify and reflect the rich plurality of Africa's ethnic heritage. But fortunately only a small minority of parents is ever likely to adopt indigenous names from groups other than their own. It is the very smallness of the minority which would constitute its strength. Trans-ethnic names would be a symbol of cultural Pan-Africanism without eroding Africa's diverse ethnic identities.

A second reform worth considering for the future is a pool of androgynous African names. By 'androgyny' we mean the elimination or minimisation of differences in gender. Most societies have different names for boys from those used for girls. You can usually tell from the first name whether the person referred to is a man or a woman.

There are some names in the international pool which have already become androgynous. I have a son called Kim. Yet the film star Kim Novak was a woman. The shortened name Chris in the West can either be a woman called Christina or a man called Christopher. Yet, to complicate matters, I have a brilliant professorial academic colleague at the University of Michigan who is called Christopher Roberts. She is American, Black – and decidedly feminine. Robin is more clearly gender-neutral.

In Africa there are a few Muslim names which are androgynous. I have come across a man called Aziza – and several women by the same name. On the other hand, the name Haruna in Uganda is *not* the feminine of Harun (both are masculine names), but the name Amina is almost always the feminine of Amin.

Indigenous cultural traditions also have a few androgynous names. Among the Baganda the arrival of twins causes some renaming in the family. The child that was born immediately before the twins arrived is renamed Kigongo, regardless of whether the elder child is a boy or a girl. The arrival of twins also produces a name in advance for the child that may follow the twins. The subsequent child is Kizza, regardless of sex. All this is without prejudice to having a separate clan name for each child.

It is worth noting that the parents of twins also acquire an additional name: the mother of twins becomes *Nalongo* and the father *Salongo*. The difference between the two names is a single letter but it is enough to make the names gender-specific.

The question which arises is whether an African organisation should deliberately collect from different African traditions gender-neutral or androgynous names which would be made available to parents all over the continent for consideration. The primary purpose of this enterprise is to contribute to the gradual breaking down of rigid cultural barriers between the sexes. Only a minority of men and women need carry gender-neutral names but that could itself be a psychological preparation for the wider androgynisation of African life-styles and the minimisation of Africa's sexual division of labour. The proper way to merge identities between men and women in Africa is not to force married women to adopt the 'surnames' of their husbands but to encourage the dissemination of gender-neutral personal names in African societies.

The third innovation worth considering is the ecumenicalisation of names – encouraging Christians to use 'Muslim' names and promoting 'Christian' names among Muslim parents.

To some extent parts of Africa are already tilting in that direction slightly. Because African families are so ecumenical, with different brothers some-times belonging to different religions, the same family can sometimes display the entire triple heritage of names.

There are also religious shifts from one generation to the next, a father may be a Muslim and a son Christian or vice versa. This may sometimes be reflected in the names.

Tanzania's most celebrated poet is Shaaban Robert, an ecumenical com-bination of names. Nigeria has produced one Christian minister called Reverend Muhammed. And names such as Shehu, Saidu, Ali and Idi in northern Nigeria have become virtually religion-neutral.

Nevertheless, the strategy of ecumenicalising African names may have to be pushed further, creating a special form of ecumenical Pan-Africanism. A pool of names may again have to be promoted for parents to choose from, blurring the sharp religious divide in Africa's nomenclature. One day names such as Ali, Abdullah, Peter, Aisha, John and Margaret may cease to proclaim the private god worshipped by the person bearing the name. And a name such as Reverend Muhammed of the Protestant faith may well cease to be an anomaly in that ecumenical future.

These then are the proposed new frontiers of Africa's culture of names. The legacy of names in modern Africa amounts to a triple heritage. There is a pool of names inherited from Africa's own indigenous ancestors, a second pool of names inherited from the Semites (especially Hebraic and Islamic names) and a third pool of European names, often an overflow of the Hebraic legacy. An alternative formulation of the triple heritage is to see it as consisting of indigenous, Islamic and Euro-Hebraic names.

But behind the triple heritage of names is that dual social mythology which provides the psychic foundations of every primordial human community: the myths of origin and collective uniqueness. Islam and Christianity, by being universalistic and monopolistic legacies, have sometimes endangered Africa's own uniqueness and Africa's own myths of origin.

But the search for a balanced synthesis continues. And part of the drama of this confluence of cultures is being played out in the theatre of personal names and on the stage of Africa's changing identity.[4]

Conclusion

In this chapter we have attempted to touch on the conflicts and tensions of cultures in dialectical interaction with each other. In the beginning was a basic culture contact as indigenous traditions were touched by the advent of Islam and later of Western civilisation.

In time, culture contact leads to culture conflict as two or more systems of values discover areas of incompatibility, areas of dissonance.

If one of the cultures begins to gain ascendancy, the process of culture conquest has begun. This has certainly been the tendency of Islam in north Africa and in parts of western and eastern Africa and in the Horn of Africa. But in much of central and southern Africa Islam has been frozen at the level of culture contact, without the strength to undertake credible conquest.

Western culture, on the other hand, is more evenly distributed in the African continent and has shown a remarkable capacity for both conquest and disruption. The disruption has resulted in cultural confusion, as the same individuals are torn by contending forces and their psychological equilibrium is no longer fully assured. The people are, in the words of literary judges, 'no longer at ease'. Pre-eminent among the illustrations is the phenomenon of corruption in Africa's experience, a phenomenon of values in transition, perspectives in collision.

A state of confusion generates its own attempts to escape. Some Africans reach out for a cultural revival, a restoration of authenticity. Others capitulate to the new civilisation, engage in cultural surrender. And many become alienated – 'bewitched, bothered, and bewildered'.

What therapies might be considered as cures for Africa's cultural

To the left of this modern highway in Nigeria, people continue to live aboard old tin-roofed waterboats

malaise? The first set of remedies could be categorised as examples of *indigenisation* or *domestication*. The progress of Swahilisation in east Africa has been outlined earlier in this chapter. In west Africa there has been no comparable advance of an indigenous language, no comparable adoption of an African language as a national or official language. In parts of west Africa, African languages have been adopted as a lingua franca beyond the ethnic boundaries of that language, for example, Wolof in Senegal and Hausa in the north of Nigeria and in parts of neighbouring states. There may be, at present, political reasons why Hausa should not be adopted as the national language in Nigeria alongside English as the official language, but there are stronger cultural reasons why Wolof should be the national language in Senegal alongside French as the official language, and fewer political objections. Senegal has already become the scene of another form of African revival, with the recent rise in status there for non-Western dress.

A second group of therapies to help revive African culture involves diversification. Imported music and film, for example, could be selected less exclusively from the West and more from places such as India. Even in the West, Indian music and film have an increasing number of devotees. The Arab cultural impact in non-Muslim areas could be increased, for example in architecture. Sources of art and literature could also be diversified. Why should educated Africans read the literature only of Africa and the West instead of also the literature of Asia, Latin America and Black America? Why should literature syllabi in African secondary schools and universities exclude the literature of the rest of the Third World even if they now include the literature of Africa?

Changing aspirations

Another set of remedies for Africa's cultural malaise concerns cultural interpenetration, the spread of African culture around Africa, from country to country and region to region. There could be more interchange in literature. Achebe is taught widely in Kenya but Ngugi could be taught far more in Nigeria. English-speaking Africa and French-speaking Africa could teach each other's literature more extensively in the schools and universities. The popular music of Zaire – the Congo jazz of Luambo Makiadi (Franco) and Tabu Ley (Rochereau) – has already shown itself to be a force for cultural Pan-Africanism. Congo jazz is extremely popular in east Africa, and has also made a big impact on Nigeria, Ghana and Ivory Coast and some of the township bands in South Africa. With African popular music, it is possible to say that it is a force not only for cultural interpenetration within Africa but also for cultural counter-penetration outside the continent. Franco, Rochereau, Osibisa of Ghana and other African musicians have toured western Europe and generated enthusiasm for African music especially in Britain, the Netherlands, Belgium, France and West Germany – and among white youth more than among the youth of the Black Diaspora.

In Africa we should look at aspects of various ethnic cultures which could be nationalised, at sub-regional cultures which could be regionalised and at regional cultures which could be Pan-Africanised. It will be necessary to expand the participation of different groups in each other's cultures. To do that, it will be necessary to respect our various African cultures, that of our parents and those of other Africans. It will also be necessary to avoid blind conformity with one's own local culture or blind imitation of alien culture.

Between Society and the State

The state was not a universal category in pre-colonial Africa. As we have noted earlier, from the political point of view the continent of Africa was a miracle of diversity – ranging from empires to stateless societies, from elaborate thrones to hunting bands, from complex civilisations to rustic village communities. But in this chapter we address ourselves to the emergence of the state in Africa. We shall relate that phenomenon to the triple political and cultural heritage of the African continent – the indigenous, the Islamic and the Western.

The modern African state is a child of three forces in world history: Semitic absolutism, European organisation and African land-reverence. Semitic beliefs about the 'Almighty', about a God who is omnipotent and omniscient, contributed to ideologies about absolute monarchies. European genius in organisation contributed to the theme of organised centralisation in state-formation. Africa's historical reverence for land has now interacted with the principle of territoriality and forged a new emphasis on boundaries and frontiers. The state in Africa is part of *world* history and not merely a chapter in the region's own past.

Monotheism and the Origins of the State

The most important political contributions to world culture that the Jews and the Arabs have made include ideas of centralised government and the principle of patriarchy. Both of these contributions have been of immense relevance to the evolution of the modern sovereign state.

People's ideas about God can condition their ideas about government and vice versa. It is not always easy to determine where theology ends and political philosophy begins. In Semitic terms, the first world government was the Government of God on Earth. Planet Earth itself was not a state, but God was certainly king. The Semitic concept of God envisaged God in anthropomorphic, royal, masculine and judgmental terms. God was Man writ large, and was king and ultimately male. The Almighty expected loyalty and obedience. Indeed, in Christian terms, the original sin was the sin of disobedience – and God was supreme judge. The Hereafter was intended to be a centralised and absolutist dominion, divided between the paradise of the pious and the ghetto of sinners under the kingdom of God.

The supreme subversive in God's government was Satan who was supposed to be peddling treasonable literature. He was fostering disobedience to the king of all kings in history – God!

opposite, Friday prayers outside the palace, Zaria, Nigeria

Engravings by Gustave Doré illustrating, *left*, God banishing Satan and, *right*, Satan approaching the confines of Earth, from Milton's *Paradise Lost*

The idea of a supreme subversive incarnated in Satan ran into difficulties when liberalism started to glorify opposition to absolutism. Nobody felt this more keenly than the English seventeenth-century essayist and poet John Milton, author of one of the most eloquent defences of liberty, *Areopagitica*, and, at the same time, defender of the ways of God to Man, in *Paradise Lost*. This lover of earthly freedom was also a defender of divine absolutism. And yet the love of freedom crept into Milton's treatment of divine absolutism. Satan in the earlier phases of the poem certainly assumes heroic proportions. After all, he is rebelling against a king who demands absolute obedience, and seems to enjoy the servility of constant prayer and hymns in His glory. God seems to revel in creating politically conscious creatures who are challenged to declare their unqualified allegiance to the Creator. God becomes absolute vanity. Satan becomes a freedom fighter, rebelling against the absolutism of the Almighty.

Semitic universalism has been towards one God and one humanity. Monotheism has influenced the emergence of sovereign absolutism, while the story of Adam and Eve has influenced the idea of a single human race. But these developments in turn created a new dialectic. There emerged a tension between ideas of sovereign absolutism (derived from monotheism) and ideas of shared humanity (derived from genesis). Western political philosophy moved towards notions of the sovereign state and notions of shared fraternity at about the same time in the seventeenth century and the two trends were ultimately contradictory.

At least for a while, the factor which tilted the balance in favour of state sovereignty was patriarchy. The Semitic impact on patriarchy helped to move the world towards emphasising the sovereign state rather than shared humanity. In other words, the trend towards monotheism in world history has been a trend towards divine masculinity and absolutism. Polytheistic or pantheistic traditions in world history – including those of ancient Egypt, ancient Greece and Rome, and the 'tribal' religions of the world – allowed considerable room for female deities. But Semitic monotheism was the great destroyer of the female factor in the character of the deity. From the Semites onwards the great symbols of fertility became masculine. This is in spite of the matrilineal principle in the lineage system of the Jews. No more goddesses – only one God, and it is a 'He', with a capital 'H'!

Suffice it to say for now that the 'God standard' in politics was in part the cradle of the sovereign state. The Semites were ironically the midwives of the concept of sovereignty.

Europe's Spirit of Organisation

Three inter-related European movements were to play a critical role in the emergence of modern Europe and the development of a new spirit of organisation in that continent – the Renaissance, the Reformation and the Enlightenment.

The Renaissance (from the fourteenth century of the Christian era) was a cultural revival after 1000 years of what the Italian poet Petrarch characterised as an age of darkness. Europe began to revive the spirit of its ancient and classical past, innovative and dynamic. The Renaissance helped to free European art and philosophy from excessive service to God and Church, and laid the foundations of aesthetic and intellectual individualism.

The Protestant Reformation was launched by a German Augustinian friar, Martin Luther, who posted his ninety-five theses on the door of the castle church at Wittenberg in 1517 – one of the great gestures of protest of all time. Luther proclaimed that faith was the true salvation and the truly repentant did not need priestly intercession or the Church's indulgences.

The Enlightenment (during the seventeenth and eighteenth centuries), with scientists such as Galileo and Newton, and philosophers such as Francis Bacon, Descartes, John Locke, Voltaire, David Hume and Rousseau, helped to secularise European science and scholarship and gave new prominence to the role of reason instead of faith.

What should be borne in mind is that these three European movements were part of the origins of the sovereign state, on the one hand, and of European capitalism, on the other. Together they constitute the roots of Europe's organisational and technical genius.

The Renaissance generated artistic independence and innovative individualism. But the Renaissance was also the period of the New Monarchies and the renewed doctrines of royal absolutism. The years of new individual liberation in the arts were also the years of the new political centralisation of

Martin Luther (1483–1546) nailing his theses to the door of the castle church in Wittenberg, 1517

the state. The glories of the palace of Versailles as an artistic achievement are inseparable from the politics of Louis XIV – who proclaimed, 'I am the state'. Artistic individualism was in the service of royal absolutism in Versailles.

The Protestant Reformation was linked both to the origins of the modern sovereign state and to the origins of Western capitalism. Luther had been motivated to protest not only by the abuses of indulgences under Pope Leo X but also by strong German nationalist resentment at the domination of the Catholic Church by Italians. In the evolution of the state system, the Reformation contributed not only to the break-up of the Catholic Church but to the break-up of what remained of the Holy Roman Empire. Quarrels among the different principalities resulted in the Treaty of Augsburg of 1555, which formulated a state sovereignty based on the principle of religious non-intervention. Hence the convention or *modus vivendi* agreed upon between European princes was founded on the idea that the religion of the ruler was to be counted as the religion of the society – *Cuius regio eius religio*. The exercise was designed to reduce interference and intervention across the territorial boundaries of each prince's domain. The idea of the sovereign kingdom was directly at stake in the Treaty of Augsburg.

But the 1555 Treaty did not end the religious wars in Europe which the Protestant Reformation had unleashed. Europe was later to plunge into another thirty years of conflict. Out of this particular period of internecine religious conflagration emerged at long last the Peace of Westphalia of 1648, widely regarded as the true genesis of the modern system of sovereign states which today governs the diplomacy and destiny of the human race.

Under Protestantism generally guilt was taken out of the pursuit of wealth. A new economic morality came into being and Protestant Europe and Protestant North America took the lead in the new capitalist revolution. The foundations of the West's hegemony had been set. Africa became a mere mirage of the new organisational genius of Europe – and became an extension also of the Semitic traditions in history.

African Politics and Islamic States

Among the Semitic traditions, Islam has been particularly influential in African history. We know, of course, that Africa's interaction with Islam antedates European colonisation of Africa by at least a millennium. We know that in the seventh century Islam conquered Egypt and started the process of penetrating north Africa. We have noted that Islam then spread up the Nile Valley as well as into north-west Africa. The politics of those societies responded to the impact of Islam, and some of those societies began to evolve institutions which reflected this basic interaction between Islam and indigenous culture.

Especially important in state-formation is the precise balance between trade and warfare, between economic aspects and military dimensions. The history of Islam from the days of Muhammad is partly an equation involving exchange of goods and balance of arms.

Islam's penetration of the African continent continued this dialectic between the economic and the military. When Islam became an empire, Egypt for a while became the pivot of an international Muslim economic system. There was a time when the merchant class of Egypt became what has been described as a group so influential that it 'increasingly shaped the policies of the Muslim states, developed commercial law and custom, and gave the civilisation of Islam its strong emphasis on the bourgeois virtues of saving and sobriety, avoidance of waste or ostentation, and respect for scholarship'.[1] Then the spread of Islam into west Africa betrayed another economic process. The trans-Saharan trade produced missionaries in the market places. The Muslim shopkeeper was at times the equivalent of the clergyman. Islam was spreading as an additional commodity accompanying the grand paradigm of trade.

Out of this began to emerge special kingdoms and emirates in west Africa, instances of new state-formation. There is a Hobbesian concept of absolutism in Islamic statecraft — encouraging obedience to those who exercise authority provided they do not violate the principles that Muhammad advocated and God willed. This side of Islam is concerned with submissive fatalism, a readiness to accept the inevitable. The same Islam which fought so hard against European colonisation in the late nineteenth century later seemed to be ready to accept the inevitable hegemony of the West. No one has put it better than the British Africanist, Michael Crowder,

Islam, whose hatred of subjection to the infidel would have provided, as it did for a short while between 1889 and 1893 in the Western Sudan, a unifying theme for resistance against the French and British, also held the seeds of a fatalist acceptance of the inevitable.[2]

But subsequently Islam profoundly influenced the colonial policy of at least one major imperial power, Great Britain. My own thesis is that the British policy of indirect rule was born out of a marriage of Islam, on one side, and the theories of the Anglo-Irish philosopher Edmund Burke, on the other. In a sense the legacy of Edmund Burke is what British political culture is all about. As a rule of political prudence Burke advised, 'Neither entirely nor at once depart from antiquity.' If a society aspires to change direction, it will be a mistake to do it either totally or in one sudden move. Political prudence, according to Burke, requires political sensitivity to history. As he put it, 'People will not look forward to posterity who never look backward to their ancestors.'[3] British political culture is a reflection in part of this broad political philosophy. The British are reluctant to turn their backs on antiquity either entirely or at once. So they maintain ancient institutions and modernise them as they go along, and they are slower to modify traditional habits than are many nations. This same Burkean gradualism in British domestic political culture came to influence British colonial policy. Indirect rule was based on a Burkean principle of gradualism.

Where was indirect rule to find its paradigmatic formulation? Lord Lugard, the architect of Britain's policy of indirect rule, looked for those institutions in the monarchical, conservative and undemocratic emirates of northern Nigeria. As Lord Hailey put it in *An African Survey*,

> It was in northern Nigeria that this procedure of using Native Authorities was given a systematic form by Lord Lugard during the years which followed the declaration of the Protectorate in 1900. The area which was brought under British protection was the scene of the most effectively organised system of indigenous rule to be found south of the Sahara. Most of the old-established Hausa Kingdoms had embraced the Islamic faith, and under its influence there had by the early sixteenth century developed a well-organised fiscal system, a definite code of land-tenure, a regular scheme of local rule through appointed District Heads, and a trained judiciary administering the tenets of the Muhammedan law.[4]

The Fulani, who gained the ascendancy in the greater part of the Hausa country during the jihad of Uthman dan Fodio at the beginning of the nineteenth century, used and helped to develop further this organised system of administration. And then Lugard and the British arrived. In the words of another writer, Cyril Whittaker,

> Like the Fulani conquerors, Lugard perceived that a solution for his problems presented itself in the form of the already effectively functioning system of government, which by then offered such obvious additional advantages as religious justification for authority, a formal code of law [the Islamic Shari'a], specialised judicial institutions, a more centrally controlled apparatus of administration, the custom of taxation and, above all, the people's habit of obeying state authority.[5]

Young Fulani woman, Nigeria

From this appraisal of the Hausa-Fulani institutions the British then evol-

ved an elaborate system of Native Authorities in Nigeria, utilising existing structures for indirect British control. Northern Nigeria in particular had local instruments which gave to the British opportunities for indirect imperial rule. The old absolutist institutions of the Hausa-Fulani states became part of the new absolutist institutions of the colonial state.

This appeared to be a healthy strategy of transition. African societies were not being disrupted precipitately, and their habits and life-styles were not ignored. African societies were ruled through institutions they had come to understand across generations but institutions which were subject to gradual change. 'Neither entirely nor at once depart from antiquity.'

And yet, indirect rule in Nigeria aggravated the problems of creating a modern nation-state after independence. The different groups in the country, by being ruled in part through their own native institutions, maintained their separate ethnic identities. Northern Nigeria became particularly distinctive in its fusion of Islam and Africanity. The missionaries were kept out of that part of Nigeria and missionary education which helped to Westernise the south fairly rapidly was relatively inaccessible in large parts of northern Nigeria. Different sections of the population perceived each other as strangers, sometimes as aliens, increasingly as rivals, and ominously as potential enemies. As it happens, the stage was being set for the events which led first to the military coup in Nigeria in January 1966, then to the slaughter of the Ibo in northern Nigeria in the same year, and then to the outbreak of a civil

A Zanzibari elder

Kabaka Mutesa II, the last of the kings of Buganda

Milton Obote of Uganda, the only African leader who made a comeback after having been overthrown by the military — only to be overthrown a second time five years later

war from 1967 to 1970. The preservation of pre-colonial state institutions, especially in northern Nigeria, had made the consolidation of post-colonial national institutions more difficult.

The Sultanate of Zanzibar in east Africa presented distinctive problems of its own without altering the basic tension between the pre-colonial and post-colonial African state. From the days before European colonial rule (1890–1963) Zanzibar had been a racially and ethnically plural society. By the end of the eighteenth century the ascendancy of the Arabs was already clear. It was consolidated by the rise of Seyyid Said bin Sultan. Sultan Barghash later provided the transitional rule from pre-European Arab ascendancy to the Arab oligarchy under European overlordship. Once again the British, having recognised monarchical institutions in Zanzibar reminiscent of their own in England, proceeded to give some kind of validity to those monarchical institutions and use them as a basis of indirect rule. In one sense the Arabs of Zanzibar were equivalent to the Hausa-Fulani of northern Nigeria. In both cases the maintenance of their particular political institutions from pre-colonial days augured ill for the transition to post-colonial nationhood. In the case of Zanzibar the tensions between the privileged ethnic group and the others could not be mitigated by a shared rivalry of all of them against still other groups elsewhere. After all, the tension between the Hausa-Fulani and others in northern Nigeria was helped by the fact that all northerners had a sense of defensiveness against southerners. Zanzibar was too small a society to have those built-in safeguards of cross-cutting alignments. The result was the disastrous revolution of January 1964, barely a month after the British had departed, when the Sultan's government was overthrown by an African uprising and thousands of Arab civilians were killed. Those very Arab institutions of statehood which the British had so affectionately protected became the Achilles heel of the new nation as it struggled to have modern statehood after independence.

The Kingdom of Buganda, on the eve of colonial rule, was a unique example of a multi-cultural state where the political aristocracy were divided among adherents of traditional religion, Islam and either Catholic or Protestant Christianity. Buganda was a racially and ethnically homogeneous but religiously plural society in the 1880s. Buganda had a centralised and organised system of government and administration which led the British, although Buganda was only partly a Muslim state, to use the monarchical and chiefly aspects of the local institutions as the basis of their own colonial rule — as they did in northern Nigeria and Zanzibar. Before his activities in Nigeria, Lugard had been the first British administrator in Buganda and in Uganda generally. One of his successors, Harry Johnston, in the famous 1900 Agreement confirmed and defined the functions of the traditional Baganda rulers in Buganda, an autonomous unit within Uganda. The Agreement strengthened the special position of the Buganda within Uganda as a reward for the loyalty of its Christian leaders to Britain. Buganda's recent annexation of several counties from Bunyoro was confirmed. The kabakaship remained and the kabaka retained the power to appoint chiefs. Buganda was given a parliament of chiefs and notables called the Lukiiko. In what came to be described later as Baganda sub-imperialism some of the Baganda chiefs helped the British to conquer other parts of Uganda and many were used as colonial administrators in Bunyoro, Busoga, Bukedi and Bugisu by the British.

After independence, Uganda witnessed an almost inevitable struggle for power between the Baganda and the rest of the country, between Kabaka Mutesa II as a regional king and Milton Obote as a national prime minister, between an ancient institution and a modern state. This confrontation reached a climax in May 1966 when Obote sent the army under Colonel Idi Amin to attack the Kabaka's palace. Mutesa fled to England and died in 1969.

From the Pre-Colonial to the Post-Colonial State

There is another triple heritage concerning state-formation in Africa – the heritage of the city-state, the empire-state and the nation-state. To some extent Zanzibar was a city-state, though it gradually established enough hegemony in parts of what is today coastal Kenya and coastal Tanzania to be on the verge of becoming a proper empire-state. In the case of Zanzibar the empire in the making was a dynastic empire, with an Arab Sultanate at the top. In the history of Europe the city-state antedated the empire-state. Athens and Sparta antedated, of course, the Austro-Hungarian Empire. In African history it is more difficult to disentangle the origins of the city as against the empire. Some of the Emirates in Nigeria, for example, Kano and Zaria, were at once city-states and part of a wider empire at the same time.

The most durable of all Africa's empire-states turned out to be Ethiopia. Its last emperor was Haile Selassie. I was privileged to meet that remarkable, if controversial, character more than once. On the first occasion I was introduced by one legacy of pre-colonial statehood, the Kabaka of Buganda, to this Ethiopian legacy of pre-colonial statehood. Haile Selassie was visiting Uganda in 1964 where our paths crossed. I should have known even then that both he and Kabaka Mutesa II were incarnations of pre-colonial statehood about to confront sooner or later post-colonial statehood. Mutesa had his confrontation with President Milton Obote in 1966.

The last time I saw Emperor Haile Selassie was in Africa House in Addis Ababa. The meeting was that of the International Congress of Africanists (later renamed the International Congress of African Studies). The Congress had asked me to propose the vote of thanks to the emperor after his speech opening the Congress. Even then I sensed a basic conflict within the demands of a dynastic ancient empire and the responsibilities of a modern nation-state. Ethiopia in 1973 had a severe famine which was underpublicised, seemingly because a famine of such magnitude was considered by the Royal Household to be an embarrassment to the empire. And yet, there we were in Addis Ababa from different countries of the world about to begin a congress on issues of development in Africa. Could we hold such a congress

The devastating effect of one of the many famines in Africa

An Ethiopian soldier in Addis Ababa, Ethiopia

in a country with large-scale starvation without referring at all to those who were starving? Were we obliged to spare the dynastic empire embarrassment, in spite of the fact that Ethiopia as a nation-state had responsibilities to alleviate the suffering of the masses? Could we expect our Ethiopian colleagues to discuss the famine in the face of the apparent ban on publicity of the famine at the behest of the Ethiopian palace?

In that assignment to propose a vote of thanks to His Imperial Majesty I felt an obligation to try to solve the conflict between courtesies of a dynastic empire on the one hand, and the obligations of a modern nation-state on the other. In my vote of thanks I therefore mentioned the unmentionable – the famine. I championed what was not to be championed – an open discussion of the famine at the congress as part of our deliberations. I argued the ultimate sin of all – that the congress itself should establish its own internal fund to raise at least a symbolic contribution from its own participants towards the alleviation of the suffering of the Ethiopian people.

It was not a long speech. It was, as votes of thanks ought to be, relatively brief. But it was deliberately calculated to break the ice on the issue of famine in front of His Imperial Majesty. If the subject was no longer taboo at a plenary session, I had argued to myself, it would not be taboo in later sessions of the Congress. In this reasoning I was abundantly vindicated. The issue of the famine became an open topic at the Congress. The Emperor had listened to the vote of thanks with his usual impassive appearance. He had not subsequently objected to the tone of the vote of thanks. Open discussion of the crisis could be undertaken without violating the courtesies of a dynastic empire-state. Recommendations could be made to Ethiopia as a modern nation-state trying to reconcile itself to its legacy of an imperial dynasty.

Two months after the Congress the Ethiopian revolution began. It has been suggested that a major contributor to the revolution was the famine and the long delay by the Imperial Order in responding to it. The creeping revolution of Ethiopia began in February 1974. By that time, it appeared that the dynastic empire-state would no longer be permitted to masquerade as a modern nation-state. The soldiers of Ethiopia, for a while cheered by the students and peasants of Ethiopia, solved the dilemmas by abolishing the ancient imperial statehood and replacing it with a modern ideology dedicated to the Marxist principle of the 'withering away of the state' itself. A new European concept of organisation was put into practice in Ethiopia.

We might therefore conclude that one of the difficulties in the transition from a pre-colonial to a post-colonial state is precisely the normative and moral gap between the two. The values have fundamentally changed, the responsibilities have been redefined, the perspectives are newly focused and the policies demand reformulation.

On Equality and Land Reverence

An important disruptive factor was the evolution of the principle of equality. In Africa this principle was by far better realised among the so-called stateless societies than among either city-states or empire-states. Many indigenous societies along the Nile Valley, or societies such as the Tiv of Nigeria and the Masai of Kenya and Tanzania, have relatively loose structures of control and substantial egalitarianism. In contrast, societies such as those of Buganda, northern Nigeria, Ashanti and other dynastic empires of west Africa were hierarchical and basically unequal.

The new post-colonial nation-state provides a basic contradiction. It champions almost as much equality as the so-called 'primitive' and stateless societies which did not have kings or identifiable rulers, yet it asserts what Max Weber called the state's 'monopoly of legitimate use of physical force'.

This basic tension between moral equality from acephalous societies in Africa and political hierarchy from monarchical societies in Africa, has been one of the central divisive elements in the post-colonial experience. In places such as Rwanda and Burundi this dialectic pitched hierarchical Tutsi against egalitarian Hutu, causing ethnic massacres in the 1960s and 1970s; in Nigeria it pitched deferential Hausa against individualistic Ibo; in Uganda it pitched monarchical Baganda against neo-republican Nilotes.

Another area of tension between the pre-colonial African states and the post-colonial states concerns attitude to territoriality. Most African societies have a high degree of land reverence. On the other hand, the principle of the Western nation-state included a high sensitivity to territoriality.

The mystique of land reverence in Africa is partly a compact between the living, the dead and the unborn. Where the ancestors are buried, there the soul of the clan resides, and there the prospects of the health of the next generation should be sought. Land was quite fundamental to both stateless African societies and to empires and city-states.

Opoku Ware II, the Asantehene (King) of the Ashantis in Ghana

On the other hand, territory became increasingly important in Europe and became almost sacrosanct in the legacy of the Peace of Westphalia of 1648. Political communities under the new doctrine of the nation-state became increasingly definable in terms of boundaries between one nation-state and another. Sovereignty was subject to territoriality; power was landbound. Once again Aimé Cesaire's lines are relevant. The pre-colonial African state carried the legacy of land reverence,

> . . . My negritude is neither a tower nor a cathedral;
> It plunges into the red flesh of the earth . . .[6]

But while the pre-colonial African states have indulged in this land worship in relation to both agriculture and the burial of ancestors, the post-colonial state indulged in the worship of territory in relation to power and sovereignty. The dichotomy between the land worship of old and territorial worship in post-colonial states has not yet been resolved. All we know is that the last legacy of the colonial order to be decolonised is likely to be the territorial boundary between one African country and another. That colonial boundary currently helps define one African political entity against another. So far, there has been not a single example of a post-colonial African state accepting any changes in those territorial boundaries that were so arbitrarily created during the European partition of the continent – apart from the union of states as in Tanzania and Senegambia. The ghosts of ancestors and land worship have been overshadowed by the imperative of sovereignty and territorial possessiveness, inherited from the Treaties of Westphalia.

Conclusion

We have sought to demonstrate in this chapter that the history of the contemporary state is, at least in part, a transition from Semitic ideas to European techniques.

From the point of view of world order, this grand cultural transition has given birth to two mighty forces of the past few hundred years – the power of the sovereign state and the force of capitalism. The modern sovereign state can be traced back to a marriage between Semitic ideas and European experience. The transition was from God as king to the king as God's anointed. And then the absolute monarchy became the absolute state.

As for what has happened within Africa itself, we have attempted to demonstrate in this chapter that there are two other levels of the triple heritage of state formation. At one level the triple heritage does indeed consist of the indigenous heritage, the Afro-Islamic heritage and the Western heritage of state formation. But the Afro-Christian component in the history of state formation in Africa did not always include European stimulus. Striking exceptions to *European* Christianity in Africa are to be found in north Africa and Ethiopia.

We have also attempted to demonstrate in this chapter another level of the triple heritage – the heritage involving the city-state, the empire-state and the new modern nation-state. Places such as Kano and Zanzibar were partly settings for the city-state. But Songhay, Ghana, Mali, the Hausa-Fulani empire, Ashanti, and possibly the Empire of the Mutapa in Zimbabwe, were manifestations of the second tradition of empire-states. The third structure of statehood was the nation-state or the modern sovereign state, very much a product of European history and very much a legacy of the Peace of Westphalia of 1648.

This chapter has attempted to point out a basic discontinuity between the pre-colonial African state and the post-colonial state. In the transition the British especially attempted to provide a ceremony of transition from pre-colonial to post-colonial statehood. This *rite de passage* was the British policy of indirect rule, which attempted to use native institutions of government as instruments for colonial control and as intermediate stages before full African incorporation into the global state-system.

But in the ultimate analysis the transition from pre-colonial statehood to post-colonial statehood was bedevilled by two crises – the crisis of egalitarianism and the crisis of territoriality. The crisis of egalitarianism arose because African city- and empire-states were, on the one hand, less egalitarian than African stateless societies; and, on the other hand, less egalitarian also than the new evolving European nation-states. The nature of responsiveness to land also distinguished pre-colonial statehood from post-colonial manifestations. Pre-colonial statehood had a mystical deference to land, an obsession with the aesthetics and religiosity of the soil.

A second major cleavage between the pre-colonial and the post-colonial is not land but morality. This is a conflict of values and principles, a tension between preferences. The pre-colonial state was basically non-egalitarian, tracing its roots to hierarchy, privilege and power. Indeed the pre-colonial state sometimes began as a city-state and then acquired enough expansionism to become an empire-state.

Perhaps the state-system, whatever its origins, ought to give way to a more humane and more equitable global-system. But while the state-system persists, it is important to realise that its African manifestation is tripartite in two fundamental senses. It covers the basic interaction among indigenous cultures, Islam and Westernism and this also includes the accompanying tripartite communication between the city-state, the empire-state, and the nation-state in the agonising tensions of Africa's political experience.

But even more fundamental is the *world-history* of the state. We have already referred to Semitic absolutism as the mother of the principle of sovereignty. Europe's genius of organisation facilitated the process of political centralisation. As for Africa's land reverence, this has merged with territoriality, and resulted in the African state's preoccupation with boundaries and political frontiers – at once promising and ominous, at once unifying and divisive, at once territorially specific and politically hazardous. These are some of the diverse tensions of the triple heritage of statehood as it continues to work itself out in Africa's historical experience.

Between War
and Peace

The Berlin Wall which separates East and West Berlin is the most obvious and most powerful symbol of the partition of Europe in the second half of the twentieth century. But Berlin was also the venue of a conference committed to the partition of Africa in the nineteenth century. Is there a historical or even a spiritual link between the two partitions?

Division of Europe and Partition of Africa

Like the ancient Greeks, we Africans are sometimes what others call 'super-stitious'. My own people, the Waswahili of east Africa, have a proverb 'mchimba kisima huingia mwenyewe' ('He who digs a well falls in himself'). It is like being 'hoist with one's own petard'. But the Swahili proverb is more mystical – involving the intervention of fate.

I am reminded of the ancient Greeks, who also deeply believed in fate and destiny. Two Greek myths come to mind – those of Narcissus and Nemesis.

> Narcissus was a Thespian, the son of the blue Nymph Leiriope whom the River-God Cephisus had once encircled with the windings of his streams, and ravished. The seer Teiresias told Leiriope, the first person ever to consult him: 'Narcissus will live to a ripe old age, provided he never knows himself.'[1]

On no account was Narcissus to see himself. To see himself was to fall in love with himself and that would result in self-destruction. Narcissus subsequently saw himself in a reflection in a pool, and self-love led to self-destruction.

Similarly, Europe's self-love in the twentieth century nearly led to self-destruction. In her empire Europe had seen a reflection of herself. Like Narcissus enraptured with his own reflection in the pool, Europe had sought her own grandeur in embracing the empire. In the pool of her imperial history, Europe had seen herself – beautiful but wounded! Was it a prophecy of the Berlin wall?

Alternatively, consider the Second World War as Africa's revenge upon Europe. Many Africans believe in forces very similar to the classical Greek concept Nemesis, 'Divine vengeance'. Did the African spirits exact their own revenge? Were these dedicated to the mission of punishing Europe for the partition of Africa? Was Europe to be penalised for the sin of arrogance? Was Europe sentenced to its own partition into Soviet and American spheres of power?

Were the African spirits especially aroused by the Italian invasion of

opposite, General Gordon's Last Stand, by W. G. Joy

Ethiopia – the remaining proud symbol of Africa's independence – acquiesced to even by those European nations, Britain and France, which half-heartedly applied the League of Nations economic sanctions against the aggressor? Indeed, I and other African political scientists and African historians believe that the Second World War did not begin in 1939 following the violation of the territory of Czechoslovakia and Poland. It began in 1935 following the violation of Ethiopia's sovereignty by Mussolini's Italy. The fact that Mussolini succeeded with his own aggression in Africa whetted the appetites of the Nazi and Fascist dictators nearer home. Once again Africa's Curse of Nemesis might have been at work as Europe's external territorial appetites abroad were mercilessly internalised, turning European against European. From a global point of view, the origins of internal European expansionism in the 1930s could be traced to external European imperialism a little earlier. Nazi Germany's rape of Poland in 1939 could, in a sense, be traced to Fascist Italy's rape of Ethiopia in 1935. And both could further be traced to the general spirit of imperialism which the Berlin Conference of 1884–5 had helped to legitimise.

Abyssinian troops marching near the northern frontier, 1935

There is therefore at least a historical link between the Berlin Conference

in 1885 and the outbreak of the Second World War. The subsequent partition of Europe owes much to the decisions made at two other conferences towards the end of that war. In February 1945 the Allied leaders (including President Franklin D. Roosevelt, Prime Minister Winston Churchill, and Premier Joseph Stalin) met at Yalta in the Crimea. Their agenda was to plan the method of the final defeat of Germany. The Allies reaffirmed their insistence on the unconditional surrender of the Axis Powers. It was also agreed that defeated Germany should be subjected to a four-power occupation (Great Britain, the United States, the Soviet Union and France). Yalta recorded a number of concessions from Britain and the United States to Joseph Stalin concerning eastern Europe.

Later in 1945, between 17 July and 2 August, another conference took place, this time in Potsdam outside Berlin. Its main participants were President Harry S. Truman, Prime Minister Winston Churchill and Premier Joseph Stalin. Churchill was later replaced by Clement Attlee, who became Britain's Prime Minister in the course of the conference. The Potsdam meeting discussed not only military operations against Japan, but also the substance and procedures for the comprehensive peace settlement in Europe.

The international actors did not realise it at the time, but they were engaged in a *partition of Europe* at least as historically momentous as the *partition of Africa* sixty years previously. The Europeans had divided Africa into, *inter alia*, linguistic units (Francophone, Anglophone, Lusophone, etc.). The Potsdam and Yalta agreements divided Europe into ideological units (capitalist, socialist and neutral Europe). The obstinacy of the colonial boundaries created by Europe in Africa was equalled by the stubbornness of the post-war boundaries imposed upon Europe by the new confrontation between capitalist America and the Union of Soviet Socialist Republics.

left to right, Winston Churchill, Franklin D. Roosevelt and Joseph Stalin at the Yalta Conference, February 1945

In Christian theology Europe could be punished for the sin of pride. In this case, imperial pride. But in African mythology it could be the four winds of East, West, North and South fighting it out across both space and time. In the mind of at least one north African poet, the southern wind is the daughter of the Mountains of the Moon in the middle of Africa:

> Ismitta, the embodiment of the southern wind is ... a beautiful slender negro-girl, intimately close to the divine image of the sources of the Nile in the Egyptian mind which goes back to ancient Egyptian cosmology. She is the 'daughter of the Mountains of the Moon' whose laughter is lightning and whose tears are torrential rains.[2]

The image is not identical with the Greek concept of Nemesis, but the question has arisen whether after the 1880s Ismitta undertook a new assignment. After all, European imperialism had used the Nile Valley as a major factor behind Africa's partition and colonisation. British debates in the cabinet about Uganda were, in effect, debates about Egypt. The imperial mind was often concerned about the unity of the Nile Valley. Whoever controlled Egypt needed to control the Sudan and the source of the White Nile as well. As for the source of the Blue Nile in Ethiopia, the European imperialist powers neutralised each other and jointly agreed to leave

Belgian Colonial troops from the Congo cleaning their equipment after disembarking at a port in British West Africa, 1944

Ethiopia alone. Uganda was the source of the White Nile. Could Britain, the ruler of Egypt, afford to let Uganda fall into 'hostile hands'? That sealed the colonial fate of Uganda. The country became a British 'protectorate'. But the way to Uganda from the sea ran through what later came to be known as Kenya. So Kenya, too, was colonised.

It is because of all these considerations that the Nile Valley is widely regarded as one of the major stimulants of the European scramble for Africa. Is it surprising that Ismitta, the divine embodiment of the sources of the Nile and daughter of the Mountains of the Moon, should appear to be the nearest African equivalent to the Greek goddess Nemesis, sometimes called 'daughter of Oceanus', and sometimes 'the Moon Goddess'?

The instrument of revenge came with those two conferences at Potsdam and Yalta. Europe was then sentenced to the same fate to which Europe had previously condemned Africa – partition and artificial frontiers. Just as the imperial British doctrine of the 'Unity of the Nile Valley' had once cast a shadow over the destiny of Africa as a whole, so the new Soviet doctrine of 'proletarian internationalism' has cast a shadow over the fate of Europe as a whole. A grim historical debt had been paid.

The Second World War and Africa's Liberation
But the effects of the Second World War were more complicated than that. While the war condemned Europe to a new partition, it helped to liberate Africa from an old colonialism.

The Second World War prepared the way for Africa's political decolonisation through a number of side-effects and after-effects. First, the war weakened Britain's capacity to retain a world-wide empire. Britain emerged from the war exhausted and impoverished. This led to the break-up of the British Empire in Asia which helped the cause of decolonisation elsewhere. India and Pakistan, in 1947, led the way in liberation. Meanwhile, the initial defeat and humiliation of France by the Germans (in 1940) helped to destroy the myth of imperial invincibility. Britain's defeat by Japan in South-East Asia, in 1941–2, had a similar effect.

Africans who served in action abroad had their political horizons broadened. They saw the world and acquired new expectations. Africans who stayed at home and tried to follow the fortunes of the war also had their horizons made international. Many were politicised by war conditions at home: by the massive increase in forced labour to produce raw materials for new factories, especially in French Africa; by the diversion of farm work away from food production; by the system of so-called 'voluntary' subscriptions to the war effort; and by the burden of runaway wartime inflation.

The white man was humanised by being demoted from the mythology of the demi-god. A frightened white man next to an African in battle was a new experience, especially in the jungles of Burma where African and Japanese soldiers both adjusted more easily to the difficult conditions than did white soldiers.

The moral case for the war, summed up as opposition to tyranny, and to foreign invasion in Europe, prepared the way for the principle of self-determination in the colonies. The Atlantic Charter between Roosevelt and Churchill was a declaration of new values. And yet, in spite of all this, imperial Britain and imperial Europe still resisted these forces of decolonisation even in the midst of defending Europe's own liberties. No war-time European figure symbolised this paradox more eloquently than Winston Churchill, Britain's wartime premier. He was at once the most poignant defender of European freedom and the most stubborn opponent of Afro-Asian liberation. He became a founding father of post-war west European unification and at the same time a major preserver of divisive colonial frontiers.

But while Churchill succeeded in helping to defeat German Nazism, he failed to vanquish Afro-Asian nationalism. It is to this saga of Winston Churchill as the supreme embodiment of both courage in the Second World War and obstinacy in imperial matters that we now turn.

Churchill: The Last Imperial Defence
On 10 May 1940 Churchill became Prime Minister of the Coalition Government in Britain, a role which gave him his most important place in the history of the world.

From the point of view of colonial aspirations he was cast in a role full of contradictions. He managed to inspire the empire and dominions to close

Mahatma Gandhi in London

ranks behind Great Britain in its moments of peril. He was eager to defend and preserve not only Britain's freedom but also Britain's power to rule others. He stood for Britain's independence and against the independence of Britain's colonies. He saw Britain's survival in terms both of its freedom and of its imperial power. To him the collective relationship within the empire even implied a long-time partnership. In the course of Britain's darkest hour, Winston Churchill said to his countrymen,

> Let us therefore brace ourselves to our duties, and so bear ourselves that, if the British Empire and its Commonwealth last for 1000 years, men will still say 'This was their finest hour'.

We now know that the British Empire did not last 1000 years. And among those who ensured that it did not was an Indian whom Winston Churchill dismissed as a 'naked Fakir' – Mahatma Gandhi. In the mythologies of independent India Gandhi, too, was destined to be placed within his country's 'finest hour'. Winston Churchill did not recognise his fellow traveller on the historical train of the twentieth century. He recognised even less the African stirring for dignity and freedom.

The contradictions of Winston Churchill's role as champion in the Second World War caught up with him when he signed the Atlantic Charter with President Franklin D. Roosevelt of the United States in August 1941. The Charter was basically a declaration of shared Anglo-American principles. It did not use the term 'self-determination' as such, but the Charter did say that the United States and the United Kingdom,

> Respect the right of all peoples to choose the form of government under which they will live; and they wish to see sovereign rights and self-government restored to those who had been forcibly deprived of them.[3]

The impact of the Atlantic Charter on the literate intelligentsia of the colonies was considerable. Nor was this merely within the British colonies. The Algerian nationalist, Muhammad Harbi, has drawn attention to its influence among Algerians. 'Recognition of the right of people to liberty and self-determination gave to nationalism the sanction of the Great Powers.'[4]

At the other end of the continent, the African National Congress of South Africa, meeting in December 1941, made the Atlantic Charter the subject of its own resolution and authorised its president to 'appoint a committee to go into the question of the Atlantic Charter and to draft the Bill of Rights to be presented to the Peace Conference at the end of the Present War'.[5]

As Basil Davidson has noted, the ANC's Atlantic Charter Committee had few illusions, but it did note for the record and with satisfaction that,

> The twenty-six other nations which subscribed to the Atlantic Charter on 2 January 1942 made it quite clear that the freedoms and liberties which this war is being forced to establish in countries which have been victims of aggression in this war, must be realised by the Allied Powers 'in their own lands as well as in other lands'. This is the common cry of all subject races at the present time.[6]

Winston Churchill was rudely awakened to the general imperial ramifications of the Charter that he had co-signed. From the House of Commons Churchill was soon to disillusion attentive nationalists in Asia and Africa. Churchill said to the Commons,

> At the Atlantic Meeting we had in mind primarily, the restoration of sovereignty [and] self-government ... to States and Nations of Europe under Nazi yoke ... so that this is quite a separate problem from the progressive evolution of self-governing institutions in the regions and peoples which owe allegiance to the British Crown.[7]

Churchill was unwilling to unravel the imperial partition of Africa. But Churchill had already exposed himself to demands for an extension of the principle of self-government to subject peoples elsewhere. The Atlantic Charter certainly stirred the national aspirations of politically conscious west Africans. In April 1943 the West African Students' Union in London sent a demand to the Colonial Office for dominion status. A group of west African editors, with Nnamdi Azikiwe as leader, prepared a memorandum entitled 'The Atlantic Charter and British West Africa', visited Britain, and asked for substantial political reforms. And among the resolutions passed by the Pan-African Congress of Manchester in 1945 (which included amongst its participants Kenya's Jomo Kenyatta and Ghana's Kwame Nkrumah) was a resolution which demanded that the 'principles of the ... Atlantic Charter be put into practice at once'.[8]

White Freedom, Black Bondage

Winston Churchill seemed to be in favour of self-determination for white people, but not for the non-white peoples of Asia and Africa – least of all if their self-determination was being violated by Great Britain.

But Churchill's American co-signatory disagreed. Franklin D. Roosevelt reaffirmed that the principles of the Atlantic Charter 'applied to all humanity'. Roosevelt was more sympathetic to the cause of undoing the partition of Africa.[9] This was only one of the occasions when Churchill and Roosevelt disagreed on colonial policies. Roosevelt was often critical especially of Britain's policy in India. Churchill felt that just as the English people at home could be racially broadminded, since at the time they had so few coloured people in the streets of Birmingham and Manchester, so the United States could claim to be broadminded in imperial affairs in the comfortable knowledge that it did not have a significant territorial empire of its own. In Winston Churchill's own phraseology in subsequent years,

> In countries where there is only one race, broad and lofty views are taken of the colour question, states which have no overseas colonies or possessions are capable of rising to moods of great elevation and detachment about the affairs of those who have.[10]

To the end of his political days, Winston Churchill remained an unrepentant imperialist. His contacts with Africa had been varied. Ugandans to the present day quote with pride Winston Churchill's tribute to their country as the Pearl of Africa, following his visit there in 1907 as a Colonial Office junior minister. Churchill served in the Colonial Office from time to time in varied roles, helping to shape the destiny of the British Empire. And as Prime Minister during the Second World War he helped in the decisions to liberate Ethiopia from Italian occupation, and the decisions which enabled the French colonies to make a contribution to the war effort in spite of the occupation of France by the Germans.

Above all, precisely by standing up to the Nazis, Winston Churchill helped to keep the extremes of racism from conquering the world. On Churchill's death in 1965, President Kwame Nkrumah of Ghana described him as one of the greatest leaders of the twentieth century. 'The memory of his inspiring leadership will long survive.'

Two more things were noted on Churchill's death which had considerable implications for Africa. One was Churchill's status as one of the founding fathers of the United Nations; the other was his status as one of the founding fathers of west European unification after the Second World War.

The man who had believed so fervently that power was a trust became one of the major architects of a global experiment in humanising power. The United Nations as a collective instrument to discipline power in humane directions was launched more by the post-war Labour Government (1945–51) in Britain than by Winston Churchill, but Churchill's role in global thinking and policymaking before he ceased to be Prime Minister was part of the background to that world body.

We must not deceive ourselves about Winston Churchill. In some respects Churchill shared the racial paradigm of Adolf Hitler. Churchill's vision of the world could accommodate the role of racial genius in historical change. Although Churchill belonged to a more liberal culture than Hitler, he remains the man who liberated Europe while refusing to liberate the Empire. Perhaps he sensed that Nemesis was closing in. After all it was Churchill who coined the phrase the 'Iron Curtain', recognising with horror that such a curtain was coming down right across Europe. It was dividing east from west, with the same sense of doom that Africans must once have felt when they put away their futile spears and resigned themselves to the European imperial curtain at the end of the previous century.

Meanwhile the Second World War had pushed western Europe off the centre-stage of world power and put it under the shadow of the United States and the Soviet Union. This not only partitioned Europe, it also helped to loosen Europe's hold on Africa. What is more, these new post-war super-powers had a tradition of opposition to western European-type imperialism and put pressure on western Europe to speed up the decolonisation of Africa.

But the most important factor behind Africa's liberation was Africa's own will to recapture its sovereignty. While this will was aided by the aftermath of the Second World War, it was much older than the war, going back to the original European scramble for Africa, and being expressed by frequent and prolonged resistance to colonial rule. In fact, Africa has experienced three traditions of political resistance to colonial rule – indigenous forms of resistance, Islamic forms of combat, and Western-inspired forms of agitation, partly related to Indian-inspired forms of rebellion.

Indigenous Forms of Resistance

'Primary resistance' in the chronological sense of 'primary' means resistance by African people at the very time of European penetration and conquest. Many African societies decided not to accept colonialism but to fight it as it arrived. Resistance ranged from the Ashanti Wars in Ghana to the Zulu Wars in South Africa and the Ndebele-Shona in Zimbabwe, from Bunyoro in Uganda to Yorubaland and Dahomey in west Africa, from the Hehe in Tanzania and the Nandi and Giriama in Kenya to the city-states of the Niger Delta and the Baoule of the Ivory Coast.

'Primary resistance' in the cultural sense of 'primary' means resistance on the basis of indigenous fighting symbols regardless of chronology. The Mau Mau fought the British as late as the 1950s – but on the basis of Kikuyu values and related religious beliefs, the symbolism of indigenous combat cultures, from oath ceremonies to the drinking of menstrual blood. The Mau Mau were militarily defeated by the British, but were nevertheless politically triumphant in the sense that Mau Mau broke white settler political will and

The so-called 'Kaffir Wars': the capture of Fort Armstrong, 1851

opened the doors for Black majority rule. The Mau Mau emergency in Kenya lasted from 1952 to 1960.

The Maji Maji War of 1905 to 1907 in Tanganyika (mainland Tanzania) was primary resistance in an intermediate sense between chronology and pure culture. Chronologically it occurred quite early in Tanzania's colonial experience. It was also inspired culturally by indigenous beliefs – including the fatal belief that Maji baptism (Maji is Kiswahili for water) was adequate protection against German bullets. The movement was crushed but it helped to inspire the Germans to formulate less repressive imperial policies.

Islamic Forms of Resistance

African 'primary resistance' in the chronological sense was sometimes Islamic rather than purely indigenous – at least in symbolism. When it was Islamic the clarion call was usually the jihad (struggle in the path of God). The resistance of African Muslims to European imperialism was sometimes couched or framed in religious terms of opposition. In these cases, jihad was not aggressive, as in the nineteenth-century conquest of the Hausa states by the Fulani led by Uthman dan Fodio, but defensive. Islam has a long history of defence against aggression by its enemies. Indeed, it goes all the way back to the life of the prophet Muhammad. Against the political establishment of Arabia in his own day, Muhammad decided that his duty was to resist or to go into exile. Under pressure he decided to flee from Mecca to Medina.

It was in this tradition of defensive resistance that Islam was mobilised to resist European imperialism. Indeed, a substantial portion of Africa's primary resistance to European colonialism was Muslim-inspired:

> Militant Islam presented the greater challenge and mobilised the sternest resistance to the European occupation of Africa in the nineteenth century. Muslim policies, with their written languages, their heritage of state-making, and the cohesive force of a universal religion preaching the brotherhood of all believers, could generally organise resistance on a wider scale than political units whose extent was limited by the tide of common ancestry. Muslims also had a strong incentive to oppose the advance of Christian power.[11]

When European pressure was becoming too strong for the leadership of the Sokoto Caliphate in nineteenth-century Nigeria, the leadership thought of the Hijra, the 'obligatory flight from the infidels'. Sultan Attahiru Ahmadu led a Hijra after the fall of Sokoto, going eastwards. As the historian Michael Crowder has put it,

> The British finally overtook him at Burmi and killed him. However, many of his followers continued to the Sudan where their descendants still live today under the chieftaincy of his grandson, Mohammadu Dan Mai Wurno.[12]

On the other side of Africa, Islam also displayed its own versions of defensive fanaticism, opposing the encroachment of European power and statecraft. The jihad tradition manifested itself in the Sudan with the Mahdiyya, Mahdist opposition to British penetration. Mohammad Ahmed el-Mahdi of Sudan was the precursor of Sudanese nationalism, rallying religion behind nationalistic causes, marrying piety to patriotism.

The jihad tradition also manifested itself in Somalia in the sacralised nationalism of Sayyed Muhammad Abdille Hassan, whom the British called the 'Mad Mullah' but who was decidedly sane as a patriot in his resistance to Britain for over two decades, from 1899 to 1920. In the words of a British historian, I. M. Lewis,

> Muhammad Abdille Hassan's burning passion was to quicken his countrymen's devotion to Islam and to secure universal and absolute adherence to all the ordinances of their faith … He had thus a deeply felt mission to fulfil amongst his people whose ancient belief in Islam he saw as perilously threatened by Christian colonisation.[13]

There were similar examples of Muslim jihadist resistance to the French in west Africa – by Lat-Dior Diop, ruler of Cayel, and Mahmadou Lamine, ruler of the Sarrakole, both in Senegal, by Ahmadu, emperor of the Tokolor, and by Samori Toure, emperor of the Mandinka, in the 1880s and 1890s.

The fear of future jihads profoundly influenced British colonial policies from Muslim areas in Africa generally. It is arguable that Britain's decision to let northern Nigeria enjoy substantial autonomy during the colonial period was partly influenced by Britain's reluctance to risk offending Muslim feelings through direct British control of the north. Britain's colonial policy of indirect rule in northern Nigeria was in part intended to reduce the risk of any further jihads in the area. Western missionary education was also discouraged in Muslim areas for similar reasons. Some caution was also shown by France in her own policies towards Muslim colonial subjects.

In north Africa opposition to European imperial rule was often reinforced by some Pan-Islamic sentiment, largely inspired by a great scholar, Al-Afghani, a teacher at Cairo's Al-Azhar university, though nationalism in Egypt against British occupation became increasingly secular in the twentieth century.

The rise of Islamic sentiment in British India in favour of creating a separate country (Pakistan) created some concern in west Africa about separatism and secessionism in African Muslim areas as well. After the Second World War Christian African nationalists such as Nnamdi Azikiwe and Kwame Nkrumah worried about Islam as a potentially separatist force in west Africa. But while west African history has witnessed Islam as an expansionist force and at times as a liberating force, west Africa has not experienced separatist Islam of the magnitude which created Pakistan.

Indo-Western Forms of Resistance

While some African nationalists in the 1930s and 1940s were nervous about religious tension of the kind which was affecting India, Africans were also often impressed by the achievements of the Indian nationalist struggle for independence. One Indian leader was for a while particularly influential as a source of ideas for distant African nationalists. This was Mahatma (Mohandas) Gandhi, the moral leader of India's nationalist movement. He represented a fusion of Western liberalism and Hinduism.

Kwame Nkrumah used Gandhian ideas as a basis for his strategy of

A ZANU rally at Mutare, Zimbabwe

'Positive Action' against the British in Ghana in the late 1940s and early 1950s. Kenneth Kaunda of Zambia was also a disciple of Mahatma Gandhi. At one time Kaunda was 'opposed to violence in all its forms' as a political strategy of decolonisation. Gandhi had championed Satyagraha or 'Soul Force' as a strategy of non-violent passive resistance. Kaunda found this philosophy attractive. The responsiveness of Nkrumah and Kaunda was partly due to their Christian upbringing. African conversion to Gandhiism was partly a consequence of Africa's Westernisation.

Africa's opposition to armed struggle was also evident at the All-Africa People's Conference held in Accra, Ghana, in 1958. The Algerians, who were at war with France at the time, found it difficult to obtain Pan-African endorsement of their struggle.

Why did armed struggle lack legitimacy among so many African nationalists at that time? Why were Gandhian ideas more popular? What was it which changed African attitudes to the use of force and violence in liberation movements?

One reason for the reluctance to resort to armed struggle was, as we have indicated, the influence of the West and Christianity. The leaders of African struggles for independence were disproportionately Western-educated or educated in Western-type schools and colleges, most of them Church missionary institutions. These leaders included figures such as Nkrumah, Senghor, Nyerere, Azikiwe, Awolowo, Banda, Kaunda, Houphouet-Boigny and many others.

Another reason why armed struggle was rejected by many modern African nationalists was a sense of political realism. In Tanganyika, for example, many Africans remembered the crushing defeats of those early nationalists who fought unavailingly against the Germans in the Hehe and Maji Maji wars. In Julius Nyerere's words,

> It was therefore necessary for TANU [Tanganyika African National Union] to start by making the people understand that peaceful methods of struggle for independence were possible and could succeed. This does not mean that the people of this country were cowardly, particularly fond of non-violence; no, they knew fighting; they had been badly defeated and ruthlessly suppressed.[14]

A third factor which won support for Gandhian tactics of non-violence in the struggle for independence in Africa was the very success of Gandhiism in India itself, as the British made concession after concession to the nationalist movement – including the final concession of independence itself, which took place in 1947.

What caused some African liberation movements to turn away from Gandhian non-violence and resort to armed struggle? There is one common factor which motivated armed guerrilla resistance in Kenya, Algeria, Portuguese Africa and the white-ruled countries of southern Africa: the sheer stubbornness of white settlers in the face of demands for political freedom by the African majorities.

The Mau Mau in Kenya, the FLN in Algeria, the various liberation movements in Angola and Mugabe's ZANU and Nkomo's ZAPU in Zimbabwe all failed to win outright victory over the colonial power or the settler regime, and the Mau Mau was defeated in the military sense. Yet all these movements succeeded in seriously weakening the will of the colonialists to continue ruling over an African majority and therefore were victorious in the political sense. In Guinea-Bissau the PAIGC won outright victory over the Portuguese, and in Mozambique FRELIMO liberated a large part of the country before Portugal conceded to FRELIMO control of the rest. In all these cases it was realised, sooner or later, that only armed struggle would achieve independence and majority rule, either by the military victory of guerrilla armies or by winning concessions from diehard white settlers who would not be moved by non-violent, semi-constitutional protest.

The armed struggle continues in Namibia (South-West Africa) and South Africa, in the form of guerrilla resistance by, respectively, SWAPO (South-West African People's Organisation) and Umkhonto we Sizwe (Spear of the Nation), the military wing of the ANC (African National Congress). SWAPO, under Sam Nujoma's leadership, began its war of independence in 1966, the same year that the United Nations General Assembly ended South Africa's mandate to rule the territory. SWAPO has units operating inside Namibia but, since Angolan independence in 1975, it has operated largely from Angola. Umkhonto we Sizwe was formed in 1961 by Nelson Mandela and other ANC radicals after the failure of the ANC's Gandhian tactics in the 1950s to win concessions from the Afrikaner-backed Nationalist Party

Nelson Mandela, the prominent African lawyer who was first charged with treason by the South African Government in 1956. He has been continuously imprisoned since 1962.

government which was busy entrenching and extending 'apartheid'. Since Mandela's arrest in 1962 and subsequent continuous imprisonment the ANC's armed struggle has been led in exile by Oliver Tambo and others. In the 1980s ANC military operations inside South Africa have been stepped up, in the form of sabotage of vital installations.

The argument about whether to use Gandhian tactics or the armed struggle to defeat colonialism has in Africa been an argument not about ideology but about means. Gandhians and guerrillas alike may separately have adopted tactics suitable to their particular local situations. Their ultimate objectives are broadly the same: to regain independence and political freedom. Guerrilla-based movements may tend to adopt more radical rhetoric, largely because the military technology they use against white settler regimes (or colonial regimes that defend settlers) comes not from the West but from the East, from the socialist and communist countries. On the other hand, the leaders even in African liberation movements that have engaged in armed struggle come mainly from among the culturally Westernised Africans. Across time these have included Amilcar Cabral of Guinea-Bissau, Eduardo Mondlane of Mozambique, Agostinho Neto of Angola, Robert Mugabe and Joshua Nkomo of Zimbabwe and Nelson Mandela of South Africa.

The West (America and western Europe) may not supply guerrillas fighting against white majority rule with arms, but it has provided them with other weapons. The West has, albeit unintentionally, inspired African resistance through various means including Western education, Christianity, Western political ideologies (nationalism, liberalism and socialism), and alliance with metropolitan political parties or organisations, especially in French-speaking Africa. Indeed, by producing Westernised African nationalists, European imperialism helped to dig its own grave, whether the executioners were Gandhians or guerrillas.

Europe's Residual Sorcery

Has the equation between the fate of Europe and the destiny of Africa in the second half of the twentieth century been completed? Does the balance sheet end with liberation for Africa and partition for Europe? Has Africa's 'Nemesis', the Black and elegant Ismitta, completed her revenge triumphantly?

Alas, European powers for both good and evil are by no means exhausted. The most powerful of all the skills of sorcery of the white man in Africa was strengthened rather than weakened by the Second World War. The African goddess, Ismitta, has so far been helpless against that particular northern wind, the dual wind of capitalism and the sovereign state.

While the Second World War was indeed congenial to subsequent political liberation, the same war helped to suck Africa more deeply into the Western capitalist system. This happened because of another set of side-effects and after-effects of the war. The war accelerated Europe's need for

Africa's raw materials, minerals and food products. The production of these commodities in Africa deepened the export-bias in Africa's economies and helped to consolidate the emerging, uneven 'interdependence' between North and South. The Korean War in the early 1950s, which was itself one of the outcomes of the Second World War, helped to sustain the momentum of Africa's incorporation into the capitalist system as Western demand for raw materials and agricultural products was maintained.

The War helped to shift Great Britain's colonial policies from mere 'law and order' issues to issues of 'development'. British investment in Africa's 'development' helped to forge new economic links between the centre and the periphery. These included the role of the Colonial Development and Welfare Fund. The new 'developmental' ethos of colonisation had an educational component. The development of such university campuses as Ibadan in Nigeria, Legon in Ghana, Makerere in Uganda, Dakar in Senegal, as well as the older Fourah Bay College in Sierra Leone, helped to accelerate the emergence of a bourgeois and petit bourgeois class with a vested interest in maintaining cultural and economic contact with the Western world. The emergence of new social and economic classes in Africa helped to make Africa a better market for Western products and, in time, expanded Africa's purchasing power for Western goods and commodities.

The uncertainties of the nuclear age gave a new strategic significance to Africa's minerals, especially cobalt and uranium in Zaire and southern Africa. Africa's extractive industries became even more deeply tied to the West, as new mineral explorations were undertaken.

The aftermath of the Second World War accelerated America's economic penetration into western Europe which, in turn, prepared the way for new Euro-American ventures into Africa. The Second World War thus helped to inaugurate a new era in multinational or transnational corporations, including such firms as the Anglo-American Corporation in the mining economies of southern Africa.

The post-war era inaugurated a new international monetary system – initially based on the supremacy of the American dollar as a medium of international exchange. The stage was set for Africa's incorporation into a Western-dominated monetary system.

The lessons of the war made western Europe less competitive and more unified, leading to the formation of the European Economic Community (EEC) in 1958. Africa's association with the EEC (1963 Yaoundé Convention; extended in 1969 to Kenya, Tanzania and Uganda in the Arusha Agreement) helped to perpetuate and stabilise Africa's interdependence with Europe.

Meanwhile that other bequest from Europe to Africa – the modern sovereign state – was taking its own toll.

Partition and the Sovereign State

For our purposes here we still accept the definition of the state as a structure of power and authority, which claims sovereign jurisdiction over a given territory, and seeks to monopolise the legitimate use of physical force within those boundaries.

As we have indicated, pre-colonial Africa encompassed both states and stateless societies. The states included elaborate empires such as ancient Ghana, Mali and Songhay, as well as city-states such as pre-imperial Sokoto or pre-imperial Zanzibar. Stateless societies ranged from the Nuer in the Sudan to the Tiv in west Africa.

However, our concern in this section is with the colonial and post-colonial state, perhaps Europe's most important bequest to the new rulers of Africa. How is it faring under the stresses of independence in Africa? And how does it relate to other aspects of the post-colonial scene with special reference to the risk of war and the search for peace within Africa?

The first factor to bear in mind is the relevance of the Berlin Conference of 1884–5 and the ensuing partition. Even in those parts of Africa where the state had not existed before European colonisation, it can be argued that state-formation began as soon as the colonial order established structures of control. The entire colonial period was therefore an experience in state-building, a phase in the growth of the modern African state. The European scramble for Africa was an essay in state-formation. But before independence the colonial state was part of a wider system of power, a wider empire. Independence was a *rite de passage*, an initiation into autonomous statehood. There were also high hopes for stability.

However, it was soon clear that the post-colonial African state was inherently fragile domestically as well as in relation to the outside world. Externally, a few European mercenaries could at times play havoc with political order in an African state. Domestically, the African state has sometimes lacked a national consensus behind it. The legitimacy of the state is not yet assured. Conditions are difficult for stability. The African state has been unable to assert a monopoly of the legitimate use of physical force. The partition of Africa has left a new tradition of violence in the post-colonial era.

But is there a triple heritage of violence in Africa? Under the influence of Islam, violence is more likely to be for public purposes than for private economic gains. Of the ten biggest cities of the world, Cairo may well be the least violent in terms of mugging and other violent individual economic crimes. Yet the city has known its assassinations and riots.

Zanzibar is the literal 'Dar es Salaam' (Heaven of Peace) of Tanzania from the point of view of safety from violent robbers, yet the island experienced the worst political and revolutionary convulsion in the modern history of Tanzania. The prison-house of Lamu has very few violent criminals – the city can be described as a beehive of vice without the sting of violence. But the prison house has sometimes accommodated political offenders. Violence in pursuit of private economic gain is more a consequence of the impact of the West on Africa than of anything else. Indigenous culture can be violent for ethnic reasons, Islam can be violent for religious reasons. Westernism in Africa is often violent for economic reasons.

A casualty of the Chad civil war awaits evacuation

The majority of major civil wars in Africa including those in Sudan, Nigeria, Chad, Eritrea, the Ogaden, have had an Islamic component. All civil wars in Africa have been substantially ethnic, including all those in the above Islamic list, with the addition of Angola and perhaps Zimbabwe and Zaire. The West has provided those artificial borders which have enclosed the battlegrounds – the borders inherited from Africa's partition.

But the West has also produced white settlers in southern Africa. The most racist component of the triple heritage is the Western legacy. Racial conflict in southern Africa is part of the triple heritage of violence.

As we have shown, Africa's triple heritage of military combat included the warrior tradition (indigenous), the jihad tradition (Islamic) and guerrilla and 'conventional' warfare (so-called 'modern' war, based on Western technology). We have indicated how the warrior tradition ranges from Zulu wars to the Mau Mau conflict, and how the jihad tradition includes Uthman dan Fodio and the Sudanese Mahdiyya. Guerrilla war in recent years has been especially important in southern Africa. 'Conventional' warfare in the Western sense has been either between states (Tanzania versus Uganda, or Ethiopia versus Somalia), or as part of a civil war (for example, in Nigeria, Chad or Sudan).

Even the external wars in which Africa has been involved have to some extent a triple heritage of their own. The two world wars were primarily Western wars. Africa participated militarily in both. The cold war (since the Second World War) is a confrontation between the West and the Soviet Union and its allies. Africa is involved politically, diplomatically and strategically. The Horn is one arena of super-power rivalry. The Middle East, the Nile Valley and the Indian Ocean are inter-related areas strategically. The Arab-Israeli conflict has always involved both the West and the Muslim world. It has now involved the Africans as well. Against none of its own former colonial masters has Africa lashed out with as much consensus as it did when it broke with Israel in 1973.

Westerners and/or Arabs have in turn taken part in such sub-Saharan conflicts as the Nigerian civil war (using British arms and Egyptian pilots), the Shaba conflicts of Zaire (Belgian troops were used in 1960–3 and Moroccan troops fought alongside French soldiers in 1978), and conflicts in the Horn of Africa (for example, the wars in Eritrea, Ogaden and Somalia). The Sudanese civil war was Afro-Arab and encompassed a triple religious heritage – the three religious legacies were at war. As for Chad, Westerners and Arabs chose their proxies once again in 1983, with the French and Americans backing President Hissene Habre and the Libyans supporting ex-President Goukouni Oueddei.

Is there a triple heritage of revolution in Africa? In post-colonial Africa the two main revolutionary forces are leftist radicalism and Islam. Indigenous culture is a sleeping giant which has yet to rise to the drums of revolution.

The first post-colonial socialist revolution in Africa was in Egypt from 1952 onwards, when Nasser's Free Officers seized power. The first one in west Africa was in Guinea (Conakry) from 1958 until Sékou Touré's death in 1984. The first in east Africa was in Zanzibar from 1964 onwards, after the overthrow of the Sultan. In the Horn of Africa Somalia went socialist before Ethiopia. All these early revolutionary experiments were in Muslim societies. But although Islam was inextricably bound up in the political culture of those societies, the revolutions were a *combination* of Islamic and Leftist radical elements.

The most explicitly Islamic revolution in Africa so far is perhaps the Libyan experiment under Qaddafy. Libya has also been the most keen to export revolution.

The Leftist radical revolutions which are not Muslim and accept being called Marxist include Mozambique, Angola, Ethiopia and the Congo (Brazzaville). Algeria's revolutionary changes have been socialist but neither Muslim nor Marxist.

There is as yet no revolutionary government which stands for the defence of indigenous values and customs. Yes, the giant of Africa's indigenous legacy continues to sleep! And when it dreams, it dreams of dances complacently – while mullahs, Marxists and mafuta-mengi (the fattened ones) take over Africa.

Even the warrior tradition is in tatters in many places: Zulu warriors pull rickshaws in South Africa; Masai warriors take jobs as night watchmen in Kenya; warrior dances as tourist attractions are to be found all over Africa.

But while no social revolution has so far been carried out in the name of indigenous culture, some military coups have included indigenisation policies. Amin's coup in Uganda sought to revive African culture (for example, by legalising polygamy) and to indigenise Asian businesses; Doe in Liberia started with the intention of re-indigenising the power structure of

Liberia and reducing the power of Americo-Liberians; Mobutu in Zaire has sounded the clarion call of authenticity (for example, by Africanising place names and personal names). But none of these good intentions has resulted in a genuine structural revolution on the side of African values.

As for riots in Africa, the religious ones are usually Islamic or indigenous. Established Christianity has not taken to rioting in the name of religion as yet. When African riots are not religious, they are either class-related (including food riots) or ethnic-related (such as the political riots in Yorubaland) or generational (such as student riots). Market women's riots are more likely to be class-related than concerned with the rights of women *per se*.

Africa's colonial boundaries may be the biggest single cause of Africa's tensions, especially in countries such as Chad under pressure from Libya, Sudan divided between north and south, Somalia shared out by colonialism into five fragments, and Morocco in the throes of a war over a separatist western Sahara, seeking its own independence.

The Berlin Conference of 1884–5 has left a legacy of continuing tension even after Europe's formal withdrawal from colonial jurisdiction in Africa. The curse of Berlin haunts both Africa and Europe. The Berlin Wall is casting its shadow over two continents.

Conclusion

What then is the final equation between Europe and Africa following the Second World War? The war resulted in the partition of Europe and the liberation of Africa. The 'daughter of the Mountains of the Moon' is triumphant up to that point. Europe is in disarray ideologically – just as Africa is in disarray economically. Vengeance has been exacted. The Berlin Wall stands in silent accusation.

But Europe has a residual secret force for mischief in Africa – the dual force of statism and capitalism. European influence in Africa remains considerable – and the colonial boundaries remain frozen in spite of the post-colonial glare of the tropical sun.

In the battle of the gods between Europe and Africa, the result so far is at best a draw. The daughter of the Mountains of the Moon may be licking her bruises. New battles are on the horizon – new powers of resistance need to be mobilised. The struggle continues.

Muntu: A Conclusion

We have referred in this book to the curse of the ancestors. The compact between this generation of Africans, on one side, and the twentieth century, on the other, has been characterised by cultural and moral imbalance. The ancestors are disturbed that inadequate allowance has been made for their own contribution to Africa's indigenous personality. The compact has been deficient in authenticity.

We have explored two routes towards Africa's redemption. One is the imperative of looking inwards towards Africa's ancestors. The other is the imperative of looking outwards towards the wider world. Indigenous culture has been the foundation of the inward imperative towards ancestry. Islam and Western culture have constituted the beginnings of looking outwards towards the wider world of humanity at large. But looking inwards at today's village is not identical with looking inwards at yesterday's Africa. The solution to Africa's war of culture does not lie in a mere geographical pronouncement that 'small is beautiful'. It must include a historical pronouncement that the 'ancestral is authentic'. A reconciliation lies in a special transition from the tribe to the human race, from the village to the world.

Muntu is an indigenous African word meaning person, and sometimes meaning Man in the generic sense of humankind. In a sense it is the theme of humanism in Africa's philosophical and political experience, involving a major transition in perception across the centuries.

There was a time for many African societies, in some cases fairly recently, when the village was the world. The myths and legends of the society focused on the immediate human community, and the people concerned sometimes visualised themselves as directly linked to the origins of humankind. The ancestry of the 'tribe' was often equated with the ancestry of human beings generally. There was a tendency to globalise the village or globalise the 'tribe'. What Africa has experienced, especially in the twentieth century, is the momentous transition from the village globalised ('my people are the world') to the world villagised ('the people of the world are my people'). A rude shock has occurred all over the continent and beyond – the shock that the village is not the world; on the contrary, the world is a village. The concept of the global village is at hand, and the idea that planet Earth is a lonely island in the cosmos is competing with more ancient myths and legends in Africa. As a Francophone wit has put it,

Africa has its feet in the neolithic and its head in the thermonuclear age. Where is the body? It is managing as best it can.[1]

opposite, The UN's 1985 women's conference was held in Nairobi

Muntu: A Conclusion 295

What are the real implications of this African condition from the image of the village as the world to that of the world as a village? How has it affected Africa's relations with other peoples and cultures? How has it conditioned the concept of Muntu in world affairs? It is to these issues that we now turn.

Africa's Myths of Ancestry

As we have mentioned in an earlier chapter, every society has two myths — the myth of ancestry concerning the origins of that society and the myth of purpose or mission, emphasising the uniqueness of that society.

We have noted that the most successful tribal myth of ancestry is that of the Jews. The story of Adam and Eve, the legend of the Garden of Eden and how death came into the world, has now triumphed over many cultures on Earth. Many African societies have given up their own myths of origin in favour of the Semitic one from Genesis. The legend of Adam and Eve is something jointly shared by all of the three Semitic religions — Judaism, Christianity and Islam. The Swahili word for human being is *mwanaadamu*, child of Adam.

Yet some indigenous African myths of origin have shown remarkable similarity to the Jewish one. Oyekan Owomoyela of Nigeria tells us about the days when the Sky God of Africa had His abode very close to the world of men. These were the days of abundance. The sky could be reached almost with the stretching of the arm, and fruit and other delicacies could be plucked by humans. In their greed the humans plucked and gathered more than they could eat, causing the Sky God considerable pain over all that waste. And when the human women pounded corn in their mortars they raised their pestles so high that they kept hitting the sky on the upstroke. The Sky God was alienated but instead of expelling humans from a bountiful garden, God Himself created a distance away from human beings. In an African sense, the sky was now the limit — it was far away because God had distanced himself from the waste and insensitivity of human beings.

The myth combines elements reminiscent of Genesis, on one side, and John Locke's ideas about the origins of private property, on the other. In both Genesis and the African myth there is a tendency to make women bear extra responsibility for destruction. But while the Semitic myth refers to a fruit which ought not to have been eaten but was, the African myth refers to wasted fruit that ought to have been eaten but was not. It is this latter aspect that makes the African myth share an idea with an English philosopher about the origins of private property.

John Locke believed that God had intended to give the world to humankind as a shared bounty. Men and women could avail themselves of the fruit of the world, and the rivers and springs, in perpetual partnership. What made something your property was the labour you put into acquiring it or making it.

But in Lockean terms there was a limitation. Nobody was to take more than they needed, and certainly not more than they could use sensibly. The limit of gathering and plucking was the borderline between sensible use and sheer waste. While the Semitic Genesis had made consumption without permission the Original Sin, John Locke and African mythology made wasteful greed the original vice. But curiously, while John Locke's ideas on the origins of private property and his opposition to waste led to the ideology of efficient capitalism, the African myths of opposition to waste led primarily to rural communalism.[2]

Many myths of 'tribal' origin include also the origins of death. A myth from Sierra Leone relates that Death once lived with God, and kept on pleading to God to let it go. But God had promised Man that although Death had been allowed to come into the world, Man would not die. There are two things that God had to reconcile; liberating Death, letting it go where it pleased, on one side, and saving Man on the other. God decided to send Man new skins which would protect him from the elements and save him from Death. But the messenger with the skins was waylaid by a snake who stole the skins. Was the snake liberated Death in disguise? Man discovered too late that the skins of protection from Death had been stolen.

> From that day onwards, Man has always borne a grudge against the Snake, and has always tried to kill him whenever he sees him. The Snake, for his part, has always avoided Man, and has always lived alone. And because he still has the basket of skins that God provided, he can always shed his old skin for a new one.[3]

This Sierra Leonean myth echoes the Semitic myth of the fall of Adam through the special use of a snake or serpent. Satan, like Death in the African myth, had once lived with God and then wanted to break out into liberty. What the Sierra Leonean myth has done is to fuse the concept of Satan with the concept of Death into a single being. In Genesis, on the other hand, Satan was instrumental in creating death for humankind but was not himself Death.

These different myths of either national ancestry or the subculture of death were based on a conception of the world which did not distinguish the history of the human species from the history of the particular society. The village was the world; the nation was the universe. Even the ancient Egyptians, the first urban rather than village-based civilisation in the African continent, still tended to equate their own destiny with the destiny of the human race. Like the Jews after them, the ancient Egyptians regarded themselves as the Chosen People. The Egyptians believed that the great gods had first manifested themselves in and through Egypt. It was in Egypt that the sun god ruled and fought as king. At their most arrogant, the ancient Egyptians saw only themselves as 'men' (*ronet*). The rest of the human species, whether white or Black, were the equivalent of what the Chinese have called 'barbarians', and the Jews have called 'gentiles'. All these three ethnocentric traditions were variations of the image that the village is the world, the 'tribe' is the human race.[4]

There are, of course, other myths of origin all over Africa that sustained

Mount Kenya

this equation between the origins of the human race and the origins of particular 'tribes'. The snow-capped Mount Kenya is associated with the House of Mumbi of the Kikuyu – and the origins of the Kikuyu are interlinked with the mountain as the abode of divinity and the coming of the first human being.

Buganda's myth of origin concerns Kintu, the first Muganda, but also, in some versions of the myth, the first human being. Competition between good and evil is again captured in the myth of Kintu. So is the story of the origin of death. Kintu, according to Ganda mythology, came from the sky not only with his wife Nnambi Nantuttululu but also in the company of her brother Walumbe (Death).[5]

When African myths of ancestry intermingle with myths from outside Africa, the usual mixture has been with Jewish, Arab or other Semitic traditions. The legend of Solomon and Makeda, the Queen of Sheba, as the origins of the Ethiopian imperial dynasty is among the most famous. In this case we are tracing the legendary ancestry of the ruling house, rather than the genesis of the human species as a whole. Makeda, Queen of Sheba and Ethiopia, visited King Solomon and was well-received. The virile king propositioned the visiting queen but was turned down. The king wanted to know under what circumstances the queen would agree to surrender to him. The queen said under no circumstances. The king asked, 'What if you took a thing of mine without my permission? Would you then let me take you into my arms?' The queen emphatically declared that she would never take anything of his without his permission. That evening the banquet had food which was highly spiced and salted. The degree of spicing was deliberate – to ensure long-lasting thirst. At night, when Makeda was trying to sleep, the thirst was too great. She looked for a jug of water in her own room but there was none. She tiptoed out of her own room, and beheld a jug in splendid isolation within the king's chamber. She sneaked towards it, in the hope of not being observed and not waking anybody. Just as she started to drink from it a hand caught hold of her arm. She had broken her pledge. She was consuming something belonging to the king without his permission. Being a woman of honour, she kept her word and surrendered her body. The future Menelik the First, great emperor of Ethiopia, was conceived that night.

Like the story of Adam and Eve, the Solomon and Makeda tale also has something that was forbidden. In this story, it was forbidden water rather than forbidden fruit. Solomon played his own Satan and his own serpent – engaged in both seduction and deception of Makeda, playing Eve. But in this royal tale of Solomon and Makeda, the seduction scene did not lead to the beginning of death; it led to a new dynasty in the Horn of Africa.

Although the last of the Solomonic emperors of Ethiopia was overthrown in 1974, and a Marxist revolution has succeeded the dynasty, there is no doubt that the legend of Solomon and Makeda is still widely believed in the highlands of Ethiopia. The legend has, to all intents and purposes, the standing of a religious doctrine in the Ethiopian Orthodox Church. The Church claims to have inherited the original Solomonic covenant, which it still holds in custody in a monastery at Axum. Again, the Ethiopians were claiming to be the custodians of a universal covenant for humanity. Here is an intermediate stage between claiming that one's own people are the totality of the

This painting depicts the life of Solomon

human race (as ancient Egyptians sometimes claimed) and asserting that the totality of the human race, wherever they may be, are one's people.

The Ethiopian dynasty also claimed the title of 'king of kings', sometimes implying suzerainty over all other royal houses. The ethnocentric principle was still manifest in the self-image of the Solomonic dynasty in Ethiopia — 'My plateau is the world, my people are the human race!'

Another major African group whose origins have been traced to the other side of the Red Sea are the Yoruba, now mainly concentrated in Nigeria and Benin. One legend has it that the Yoruba are the remnant of the children of Canaan, who were of the 'tribe of Nimrod':

> The cause of their establishment in the West of Africa was . . . in consequence of their being driven by Yarrooba, son of Kastan, out of Arabia to the Western coast between Egypt and Abyssinia. From that spot they advanced into the interior of Africa till they reached Yarba, where they fixed their residence.[6]

According to a related mythological tradition, the Yoruba migrated from Mecca to their present abode, having been forced out of Mecca following a civil war involving Oduduwa, a son of King Lamurudu of Mecca. Oduduwa became the common ancestor of the Yoruba as a Black African people, and Ile-Ife was the place from which Yoruba culture flowered in west Africa.[7]

An aspect of the myth is very similar to the Islamic principle of the Hijra, political exile to escape persecution. As we indicated in an earlier chapter, the Prophet Muhammad had to flee from Mecca and go into exile in Medina. Similarly, the founding father of the African Yoruba had to flee from Mecca to Ile-Ife to escape persecution. Muhammad later returned to Mecca in triumph. Oduduwa also dreamt of returning to Mecca but, instead, his descendants spread out in west Africa and populated new kingdoms.

As can be seen, both the Yoruba and the Amhara of Ethiopia link their own myths of ancestry with elements of Semitic traditions under the Jews and the Arabs. The actual geographical area from where Oduduwa left for Africa and the Sheba whose Queen was seduced by Solomon may be much closer than we once assumed. Certainly this would be the case if Professor Kamal Salibi is justified in his theory that the Israelite kingdom of David and Solomon was not in present-day Israel but in the Saudi provinces of Hejaz and Asir. (See Chapter 4.)

It is in this sense that the myth of seduction between Solomon and Makeda and the myth of Oduduwa's exile might have occurred in close geographical proximity to each other, though separated by centuries of history. What is more, Salibi's theory not only brings the Old Testament closer to history, it also brings the mythology of the Queen of Sheba closer to credibility. Salibi himself has argued that he, as a Christian and a Protestant, conceives of his theory not as refutation of the accuracy of the Old Testament events, but as a strengthening of the Bible as history. The new geographical location, with historically identifiable names, would help to lift the Bible from theology to history.[8]

It can similarly be argued that if the real ancient Israel was located between Mecca and Yemen in south-west Arabia, it was much closer to the Horn of Africa and therefore more easily reachable by an Ethiopian queen 3000 years ago. Linkages between southern Arabia and the Horn of Africa are already a matter of established history and linguistic evidence. That an Ethiopian queen should have visited a Jewish king somewhere between Yemen and Mecca three millennia ago is geographically more believable than a journey to Palestine at that time.[9]

What we are witnessing in these links between African myths and wider Semitic myths is the beginning of a shift from that ethnocentric doctrine that the 'tribe' is the human race to the universalistic doctrine that the human race is a family.

Semites, Whites and the African Diaspora

The first forces to teach the world that the human race was *one* were religious forces. The most universalist of all religions were Semitic religions, especially Christianity and Islam. Precisely because Christianity and Islam wanted to convert every human being, they were the most militantly globalist of all cultures. Their ambitions exceeded their communications, and exceeded also at times their own sincerity of purpose.

The Semites had a consciousness of a *single world*. It is true that part of that story has resulted in religious bigotry, part of it has gone on into militarism and conquest, and much of it over the centuries has included some degree of either religious discrimination or outright religious persecution. But when all is said and done, there has been a Semitic belief in the oneness of the human race, for better or worse. Indeed, the two biggest contributors to world culture to date have been the Semites and Europeans. The Semitic peoples (especially Jews who developed Judaism and Christianity, and Arabs, who developed Islam) helped to change the world through religion – a *theocratic* approach to cultural universalism. Europeans, on the other hand, have helped to change the world through technology and science – a *technocratic* approach to cultural universalism.

Africa has been caught up in these forces of change and universalisation, a brutal transition from the ethnocentrism of the village as the world to a fragile and incoherent universalism aspiring to make the world a true village.

We may therefore say that the absorption of Africa into a global scheme of things was accomplished in a variety of stages, some of them brutal. The most insensitive role was, of course, the slave trade which uprooted millions of Africans and placed them in other parts of the world. This brutality was a form of universalisation, for the slave trade created a permanent African presence in countries such as the United States, Brazil, the Caribbean Islands, the Arabian Peninsula and, more recently, Europe. Because of the slave trade, there has been a partial Africanisation of the Western world, especially of the Americas. Africa's exported sons and daughters have in part become a transmission belt for African culture and myths, for African music and dance. Jazz, the blues, reggae, rumba, calypso, and even rock 'n' roll have all been rhythms partly derived from the African experience, and transmitted into world culture through the African Diaspora.

We mentioned in an earlier chapter that the Diaspora had been dis-Africanised by the West, and yet at the same time racialised in identity. 'Forget you are African, remember you are Black!' The African geographical and cultural ancestry was originally suppressed among African sons and daughters of the Diaspora; while the focus of identity turned more firmly to the physical characteristic of being Black. But there are indications of a partial re-Africanisation in the Diaspora, of a search to re-create the myth of ancestry. With such a re-creation Africa could at last rediscover its bonds with those who were forcibly exported centuries ago.

From a political point of view, Black America especially is Africa's most important external human resource, precisely because it constitutes a large concentration of people of African ancestry lodged in the most powerful nation in the world, and certainly a nation with immense capacity to do Africa harm or good. A re-Africanisation of Black American allegiance and sympathies could help to re-orient American foreign policy towards Africa, and transform it in the direction of greater sensitivity and sympathy with African aspirations and values.

There are twice as many Black Americans as there are Jews in the whole world including, of course, the Jews of Israel. And yet the Black American impact on American foreign policy towards Africa is still only a tiny fraction of the impact of the Jewish Americans upon American policy towards the Middle East. Should the gap in power and influence between African Americans and Jewish Americans narrow in the years ahead, Black America could one day fulfil its destiny as one of Africa's advocates in international courts of judgement; one of Africa's ambassadors in the chanceries of humanity. The increasing influence of Black American organisations such as TransAfrica, a congressional lobby designed to influence legislation favourable to African interests, is one measurement of the slow but still promising re-Africanisation of the Black American psyche.

It is partly in this sense that the African presence in the outer world has been part of the universalisation of Africa, part of the transition from the ethnocentric image of the 'tribe' as the world to the universalistic image of the world as a family.

We must remember that historically there are two African Diasporas and not just one. There is first the Diaspora created by the slave trade, the dispersal of people of African ancestry sold as slaves both across the Atlantic and across the Indian Ocean and the Red Sea. The overwhelming majority of these Africans are Black, drawn from south of the Sahara. But there is also a Diaspora created by colonialism, by movements of population instigated or provoked either directly by the colonial experience or by the ramifications and repercussions of the colonial aftermath. The Diaspora of colonialism is not exclusively from south of the Sahara; it includes large numbers of north Africans scattered in Europe, the Arabian Peninsula and the Americas. Algerians and Moroccans in France and other parts of Europe are part of the total African Diaspora, but they are basically the Diaspora of colonialism rather than slavery. They have been displaced from their home areas by economic necessity cultural dependency, and sometimes the legacy of the competing pulls of tyranny and anarchy in post-colonial African countries.

Curiously enough, the *Black* Diaspora in the Americas is less and less brutalised by racism, though there are still large areas of injustice. In the world of the Western hemisphere, especially North America, racism is becoming less and less overt and, relatively speaking, more subtle.

On the other hand, the North African Brown Diaspora in Europe is experiencing more and more racist brutalities. The French Head of State has had to appeal publicly more than once for discipline, civility and tolerance in France towards immigrant workers, including those large numbers drawn from the Maghreb in northern Africa. Sometimes north Africans have been murdered in France in a manner reminiscent of lynching in American history. The Brown Diaspora in Europe, the Diaspora of colonialism, is confronting rising racism. The Black Diaspora in the Americas, the Diaspora of slavery, has begun to witness declining racism. But both are trends towards the universalisation of the African experience, the agonies of discovering that the world is a village.

New York policeman – part of the Black middle class

Africa: Passive or Active Continent?

This universalisation of the African experience has not simply been passive for Africa. There is indeed a strong tendency in African studies to regard Africa as the passive continent *par excellence*, a recipient of influences rather than a transmitter of effects. And insulting to both Africa and women, some have called Africa the female continent in the special sense of passivity – patient and penetrable. But the assertion that Africa is a passive continent is often a question of the angle of perception. The same evidence could be interpreted either as the effect of the outside world upon Africa or as an example of Africa's influence upon the cultural events in the outside world.

For example, it is arguable that the National Liberation Front (FLN) of Algeria, when fighting for Algeria's independence in the second half of the 1950s, helped to transform the history of metropolitan *France* for the rest of this century. While the Algerians were fighting for their own freedom, they were undermining the Fourth Republic of the French system of government, and the Fourth Republic had been a liability and a weakening factor in the destiny and stability of France. Under the weight of the dissensions and divisions generated by the Algerian war, the Fourth Republic collapsed and France turned to Charles de Gaulle. The Fifth Republic was born, created in the image of de Gaulle, and destined to give France a degree of relative stability it had not until then enjoyed in the twentieth century.

An anti-apartheid demonstration in New York, 1985

Similarly, it is arguable that the African liberation movements in Angola, Mozambique and Guinea-Bissau helped to bring down the dictatorial and sometimes fascist regime of Portugal. The strain of the colonial wars weakened Lisbon under the dictators and led to the coup in Portugal in April 1974. And the long tyranny of the Right Wing in Portugal at last collapsed under the weight of the African challenge in the colonies.

At a more general level, there is Africa's role in the broad redefinition of international morality and law. Africa, perhaps more than any other continent, has helped to make domestic racism in a particular society an issue of international relevance. Under pressure from African states, it has become increasingly impossible for South Africa to claim that apartheid is an issue of domestic jurisdiction. The conflicts and demonstrations within the Republic of South Africa have become a cause of increasing international concern; and have deepened the movement for disinvestment, the withdrawal of investment money from companies conducting business with South Africa. The death knell of institutionalised racism has been sounded by the African struggle against apartheid. When fighting for their own dignity, the Africans have not merely been helping to change their own history. They have been helping to change the history of the world.

Globally, this may be the last complete century of institutionalised racism. Biological versions of ethnocentrism (my tribe is the world, or my race is the world) are giving way to economic universalism (my economy is part of a global system). In the future people will quarrel less and less about tribal or racist versions of ethnocentrism and more and more about resources and jobs in an economically interdependent world.

The next phase in Africa's positive universalisation must surely be the rolling back of the curtain of neo-colonialism, a new phase in Africa's liberation in a global context.

One aspect of this process is to reduce the power that the Western world has upon Africa. The other aspect is to attempt to increase the power of Africa upon the Western world. The former process is a continuation of the anti-colonial struggle, a new phase in the pursuit of autonomy and self-reliance. As for increasing the power of Africa upon the Western world, this requires totally new outlooks and transformed strategies. There is a need to look at the world in a different way, and then to respond to those innovative perspectives. We propose to take as an illustration Nigeria's future rivalry with France for influence and leverage in west Africa.

It is not often realised that Nigeria's most natural rival is neither Libya nor Chad, neither Cameroon nor the Republic of South Africa, though Nigerians have been embroiled in conflicts or disputes with all these four countries. Nigeria's most natural rival is in fact France.

Given the system of sovereign states prevalent in the twentieth century, west Africa should be Nigeria's natural sphere of influence. History books in the Western world are used to ascribing spheres of influence to European and Western powers. The term used can sometimes involve 'filling the vacuum' – a Western power is expected to fill the 'political vacuum' in a country in the Third World or southern region. But even if there is such a thing as a 'political vacuum' in a Third World country, why should it be a Western power that fills it? Why cannot another Third World country, stronger either in wealth or in size or in military might, provide the stabilising prowess in a weaker southern country? In population, Nigeria is at least ten times the size of any other country in west Africa, and more than fifty times the size of a few. Again, in population, Nigeria is more than double the size of the French-speaking countries of west Africa added together. What is more, Nigerians themselves add up to virtually twice the population of France. And yet France for the time being is the most influential single country in west Africa. It exercises considerable influence in more than half a dozen countries in the region. It helps to consolidate a number of African governments and to stabilise their economies. The educational systems of many of these countries are severely penetrated by Frenchmen, French syllabi and French ideas. French personnel wield power and hold positions in a variety of contexts, both high and sometimes relatively low, but nevertheless supervisory. France has also felt free to intervene in some situations in French-speaking countries and to change governments. Among those which were blatantly changed by France was the government of Emperor Bokassa of the Central African Empire (now renamed Central African Republic) in September 1979. France also attempted, less successfully, to tilt the balance of forces in the various civil wars in Chad between 1981 and 1983. In short, there is abundant evidence that France still exercises substantial neo-colonial authority in west Africa, subsidising budgets, designing economies and influencing cultures. Nigeria is not even remotely comparable to France in those countries in terms of influence and leverage, in spite of the credentials that the country has in size, location and sheer Africanity. The real rivalry between France and Nigeria has not really started, but it is a rivalry which seems inevitable and irresistible.

There is evidence that France is aware that Nigeria is a potential rival for influence in west Africa. After all, France had reservations about the creation of the Economic Community of West African States (ECOWAS) in 1976. This organisation was correctly perceived by France as a potential constituency for Nigerian leadership and a potential mechanism for Nigerian influence in French-speaking west Africa. It is true that Nigeria has a number of times compromised its credentials for leadership in west Africa. The expulsion of illegal aliens in Nigeria coming from ECOWAS countries, both under the civilian administration of Shagari and the post-Shagari military administration of General Buhari, was hardly designed to increase Nigeria's influence over its neighbours. On the contrary, holding the illegal aliens as 'economic hostages' within Nigeria, threatening possible expulsion but never executing it, would have been a far more effective instrument of leverage over the countries to whom those individuals belonged. Playing host to foreign workers whom you can expel at short notice can sometimes be a basis of leverage over the countries to which those workers belong. Unfortunately, neither civilian nor military administrations in Nigeria have fully recognised the foundations of regional power and the sacrifices which need to be made to make that power operational. Nevertheless, if ECOWAS does survive, the organisation could become one of Nigeria's instruments in its coming rivalry with France. But for Nigeria to have the necessary qualifications for such an undertaking, Nigeria would not only have to put its domestic house in order but also attempt to put its relations with its neighbours on a more even keel.

Meanwhile, France is gradually increasing its own economic penetration of Nigeria, conceivably designed in part not only to increase French economic returns but also to deepen French political leverage on Nigeria in the days ahead.

It is arguable that France initially attempted to weaken Nigeria by a strategy of fragmentation before Paris resolved to neutralise Nigeria by a strategy of penetration. The strategy of fragmentation was with special reference to French support for Biafra both directly and through the Ivory Coast and Gabon. Although Paris did not recognise Biafra as it was seeking to break away from Nigeria, there is ample evidence that Paris encouraged the governments of the Ivory Coast and Gabon to extend diplomatic recognition to the separatist region of Nigeria. The government in Paris may also have turned a blind eye to Biafra's procurement of arms from France.

As for the French strategy of penetrating Nigeria, this can be traced back at least to 1973 when Franco-Nigerian relations were normalised following the damage done to them by the civil war in Nigeria. M. André Bettencourt, Minister-Delegate for Foreign Affairs, arrived from Paris in Lagos for discussions with the Nigerian government about a *rapprochement*. New areas of economic co-operation were soon being explored. Nigerian Airways entered into a joint venture with the French airline, UTA. In 1975 an assembly plant for a French car, the Peugeot, was commissioned for establishment in Kaduna. Contacts were also made with other French industrialists and financiers about possible French participation in Nigeria's Third National Development Plan. As Dr Bassey Ate of the Nigerian Institute of International Affairs has put it,

> Since 1973, direct Nigerian-Franco business transactions have grown to such an extent that by March 1978, some twenty French companies were engaged on projects in building, road construction, the oil industry and telecommunications, worth about N2·6 billion. And incredible as it might sound, there is an unconfirmed report that the federal government plans to entrust to France the construction of the nation's comprehensive air defence system.[10]

As it happens, Nigeria did step back from so intimate an area of collaboration with France, the construction of the air defence systems. But other areas of co-operation have matured and multiplied since the normalisation of relations between the two countries in 1973. Sometimes the co-operation is triangular – Nigeria, France and a French-speaking African country; for example, Nigeria's business deals with its uranium-rich neighbour, Niger. What seems clear is that France continues to keep a close eye on the evolving role of Nigeria in west Africa, and perhaps silently celebrates when Nigeria damages its own credentials for leadership through either internal instability or the external expulsion of nationals of Nigeria's neighbours.

But the structure of the future is still there – a potential rivalry for leverage

The French Peugeot assembly plant in Kaduna, Nigeria

between France, with its credentials of historical continuities, and Nigeria, with its credentials of geographical contiguities.

There is another African country that could one day cause problems for France in terms of influence in former French colonies. This is Zaire, the largest French-speaking country in Africa and the second largest in the world after France. In area it can in fact swallow up France completely. In mineral resources it could buy France if France were for sale. As the Zairean scholar, Thomas Kanza, has put it,

> Those who speak of the Zaire Republic often forget that this is an immense territory, ten times the size of Great Britain, five times that of France, three times that of Nigeria, eleven times the size of Ghana and eight times that of Belgium. Superimposed on a map of western Europe, the Republic of Zaire would cover Belgium, France, Holland, Denmark, Sweden, Norway, Luxemburg, Spain, West Germany, Portugal and Switzerland. Thus, the size of Zaire is a permanent feature which must be taken into account when any interpretations of political events in Zaire are made or when the country is compared to other African states.
>
> The Republic of Zaire is also rich. The potential wealth of the country is enormous, whether one considers the agricultural possibilities, or the mineral, which have yet to be accurately estimated, or the potential resources of energy.[11]

In the natural order of things there is no reason why Zaire should not one day exercise considerable influence among its neighbours regardless of language, and among French-speaking Africans regardless of proximity.

Without the minerals that Zaire exports to the outside world, it is estimated that up to a third of the airpower of the North Atlantic Treaty Organisation would be in serious trouble. Defence budgets would have to increase or perhaps aeroplanes would be in short supply or perhaps both difficulties would be encountered. International civil aviation might also be affected very seriously. Aircraft could be so expensive that some of the major international airlines would shut down altogether. And yet the same country which is in a position to hold the international air traffic to ransom cannot even maintain its own modest fleet of aircraft. The national airline periodically lays off staff, or runs short of spare parts for its antiquated aeroplanes, and seeks either Israeli or Western investors to bail it out for another few years. Zaire is a tragic illustration of how Africa's resources help to industrialise the Western world, while Africa itself remains pitifully stagnant. But the potential for correcting this situation is there. An initial move is certainly to reduce the power of the West upon Africa. Nigeria could help reduce the power of the West upon west Africa, regardless of language; and Zaire could one day reduce the power of France in French-speaking African countries.

Apartheid: Humanity in Fragments

At least as fundamental as the issues raised above is the struggle in southern Africa, as the confrontation there reaches new levels. It is true that the new collaboration between the Marxist governments of Mozambique and Angola, on one side, and the government of the Republic of South Africa, on the other, has inflicted a serious blow on the combat effectiveness of both the

South African police clear a SWAPO demonstration in Windhoek

African National Congress (ANC) of South Africa and the South-West Africa People's Organisation (SWAPO) in Namibia. But the struggle for Namibia is close to fulfilment in any case and should be solved before the 1990s. However the struggle for South Africa could be drawn out to the last years of the twentieth century.

It is true that agreements that South Africa has reached with its neighbours about controlling the ANC have once again pushed the frontline northwards into Tanzania where it previously was in the 1960s.

There is another consequence of the Nkomati Accord which may already be manifesting itself, and this is to force the struggle against apartheid into the interior of the Republic of South Africa instead of operating from neighbouring countries. The ANC is torn between two political tendencies – the tendency towards internalising the struggle and the tendency towards operating from further north. The formal areas of training and consolidation have already moved northwards; but the need for domestic cells of operation has now become greater than ever. And the unrest which has been unleashed from 1985 by the new brutalities of the South African government has created an opportunity for leadership. It is a resource to be tapped; a diversion which could facilitate sabotage in other areas.

In reality the South African government cannot be effectively threatened until the internal struggle becomes strong enough. Apartheid will not collapse by remote control from either Dar es Salaam or such sympathetic anti-colonialist capitals as Moscow. The Achilles heel of apartheid in South Africa is the Black population of the country itself, and its capacity one day to be sufficiently mobilised for effective combat with the system.

The struggle in the Western world for disinvestment in South Africa, the efforts to persuade Western firms to withdraw their inputs into the apartheid system, will certainly be an important stage in the general evolution from the ethnocentrism that 'my people are the world' to the universalism that 'the people of the world are my people'. The international struggle for disinvestment from South Africa is important as a symbol of human solidarity but its impact on South Africa will be of secondary significance. The primary instrument of struggle has to be armed and mobilised freedom fighters from within the erring republic.

When that struggle finally succeeds, one major change will be the status of Black South Africans. In the twentieth century these have been the most humiliated Blacks of them all. But in the twenty-first century Black South Africans are likely to become the most privileged and powerful Blacks of the world. The immense wealth that the country has, the industrial base which whites and Blacks have all helped to construct, the courage hardened by struggle, the sophistication drawn from being part of a global drama, will all contribute towards making South African Blacks a potentially enlightened aristocracy in the world of Blacks, and certainly a major force for Black power in the world economy.

A stratified Black world could not be an end in itself; nor can the twenty-first century be expected to be the final fulfilment of either African or more broadly human ideals. The struggle to move from privilege to equity will no doubt continue throughout the twenty-first century, but taking new forms and focusing on new issues. The transition from ancestral African beliefs that the tribe is the human race will have gone a long way towards the new universalist dream that the human race is a family.

Africa's role in this transition cannot limit itself to reducing the power of the West over Africa. Decolonisation was indeed necessary, and the struggle against apartheid is absolutely inescapable. The need for countries such as Nigeria and Zaire to displace countries such as France in influence within Africa will remain persistent and demanding for decades to come. But all these are areas where the focus is to reduce the power of outsiders upon Africa. The question still remains as to how Africa can increase its own power over the world beyond. Diluting Western influence on African options is one goal; increasing African influence on Western options is another. It is this second part of the equation to which we now turn.

Power of Numbers and Mineral Wealth

Africa's capacity to influence events partly rests on the numerals of power and the minerals of wealth. Were the world a more democratic place, numerals of power would count for more. We might define 'numericalism' in intergroup or international relations to be that collection of attitudes or general principles which put a moral premium on numerical advantage. The range of forms which numericalism takes is from the moral complexities of 'majority rule' to the simple adage that 'there is strength in numbers'.

What manifestations has numericalism had in international relations? And with what practical effects? The ethic of numerical supremacy has played an important part in multiplying the number of sovereign states in the international community since the end of the Second World War. We know that in the history of colonial liberation the principle of 'one man, one vote' was often crucial. And the appeal of this principle for the colonised lay in the assumption that if 'one man, one vote' were conceded, power would inevitably pass to the majority of the people. In practice two concepts of 'majority rule' have tended to operate. One concept requires that the rulers should be responsive and institutionally answerable to a majority of those they rule. This is the normal liberal concept. The other concept of majority rule simply requires that the rulers should broadly be of the same ethnic or racial stock as the majority of those they rule. In this latter sense, the rulers are to be 'representative' in the sense of being ethnically 'typical' rather than democratically accountable. The idea of 'Black majority rule' is in this latter sense of representativeness. In the history of colonial liberation movements generally in the Third World it has been the ethnic conception of majority rule, rather than the orthodox liberal one, which has been crucial.

The Western world, assisted by other countries at the time, especially the Soviet Union, constructed the United Nations system after the Second World War. This system was primarily based on the idea of votes and decisions being taken by majorities in different institutions. Strictly in numerical terms, Africa is quite influential within the United Nations and in almost all of its agencies. When in alliance with other countries from the Third World, the preferences of the developing countries can at least be proclaimed in resolutions and in votes even if they are not proclaimed in implementation.

Sometimes the Western world has resented this transition from voting power manipulated mainly by the United States in the first twenty years of the United Nations' existence to voting power mobilised by a genuine majority of the human race under the banner of Third World solidarity. Western resentment has sometimes taken the form of threatening to withhold aid to poor countries who voted the 'wrong' way. The Nixon and Reagan administrations were often particularly blunt with this kind of threat. The United States also deprived Africa of the chance of having its first Secretary-General of the United Nations, Salim Ahmed Salim of Tanzania. The main stumbling block to his election was American opposition, and this was based on an image of Salim and of his country as Third World activists. So a quieter diplomatic figure from the Third World was chosen – and Latin America took its turn in directing the destiny of the world body, with Perez de Cuellar's tenure from December 1981.

A third way in which the Western world has attempted to fight majority votes in the United Nations is by actually withdrawing from specific United Nations agencies or at least threatening to withdraw. The most highly publicised of these disputes has concerned the United Nations Educational, Scientific and Cultural Organisation (UNESCO). The Director General of UNESCO, Mukhtar M'bow of Senegal, was the highest-ranking official from Africa within the United Nations system when the United States attacked him in 1984–5. He was accused of mismanagement, budgetary waste, a dictatorial style and sometimes outright corruption. It is ironic that the charge of budgetary waste and mismanagement came from an American administration which had managed to accumulate the biggest budgetary deficit in American history, in spite of pledges to force the nation to live within its means. Under that administration the United States actually crossed the boundary from a creditor nation to a debtor nation in absolute terms. As for the other charges against Mr M'bow, the evidence was at best ambiguous and sometimes outright misleading.

In the final analysis, the Western powers, bound by their own ideologies to the principle of majority rule, were nevertheless unwilling to concede that principle in foreign policy and international affairs. In the theatre of international discourse Western ambassadors cried out against the 'tyranny of the majority' – when in fact they simply meant that they themselves were bad losers in United Nations' votes.

It is one thing for the Third World to have influence within the United Nations; it is quite another for the United Nations to have influence upon the world. The world body is only as powerful as its members are prepared to let it be. The most powerful of its members are not prepared to let it assert greater control over the destiny of this shared planet. The world may be in the process of becoming a village, but this particular village council has yet to become authoritative. The numerals of power can only work effectively when not only the council but also the population of the village has accepted democracy in both intention and in implementation.

This is where Africa and the rest of the Third World have therefore to look for other levers in the global system. From Africa's point of view this is partly a transition from the numerals of power to the minerals of wealth. As Victor LeVine has reminded us, in 1980, about 41 per cent of the United States' crude oil imports came from Nigeria, Algeria and Libya; by 1984 the Libyan share had diminished but the African percentage of America's need had remained constant, with new additional supplies from Angola, Cameroon and Congo. LeVine lays particular emphasis on the non-fuel minerals that have continued to be so important to Western industrialisation:

> These include manganese, crucial to the manufacture of steel, found in Gabon and South Africa; over 50 per cent of the West's imports come from these two countries. They also include chromium (98 per cent of the world's known reserves are concentrated in South Africa and Zimbabwe), cobalt (used for alloys and found mainly in Zaire, Zambia, and Morocco), vanadium (over 50 per cent of the West's imports come from South Africa), plus platinum, germanium, tungsten and several other rare minerals.[12]

And so they dig up Africa faster than they have ever done before. Yet it is one of the cruel ironies of the world economy that a continent so well endowed in natural resources should at the same time be so poor in living standards. Why? Something has gone wrong in the transition towards the human race as one family, tragically wrong especially in the partnership between Western technology and African resources. The digging for those resources continues. Is the digging for wealth? Or is it for the collective burial of a people?

The answer partly depends upon whether Africa's minerals are a cause of Africa's dependency or an instrument of Africa's power over those who need the minerals. If a country has something that other people need, does that make the country more vulnerable to manipulation or exploitation, or does it give the well-endowed country extra influence upon those who need its products? Unfortunately, except for oil, most African resources so far have been a basis for dependency rather than delivery, a cause of vulnerability rather than a source of power.

Even in the case of oil, it was not until OPEC was formed and became more assertive that the benefits of oil became more evenly distributed to their producers. Should African countries with minerals other than oil follow the same path? There may indeed be a case for producer cartels in some instances. Some of the cartels may not be as powerful as OPEC was in the 1970s but organised unity could still make a difference to the price they get and the level of returns. Zaire, Zambia and Morocco could themselves hold the world to ransom over the price of cobalt – not necessarily to push the market too far, but to ensure a fairer return for what they produce. When that happens, this digging and processing of metals from the African earthly body will become not a symbol of weakness, as it now generally is, but a symbol of a capacity for self-protection and self-development; not a symbol of exploitation and unequal exchange but a symbol at last of effective partnership and equitable interdependence.

It is up to mineral-rich African countries to look beyond their immediate horizons of political convenience in their relations with their customers and begin to calculate how best to ensure equitable long-term returns. Producer organisations and co-ordination are probably indispensable if long-term economic justice is to be achieved.

Africa: In Search of Counter-Power

In addition to the numerals of power and the minerals of wealth as bases for leverage, there is the scale of debt. Among Third World countries Africans are not the worst indebted in scale, but the solution to the debt problem among Third World countries may require co-operation and collaboration, especially between African and Latin American countries.

In his role as chairman of the Organisation of African Unity (OAU), Julius Nyerere chose as one of his missions a sustained attack on the system of loans and debts in the world. Nyerere accused the Western world of using economic power in the second half of the twentieth century the way they had once used the power of gunboats to exercise control over the Third World. He told the Royal Commonwealth Society in London in March 1985,

> If the rich refuse to discuss methods by which the Third World can repay its debts, should we continue to try to pay on the terms set – even at the cost of letting our people starve? What I am saying is that the Third World should begin to work together and use its combined power – including the power of debt – to force upon the developed world a series of interlocked discussions. There needs to be an urgent discussion about how and on what

The United Nations in session

terms the debt problem can be dealt with. There also needs to be a wider discussion directed at a reconsideration and reform of an international economic system which is working iniquitously and inexorably against the interests of the poor.[13]

The idea of using debtor power arises out of the assumption that there is a scale of indebtedness which makes the creditor at least as vulnerable as the debtor. If I owed my small bank in Plateau State, Nigeria, $10,000, I am in real trouble; but if I owed the bank $1 billion, the bank is in trouble. In the escalation of indebtedness there comes a time when vulnerability is almost reversed. The creditor is terrified of not being paid back. The threat of default on the part of the debtor becomes *counter-power*.

The Western banks that extend this credit do themselves meet to consult and agree on procedures and strategies; but the indebted nations themselves do not normally meet to co-ordinate their own response, although Argentina has sometimes succeeded in persuading its fellow Latin American debtor nations at least to have joint discussions about their shared predicament.

Is there life after *debt*? It partly depends upon the actions that the Third World countries take as counter-power. The idea is not necessarily to default in paying the debt. The aim is to make the threat of default sufficiently credible that discussions are undertaken to review the terms of the debt, the timetable for the payments, the possibility of a moratorium, and the possibility of declaring certain debts as definitely bad and therefore terminable. A trade union of the indebted is called for; a lobby against the Shylocks of the international banking system.[14]

The fourth kind of counter-power potentially available for Africa (after numerical strength, mineral wealth and debtor power) is some kind of military power, including the possibility of cultivating a nuclear capability. We define 'counter-power' as power exercised by those who, in absolute terms, are weaker upon those who are, by absolute measurements, stronger. Counter-power can be used to attain liberation within the weaker countries; but it can also be used to influence change in the stronger countries.

In the military field, it seems unlikely that Africa will be able to cultivate a sufficient level of counter-power to sustain the idea of military victory against the powerful. What Africa could cultivate is a sufficient degree of nuclear capability to force the powerful in the direction of reconsidering the legitimacy of nuclear weapons.

But why should Africa engage in nuclear proliferation? By a strange destiny only the nuclearisation of Africa could really complete the transition from the image that the village is the world to the vision that the world is a village, from the arrogance that the tribe is the human race to the compassion that the human race is a family. There is a strong possibility that the nuclearisation of Africa is the catalyst that could create consternation among the big powers. The very distrust of Africa and its underdevelopment and instability could begin to induce a true recognition that nuclear weapons have to be denied to all if they are to be denied to anyone. The world cannot be divided for long between nuclear Brahmins and non-nuclear Untouchables, between nuclear haves and non-nuclear have-nots. The egalitarian force in world reform demands equalisation. In order to ensure that no one will have nuclear weapons, it may be necessary for a while to ensure that some more countries have them – especially those least trusted with such a responsibility. The world needs a sense of urgency about nuclear weapons. This sense of urgency has not been created by the super-powers' acquisition of more sophisticated arsenals of destruction. Maybe the sense of urgency will be created by too many small countries acquiring nuclear bombs of their own. A nuclear innoculation is needed to shock the world into nuclear immunisation.

Muntu, Man, is facing his most complete crisis. He needs a final scare to convince him that the world is indeed a village; that the human race is indeed a family.

Appendix

This appendix indicates which chapters relate to each television programme.

Themes of Television Programmes	Book Chapters
1 Environment	Chapter 1 Where is Africa?
	Chapter 2 Anatomy of a Continent
2 Identity and Culture	Chapter 3 The Indigenous Personality
	Chapter 4 The Semitic Impact
	Chapter 5 The Western Aftermath
	Chapter 6 Africa at Play
3 Religion	Chapter 7 Africa at Prayer
4 Technology and Development	Chapter 8 Tools of Exploitation
5 Stability and Political Conflict	Chapter 9 In Search of Stability
6 Political Modernisation and Institutionalisation	Chapter 10 Is Modernisation Reversible?
7 Economic Dependency	Chapter 11 In Search of Self-Reliance
8 Cultural Fusion	Chapter 12 Towards Cultural Synthesis
	Introduction: A Celebration of Decay?
9 Africa in the World	Chapter 13 Between Society and the State
	Chapter 14 Between War and Peace
	Chapter 15 Muntu: A Conclusion

Notes

Introduction

1 Edmund Burke, *Reflections on the Revolution in France* (London, 1790), *Works* (London: World's Classic Edition, 1907), Volume IV, p. 109.

2 The Nigerian novelist, Chinua Achebe, has captured the curse of the ancestors in a related way in his first novel *Things Fall Apart* (London: Heinemann Educational Books, 1958; New York: Astor-Honor, 1961). There are Shakespearian echoes.

1: Where is Africa?

1 This section of the chapter is indebted to my first BBC Reith Lecture. See Mazrui, *The African Condition. The Reith Lectures*, Lecture 1. (London: Heinemann Educational Books and New York: Cambridge University Press, 1980), pp. 3–6.

2 C. McEvedy, *The Penguin Atlas of African History* (Harmondsworth, Middlesex: Penguin Books, 1980).

3 P. Bohannan, *African Outline* (Harmondsworth, Middlesex: Penguin Books, 1966), p. 42.

4 See R. R. Palmer in collaboration with J. Colton, *A History of the Modern World* (New York: Knopf, 1962), 2nd edition, p. 13.

5 See Herskovits's contribution to Wellesley College, *Symposium on Africa* (Wellesley College, Massachusetts, 1960), p. 16.

2: Anatomy of a Continent

1 Consult also Mazrui, *The African Condition. The Reith Lectures*, Lecture 1 (London: Heinemann Educational Books and New York: Cambridge University Press, 1980).

2 Poem by Ali A. Mazrui, not previously published.

3 J. H. Driberg, *The Lango*, cited by Okot p'Bitek in *Religion of the Central Luo* (Nairobi: East African Literature Bureau, 1971), p. 50.

4 B. A. Ogot, 'Concept of Jok', *African Studies*, No. 20 (1961).

5 The English word 'animism' derives from the Latin word 'anima', meaning 'soul', and is very different in meaning and insinuation from 'animalism' which refers to brutishness and sensuality.

3: Africa's Identity: The Indigenous Personality

1 This rendering in the English language is from S. W. Allen's translation of

Jean-Paul Sartre's introduction to African poetry, *Black Orpheus* (Paris: Presence Africaine 1963), pp. 41–3.

2 Ibid.

3 I first encountered this distinction between romantic gloriana and romantic primitivism at a special conference organised by the Rockefeller Foundation held at the Villa Serbelloni in Italy on the subject 'African Cultural and Intellectual Leaders and the Development of the New African Nations'. The subsequent report was edited by Robert W. July and Peter Benson, *African Culture and Intellectual Leaders* (New York: The Rockefeller Foundation and Ibadan: The University Press, 1982).

4 Julius K. Nyerere, '*Ujamaa*. The Basis of African Socialism', *Freedom and Unity* (Dar es Salaam and London: Oxford University Press, 1968), p. 12.

5 I first discussed the archival tradition in relation to the oral tradition at the Seventh Biennial Conference and Seminar of the East and Central African Regional Branch of the International Council on Archives, which was held in Harare, Zimbabwe, in September 1982. See Ali A. Mazrui, 'African Archives and the Oral Tradition' *Courier* (Paris: UNESCO, February 1985), and Ali A. Mazrui, 'The Archival Tradition and International Stratification: The Case of Africa's Marginality', ECARBICA 7 *Proceedings of the 7th Conference of the East and Central African Regional Branch of the International Council of Archives* (Harare: ECARBICA, 1983), pp. 142–55.

6 This rendering in English is from Muhammad Abdul-Hai, *Conflict and Identity: The Cultural Poetics of Contemporary Sudanese Poetry* (Khartoum: Institute of African and Asian Studies, University of Khartoum, African Seminar Series No. 26, 1976), pp. 43–4.

4: Africa's Identity: The Semitic Impact

1 Consult *The Jewish Communities of the World* (London: André Deutsch, 1971), prepared by the Institute of Jewish Affairs in association with the World Jewish Congress. Third revised edition.

2 For America's twin myths consult Max Lerner, *America as a Civilisation: Life and Thought in the United States Today* (New York: Simon and Schuster, 1957), p. 162.

3 *Daily Telegraph* (London), 13 August 1984. See also *Sunday Times* (London), 12 August 1984 and 19 August 1984. Consult also the *International Herald Tribune* (Paris and London), 23 August 1984.

4 Kamal Salibi, *The Bible Came from Arabia* (Bonn: Spiegel, 1984 and London: Jonathan Cape, 1985).

5 *Europa Yearbook 1984* (London: Europa, 1984).

5: Africa's Identity: The Western Aftermath

1 Bernard Lewis, *The Emergence of Modern Turkey* (London: Oxford University Press, 1961). See especially his 'Introduction: The Sources of Turkish Civilisation', pp. 1–17.

2 Melville J. Herskovits, 'Does "Africa" Exist?', Wellesley College,

Symposium on Africa (Wellesley College, Massachusetts, 1960), p. 15.

3 Max Beloff, 'The Prospects for Atlantic Union', *The Times* (London), 2 February 1962.

4 See Nyerere's contribution to *Symposium*, Wellesley College, *op. cit.*, p. 149.

5 *Education in African Society*, Colonial Paper No. 186, 1944, p. 55.

6 Nyerere's 'Africa's Place in the World', *Symposium*, Wellesley College, *op. cit.*, p. 149. For a brief analysis of his argument see my article 'On the Concept of "We Are All Africans"', *The American Political Science Review*, Vol. LVII, No. i, March 1963. Consult also Mazrui, *Towards a Pax Africana: A Study of Ideology and Ambition* (London: Weidenfeld and Nicolson and Chicago: University of Chicago Press, 1967).

7 Alex Haley, *Roots*, (Garden City, N.Y.: Doubleday, 1976, London: Hutchinson, 1977), p. 255.

8 *Ibid.*, p. 255.

9 James Baldwin, 'How I Stopped Hating Shakespeare' *Insight* 11 (Ibadan: British High Commission, 1964), pp. 14–16.

6: Africa at Play: A Triple Heritage of Sports

1 *Ethiopian Festivals* (Addis Ababa: Ethiopian Tourism Commission, 1982), p. 15.

2 *Ibid.*, p. 8. This author was a member of a BBC television team which filmed *Feres Gugs* in Addis Ababa early in 1984.

3 Paul Weiss, *Sport: A Philosophical Enquiry* (Carbondale: Southern Illinois Press, 1969), p. 39.

4 Paul Crispin, 'The Essence of Fattening', *Democrat Weekly*, Lagos, 29 July 1984.

5 David Martin, *General Amin* (London: Faber and Faber, 1974), p. 15.

6 James M. Macpherson, Laurence B. Holland, James M. Banner, Jr, Nancy J. Weiss and Michael D. Bell, *Blacks in America: Bibliographical Essays*, (Garden City, N.Y.: Doubleday and Co., 1972), p. 298.

7 *Ibid.*, p. 297.

8 Jesse Kornbluth, 'Muhammad Goes to the Mountain', *New Times* (USA), Vol. 3, No. 5, 6 September 1974, p. 55. Idi Amin once sent a cable intended to insult President Nyerere stating *inter alia*, 'I love you very much and if you had been a woman I would have considered marrying you even though your head is full of grey hairs' – cited in *Facts on File*, Vol. xxxxii, No. 1660 (20–6 August 1972), p. 659.

9 Consult for women's point of view Ann Scott, 'Closing the Muscle Gap', in *MS* (US magazine), September 1974.

7: Africa at Prayer: New Gods

1 *The Bible*, Romans 10, 12 (Revised Standard Version).
2 D. B. Cruise O'Brien, *The Mourides of Senegal* (Oxford: The Clarendon Press, 1971).

8: Tools of Exploitation: A Triple Heritage of Technology

1 Caryl P. Haskins, 'Atomic Energy and American Foreign Policy', *Foreign Affairs*, Vol. 24, No. 4, July 1946, pp. 595–6.
2 Kwame Nkrumah, *I Speak of Freedom: A Statement of African Ideology* (London: Heinemann, 1961), p. 213.
3 Edward S. Ayensu, lecture on 'Natural and Applied Sciences and National Development', delivered at the Silver Jubilee celebration of the Ghana Academy of Arts and Sciences (Accra) 22 November 1984.
4 The two Ghanaian visitors were Professor Alexander Kwapong, Vice-Rector of the United Nations University in Tokyo, and Professor Edward Ayensu of the Smithsonian Institution in the United States. See Ayensu's lecture (mimeo), Ghana Academy of Arts and Sciences (Accra), *ibid.*
5 The Voice of America's African Service broadcast a recording of both Nyerere's speech and Nyerere's press conference. One such broadcast by VoA African Service was on 24 November 1984.

9: In Search of Stability

1 Julius K. Nyerere, 'Democracy and the Party System', *Freedom and Unity* (Dar es Salaam and London: Oxford University Press, 1966), p. 198.
2 Nyerere, '*Ujamaa*: The Basis of African Socialism', *Freedom and Unity* (Dar es Salaam and London: Oxford University Press, 1966), p. 170.
3 *Ibid.*, p. 170.
4 See *Transition* (Kampala), Vol. 3, No. 11, November 1963, p. 6. Mboya's critic was also an east African – C. N. Omondi. The critic's letter first appeared in *Kenya Weekly News* (Nairobi) 2 August 1963.
5 Consult also Mazrui, *Political Values and the Educated Class in Africa* (London: Heinemann Educational Books and Los Angeles and Berkeley: University of California Press, 1978). See also Mazrui, 'Marxist Theories, Socialist Policies and African Realities', *Problems of Communism*, (September–October 1980), pp. 44–53.
6 James Mittleman has attempted to quantify this increasing Tanzanian dependency internationally in spite of its domestic efforts to pursue the socialist path of development. Some might even argue that the deepening international dependency might in part be due precisely to the domestic socialist experimentation.
7 For comparative state-formations in recent history consult the special issue 'On the State', *International Social Science Journal* (Paris), Vol. XXXII, No. 4, 1980, and the special issue 'Capitalism, Socialism and the State', *Survey: A Journal of East and West Studies* (London), Vol. 26, No. 1 (114), Winter, 1982.

10: Is Modernisation Reversible?

1 Robert W. July, *A History of the African People*, 3rd edition (New York: Charles Scribner and Sons, 1980), p. 229.

2 See July, *ibid.*, p. 228. Egypt was technically under the Ottoman Empire with a Viceroy, but in fact the Turks were forced to give a good deal of independence to the Viceroy of Egypt except when the Turks were under pressure from western European imperialist powers. It should be mentioned that Muhammad Ali was an Albanian Turk not a native Egyptian but he was, of course, a Muslim.

11: In Search of Self-Reliance: Capitalism without Winter

1 Aimé Cesaire, *Return to My Native Land* (Paris: Presence Africaine, 1939). See Chapter 3, note 1 for translation details.

2 I am indebted to Peter Bate of the BBC, Diana Frank of WETA and Christopher Davis of the University of Michigan for stimulation and criticisms of these ideas.

3 See A. Heath, R. Jowell and J. Curtice, *How Britain Votes* (Oxford: Pergamon Press, 1985).

12: Towards Cultural Synthesis

1 Achebe, *No Longer at Ease* (London: Heinemann Educational Books, 1960 and New York: Astor-Honor, 1961), pp. 87–8.

2 See Colin Leys, 'What is the Problem About Corruption?' *The Journal of Modern African Studies*, Vol. III, No. 2, 1965, p. 225. Consult also M. G. Smith, 'Historical and Cultural Conditions of Political Corruption Among the Hausa', *Comparative Studies in Society and History*, January 1964, pp. 164–98.

3 Letter, Secretaries to Missionaries in Yoruba, 17 February 1857; CNS Ca2/L2. Cited by J. F. A. Ajayi, *Christian Missions in Nigeria, 1841–1891: The Making of a New Élite* (Harlow, Essex: Longman, 1981 edition), p. 107.

4 In cross-checking my data in this section, I am indebted to the novelist and playwright Nuruddin Farah, Dr John Munene of the Department of Psychology at the University of Jos, Nigeria, and to my ward and assistant, Mr Sam Max Sebina of Uganda.

13: Between Society and the State

1 Basil Davidson, *The African Genius* (Boston: Little, Brown, 1969), pp. 211–2.

2 Michael Crowder's editorial introduction, *West African Resistance* (New York: Africana Publishing Corporation, 1971), p. 15.

3 Edmund Burke, *Reflections on the Revolution in France* (1790), *Works* (London: World's Classic Edition, 1907), Volume IV, p. 109.

4 Lord Hailey, *An African Survey* (London: Oxford University Press, 1957), revised edition, pp. 453–4.

5 C. S. Whittaker, Jr, *The Politics of Tradition: Continuity and Change in*

Northern Nigeria, 1947–1966 (Princeton: Princeton University Press, 1970), pp. 26–7.

6 Aimé Cesaire, *Return to My Native Land* (Paris: Presence Africaine, 1939). See Chapter 3, note 1 for translation details.

14: Between War and Peace

1 Robert Graves, *The Greek Myths*, Vol. 1 (Harmondsworth and New York: Penguin Books, 1960 edition), pp. 286–8.

2 Consult Muhammad Abdul-Hai, *Conflict and Identity: The Cultural Poetics of Contemporary Sudanese Poetry*, (Khartoum: Institute of African and Asian Studies, University of Khartoum, African Seminar Series No. 26, 1976).

3 'The Atlantic Charter', *United States Executive Agreement Series*, No. 236, Department of State Publication No. 1732 (Washington, D.C.; U.S. Government Printing Office, 1942).

4 Muhammad Harbi, quoted in Basil Davidson, *Africa in Modern History: The Search for a New Society* (London: Allen Lane, 1978) pp. 202–3.

5 African National Congress, December 1941, as quoted in Davidson, *ibid.*, pp. 202–3, 411.

6 Cited by Basil Davidson, *Africa in Modern History: The Search for a New Society* (London: Allen Lane, Penguin Books, 1978), pp. 202–3, 411.

7 Speech to the House of Commons, 9 September 1941. See Charles Eade (Editor), *War Speeches of Winston Churchill* (London: Cassell, 1952), Vol. 2, pp. 71–2.

8 See the resolutions cited in Colin Legum, *Pan-Africanism* (New York: Praeger, 1962), Appendix 2.

9 *The Times* (London), 16 September 1941.

10 Winston S. Churchill, *The Second World War*, Vol. IV; *The Hinge of Fate* (Boston: Houghton Mifflin Co., 1950), p. 209.

11 A. S. Kanya-Forstner, 'Mali-Tukulor', in Michael Crowder (editor), *West African Resistance* (London: Hutchinson, 1971; New York: Africana Publishing Corporation, 1971), p. 53.

12 Michael Crowder's 'Introduction', *West African Resistance, ibid.*, p. 15.

13 I. M. Lewis, *A Modern History of Somalia* (London: Longman, 1980), pp. 80–1.

14 Julius K. Nyerere, *Freedom and Unity* (Dar es Salaam and Oxford University Press, 1966), pp. 2–3.

15: Muntu: A Conclusion

1 Quoted by Elliott P. Skinner and Gwendolyn Mikell, 'A Conflict of Cultures', *The Africans: A Reader*. Edited by Ali A. Mazrui and Toby Levine (New York: Praeger Publishing House, 1986).

2 For this specific African myth of the Sky God's anger over human waste I have borrowed the formulation from Oyekan Owomoyela, *African Literatures: An Introduction* (Waltham, Massachusetts: Crossroads

Press, African Studies Association, 1979), p. 3.

3 See Margaret Carey, *Myths and Legends of Africa* (Melbourne and London: Sun Books, Hamlyn Publishing Group, 1970), pp. 18–19.

4 Consult Adolf Erman, *Life in Ancient Egypt* (translated by H. N. Tirard), (New York: Dover Publications, 1971), pp. 32–3.

5 I am indebted to Sam Max Sebina, John Munene, Brenda Kiberu and Omari Kokole for information about the myths of the Baganda.

6 This form is cited by N. A. Fadipe, *The Sociology of the Yoruba*, edited by Francis Olu Okediji and Oladejo Okediji (Ibadan: Ibadan University Press, 1970), p. 31.

7 *Ibid.*, pp. 32–4.

8 See Kamal Salibi, *The Bible Came from Arabia* (Bonn: Spiegel, 1984 and London: Jonathan Cape, 1985).

9 I am indebted for stimulation on some of these issues to my conversations with Michael Tidy, my literary editor, and to Lemuel Johnson, my colleague at the University of Michigan.

10 N. Bassey Ate, 'France in Central Africa: The NATO Dimension and Implications for Nigeria', *Nigerian Forum* (Lagos: Nigerian Institute of International Affairs), Vol. 1, No. 6, August 1981, p. 234.

11 Thomas Kanza, 'Zaire's Foreign Policy' in Olajide Aluko (editor), *The Foreign Policies of African States* (London: Hodder and Stoughton, 1977), p. 235.

12 Victor LeVine, 'Africa in the World', Chapter in *The Africans: A Reader*, *op. cit.* LeVine also refers to an earlier article by Philip L. Christenson, 'Some Economic Facts of Life', *AEI Foreign Policy and Defense Review*, Vol. 1, No. 1 (1979), pp. 38–41, which is included in an appendix to LeVine's chapter.

13 'Nyerere Hits IMF "Ritual Compassion"', *The Times* (London), 22 March 1985.

14 I first discussed the idea of the solidarity of the indebted in an article written for *The Times Higher Education Supplement* (London, 19 March 1983).

Select Bibliography

Achebe, C. *Things Fall Apart* London: Heinemann Educational, 1958; New York: Astor-Honor, 1959.

Achebe, C. *No Longer at Ease* London: Heinemann Educational, 1960; New York: Astor-Honor, 1961.

Achebe, C. *Arrow of God* London: Heinemann Educational, 1964; New York: Doubleday, 1982.

Achebe, C. *A Man of the People* London: Heinemann Educational, 1966; New York: Doubleday, 1966.

Adams, J. *The Unnatural Alliance: Israel and South Africa* London: Quartet Books, 1984; Salem, NH: Merrimack Publishing Circle, 1984.

Ajayi, J. F. A. *Christian Missions in Nigeria 1841–1891: The Making of a New Élite* Evanston, Ill: Northwestern University Press, 1965; London: Longman, 1969.

Ake, C. *A Political Economy of Africa* Harlow and Chicago: Longman, 1981.

Akintoye, S. A. *Emergent African States: Topics in Twentieth-Century African History* Harlow and Chicago: Longman, 1976.

Al-Hakim, T. *Fate of a Cockroach and Other Plays* London: Heinemann Educational, 1973; Washington, DC: Three Continents, 1980.

Aluko, O. ed. *The Foreign Policies of African States* London: Hodder and Stoughton, 1977; Atlantic Highlands, NJ: Humanities, 1977.

Armah, A. K. *The Beautyful Ones are Not Yet Born* Boston: Houghton Mifflin, 1968; London: Heinemann Educational, 1969.

Ayisi, E. O. *An Introduction to the Study of African Culture* London and Portsmouth, NH: Heinemann, 1972 n.e. 1979.

Bakari, M. B. M. *The Customs of the Swahili People* edited by J. W. T. Allen. Berkeley, CA: University of California Press, 1982.

Biko, S. *I Write What I Like: A Selection of his Writings* London: Heinemann Educational, 1979; New York: Harper and Row, 1979.

Blyden, E. W. *Christianity, Islam and the Negro Race* London: Whittingham Press, 1887.

Blyden, E. W. *Black Spokesman: Selected Published Writings of Edward Wilmot Blyden* edited by H. R. Lynch. London: Frank Cass, 1971; New York: Humanities, 1971.

Boahen, A. A. *Topics in West African History* London: Longman, 1965, n.e. due 1986.

Boahen, A. A. 'Africa under Colonial Domination, 1880–1935' in *Unesco General History of Africa* Vol. 2 *Ancient Africa* edited by G. Mokhtar. Berkeley, CA: University of California Press, 1980.

Bond, G. et al *African Christianity: Patterns of Religious Continuity* New York and London: Academic Press, 1979.

Chraibi, D. *Heirs to the Past* London: Heinemann Educational, 1971.

Clark, J. P. *America, Their America: Autobiography* London: Heinemann Educational, 1964; New York: Holmes and Meier, 1969.

Collins, J. *African Pop Roots: The Inside Rhythms of Africa* Slough: W. Foulsham, 1985.

Crowder, M. ed. *West African Resistance: The Military Response to Colonial Occupation* New York: Africana Publishing Corporation, 1971; London: Hutchinson, 1971.

Cruise O'Brien, D. B. *The Mourides of Senegal: The Political and Economic Organisation of an Islamic Brotherhood* Oxford: The Clarendon Press, 1971.

Curtin, P. D. et al *African History* 1964. Boston: Little, Brown, 1978; Harlow: Longman, 1979.

Danquah, J. B. *The Akan Doctrine of God: A Fragment of Gold Coast Ethics and Religion* 1944. London: Frank Cass, 1968.

Davidson, B. *Africa in Modern History: The Search for a New Society* London: Allen Lane and Penguin Books, 1978.

Davidson, B. *The African Genius* Boston: Little, Brown, 1969.

Davidson, B. *Discovering Africa's Past* London: Longman, 1978.

Davidson, B. *Modern Africa* London and Chicago: Longman, 1983.

Davidson, B. *The People's Cause: A History of Guerrillas in Africa* Harlow: Longman, 1981.

Decalo, S. *Coups and Army Rule in Africa: Studies in Military Style* New Haven and London: Yale University Press, 1976.

De Graft, J. C. *Muntu* London and Portsmouth, NH: Heinemann Educational, 1977.

Deng, F. M. *Africans of Two Worlds: The Dinka in Afro-Arab Sudan* New Haven and London: Yale University Press, 1978.

Denoon, D. and Nyeko, B. *Southern Africa since 1800* London: Longman, 1972 n.e. 1984; New York: Praeger, 1973.

Du Bois, W. E. B. *The World and Africa: An Inquiry into the Part which Africa has Played in World History* New York: Viking Press, 1947; Millwood, NY: Kraus International, 1976.

El Zein, A. H. M. *The Sacred Meadows* Evanston, Ill: Northwestern University Press, 1974.

Equiano, O. *Equiano's Travels: His Autobiography* 1789. Abridged edition edited by P. E. Edwards. London: Heinemann Educational, 1967.

Farah, N. *From a Crooked Rib* London and Portsmouth, NH: Heinemann Educational, 1970.

Geertz, C. *The Interpretation of Cultures* New York: Basic Books, 1973; London: Hutchinson, 1975.

Gilsenan, M. *Saint and Sufi in Modern Egypt: An Essay in the Sociology of Religion* Oxford and New York: The Clarendon Press, 1973.

Gutteridge, W. *Military Regimes in Africa* London and New York: Methuen, 1975.

Haley, A. *Roots* Garden City, NY: Doubleday, 1976; London: Hutchinson, 1977; Picador, 1978.

Harrison, D. *The White Tribe of Africa: South Africa in Perspective* London: BBC Publications, 1981; Ariel Books, 1985; Berkeley, CA: University of California Press, 1982.

Hastings, A. *A History of African Christianity, 1950–75* Cambridge and New York: Cambridge University Press, 1979.

Hay, M. J. and Stichter, S. *African Women South of the Sahara* Harlow: Longman, 1982.

Hiskett, M. *The Development of Islam in West Africa* Harlow: Longman, 1984.

Hull, R. W. *Modern Africa: Change and Continuity* Englewood Cliffs, NJ and Hemel Hempstead, Herts: Prentice-Hall, 1980.

July, R. W. *A History of the African People* London: Faber, 1970; New York: Scribner, 1970, n.e. 1980.

Kenyatta, J. *Facing Mount Kenya: The Tribal Life of the Kikuyu* 1938. London and Nairobi: Heinemann Educational, 1971; New York: AMS Press, n.e. 1978.

Kitchen, H. *United States Interests in Africa in the 80s* New York: Praeger, 1983.

Kunene, M. *Anthem of the Decades* London: Heinemann Educational, 1981.

Kwamena-Poh, M. A. et al *African History in Maps* Harlow and Chicago: Longman, 1982.

Lan, D. *Guns and Rain: Guerrillas and Spirit Mediums in Zimbabwe* London: James Currey, 1985.

Lanning, G. and Mueller, M. *Africa Undermined, Mining Companies and the Under-development of Africa* Harmondsworth: Penguin Books, 1979.

Laye, C. *The African Child* London: Collins, 1955; Fontana edition called *The Dark Child* 1959; New York: F. S. and G, 1955.

Laye, C. *A Dream of Africa* London: Collins, 1966.

Le Vine, V. T. and Luke, T. W. eds *The Arab–African Connection* Boulder: Westview Press, 1979.

Leape, J. et al *Business in the Shadow of Apartheid: U.S. Firms in South Africa* Lexington, MA: Lexington Books, 1984.

McEvedy, C. *The Penguin Atlas of African History* Harmondsworth, Penguin Books, 1980; New York: Facts on File, 1980.

MacGaffey, W. *Modern Kongo Prophets: Religion in a Plural Society* Bloomington: Indiana University Press, 1983.

MacPherson, J. M. et al *Blacks in America: Bibliographical Essays* Garden City, NY: Doubleday, 1971.

Mahfouz, N. *Children of Gebelawi* London: Heinemann Educational, 1981; Washington, DC: Three Continents, 1981.

Mandela, N. *No Easy Walk to Freedom: Articles, Speeches and Trial Addresses* London: Heinemann Educational, 1965.

Martin, M-L. *Kimbangu: An African Prophet and his Church* Oxford: Basil Blackwell, 1975; Grand Rapids: Eerdmans, 1976.

Mazrui, A. A. *The African Condition: the Reith Lectures 1979* London: Heinemann Educational, 1980; New York: Cambridge University Press, 1980.

Mazrui, A. A. *The Africans: A Reader* New York: Praeger, due 1986.

Mazrui, A. A. *Africa's International Relations: The Diplomacy of Dependency and Change* London: Heinemann Educational, 1977; Boulder: Westview Press, 1978.

Mazrui, A. A. *Political Values and the Educated Class in Africa* London: Heinemann Educational, 1978; Berkeley: University of California Press, 1978.

Mazrui, A. A. and Tidy, M. *Nationalism and New States in Africa from about 1935 to the Present* London and Portsmouth, NH: Heinemann Educational, 1984.

Mazrui, A. A. and Tidy, M. *The Trial of Christopher Okigbo* London: Heinemann Educational, 1972; New York: Okpaku Communications, 1972.

Mbiti, J. S. *African Religions and Philosophy* London: Heinemann Educational, 1969; New York: Doubleday, 1970.

Mbiti, J. S. *An Introduction to African Religion* London and Portsmouth, NH: Heinemann Educational, 1975.

Mertz, P. M. and R. A. *Arab Aid to Sub-Saharan Africa* Boulder: Westview Press, 1983.

Mwangi, M. *Going Down River Road* London and Portsmouth, NH: Heinemann Educational, 1976.

Mwangi, M. *Kill Me Quick* London and Portsmouth, NH: Heinemann Educational, 1973.

Mwase, G. S. *Strike a Blow and Die: A Narrative of Race Relations in Colonial Africa* London: Heinemann Educational, 1969, n.e. 1975; Cambridge, MA: Harvard University Press, 1970.

Myers, III, D. et al *U.S. Business in South Africa: The Economic, Political and Moral Issues* Bloomington: Indiana University Press, 1980; London: Rex Collings, 1981.

Nation, R. C. and Kauppi, M. V. eds *The Soviet Impact in Africa* Boston: D. C. Heath, 1984.

Ngugi wa Thiong'o *Detained: A Writer's Prison Diary* London: Heinemann Educational, 1981.

Ngugi wa Thiong'o *Devil on the Cross* London: Heinemann Educational, 1982.

Ngugi wa Thiong'o *Petals of Blood* London: Heinemann Educational, 1977; New York: Dutton, 1978.

Nkosi, L. *Tasks and Masks: Themes and Styles of African Literature* Harlow and White Plains, NY: Longman, 1981.

Nkrumah, K. *Consciencism: Philosophy and the Ideology for Decolonisation* London: Panaf Books, n.e. 1970; New York: Monthly Review Press, 1970.

Nkrumah, K. *Neo-Colonialism: The Last Stage of Imperialism* London: Panaf Books, 1965; Heinemann Educational, 1968; Canton, Ohio: International Publishing, 1966; New York: State Mutual Books, 1981.

Nyerere, J. K. *Ujamaa: Essays on Socialism* Dar es Salaam and London: Oxford University Press, 1968.

Ogot, B. A. and Kieran, J. A. *Zamani: A Survey of East African History* Nairobi: East African Publishing House, 1968, n.e. 1974; New York: Humanities, 1968.

Olaniyan, R. ed. *African History and Culture* Harlow: Longman, 1982.

Olaniyan, R. *Nigerian History and Culture* Harlow: Longman, 1984.

Osia, K. *Israel, South Africa and Black Africa: A Study of the Primacy of the Politics of Expediency* New York: University Press of America, 1983.

Ousmane, S. *The Money Order* with *White Genesis* London: Heinemann Educational, 1972.

Ousmane, S. *Xala* London: Heinemann Educational, 1976.

Oyono, F. *Houseboy* London: Heinemann Educational, 1966; published in U.S. as *Boy!* New York: Collier Books, 1966.

Oyono, F. *The Old Man and the Medal* London: Heinemann Educational, 1970; New York: Collier Books, 1971.

Parfitt, T. *Operation Moses: The Story of the Exodus of Falasha Jews from Ethiopia* London: Weidenfeld and Nicolson, 1985.

P'Bitek, O. *African Religions in Western Scholarship* Kampala: East African Literature Bureau, 1970.

P'Bitek, O. *Song of Ocol* and *Song of Lawino* Nairobi: East African Publishing House, 1970–3. Published in one volume London: Heinemann Educational, 1984.

Ranger, T. O. *Peasant Consciousness and Guerrilla War in Zimbabwe* London: James Currey, 1985.

Rogers, B. *White Wealth and Black Poverty: American Investments in Southern Africa* Westport, Conn. and London: Greenwood Press, 1976.

Senghor, L. S. *Prose and Poetry* selected and translated by J. Reed and C. Wake. London: Oxford University Press, 1965; Heinemann, 1976.

Shaw, T. M. and Heard, K. A. *The Politics of Africa: Dependence and Development* New York: Holmes and Meier, 1979; Harlow: Longman, 1982.

Soyinka, W. *Aké: The Years of Childhood* London: Rex Collings, 1981; New York: Random House, 1983.

Soyinka, W. *Myth, Literature and the African World* Cambridge and New York: Cambridge University Press, 1976.

Soyinka, W. *The Man Died: Prison Notes of Wole Soyinka* London: Rex Collings, 1972; Penguin Books, 1975; New York: Harper and Row, 1972.

Sweetman, D. *Women Leaders in African History* London: Heinemann Educational, 1984.

Sylvester, A. *Arabs and Africans: Five Years of Arab–African Economic Co-operation* London: The Bodley Head, 1981.

Tangri, R. *Politics in Sub-Saharan Africa* London: James Currey; Portsmouth, NH: Heinemann, 1985.

Tidy, M. and Leeming, D. *A History of Africa, 1840–1914* London: Hodder and Stoughton, 2 vols, 1980–1; New York: Holmes and Meier, 1981.

Trimingham, J. S. *The Influence of Islam upon Africa* Harlow: Longman, 1968, n.e. 1980; New York, Praeger, 1968.

Wai, D. M. ed. *Interdependence in a World of Unequals: African–Arab–OECD Economic Co-operation for Development* Boulder: Westview Press, 1982.

Webster, J. B. et al *The Revolutionary Years: West Africa since 1800* Harlow and New York: Longman, 1967, n.e. 1980.

Worku, D. *The Thirteenth Sun* London: Heinemann Educational, 1973; Atlantic Highlands, NJ: Humanities, 1973.

Zahan, D. *The Religion, Spirituality and Thought of Traditional Africa* Chicago: University of Chicago Press, 1979.

Zell, H. M. et al *A New Reader's Guide to African Literature* London: Heinemann Educational, n.e. 1983; New York: Holmes and Meier, 1983.

Index

Page numbers in *italic* refer to illustrations

Picture Credits

Page 22 Ronald Sheridan; 25 Hirmer Fotarchiv, Munich; 26 *left* Mary Evans Picpue Library, *right* Mansell Collection; 27 BBC/David Harrison; 29 BBC Hulton Picture Library; 34 & 35 Picturepoint, London; 37 Frank Spooner Pictures/Abbas; 38 *top* The Photo Source, *bottom* BBC Hulton Picture Library; 39 Camerapix; 40 Robert Harding Picture Library/Ross; 41 Popperfoto; 42 & 03 BBC/Tim Copestake; 44 Mansell Collection; 45 Hutchison Library; 46 Ronald Sheridan; 47 *top* Ashmolean Museum, *bottom* Eric Kay; 48 Ronald Sheridan; 49 British Museum; 50 Ashmolean Museum; 51 Ronald Sheridan; 54 *left* Hutchison Library, *right* Robert Harding Picture Library/Garner; 55 J.Allan Cash Photolibrary; 57 BBC Hulton Picture Library; 59 Ministère des Affaires Culturelles, Ivory Coast; 62 John Hillelson Agency/Seed; 64 British Museum; 66 World Bank; 67 Hutchison Library; 69 Mary Evans Picture Library 70 Picturepoint, London; 71 BBC/David Harrison; 72 Hutchison Library; 73 Camera Press; 74 Hutchison Library; 75 Camera Press; 80 & 83 J.Allan Cash Photolibrary; 84 Camera Press; 85 J.Allan Cash Photolibrary; 86 *left* David Coulson, *right* Popperfoto; 87 David Coulson; 89 Frank Spooner Pictures/Cilo; 91 Hutchison Library; 93 Camera Press; 94 Camerapix; 98 Mary Evans Picture Library; 100 from *Fun Magazine* 4.12.1875; 102 Royal Geographical Society; 103 BBC Hulton Picture Library; 104 New York Historical Society; 105 Werner Forman Archive; 106 from *Fun Magazine* 26.6.1875; 107 BBC Hulton Picture Library; 108 Mary Evans Picture Library; 109 Rex Features; 111 Frank Spooner Pictures/Adams; 112 Picturepoint, London; 113 *both* Popperfoto; 114 All-Sport; 116 Robert Harding Picture Library/Mackenzie; 118 *top* Peter Fraenkel, *bottom* Picturepoint, London; 121 *both* Camera Press; 122 *left* All-Sport, *right* Kodak Ltd; 123 All-Sport; 126 The Photo Source; 129 Anna Tully; 130 Peter Fraenkel; 131 All-Sport; 134 *all* Ministère des Affaires Culturelles, Ivory Coast; 138 & 139 J.Allan Cash Photolibrary; 140 Middle East Photographic Archive; 142 Hutchison Library; 145 BBC/Chris Terrill; 147 *both* Hutchison Library; 148 *top* Mansell Collection, *bottom* H.Roger-Viollet; 150 J.Allan Cash Photolibrary; 151 *left* BBC/Chris Terrill, *right* Mansell Collection; 154, 155 & 156 BBC/J.Chiasson; 158 Hutchison Library; 160 British Museum/Bridgeman Art Library; 162 Hutchison Library; 163 BBC/Penelope Breese; 164 Frank Spooner Pictures/Abbas; 167 Hutchison Library; 168 *top* The Photo Source, *bottom* Popperfoto; 171 Frank Spooner Pictures/Abbas; 174 Hutchison Library; 175 Robert Harding Picture Library; 178 & 180 BBC/David Harrison; 182 *left* Popperfoto, *right* Camera Press; 183 BBC/Anna Tully; 186 The Photo Source; 187 Camera Press; 190 Hutchison Library; 194 John Hillelson Agency/Nogues; 195 BBC/David Harrison; 198 *left* Hutchison Library, *right* Anna Tully; 199 John Hillelson Agency/Campbell; 200 Oxfam; 202 & 203 Hutchison Library; 205 BBC/David Harrison; 206 John Hillelson Agency/Roger; 207 John Hillelson Agency/Barbey; 208 Camera Press; 210 Bruce Coleman/Reinhard; 211 BBC/David Harrison; 212 Robert Harding Picture Library/Griffiths; 214 J.Allan Cash Photolibrary; 215 Robert Harding Picture Library/Rawlings; 216 Picturepoint, London; 218 Bruce Coleman/Newby; 219 The Photo Souce; 221 Robert Harding Picture Library/Sassoon; 222 *top* Rex Features, *bottom* Hutchison Library; 225 Robert Harding Picture Library/Griffiths; 226 BBC/Anna Tully; 227 Compix, Commonwealth Institute; 229 Mozambique Historical Archives, Maputo; 230 BBC/David Harrison; 231 Avon County Library; 235 BBC/David Coulson; 238, 242 & 243 Hutchison Library; 246 *left* Peter Fraenkel; 246–7 Rex Features; 247 *right* Peter Fraenkel; 250 Picturepoint, London; 251 J.Allan Cash Photolibrary; 254 Robert Harding Picture Library/Watts; 258 Frank Spooner Pictures/Abbas; 259 Hutchison Library; 260 BBC/Judy Andrews; 262 *both* & 263 BBC Hulton Picture Library; 266 Hutchison Library; 267 BBC/David South; 268 *both* Popperfoto; 270 *top* BBC/Chris Terrill, *bottom* J.Allan Cash Photolibrary; 271 BBC/Anna Tully; 274 The Gordon Boys' School, Woking/E.T.Archive; 276 The Photo Source; 277 Popperfoto; 278 Imperial War Museum; 280 Camera Press; 283 National Army Museum; 286 BBC/David Harrison; 288 Camera Press; 291 Robert Harding Picture Library/Lomax; 294 Rex Features; 298 Picturepoint, London: 299 Prof.Richard Pankhurst; 303 J.Allan Cash Photolibrary; 304 IDAF; 307 BBC/Anna Tully: 309 IDAF; 314 Rex Features.

Maps on pages 30–1 drawn by Line and Line.